T0267890

prism

Volume 20 / Issue 2 / September 2023

THEORY AND MODERN CHINESE LITERATURE

Classicism in Digital Times: Cultural Remembrance
as Reimagination in the Sinophone Cyberspace
ZHIYI YANG and DAVID DER-WEI WANG,
Special issue editors

249 | Classicism in Digital Times: Cultural Remembrance
as Reimagination in the Sinophone Cyberspace
ZHIYI YANG and DAVID DER-WEI WANG

265 | *Xiqu* 2.0: Expanded Chinese Opera in Digital Times
ROSSELLA FERRARI

297 | Avant-Garde Anachronism: *Dream of the Red Chamber*
in the Forty-Ninth Century
FANGDAI CHEN

315 | The Thrill of Becoming: Writing Poetry in Digital Times
XIAOFEI TIAN

341 | Writing in the Digital Sand: Technological Transformation
and Classicist Poetry Writing in China's Fluid Cyberspace
ZHIYI YANG

367 | Gaming Sinographs beyond the Ludic: *Word Game* and
the Digital Sinophone
MICHAEL O'KRENT

395 | China in the Skin: In Search of a Chinese Video Game
YEDONG SH-CHEN

417 | Classicist Drama in Digital Times: Reimagining the Past
in Chinese Cyberspace
MICHELLE YEH

442   The Digital Classicism of the Cantonese Opera Film
White Snake
LIANG LUO

462   Surface Classicism: Aesthetics, Poetics, and Remediation
in Digitally Enhanced Chinese Performance
TARRYN LI-MIN CHUN

487   Writing the Heart Sutra Online
LAURA VERMEEREN

503   The Body That Counts: On the Digital Techniques
of the Chinese Modern Dance
CHIEH-TING HSIEH

ZHIYI YANG and DAVID DER-WEI WANG

Classicism in Digital Times
Cultural Remembrance as Reimagination in the Sinophone Cyberspace

ABSTRACT This article, the introduction to the special issue, proposes "Sinophone classicism" as a new paradigm to investigate Chineseness as an identity shaped by cultural and digital memories in the global cyberspace. Digital technology has drastically transformed the world we inhabit, particularly the way in which we symbiotically remember and imagine our cultural legacies and visions. To rethink the relations between the humanities and digital technicity, we seek to invoke "classicism" as a keyword through which to engage questions from temporality to virtuality and "Sinophone" as a topos through which to discover the pluriverse of China. Being "Chinese" in cyberspace, therefore, entails a constant and dynamic process of remembering, performing, (re)imagining, and (re)negotiating one's cultural identities.

KEYWORDS classicism, Chineseness, the Sinophone, digital enframing, being-in-cyberspace

On April 30, 1993, the World Wide Web (the Internet) became commercially available. In less than thirty years, it has fundamentally changed the way people around the world communicate, access information, and form group identities. It has greatly furthered the trend of digitization in cultural production that began when the world's first word processor for personal computers was made commercially available in the mid-1970s. And the recent global COVID-19 pandemic did its part in eliminating some last strongholds of resistance against the digital revolution.

Nestled under this global rhythm of instant contemporaneity, however, is a contradictory pull toward separate digital ecosystems in non-English languages and cultures. A global Sinitic-language (or "Sinophone," Shu-mei Shih's term; see below) cyberspace, for instance, has empowered cultural and pop cultural trends that quickly sweep across geographically scattered, politically divided, and vernacularly distinct communities, creating a mediascape. Some of the most notable trends may be described as contributing to a "classicist revival," if we understand every purported revival of the tradition as reinvention and reimagination. Literary and cultural articulations evoking China's classical past instantly travel through a rhizomatic network of dynamic cultural production, dissemination,

PRISM: THEORY AND MODERN CHINESE LITERATURE • 20:2 • SEPTEMBER 2023
DOI 10.1215/25783491-10991578 • © 2023 LINGNAN UNIVERSITY

and consumption. Platforms of "knowing" and "learning" about the antiquity, too, are increasingly digital: databases, search engines, and digital preservation projects have fundamentally transformed the way we access and interpret Chinese classics, generating not only the interface but also the metaverse of canons and memories.

To illustrate how digital media help recruit individuals to become agents of cultural remembrance and imagination, consider the following true case. Lee, born in 1996, is a Malaysian woman working in Singapore who likes to wear Hanfu 漢服, a kind of reinvented ethnic clothing inspired by ancient Chinese sartorial traditions.[1] Her family migrated from the coastal region around Quanzhou to Malaysia four generations ago. She speaks Mandarin, Hokkien, English, and Malay, in that order of proficiency. She went to a Chinese-language primary school and a national (Malaysian) middle school, before going to Singapore for a college degree in information technology. She has always identified herself as Chinese culturally: her family are practicing Daoists, and she learned *guzheng* (a Chinese plucked zither) in school. Her fascination with China's literary past began with *Dynasty Warriors*, a Japanese video game based on the Chinese classical novel *Romance of the Three Kingdoms*. She also watched the eponymous historical drama produced in mainland China (CCTV, 1994), which was shown on local TV when she was in primary school, but she watched it in full only later online. She then read the novel in Chinese, after having taken some classical Chinese classes in middle school. By 2015 she had her first smartphone. In 2019, through the Chinese app Douyin (the People's Republic of China's [PRC] version of TikTok), she saw some short videos featuring Hanfu. Reminded of the period drama characters, she clicked "like." Almost immediately Douyin began to recommend other Hanfu videos, including ones that helped her gain deeper insight into Hanfu history, designs, accessories, and matching makeup techniques. For the first time she felt an intimate connection with her ancestors' daily lives. After two years of following the "movement" and having saved enough to buy Hanfu that were high quality and historically faithful, she bought her first set on Taobao, where the so-called Hanfu renaissance had fostered domestic fashion vendors and brands, producing and selling clothes ranging from costumes to couture and quotidian wear. She purchased matching accessories too, from hairpins to embroidered slippers, many of which purchases were based on the algorithmic recommendations featured on her personalized Taobao homepage. A private person, she had been sharing her Hanfu selfies with face veiled via Instagram. In one of the portraits, her face is masked by another face cropped from a digitalized image of a Tang Dynasty silk painting (from the Astana Cemetery) that inspired her clothing, and the virtual background is photoshopped to resemble a Tang painting too. The smartphone held in her raised left hand, however, betrays the image's artful conceit.

Figure 1. Ms. Lee, self-portrait in Hanfu, 2023. Courtesy of Ms. Lee.

Lee's case illustrates the power of digital media in shaping cultural identities across geopolitical borders. First, "Chineseness" is here primarily experienced as cultural remembrance and affective affordance—of a literary and classical past imagined and reinvented. On a global scale, this digital mediascape connects every individual agent of a particular language or culture, sometimes living under other dominant cultures. And Lee is not alone: in recent years, pop music, fashion, dance theater, films, period dramas, video games, and fantasies based on or inspired by Chinese elite traditions are among the most lavishly produced and avidly consumed cultural products worldwide. This multifaceted phenomenon, which we call "Sinophone classicism in digital times," is the focus of a collaborative investigation in this special issue.

Second, thanks to China's giant strides in digital commerce and the global logistics network that online retailers can tap into, Lee further substantiates this cultural identity with physical objects. These accoutrements of cultural identity are produced by digital savvy vendors and designers inspired by a grassroots fashion trend that spread primarily online. They are sold on Chinese e-commerce platforms, delivered to their global customers within days or weeks, and then photographed to become sharable digital images, feeding a perpetual loop of an online-offline flow of information and goods. As the mediologist Régis Debray argues, memory's reinforcements cannot be reduced to sayings and writings. Rather, "the trivial, peripheral, or basely material incidentals of how any given message, doctrine, or idea is put across" mean as much as "exemplary lives" or "great books."[2] In Lee's case, the daily Daoist rituals performed at her parental home, the pop cultural products, and the Hanfu clothing contributed as much as, if not much more than, the classic Chinese novels in transmitting, transforming, and re-creating Chinese cultural memories for her. Together they provide an imaginative milieu for her to reinvent and substantiate a Chinese identity in postcolonial Malaysia and Singapore.

Third, as this case exemplifies, the agents involved in the transmission and transformation of cultural memory are highly diverse, each having their own agenda. *Dynasty Warriors* is a game that taps into the repertoire of shared cultural memories in East Asia and created a product that became instantly popular among the global Asian community. The CCTV dramatization of the same romance symbolizes the Chinese state media's balancing act between profit (market-oriented content creation) and propaganda (promoting national culture). The classical Chinese class Lee took in school represents the Malaysian government's concession to the demands of local Chinese communities, which see the veneration of their ancestral traditions as a source of cultural pride and a means of resisting assimilation into a dominant national culture. The Hanfu trend initially embodied a nationalist drive to visually re-create a Han-ethnic body, turning it into a battlefield against sartorial homogenization, globalization, and (purported) Westernization. It has, however, evolved into a fashion trend with diverse functions as well as a business opportunity. The Chinese state, while cautiously co-opting the popularity of this fashion, remains weary of its implied Han cultural otherness.[3] Lee herself has mixed incentives: partly aesthetic choice (the clothes are beautiful and different, as she puts it), partly cultural pride, and partly cultural envy (in emulation of the more quotidian presence of kimonos and *hanbok* in Japan and Korea). These diverse agendas and functions mean that classicism cannot be simply dismissed as cultural nationalism or fetishism but should be viewed as a multifaceted, multi-centered, multidimensional, and multifunctional phenomenon.

On October 22, 2022, the Constitution of the Communist Party of China was revised to include China's "fine traditional culture" as a major intellectual resource, together with basic Marxist tenets, for constructing "socialism with

Chinese characteristics."[4] This moment intensified a trend that had begun much earlier but has been deliberately fostered during the Xi era. This trend is the authoritarian and nationalist use of Chinese cultural classicism. It thus becomes even more urgent to wrestle this concept from state hegemony and restore its multidimensionality and multifunctionality. To investigate the diverse array of forms, functions, purposes, and mediality of Sinophone classicism in digital times, interdisciplinary scholarly effort is urgently needed. This special issue represents a first collaborative step in addressing this research lacuna and related paradigmatic challenges. Here *memory* refers to both the mnemonic act of remembering that which is long gone and the digital functionality of storing that which is reverberating in the virtual space. We seek to bring together these two kinds of memory—the classicist and the digital—providing a new platform for furthering the question of Chineseness in our time.

What Is Sinophone Classicism?

As a working definition proposed by Zhiyi Yang, *Sinophone classicism* refers to the appropriation, redeployment, and reconfiguration of cultural memories harking back to Chinese aesthetic and intellectual traditions for local, contemporary, and vernacular uses.[5] *Sinophone* is a neologism coined by Shu-mei Shih in the early 2000s as a counterpart of the Anglophone, the Francophone, or the Germanophone. It highlights the multilingual nature of the Sinitic-language spaces and has rapidly become a fast-growing field of study. The scope of Sinophone studies was first articulated by Shih as "the study of Sinitic-language cultures on the *margins of* geopolitical nation-states and their hegemonic productions" (emphasis added).[6] It aims to replace what Shih perceives as the outdated concept of "the Chinese diaspora," which presumes an immutable relation between the "center" and the "margins" of Chineseness.[7] However, when excluding Han ethnic mainland China from Sinophone studies, Shih neglects China's own heterogeneous nature and arguably reaffirms the same discursive binary that she ostensibly revolts against.[8] Thus, for a thorough decentralization of the "Sinophone," we will include mainland China in the geopolitical scope of investigation. For our purpose, the Sinophone space is defined as wherever Sinitic languages are used, in written or oral forms, and as media of cultural transmission, production, and dissemination. It is not exclusive, as one can be simultaneously Sinophone and Anglophone. The association of *Sinophone* with *classicism* will further limit the scope of our investigation to texts, images, arts, and practices deriving from or inspired by China's traditions that enjoy the prestige and veneration as being "classical."

Classicism is a nineteenth-century coinage originally used to describe a cultural war happening in France and later in Germany between, on the one hand, Romanticism, which emphasizes liberation from restraints, and, on the other, an aesthetic and political program devoted to the re-creation of an ideal of spiritual beauty and artistic purity associated with an idealized classical Greek culture.[9] Though in some cultures (as in Germany) *classicism* is commonly used to mean something derivative or inauthentic, we embrace the term precisely for its rejection of the pretense of "authenticity" as a marketing device. By claiming to venerate and emulate the past, the classicists also necessarily reinvent and reimagine the past for self-projection and novel recreation. Every form of classicism takes on characteristics of its own time, and it is our task in this special issue to examine the dynamic diversification, hybridization, and fragmentation of cultural memories that reinvent and reimagine the Chinese cultural past in our hyperconnected digital age. By consciously adopting the term *classicism*, we also intend to decouple it from its Eurocentric conceptual history. We argue that every high tradition that is venerably evoked by agents of its cultural memory to serve functions similar to Greco-Roman classicism should enjoy the same claim to the nomenclature of being "classical." Today various classical traditions—Egyptian, Indian, Arabic, Japanese, to name but a few—are riding the digital waves across media platforms and genres to endow contemporary cultures with the sheen of a distinguished past. A cross-cultural study of contemporary classicisms is urgently needed to reevaluate the meaning and functions of cultural memories for the formation of group identities in an increasingly interconnected and multipolar world.

Furthermore, the functions of classicisms are highly varied. While classicism may be employed to serve conservative, authoritarian, or hegemonic agendas, it is not intrinsically the opposite of innovation, or even of avant-gardism. Indeed, the extent to which *modernism* and *classicism* may be perceived as contradictory terms at all is due to the fact that modernism, wrongfully, "has been so strongly identified with aesthetic innovation, and because modernist studies has in turn made originality the core principle of aesthetic value."[10] In fact, geniuses of originality are never conceived in the void of cultural memories. Pioneers of Western modernism, such as T. S. Eliot, Pablo Picasso, and Igor Stravinsky, were all professed classicists.[11] After the postmodern turn, classicism may well be, in the words of Milan Kundera, a kind of "antimodern modernism," or even "the only modernism worthy of the name" today. As he points out, while being conservative used to mean being comfortable with the status quo, today the status quo is moving, so that "a person could be both progressive and conformist, conservative and rebel, at the same time."[12] Indeed, the kind of aesthetics that serves agendas of mass mobilization termed as "revolutions" may itself be conservative, as evinced by the dominant art practices under Stalin's Soviet Union or Mao's China. We may envision a kind of avant-garde classicism that rejects relentless progressivism and "revolutions" as another status quo. While we do not naively ignore the hegemonic exercise of classicism, this issue pays special attention to the diverse ends and means of various articulations of classicism, from pop to avant-garde and from aesthetic to epistemological.

As such, Sinophone classicism constantly reminds cultural producers and consumers, regardless of their vernaculars, of their shared cultural memories, often tied to the written Chinese language. It thus becomes an urgent task to rethink what the purported "Chinese traditions," in a non-static and non-statist sense of the concept, entail for the purpose of redefining Chineseness as a decentralized, multilingual, and multicultural identity. By stressing the dimensionality of Sinophone culture rather than its substantiality, we follow Arjun Appadurai's suggestion to think of culture "less as a property of individuals and groups and more as a heuristic device that we can use to talk about differences."[13] Whenever we use the epithet *Chinese* or *Sinophone* in association with culture, it is a heuristic device rather than a suggestion of any essentialized, homogenous, or overdetermined ontological entity. We argue that Sinophone classicism may at times be associated with, but must be decoupled from, Chinese cultural nationalism as well as global postmodern conservatism. Caution against the misuse of the past as chauvinistic mythology, however, should not lead to a blanket denunciation of any evocation of the past, since condemnation does not address the genuine grievance over the dystopic side of cosmopolitan homogenization. Instead, creative imagination is necessary to transform the past in the service of contemporary and local purposes. We therefore borrow the Heideggerian critique of the nature of modern technology as "enframing" (*das Gestell*) to reflect on the dangers and "saving powers" of digital technology. Today Chineseness is increasingly shaped by cybernetic data, censorship, and recommendations made by powerful algorithms, the copyrights of which belong mostly to domineering US- and PRC-based digital platforms. The paradigm of Sinophone classicism is proposed, in Yang's words, "to enable the rethinking of dynamic, multilayered, and evolving cultural exchanges among Sinophone communities,"[14] in constant vigilance against cosmopolitan homogenization, on one hand, and Han nationalism or cultural essentialism, on the other.

In recent years, both editors of this special issue have attempted to grapple with the changing notions of Chineseness and their ramifications. David Der-wei Wang has called attention to the dialecticism of "Sinophone/Xenophone changeability" within and without China as opposed to the time-honored discourse of "Sinophone/Xenophone differentiation."[15] Zhiyi Yang has proposed to redefine Chineseness as "experienced," hereby temporal and mnemonic, a proposal that localizes the social and dynamic process of identity construction in the domain of everyday subjectivity, remembrance, and imagination.[16] By defining Chineseness as cultural remembrance that constitutes "the work of the imagination,"[17] it is liberated from both the geographic border and the political authority that often control the discourse. Individuals become "Chinese" when they voluntarily or involuntarily act as agents of cultural remembrance, hereby reactivating the connection to a repertoire of collective memory in local, vernacular, and contemporaneous contexts. This understanding also acknowledges the multidimensionality of individual subjectivity and posits that one can be both Chinese and not Chinese at the same time.[18] Ms. Lee, for instance, considers herself first and foremost a Malaysian citizen and is equally comfortable with her choice to live in the highly Anglicized Singapore. Instead of being essentially "Chinese," she is equally Malay, Singaporean, and cosmopolitan, with different aspects of her identity being called-for in different constellations of contextual factors.

Digitality has exerted enormous impact on the academic and affective inquiry into classicism. We are witnessing how technologies ranging from databases to search engines, algorithms, global positioning systems, cybernetic reality, and avatar communication have profoundly transformed the instrumental aspect of our interaction with antiquity. What matters more are the conceptual, emotional, and even ontological shake-ups brought about by digital engagement *and* entanglement with classicism. As humanists, we may remain less informed regarding the mechanisms of computational protocols; this fact, however, cannot keep us from conceiving of, or even imagining, a new paradigm of accessing the past: not only the "pastness" of the past but also the "nowness" and "futurity" of the past. In other words, digital configuration has shed new light on the structure of knowledge and feeling in relation to the legacies—as well as the potentials—of tradition.

Here are a few examples drawn from recent Chinese/Sinophone literature. Liu Cixin's "Poetry Cloud" describes an extraterrestrial spectacle of Chinese poetry being transformed into a mega-database, a "poetry cloud," generating infinitely new compositions.[19] Still, how to assess the excellence of select products remains an insurmountable challenge. Wu Mingyi's "Two Thousand Meters above the Cloud" describes climate catastrophe, animalistic mystery, romantic bereavement, and rampant computer viruses at the calling of the magical word *cloud*. Whereas Tung Kai-cheung's V City fiction series offers a "virtual archaeology" of Hong Kong or Victoria City in its futurist ruination, Lo Yi-chin's *Ming Dynasty* takes us on a planetary tour through which the splendor and decadence of a bygone dynasty are brought back like a metaverse. Chen Chuncheng's "Mass of the *Dream of Red Chamber*" introduces the classic as the "book of all books" that manifests as much as conceals all secrets of humanity, a book that refuses to be "cleaned up" by hegemonic censorship. With language that includes words such as *cloud*, *virus*, and "memory," these works teach us how the invention of posthuman enlightenment entails the incantation of premodern enchantment, or vice versa.

Above all, conventional concepts such as the "book," "canon," "oeuvre," "history," and "*wen*" (literariness) are seen as subject to contestation. In particular, if "*wen*" etymologically denotes the amorphous repository of notions such as patterning, traces, inscription, craftsmanship, belles lettres, cultural upbringing, and civilization, one may find unlikely resonances in the digital humanities in which knowledge production defies the immanent, linear model, pointing to both sedimentation and proliferation, both coding and recoding, both acquisition and immersion. To be sure, we are not suggesting a simple parallelism any more than an "objective correlative" that prompts a renewed appraisal of the past. Indeed, we are suggesting a vigorous engagement with the extant paradigm.

Being in Cyberspace

What does digital media technology entail, besides serving as a channel for global, facile, and instantaneous dissemination? As Martin Heidegger argues, the essence of modern technology is not technological but a kind of "enframing," a challenging "unconcealment" that turns all things into an undifferentiated supply of the available, which he calls the "standing-reserve" (*der Bestand*).[20] Instead of being a means of liberation, technology as an enframing encloses humankind in a technologized view of the world. In this sense, we may argue that contemporary digital technology, in an unprecedented fashion, has turned all cultural memories into a "standing-reserve," an omnipresence that radically re-enframes our daily interaction in space-time. In the words of Patrick Walters and Rita Kop, "Heidegger's characterization of human beings as 'being-in-the-world' means that living in a digital environment entails an altered sense of self—being-in-cyberspace."[21] So what does it mean for this self to experience its Chineseness, epistemologically and physically, in a digitalized world?

Enframing does not simply mean a framework. Rather, *en-* suggests an active challenge, a calling-forth into revealing. Heidegger's examples of this challenge include humanity's exploitation of nature and turning it into a storage house for the standing energy reserve and our own permission to be exploited to serve the demands of technology (as in "human resource"). In his somewhat arcane words, enframing is "an ordaining of destining" in the sense of revelation.[22] Digital technology challenges the accumulated human knowledge to turn into information, potentially accessible anywhere, anytime, by anyone. Not only collective memories of cultures but also our individual memories, too, are increasingly uploaded into a cloud and become instantly sharable and (at least theoretically) permanently storable. The cloud functions as external storage of the human brain, promising to alleviate it from the burden of rote memory. The price of liberation, however, is an ever-deeper degree of codependency between man and technology. We, in this way, are in danger of becoming the standing-reserve of artificial intelligence machines, providing raw data for the latter's evolution—in other words, of becoming bio-power. Information technology, furthermore, "functions as a kind of modern formatting of experience," by not only transforming the "content" of experience into information but also preformatting how experience or being happens.[23] The profound ramifications of such transformations and pre-formatting cannot be overestimated.

Again, in Ms. Lee's case, social media, recommendation algorithms, education, and networks of migration conspire to empower Sinophone classicism as a cultural and consumerist option. Consumerism feeds on "imagined nostalgia": nostalgia for things that never were and that the nostalgic consumers never had.[24] Yet by eventually turning into an experience more encompassing and immersive, what Lee has acquired in the end seems to resemble the traditional understanding of "national identity" as a kind of destiny into which an individual is born. She laments that, in Singapore, she can no longer perform Daoist rituals, as there is a ban on burning candles or paper money. It is digital media that presents her with the alternative "standing-reserve" of cultural products tied to a foreign past, inhabited with faces and bodies that resemble her own. In trying to become like them, she "rediscovers," or perhaps "reinvents," herself, through accumulating pastiches associated with Chineseness in a world culture bazaar. In Fredric Jameson's words, such a pastiche is a performance of "older philosophical moves," as though they still had content but which have long become "simulacra, the somnambulistic speech of a subject long since historically extinct."[25] Chineseness thus becomes a simulacrum of identity as destiny.

Notably, social media connects Lee with a virtual community of people with similar interests and languages. She chooses to use Douyin instead of TikTok because the former connects her to content creators living behind the PRC firewall. She shares her photos on Instagram because this is what her friends use. Arguably, though her actual *Gemeinschaft* (community) consists of acquaintances living outside mainland China, she has chosen Douyin to connect to an expanded community—a *Gesellschaft* (society) of strangers. As Ernest Gellner argues, nationalism is "a phenomenon of *Gesellschaft* using the idiom of *Gemeinschaft*: a mobile anonymous society simulating a closed cosy community."[26] In other words, a mobile society "sharing a high (codified, literate) culture, and using it as its main tool of work, defines and delimits its members not by status but by culture, or by eligibility-into-a-culture (known as 'roots')."[27] In this case, digital technology offers both a means of resistance (against Malaysian nationalism and its program of cultural assimilation) and a channel of voluntary recruitment. It helps Lee transcend the Malaysian *Gemeinschaft* into which she was born and relocate herself, at least in certain times and contexts, into another geographically dispersed and rhizomatically connected ethno-cultural community. Digital technology hence leads to intense disruption and fragmentation of geopolitical as well as ethno-cultural communities, by building kinetic connections among atomized individuals who act as agents of cultural remembrance and imagination. The ramifications of this virtual cultural-linguistic nationalism remain to be observed in long-term academic studies.

Hybrid and Timeless Time

As we have repeatedly emphasized, cultural remembrance is simultaneously an act of cultural imagination. On the surface of it, remembrance is past oriented, while imagination is future oriented. The gap between these two acts, however, may be narrower than their vernacular uses tend to assume. To remember, we need to retrieve fragments of memory stored in various neurons and reassemble them into a plausible narrative, in a framework constantly shifting according to acquired contextual information. Memory, in this way, can be biased, manipulated, and contaminated.[28] On the other hand, imagination is critically dependent on memory, since we can only imagine on the basis of things that we already know.[29] Every instance of remembrance, in a certain sense, is a renewed imagination of the past. Classicism, as evoked cultural memory, is thus a future-oriented look at the past, which in turn is reimagined to suit the needs and desires of the present. The present thus becomes haunted and ghosted. As Rossella Ferrari's article in this special issue shows, digital technologies, by consciously reusing "material haunted by memory," are thus turned into "techniques of hauntological enhancement of the classical form." In Fangdai Chen's article, Chen Chuncheng's vision of the classical novel *Dream in the Red Chamber*'s serving as a futuristic holy text demonstrates that, when the temporality and materiality of literature are "decomposed," literature also becomes emancipated from its social determination. The classical hereby becomes a kind of overwhelming presence in the future.

In our digital times, classicism necessarily embodies hybrid notions of time, even though at times it threatens to reduce temporality to a kind of timeless presentification. Hybridity, as an essential link in Ihab Hassan's "catena of postmodern features," is described as "the mutant replication of genres, including parody, travesty, pastiche." It equalizes a model and its replicas and thereby creates "a different concept of tradition, one in which continuity and discontinuity, high and low culture, mingle not to imitate but to expand the past in the present. In that plural present, all styles are dialectically available in an interplay between the Now and the Not Now, the Same and the Other."[30] Today authenticity is increasingly revealed to be a kind of cultural construct, often implicated in marketing and consumption as a device for producing meaning and monetary value.[31] In contrast, genuinely innovative classicist literature and art are by necessity hybrid, a dynamic eclecticism of cultural influences, temporal references, and registers. In these works, the past is both celebrated for its eternal reoccurrence and ironized as a simulacrum, a reaffirmation of the contemporary as the continually self-renewing outcome of globalizing modernity. The circular and the linear logics of time, therefore, coexist in the same work. Both articles by Xiaofei Tian and Zhiyi Yang examine innovative classicist poetry in Chinese cyberspace, with different foci. Tian's article explores the boundaries between "new" and "old" poetry—a politics of form perceived as the "internal affair" of the Chinese language—and proposes a spatialized instead of temporalized view of modern Chinese poetry: that is, to envision it as a space "marked by multipolarity and hybridity." Zhiyi Yang's article explores the interaction between technology and aesthetics: how the unique ecosystem of the Chinese internet around the millennial turn had given rise to a kind of "avant-garde classicism," how the current Chinese digital platforms instead foster artistic and ideological conservatism, and the mnemonic tasks facing researchers regarding the observation and archiving of the rapid transformations of cyberspace.

Hans Ulrich Gumbrecht criticized the eagerness to fill the ever-broadening present with artifacts from the past and reproductions based on such artifacts as the desire for "presentification."[32] Such a broad present, as he argues, would end up accumulating different past worlds and their artifacts in a sphere of simultaneity. But what the network society has further actualized is the shattering of "linear, irreversible, measurable, predictable time." [33] It results not only, in Manuel Castells's words, in "a relativization of time according to social contexts or alternatively the return to time reversibility as if reality could become entirely captured in cyclical myths," but something even more profound: "the mixing of tenses to create a forever universe, not self-expanding but self-maintaining, not cyclical but random, not recursive but incursive: timeless time."[34] Technology helps transcend the context of temporal existence, and all values are selectively appropriated to serve the ever-present, as symbolized by video games. Michael O'Krent's article explores how the Taiwanese video game *Word Game* employs the uniform size of sinographs to present them as the fundamental units of on-screen images that simultaneously signify through graphical appearance and textual meaning. Its logic of game-play mechanics consists not of mathematical universals but of culturally determined relationships between sinographs. In Yedong Sh-Chen's article, the "skin" that gamers don becomes a special digital milieu where "China stories" are told and debated, and their "goodness" performed and contested. The growing trend toward classicism in digital skin design illustrates how the Chinese game industry responds to the demand of representing and reconfiguring Chineseness.

Notably, performing Chineseness is also an economic question. A fabulously beautiful classicist digital "skin" with a certain depth of material history is also fabulously expensive. Or to go back to the case of Ms. Lee explored at the beginning of this essay: it took her, an IT worker in Singapore, two years to decide to invest in Hanfu and accessories, as she demands a certain level of material-historical faithfulness. This awareness is what separates cheap Hanfu costumes from Hanfu as a venerable symbol of cultural identity. Classicist extravaganza on a grander scale is manifested in the two recent web dramas that Michelle Yeh examines. Here "Chinese style" is created through a deep commitment to material authenticity, a crucial distinction that separates "classicist drama" from "costume drama." Similarly, Liang Luo's in-depth analysis of the film version of the Cantonese opera *White Snake* (2019) shows how Sinophone regional theater also responds to the challenge of the digital turn. With digitally produced "ink painting–style Chinese aesthetics," it arguably becomes a "musical with Chinese characteristics."

But perhaps the correlation is not that simple: ultimately, what separates "deep classicism" from "surface classicism" is more than a matter of money. As Tarryn Li-Min Chun's article shows, the dance theater piece *Zhici qinglü* 只此青綠, originally a well-researched work of art with depth and dimensionality, can easily turn into a propagandist visual spectacle in the service of state power. In her words, surface classicism in contemporary Chinese performance "suggests not an immaturity of engagement with ancient models but, rather, a targeted mobilization of seemingly superficial qualities to map the classical onto the contemporary." In contrast to the digital visual extravaganza characterizing the classicist performance of Chineseness, Laura Vermeeren's article explores the platform Kuaishou 快手, favored mostly by rural and grassroots content creators. The performative copying of the Buddhist Heart Sutra in calligraphy reveals instead a more ambivalent and devotional attitude toward the classical cultural past.

Ultimately, digital technology is only a medium. What is being mediated in "digital classicism" is the cultural memory of an elevated, re-created, and reimagined past. As a result of that mediation, we—agents of Chinese cultural memory—are the ones being elevated, re-created, and reimagined in correlation to this past. This kind of "embodied digitality" is what Chiehting Hsieh skillfully explores through an examination of dance notations in modern Chinese dance and what makes it "Chinese," which requires analysis of digital techniques as techniques of the body. In his words, it is the body that counts. While classicism assigns the contemporary "being in cyberspace" a mnemonic connection to a cultural past, only when doing classicism becomes the cultural agent's muscle memory—in slowly wrapping a Hanfu skirt around the body, in holding a calligraphic brush to write a sinograph, in training one's voice to sing a piece of Cantonese opera or one's tongue to recite a classicist poem—does the past becomes truly embodied. The cultural agent thereby gains an "identity" in the sense of becoming "identified" by (as well as with) the embodied past.

ZHIYI YANG is professor of Sinology at University of Frankfurt. Her research investigates how Chinese classical lyric traditions engage with aesthetics (of nature and art) and with ethics (of private and public life). She is the author of *Dialectics of Spontaneity: The Aesthetics and Ethics of Su Shi (1037–1101) in Poetry* (2015) and *Poetry, History, Memory: Wang Jingwei and China in Dark Times* (2023). She is currently writing a monograph on avant-garde classicist poetry in the Sinophone cyberspace and collaborating with scholars on an interdisciplinary project of global Sinophone classicisms.

DAVID DER-WEI WANG is Edward C. Henderson Professor in Chinese Literature and Comparative Literature, Harvard University. He is director of CCK Inter-University Center for Sinological Studies, Academician of Academia Sinica and American Academy of Arts and Sciences. Wang's specialties are modern and contemporary Chinese and Sinophone literature, Late Qing fiction, and comparative literary theory. His recent publications include *The Monster That Is History* (2004), *Taiwan under Japanese Colonial Rule* (coedited with Pinghui Liao, 2007), *The Lyrical in Epic Time* (2014), and *Why Fiction Matters in Contemporary China* (2020). He is editor of *A New Literary History of Modern China* (2017), published by Harvard University Press.

/////////////////////////////

Notes

1   WeChat audio interview by Zhiyi Yang, October 23, 2022. We thank Yifan Dai, a doctoral candidate and Hanfu researcher at Goethe University Frankfurt, for providing the contact to Ms. Lee. For more on Hanfu, see Leibold, "More than a Category"; Carrico, *Great Han*; and Dai, "Hanfu Renaissance."
2   Debray, *Transmitting Culture*, 2.
3   Yang, "Sinophone Classicism," 9. We thank the journal editor for allowing us to use some materials from this article.
4   For the full official English translation of this text, see https://english.www.gov.cn/atts/stream/files/63591d06c6d028997c37ca9e (accessed January 24, 2024).
5   Yang, "Sinophone Classicism," 2.
6   Shih, "Concept of the Sinophone," 710.
7   Shih, "Against Diaspora."
8   Chua, *Structure, Audience and Soft Power*, 35.
9   Perry, "Classicism."
10 Hayot, *On Literary Worlds*, 4.
11 Ziolkowski, *Classicism of the Twenties*.
12 Kundera, *Curtain*, 55–56.
13 Appadurai, *Modernity at Large*, 13.
14 Yang, "Sinophone Classicism," 4.
15 Wang, "Huayi zhi bian."
16 Yang, "Sinophone Classicism," esp. 10–11.
17 Appadurai, *Modernity at Large*, 4.
18 Yang, "Sinophone Classicism," 11.
19 Fascinatingly, from the all-around artistic talent Xiaobing 小冰 (www.poem.xiaoice.com/) to classicist verse programs developed by Baidu (*weini xieshi* 為你寫詩), Tsinghua University (*jiuge* 九歌), and Huawei (*yuefu* 樂府), artificial intelligence–powered poetry machines are no longer a scientific fantasy.
20 Heidegger, "Question Concerning Technology," 14–17.
21 Walters and Kop, "Heidegger, Digital Technology, and Postmodern Education," 282.
22 Heidegger, "Question Concerning Technology," 24.
23 Ziarek, "Powers to Be," 176.
24 Appadurai, *Modernity at Large*, 77.
25 Jameson, *Cultural Turn*, 98.
26 Gellner, *Nationalism*, 74.
27 Ibid., 75.

28 On unreliable memory, see, e.g., Tversky and Kahneman, "Judgment under Uncertainty"; Plant, "On Testimony"; Gardner, "Unreliable Memories."

29 See, e.g., Abraham and Bubic, "Semantic Memory."

30 Hassan, "Pluralism in Postmodern Perspective," 506.

31 See Trilling, *Sincerity and Authenticity*; Canavan, "Post-postmodern Consumer Authenticity."

32 Gumbrecht, *Production of Presence*, 121.

33 Castells, *Rise of the Network Society*, 463.

34 Ibid., 464–65.

References

Abraham, Anna, and Andreja Bubic. "Semantic Memory as the Root of Imagination." *Frontiers in Psychology* 6 (2015): article 325. www.ncbi.nlm.nih.gov/pmc/articles/PMC4371585/.

Appadurai, Arjun. *Modernity at Large: Cultural Dimensions of Globalization*. Minneapolis: University of Minnesota Press, 1996.

Canavan, Brendan. "Post-postmodern Consumer Authenticity, Shantay You Stay or Sashay Away? A Netnography of RuPaul's Drag Race Fans." *Marketing Theory* 21, no. 2 (2021): 251–76.

Carrico, Kevin. *The Great Han: Race, Nationalism, and Tradition in China Today*. Oakland: University of California Press, 2017.

Castells, Manuel. *The Rise of the Network Society*. 2nd ed. Chichester, UK: Wiley-Blackwell, 2010.

Chua, Beng Huat. *Structure, Audience, and Soft Power in East Asian Pop Culture*. Hong Kong: Hong Kong University Press, 2012.

Dai, Yifan. "Hanfu Renaissance: The Ethno-Symbolic Reconstruction of Han Costume." MA thesis, Goethe University Frankfurt, 2019.

Debray, Régis. *Transmitting Culture*. Translated by Eric Rauth. New York: Columbia University Press, 2000.

Gardner, Graham. "Unreliable Memories and Other Contingencies: Problems with Biographical Knowledge." *Qualitative Research* 1, no. 2 (2001): 185–204.

Gellner, Ernest. *Nationalism*. New York: New York University Press, 1997.

Gumbrecht, Hans Ulrich. *Production of Presence: What Meaning Cannot Convey*. Stanford, CA: Stanford University Press, 2004.

Hassan, Ihab. "Pluralism in Postmodern Perspective." *Critical Inquiry* 12, no. 3 (1986): 503–20.

Hayot, Eric. *On Literary Worlds*. Oxford: Oxford University Press, 2012.

Heidegger, Martin. "The Question Concerning Technology." In *The Question Concerning Technology and Other Essays*, translated by William Lovitt, 3–35. New York: Harper and Row, 1977.

Jameson, Fredric. *The Cultural Turn: Selected Writings on the Postmodern, 1983–1998*. London: Verso, 1998.

Kundera, Milan. *The Curtain: An Essay in Seven Parts*. Translated by Linda Asher. New York: HarperCollins, 2007.

Leibold, James. "More than a Category: Han Supremacism on the Chinese Internet." *China Quarterly*, no. 203 (2010): 539–59.

Perry, Curtis. "Classicism." In *The Princeton Encyclopedia of Poetry and Poetics*, 4th ed., edited by Roland Greene, Stephen Cushman, Clare Cavanagh, Jahan Ramazani, Paul F. Rouzer, Harris Feinsod, David Marno, and Alexandra Slessarev, 263–66. Princeton, NJ: Princeton University Press, 2012.

Plant, Bob. "On Testimony, Sincerity, and Truth." *Paragraph, Trauma, Therapy, and Representation* 30, no. 1 (2007): 30–50.

Shih, Shu-mei. "Against Diaspora: The Sinophone as Places of Cultural Production." In *Global Chinese Literature: Critical Essays*, edited by Jing Tsu and David Der-wei Wang, 29–48. Leiden: Brill, 2010.

———. "The Concept of the Sinophone." *PMLA* 126, no. 3 (2011): 709–18.

Trilling, Lionel. *Sincerity and Authenticity*. Cambridge, MA: Harvard University Press, 1972.

Tversky, Amos, and Daniel Kahneman. "Judgment under Uncertainty: Heuristics and Biases." *Science* 185, no. 4157 (1974): 1124–31.

Walters, Patrick, and Rita Kop. "Heidegger, Digital Technology, and Postmodern Education: From Being in Cyberspace to Meeting on MySpace." *Bulletin of Science, Technology, and Society* 29, no. 4 (2009): 278–86.

Wang, David Der-wei. "Huayi zhi bian: Huayu yuxi yanjiu de xin shijie" 華夷之變：華語語系研究的新視界 [Sinophone/Xenophone Studies: Toward a Poetics of Wind, Sound, and Changeability]. *Zhongguo xiandai wenxue* 中國現代文學 [Modern Chinese Literature], no. 34 (2018): 1–28.

Yang, Zhiyi. "Sinophone Classicism: Chineseness as Temporal and Mnemonic Experience in the Digital Era." *Journal of Asian Studies* 81, no. 4 (2022): 1–15.

Ziarek, Krzysztof. "Powers to Be: Art and Technology in Heidegger and Foucault." *Research in Phenomenology* 28 (1998): 162–94.

ROSSELLA FERRARI

Xiqu 2.0
Expanded Chinese Opera in Digital Times

ABSTRACT *Xiqu* 2.0 designates an experimental approach to adapting and updating the classical theaters of the Sinophone region (*xiqu*) and a form of expanded Chinese opera in digital times. It highlights strategies of versioning and serialization of classical texts and tropes in (post-)modern performance environments and foregrounds media and textual interactivity, networking, and participatory contexts of production, reception, and circulation—including the production, reception, and circulation of cultural memory in the contemporary Sinosphere. The stage practice of Hong Kong–based multi-genre artist Danny Yung of Zuni Icosahedron and his long-term work with Tang Xianzu's *Peony Pavilion* (1598) illustrate the multiple dimensions of *xiqu* 2.0. Representative productions include the digital Kun opera *Sigmund Freud in Search of Chinese Matter and Mind* (2002, 2016) and the series *The Interrupted Dream*, launched in 2018. The latter links Tang's oneiric imaginary to the postcolonial critique of orientalism through references to seventeenth-century chinoiserie at the court of Louis XIV. Updated for livestreaming during the COVID-19 pandemic, the series served as a virtual channel of mediated memory across the digital Sinosphere in the aftermath of the 2019–20 Hong Kong protests and as a commentary on *ancien* and modern regimes, past and present revolutions, old and new Chinese dreams.

KEYWORDS Chinese opera, technology, experimental *xiqu*, *Peony Pavilion*, Zuni Icosahedron

This essay introduces *xiqu* 2.0 as an articulation of contemporary "Sinophone classicism"[1] and a form of expanded Chinese opera in digital times. *Xiqu* 2.0 designates an experimental and, often, mediated approach to adapting and updating the classical theaters of the Chinese-speaking region—collectively categorized as *xiqu* 戲曲, or Chinese opera. It refers to the repurposing of textual and performance traditions in ways that draw attention to processes of aesthetic, epistemic, and semantic expansion of the canons, conventions, and (analog) corporealities of the Sinophone theatrical heritage through techniques and technologies that destabilize the codes of the classical form. *Xiqu* 2.0 highlights strategies of versioning and serialization of classical texts and tropes in (post-)modern performance environments. It foregrounds media and textual interactivity, networking, and participatory contexts of production, reception, and circulation—including the production, reception, and circulation of cultural memory in the contemporary Sinosphere.

PRISM: THEORY AND MODERN CHINESE LITERATURE • 20:2 • SEPTEMBER 2023
DOI 10.1215/25783491-10992720 • © 2023 LINGNAN UNIVERSITY

The stage practice of Sinophone multi-artist Danny Yung Ning-tsun 榮念
曾 (1943–), co–artistic director of the Hong Kong arts collective Zuni Icosahedron 進念二十面體 (hereafter Zuni), aptly illustrates the multiple dimensions
of *xiqu* 2.0. Yung has developed a distinctive style of experimental *xiqu* through
long-term work with classical theater practitioners, and his productions routinely incorporate texts and symbols from classical Chinese culture. Representative of Yung's expanded approach to *xiqu* classicism is his long-standing
work with scenes from Tang Xianzu's 湯顯祖 (1550–1616) *Mudan ting* 牡丹亭
(Peony Pavilion, 1598), beginning with the digital *kunqu* 昆曲 (or *kunju* 昆劇;
Kun opera) *Fuluoyide xunzhao Zhongguo qing yu shi* 佛洛伊德尋找中國情與事
(Sigmund Freud in Search of Chinese Matter and Mind, 2002; hereafter *Freud*)
to the series *Jingmeng* 驚夢 (The Interrupted Dream). Inaugurated in 2018 as a
trans-Asian project, the early installments of the series connect Tang's oneiric
imaginary to the postcolonial critique of orientalism through references to seventeenth-century chinoiserie at the court of Louis XIV (1638–1715). In 2020 it
was revived with a Hong Kong cast and livestreamed on Zuni's YouTube channel, ZLive, during the COVID-19 pandemic. In the aftermath of the 2019–20
anti-Extradition Law Amendment Bill (ELAB) protests in Hong Kong, this
new virtual incarnation—followed by an updated hybrid version in 2021—
reconfigured the series as a conduit of mediated memory across the digital
Sinosphere and an incisive commentary on *ancien* and modern regimes, past
and present revolutions, old and new Chinese dreams.

The generative adaptation of tradition that characterizes Zuni's collaborations with classical performers from the Sinosphere and the wider Asian
region sheds light on the capacity of contemporary forms of reinvented classicism to resignify heritage genres and traditional bodies as transcultural
conduits of historical critique.[2] Accordingly, the intertextual and intermedial
archaeology of Yung's *xiqu* 2.0 taps into the politics of interculturalism and
cultural heritage to facilitate the articulation and sharing of trans-Chinese
relational memory.

The first part of this essay outlines various connotations of the language of
2.0 as (1) updating and upgrading, (2) versioning and serialization, and (3) participation and interactivity. It illustrates how each of these connotations informs
the definition of *xiqu* 2.0 in Yung's practice through examples of his work with
Zuni. It also explores the potential of Zuni's brand of expanded minimalism to
both destabilize and decolonize conventional *xiqu* epistemologies. The second
part elucidates how the characteristics of *xiqu* 2.0 inform the content and form
of the Interrupted Dream series by reviewing its major installments in light
of Yung's multilayered expansion of *Peony Pavilion*'s classical dreamology and
dramaturgical treatment of the dream motif as "common ground for discourse"
共通的議題.[3]

2.0 as Updating and Upgrading

The basic meaning of *2.0* suggests something new or different from an original version. It evokes the semantics of technology and notions of innovation and upgrading achieved through technical expansion. In this sense, *xiqu* 2.0 encapsulates the retro-technological mode of adapting and updating the Sinophone theatrical heritage that defines Zuni's practice of experimental *xiqu* (*shiyan xiqu* 實驗戲曲)—or, rather, experiments with *xiqu*. This distinction emphasizes that these are not new renditions of canonical pieces originating from the traditional *xiqu* community (an established but separate practice) but works of contemporary theater that incorporate and expand select musical, corporeal, and design features of *xiqu*.

The conceptual framework of *xiqu* 2.0 illuminates discrete modes of interaction between classical conventions and modern techniques. *Xiqu* 2.0 condenses, adapts, and amplifies essential aspects of the original version (the classical form) and (dis-)places them in recontextualized and, often, technologically enhanced environments. In *xiqu* 2.0 the analog theatricality of indigenous forms such as *kunqu* and *jingju* 京劇 interfaces with electronic soundscapes, multimedia installations, new digital arts, and advanced technologies such as augmented and virtual reality, digital imaging, motion capture visualization, three-dimensional audio, telematic performance, and livestreaming. *Xiqu* 2.0 resonates with contemporary definitions of new media dramaturgy as "an expanded practice of conceptual and creative labour across arts institutions and industries facilitated by recent technical developments, mainly but not exclusively in digital media."[4] Zuni co–artistic director Mathias Woo Yan-wai 胡恩威 (1968–) has been especially active in technological research for digital theater. In 2017 he initiated a dedicated platform, the Freespace Tech Lab (renamed Z Innovation Lab in 2018)—a mirror-walled, black-box-style, 3.2-meter-deep sunken stage outfitted with state-of-the-art equipment (fig. 1).

Second, the "expanded dramaturgy"[5] of *xiqu* 2.0 involves the application of contemporary (postmodernist, postdramatic) theatrical semiotics and nontraditional acting and directing methods to the production and performance of *xiqu*. It also refers to the amplification of the generic remit of *xiqu* through hybridization with techniques from other Asian theater traditions. In this sense, it denotes a form of aesthetic expansion through intergeneric and intercultural "interweaving."[6] This expansive approach is not limited to technical experimentation; as Jessica Yeung 楊慧儀 notes, "Zuni's brand of hybridity fulfills the unique function of being a cognitive tool."[7] In line with the company's stated aim of embedding theater in society, additional features of *xiqu* 2.0's expanded dimension are the intertextual assemblage of symbols and narratives from the classical literary tradition and the remediation of the nonhuman materialities of the classical performance apparatus to reactivate historical memories and reflect on current events.

FIGURE 1. *The Interrupted Dream* in the Z Innovation Lab, Hong Kong Cultural Centre, 2018. Courtesy of Zuni Icosahedron.

In other words, *xiqu* 2.0 subjects *xiqu* to a process of semantic and functional expansion achieved through "a politics of dramaturgy that is visibly about the arts connecting with the social world."[8]

As the analysis of the Interrupted Dream series reveals, such a complex mediality of transhistorical memory is central to Zuni's experiments with Asia's heritage theaters. An earlier example is *Lingxi* 靈戲 (The Spirits Play, 2011–12), a multilingual, multi-genre adaptation of Singaporean playwright Kuo Pao Kun's 郭寶崑 (1939–2002) eponymous 1998 drama. Codirected by Yung and Japan's Satō Makoto with performers from Tokyo and Nanjing, the project resulted from an inter-Asian nongovernmental network dedicated to revitalizing the region's intangible cultural heritage (ICH) of indigenous performing arts through intercultural collaboration. The production merges *kunqu*, Japanese *nō*, contemporary theater and dance, electronic music, and digital media. It cross-references Kuo's reflection on the Japanese occupation of Singapore during the Pacific War (1942–45) with comparable experiences of wartime brutality in China, such as the Nanjing Massacre of 1937 and the more recent memory of the Tiananmen Square crackdown of 1989, conveyed largely through intertextual references to figures of violated children and mourning mothers across Asia and across history.[9]

The capacity of heritage genres to activate a mnemonic echo chamber for historical and current meanings is likewise manifest in the reflection on the role and responsibility of intellectuals and artists under authoritarian regimes in *Yeben* 夜奔 (Flee by Night; various versions since 2004), a contemporary transposition of the eponymous *kunqu* classic, and *Huangshan lei* 荒山淚 (Tears of Barren Hill, 2008), named after a script by *jingju* actor Cheng Yanqiu 程硯秋 (1904–58). The politics of memory in the former address the relationship between the individual and state power and the moral imperative to flee a corrupt system. The latter reconstructs scenes from Cheng's 1932 Berlin sojourn, interposed with sequences from Leni Riefenstahl's (1902–2003) documentary on Hitler's rise to power, *Triumph of the Will* (*Triumph des Willens*, 1935), and archival footage from the Chinese Cultural Revolution (1966–76) to evoke mediated memories of modern violence across spatiotemporal boundaries and question the relationship between art and power.[10]

The implications of recasting classicism in postmodernist settings or renovating tradition through new media go beyond the design of enhanced avant-garde aesthetics. Technological expansion tackles more fundamental questions of the preservation and sustainability of indigenous performance traditions as significant expressions of Sinophone ICH. Rather than a depthless celebration of technology, *xiqu* 2.0 exposes its double-edged ontology. Technology can be alienating, overpowering, and constricting to the performer. But it also creates an expanded space for questioning, which is central to Zuni's creative philosophy.[11] Classicism in the 2.0 mode seeks to ensure the continued relevance of the classical heritage by expanding not only its theatrical semantics but also its sensory and synesthetic latitudes, its receptive horizon, and its potential for transhistorical and transcultural resignification. As an illustration of a broader global trend toward ICH technologization,[12] *xiqu* 2.0 pursues new forms of identification from shared cultural legacies. It upholds the enduring significance of articulations of classical Sinophone cultures for contemporary audiences so that cultural heritage can "become part of the community cultural development."[13] It opens up inherited traditions to new communicative capacities that can positively negotiate the challenges posed by technology and the altered circumstances of cultural production, reception, and transmission in the digital age.

2.0 as Versioning and Serialization

Second, the descriptor *2.0* evokes notions of versioning and serialization that resonate with Zuni's distinctive practice of devising multiple sequential interpretations of a dramatic text or scene; implementing creative formats across successive projects as well as across media and art forms; and developing production concepts and creative platforms as series. Yung's approach deliberately embraces strategies of repetition, replication, and "*ghosting*"[14]—to quote Marvin Carlson's influential concept—such as self-referential citation, aesthetic recycling, and the repurposing of scripts, narratives, images, bodies, and material objects. Carlson examines four dimensions of theater as an ontologically haunted and haunting medium: "the haunted text," "the haunted body," "the haunted production," and "the haunted house." His basic proposition is that every text, body, production, and venue is haunted by the ghosts of preceding texts, bodies, and production elements that have inhabited a theatrical space in the past—either literally, in the case of physical objects such as costumes and stage properties, or figuratively, through practices of intertextuality, citation, adaptation, recasting, and repetition.[15] "The present experience," Carlson writes, "is always ghosted by previous experiences and associations while these ghosts are simultaneously shifted and modified by the processes of recycling and recollection."[16] Already present in the codified "performance citationality"[17] of classic *xiqu*, these dimensions of theatrical déjà vu become most prominent in *xiqu* 2.0.

From this perspective, the definition of *xiqu* 2.0 as expanded Chinese opera foregrounds not only strategies of ontological redefinition through the operations of technology but also techniques of hauntological enhancement of the classical form through "the conscious reuse of material haunted by memory."[18] *Xiqu* 2.0 resonates with notions of theatrical doubling and "restored" or "twice-behaved behavior,"[19] and with the uncanny sense that "*we are seeing what we saw before*"[20]—but with a difference. Versioning, serialization, self-citation, and difference-in-repetition are key to Yung's hauntological approach to *xiqu*, as texts, actors, formats, media, and design elements recur across productions. Carlson associates haunting and ghosting with the mnemonic functions of the theater. Similarly, *xiqu* 2.0 is closely connected to the politics of cultural heritage and cultural memory in the Sinophone region. Several projects realized through the aforementioned Nanjing–Hong Kong–Tokyo ICH network mobilize cultural heritage to speak of cultural memory. Similarly, the 2020–21 installments of *The Interrupted Dream*, examined below, make use of technology to activate a space for memory in Hong Kong in times of protest and pandemic.

The Interrupted Dream is, moreover, a prime illustration of sequential interpretation and versioning of texts and of Yung's sustained exploration of extracts from *Peony Pavilion*—in this case, "Jingmeng" (The Interrupted Dream; scene 10). In the original scene, the aristocratic maiden Du Liniang 杜麗娘 makes love to the scholar Liu Mengmei 柳夢梅 in her dream after taking a springtime stroll in the back garden of the family mansion, which her parents have kept secret from her. The walk in the forbidden garden, amid "all the brilliant riot of the new season,"[21] awakens the sixteen-year-old's sensual desire. Liniang's dream of lovemaking by the garden's peony pavilion enacts this desire, but it is interrupted by the arrival of her mother, who scolds her for venturing out and falling asleep in the middle of the day. The inability to revive the erotic fantasy in real life increases Liniang's "secret discontent,"[22] as she sees her youthful beauty waste away in a secluded existence without the comfort of romantic companionship. Consumed by haunting recollections of her oneiric encounter, Liniang dies of her passion. She roams as a ghost in pursuit of her passion and is ultimately brought back to life by it. Adapting Carlson's comment on William Shakespeare's (1564–1616) *Hamlet* to the Ming-dynasty classic, one could argue that "the density of its ghosting" is among the highest in the Sinophone dramatic tradition,[23] as the play clusters around otherworldly reveries and spectral returns.

The "electronic Kun digital opera" (*dianzi shuma shiyan kunqu* 電子數碼實驗昆曲) *Freud* can be seen as a precursor to *The Interrupted Dream* with respect to Yung's ghosting of Tang's text. Codirected by Yung and Woo and starring Nanjing-based *kunqu* performer Shi Xiaomei 石小梅, *Freud* is itself haunted by dramaturgical repetition as it unfolds through various iterations of scene 26, titled "Jiaohua" 叫畫 (In Praise of the Portrait, aka The Portrait Examined). In this scene, Liu Mengmei takes a stroll in the ruined garden of the Du family mansion years after Liniang's death and discovers the entrancing self-portrait she painted before dying. *Freud* contrasts classical and modern renditions of the scene's music, movement, and lyrics to explore *Peony Pavilion*'s central themes of passion (*qing* 情) and dreaming (*meng* 夢) through Freudian psychoanalysis. It thus interprets the play's oneiric imaginary as an unconscious manifestation of cultural repression and unsatisfied sexual desire.[24]

The "mediated duplication" of Shi's live performance of Liu's role is central to *Freud*'s 2.0 strategies of versioning and doubling, as the "live actor confronts her mediated other through the technologies of reproduction."[25] Shi, a female performer specializing in male (*sheng* 生) roles, executes her version of "In Praise of the Portrait" twice: first in full (male) opera costume with conventional *kunqu* musical accompaniment and subsequently in plain (female) clothes amid a mediascape of electronic music and digital imagery. The scene is then reproduced a third time when a video recording of the first rendition is projected onto a mirrored back panel, intensifying the effect of endless ghosting and proliferation of the intersecting realms of reality, illusion, and self that characterize the dream state.

On the quatercentenary of Tang and Shakespeare in 2016, Shanghai-based *kunqu* actor Zhang Jun 張軍 joined Shi in a new, upgraded version. This version adds intertextual echoes of Hamlet's nightmares and media-induced doppelgängers to the haunted, oneiric assemblage and mediated recycling effect of the original production. In an expanded display of the multilayered operations of ghosting, an extract from yet another *Peony Pavilion*–inspired piece that Yung and Zhang devised in 2015, *Meng duan meng chang* 夢短夢長 (Making Dreams), opens and closes the production. In the second iteration of *Making Dreams* at the end of the *Freud* performance, Zhang holds a Hamletian skull (fig. 2), and projected texts in an earlier sequence include quotations from the Danish prince's most famous soliloquy. In another segment, Zhang's movements are recorded using motion capture technology and visualized during Shi's live performance of "In Praise of the Portrait" (fig. 3). The *xiqu* 2.0 actor is thus recast "as an intermedial agent" and mediator of "the tension between the twin logics of *immediacy*

FIGURE 2. Strategies of ghosting in the 2016 version of *Sigmund Freud in Search of Chinese Matter and Mind*, starring *kunqu* actor Zhang Jun, through citations from William Shakespeare's *Hamlet* and Danny Yung's *Making Dreams* (2015). Courtesy of Zuni Icosahedron.

FIGURE 3. Motion capture technology in the 2016 version of *Sigmund Freud in Search of Chinese Matter and Mind*, starring *kunqu* actor Shi Xiaomei (right) in the role of Liu Mengmei. Courtesy of Zuni Icosahedron.

and *hypermediacy*" inherent in the interlocking of liveness and mediatization in digital opera.[26]

Another manifestation of mediated duplication occurs during one of several renditions of the scene, which also illustrates the frequent dissociation of movement and voice elements in Yung's method of adapting *xiqu*. Sitting on a slightly elevated platform at stage left, Shi performs the spoken and sung parts of the scene dressed in full traditional costume and makeup. At the same time, Zhang stands on stage right, silently executing the scene's movements and gestures in plain clothes and without makeup, amid a soundscape of piano and electronic music. The separation of the actors' movement and vocal scores in the live sequences amplifies the "sparagmos" effect of dismemberment, disembodiment, and fragmentation that "the doubling technologies of mediation" generate in the media-enhanced sequences.[27]

The framework of "one table two chairs" (*yi zhuo er yi* 一桌二椅; 1T2C) also originates from *xiqu*, inspired by its conventional stage set. 1T2C has become a signature of Yung's style and is emblematic of his penchant for serializing creative formats across projects, media, and art forms. It was first introduced in 1997 as the curatorial concept of the series *Zhongguo lücheng* 中國旅程 (Journey to the East; hereafter *Journey*), which required participants to implement the framework in visual artworks and twenty-minute performance pieces for two performers. It was subsequently applied to many experimental *xiqu* productions and cultural exchange projects in Asia and Europe. In *xiqu*, the arrangement and position of the table and chairs signify different geographic locations, human relationships, and social hierarchies. Similarly, in *xiqu* 2.0, the table and chairs serve as communication channels and material conduits for different kinds of sociocultural, geopolitical, and affective relations. They are symbols of identitarian formations and intercultural interactions, political metaphors, catalysts of spectral appearances, and ritual tools. In the 1997 edition of *Journey*, for example, 1T2C became a tongue-in-cheek allusion to the "one country, two systems" (*yi guo liang zhi* 一國兩制) governance agreement for post-handover Hong Kong. 1T2C is both a nonhuman signifier of *xiqu* 2.0's strategies of reinvented classicism and a dialogic platform for collaboration and dialectical thinking.

Journey also exemplifies Zuni's deliberate recycling of production concepts and cultural exchange platforms, further illustrating the 2.0 tendency toward versioning and serialization. Launched in Hong Kong in the 1980s, it was redeveloped in the late 1990s as a multi-art, multiyear exchange forum for creative communities from the Sinosphere and the Asia Pacific region, involving performance makers, filmmakers, and visual artists.[28] Another example is the Toki Experimental Project on Intangible Cultural Heritage, which originated from a Sino-Japanese collaboration at Shanghai Expo 2010 and subsequently evolved into an annual trans-Asian festival based in Nanjing, with satellite events in

Tokyo and Hong Kong. Participants have included performers of Chinese *kunqu* and *jingju*, Japanese *nō* and *bunraku*, Javanese classical dance, and contemporary dance and theater, among others. Both platforms were blueprints for the One Belt One Road Experimental Theatre series, inaugurated in Hong Kong in 2017 with associated activities in Europe, Singapore, and Indonesia. This project integrated the 1T2C framework with intermedia experiments in the Z Innovation Lab. Synesthetic audiovisual effects and kinetic installations sensorily augmented the bare physicality and pure sounds of the classical performance forms in the immersive setting of the lab's media-enhanced mirror stage. The 2018 edition was also the incubator for the Interrupted Dream series. The concept grew out of a creative exchange between Shanghainese *kunqu* performer Shen Yili 沈昳麗 and Javanese classical cross-gender dancer Didik Nini Thowok, who experimented with a cross-cultural rendition of the *Peony Pavilion* scene.

Finally, the dynamics of versioning and serialization that typify the 2.0 dimension resonate with Zuni's pronounced propensity for the ghosted repurposing of bodies and material objects. Yung tends to recast actors and "interrelationships of several actors";[29] recycle video, sound, costume, and design components; and reuse props such as mirrors, sheets, drapes, pieces of A4 paper, chairs, and table-and-chairs sets in successive works. Versioning and serialization are central to Zuni's propagative approach to the task of reinventing tradition, as the company identifies its experiments with Asia's theatrical heritage: aesthetically intertextual, trans-generic, intermedial, and cognitively engaged in dialectical strategies of serial questioning of sociocultural systems at the level of both the individual and the institution, on- and offstage.

2.0 as Participation and Interactivity

Serialization and a propagative approach to artistic creation are further evidenced by the transnational dissemination of Zuni's creative frameworks, such as 1T2C, within and beyond the Sinosphere.[30] In this respect, *xiqu* 2.0 epitomizes a third connotation of the semantics of *2.0*: participation and interactivity. The descriptor *2.0* evokes web-like patterns of interaction and the facilitation of dialogic environments that resonate with Yung's dialectical practice and Asia-oriented approach to intercultural collaboration, which I have described elsewhere as "Asian theatre as method."[31] *Asian theater as method* denotes a networked mode of interculturalism that foregrounds inter-Asian relationality. It valorizes indigenous epistemologies and regional dynamics of creative mobility, as discrete textual traditions, aesthetic conventions, and modes of performative embodiment circulate transnationally and transmedially across physical and virtual borders. Inherent in this method is the elaboration of an aesthetic of minimalism that resists historical discourses of museumification, objectification, and othering of Asia's classical heritage. Methodologically, *xiqu* 2.0 expands *xiqu*'s epistemic capacities to transform the deconstructed classical form into a form of deconstructionist critique.[32] Stylistically, this epistemic expansion is achieved by undoing the aesthetic conventions of the classical form to develop new conventions: for instance, by removing or replacing elements of movement, singing, music, costume, and props. These reformed conventions challenge entrenched perceptions and preconceptions of the classical form; they destabilize what is commonly regarded as "tradition" and defy expectations of how an authentic "traditional" performance or genre should look or sound. For, as Yung has argued, "real [cultural] transmission must start with a critique of the system for transmitting culture."[33]

Ethnomusicologist Bell Yung 榮鴻曾 has examined the alienating (in the Brechtian sense) de- and re-contextualization of the aural, visual, and narrative components of *jingju* in Zuni's productions. In *Tears of Barren Hill*, for example, the actors wear no makeup and are dressed in modern suits with only sartorial citations of the conventionally elaborate costumes of *jingju*, such as the addition of water sleeves (*shuixiu* 水袖). They are also blindfolded, zeroing out the powerful emotional range that classical *jingju* actors convey through their eye movement and penetrating gaze.[34]

The crossover experiments with *kunqu*, *nō*, and other ICH genres that Zuni and their collaborators have developed within the Toki Project, such as *Making Dreams*, testify to a comparable procedure. Zhang Jun, nicknamed the Prince of Kunqu for his vocal talents, neither sings nor moves throughout the performance. He reclines in an armchair with a white sheet wrapped around his head, as if adrift in a dream. All the audience hears of his voice is a prerecorded audio sample of a one-word utterance: *meng* (dream). When, in a deliberate act of self-citation, *Making Dreams* was included to open and close the 2016 version of *Freud*, Zhang appeared onstage while a body double took the role of the reclining dreamer. Yet Zhang performed only the movement score, in silence, to the sound of his prerecorded voice track, breaking the holistic effect that would normally characterize a conventional *xiqu* performance of the scene.

In both cases, the classical form is stripped down to its bare essence. It is divested of decorative exterior features such as costumes, makeup, or props; and distinctive conventions such as the eye movement and musical accompaniment of *jingju* in *Tears of Barren Hill* and the elegant movement and singing of *kunqu* in *Making Dreams* are almost completely erased. One could argue that Yung's approach to *xiqu* classicism represents a paradoxical form of expansion by subtraction. In a letter he wrote to Shi Xiaomei in preparation for the first version of *Freud*, Yung explains that, while intending to preserve the "original essence" of the vocal and gestural elements of *kunqu*, "it is possible that we will use subtraction to reduce the work to its most succinct state."[35] While expanding the semantic and sensory range of *xiqu* through technological mediation, *xiqu* 2.0 reduces its material, corporeal, and aural characteristics to their essential qualities.

Expanded Classicism and Decolonization

The expanded minimalism, or maximalism by subtraction, that defines the 2.0 method of adapting and updating Asia's theatrical heritage stimulates new modes of perception and reception that resist Western-centric epistemologies and the orientalist practices of exoticization and cultural essentialism that haunt the hegemonic histories of intercultural theater to this day.[36] Tokenistic appropriations of aspects of "traditional Asia" for ornamental purposes are typical examples of the museumification of classical forms. Contemporary reinterpretations in the *xiqu* 2.0 mode, however, literally "dis-Orient" the viewer—especially one unfamiliar with the form's culture of origin.[37]

Yung has addressed such colonial legacies in his theater, writings, and artworks. He has likened the stage to a cage (a cipher for objectification), and classically trained actors to endangered birds (a trope for museumification), such as the crested ibis (*toki*, in Japanese) that gives the Toki Project its name. The rare bird trapped in a cage for voyeuristic display is a metaphor for the "Asian exotic," as is the theme of zoological exhibition explored in *Tiangong* 天宮 (Heavenly Palace of Monkey Business, 2018). In this work, also from the One Belt One Road Experimental Theatre series, performers of the traditional monkey roles in *jingju* and Cambodian *lakhon khol* (Khmer masked dance) wrestle with the boundaries of cage-like enclosures. Texts projected during the performance ("Is the stage a cage?") and descriptions in the promotional materials ("event at the zoo") mock the fetishization of an imaginary notion of Asian classicism that reduces traditional performers to monkeys in cages and their supposedly exotic performances to a human zoo.[38] Similarly, the critique of chinoiserie in *Fan'ersaigong de jiushi* 凡爾賽宮的舊事 (Chinois Dream at Château de Versailles, 2019; hereafter *Chinois Dream*), the first installment of *The Interrupted Dream*, draws comparisons between the theater and the museum as sites of voyeurism and (self-)exhibition. Its fragmented composition of musical and choreographic styles from Asia and Europe as "disrupted historical records in a museum" exposes the orientalist gaze and reflects on the power of seeing and being seen.[39] As Yung has stated: "Placing traditional performing arts in a museum is not the best way to preserve them. . . . Traditional performing arts are living arts, which can only be preserved and fully developed through the creativity of their practitioners. This is the true form of transmission."[40]

Expanded classicism in the 2.0 mode should be understood not only as a language of *de*—of destabilizing, dismantling, and dislocating the classical form—or of *re*, "as in *re*embody, *re*inscribe, *re*configure, *re*signify."[41] It is also one of *with*—one that values interactivity, relationality, and participation over vague cultural affinity or, conversely, essential ontological difference. On the one hand, the recasting of heritage genres in contemporary decontextualized settings defies expectations of purity and fixity regarding classical cultural forms—namely, that they should remain as they have always been, like museum pieces or caged animals for exhibition. On the other hand, it underscores the capacity of reinvented iterations of Sinophone classicism to intervene as instruments of contemporary critique. As *The Interrupted Dream* testifies, the activation of contingent meanings in contemporary adaptations of canonical texts typifies yet another facet of *xiqu* 2.0—one that both expands and decolonizes *xiqu* epistemologies and the semantic potential of *xiqu*.

Expanded Chinese Dreams in Digital Times

The Interrupted Dream mobilizes *xiqu* classicism to produce physical and virtual spaces for Sinophone relational memory through the intermedial and intertextual resignification of signs and symbols from *Peony Pavilion*'s iconic scene. Zuni's media-expanded version is not a direct adaptation of Tang's text but a multi-perspectival rendition of its "emotion-realm" (*qingjing* 情境),[42] which (de-)constructs a transhistorical archaeology of Chinese dreams and dreamers across cultural and spatiotemporal dimensions. Combining live performance, video, electronic sound mixes, multilingual voice-overs, onstage text projections, and on-screen intertitles, its expanded dramaturgy extends "the regime of dreamscapes"[43] of its source material—a proscribed play by a demoted official celebrating a rebellious heroine—to reflect on authoritarian regimes and rebellions against authority across centuries of Chinese history.[44] In keeping with Yung's characteristic practice of versioning, updating, and self-referencing, the series delivers an extended dreamology of thwarted passions, erupting desires, and political ambitions: from the Ming-era cult of *qing* to the revolutionary utopia of Mao Zedong's 毛澤東 (1893–1976) New China (Xin Zhongguo 新中國) and Xi Jinping's 習近平 (1953–) Chinese Dream, or China Dream (*Zhongguo meng* 中國夢), and from the interrupted dreams of democracy in Beijing's Tiananmen Square in 1989 to the frustrated aspirations of Hong Kong's millennial dreamers—via a detour by the extravagant *chinois* reveries of seventeenth-century Versailles.

The inaugural installment originated from a 2018 Z Innovation Lab experiment based on the 1T2C framework. The full production, *Chinois Dream*, premiered in Hong Kong in September 2019. The pan-Asian cast included classical and contemporary performers from Shanghai (*kunqu*), Taipei (*kunqu*), Hong Kong (*yueju* 粵劇), Yogyakarta (Javanese classical dance), Phnom Penh (*lakhon khol*), Hat Yai (Thai classical dance), Tokyo (contemporary dance), and Singapore (Malay classical dance; contemporary theater). Later that year, the alternate versions *In Search of a Dream* and *Journey to a Dream* toured Indonesia and Singapore respectively. During the COVID-19 pandemic, the production was updated into a digital theater version, *Gengzi jingmeng* 庚子驚夢 (The Interrupted Geng Zi Dream; hereafter *Geng Zi Dream*), with a Hong Kong–based cast. It was livestreamed worldwide in October and November 2020. The next iteration,

Jingmeng er san shi 驚夢二三事 (Two or Three Things about Interrupted Dream), was performed live in Hong Kong in July 2021 and reworked for digital screening at the InlanDimensions International Arts Festival in September and October.[45]

Chinois Dream reimagines the scene from *Peony Pavilion* as a lavish pan-Asian exotic spectacle staged at the court of Louis XIV at the height of seventeenth-century chinoiserie. The French monarch pursued relations with China through the Jesuits under the Kangxi 康熙 Emperor (1654–1722) and acquired a vast personal collection of Asian artifacts.[46] He ordered the construction of the Porcelain Trianon in Versailles, inspired by descriptions of the Porcelain Tower in Nanjing, and performances of "Chinese" dances at his court are documented.[47] The Zuni production blends classical Asian singing and choreography with contemporary dance, electronic sound, and French baroque music to undertake "a dream-state deconstruction of orientalism"[48] that questions European colonial legacies in Asia while alluding to more recent forms of cultural imperialism and political authoritarianism in China and Hong Kong. Its text and imagery weave a symbolic red thread between the French *ancien régime* under the despotic rule of the Sun King and the ideological dream regimes of Mao (the Red Sun) and Xi (the "Red Emperor," as the Chinese president has been dubbed in the media).[49] These grandiose dreams are juxtaposed with the grassroots dreams of the 1989 pro-democracy movement in China and of the then-unfolding 2019–20 Hong Kong protests, which play a more prominent role in later installments.

The production design overlays essentialist stereotypes of cultural objectification stemming from the European colonial fascination with Asian civilizations with visual and textual allusions to the motifs of the mirror and the portrait—crucial to the formation of Liniang's identity in *Peony Pavilion*—to explore power dynamics between "watching" 觀看 and "being watched" 被觀看.[50] During performances at the Hong Kong Cultural Centre, a view of the audience seats captured with a hidden camera served as a backdrop to the stage action in the final scene. Such a spatial configuration reinforced equivalences between acting and spectating, performance and surveillance, on- and offstage realities, as well as analogies between the theater stage and the Palace of Versailles as an exotic museum and orientalist dream. Furthermore, the tropes of the mirror and the portrait resonate with the multiple refractions of Liniang's dream and the multiplying reflections of her fragmented identity as a dreamer, rebel, and spectral revenant—and of dreamers watching and being watched by other dreamers—that are central to the production concept.[51]

The opening scene recasts the classic dream in the garden among familiar sights and sounds on the streets of Hong Kong during the anti-ELAB movement. Amid a soundscape of remonstrating voices, a young man dressed in black—the popular dress code of the Hong Kong protesters—lies on the ground. He could be dreaming or dead. Another man, also dressed in black, enters and places a chair over his body. He then lies next to him, becoming yet another dreamer. Others follow throughout the performance, as various scenes set in the historic court of Versailles unfold. Dreamers/protesters dressed in black and masked court ladies in white Rococo-style hoop skirts mingle on the stage, which doubles as a protest site and a palace ballroom. They inspect the man on the floor or sit on the chair towering over his motionless body, watching the scene unfold. Omnipresent in Yung's stage designs, the chair is a material index of authority in this series. The overbearing chair pins bodies to the ground, preventing movement and action/activism. This ritualistic sequence of repetitive actions and the interchange of power roles between the performers—as actors and audiences, viewers and viewed, oppressors and oppressed—"seems to satirize the repetition of history" 彷彿在諷刺歷史的重複, as Yung writes in a production note.[52] The script implicates the audience in the power play that takes place onstage: "This is the garden in *Peony Pavilion*. There is a chair. The one [who] sits on the chair can be me or you" 我們的眼前是遊園驚夢的花園，花園的裡面擺放的是一張椅子，椅子上面坐著的是我也是你們.[53] Only in the final scene does the dreamer wake up and free himself from the chair, only to pass his struggle on to another dreamer and continue his "incessant, cursed journey" 停不下來的被詛咒之旅程.[54]

A background video reinforces the motif of the endless repetition of history and of dreams through history. The camera zooms in on an archival photograph of two young men climbing one of the sculptural groups located outside Mao's mausoleum in Tiananmen Square during the "brilliant riot" of the 1989 spring of "discontent"—to adapt Liniang's despondent remarks.[55] Extreme closeups of the men's facial features alternate with details of the faces of Mao and of a revolutionary soldier sculpted on the monument (fig. 4). In the 2020–21 versions, these haunting portraits are matched with allusive intertitles about "heroes [who] come and go in history" and people falling "in the desolated public sphere called the square."[56] Thus the perturbed "stirrings of the spring's passions"[57] of the classic heroine converge with the "turbulent heart"[58] of Beijing's and Hong Kong's modern-day dreamers. The scene presents Tiananmen Square as both a site of heroism and official celebration—the center of Mao's monumental "dream of national revolution and renewal that, by the end of 2019, had become a dream of empire"[59]—and yet another theater for interrupted dreams of democracy. The combined images of the young men standing high up on the sculpture and of a black-clad body lying motionless "in the empty theatre where stage turns cage"[60] might have triggered an additional layer of memory in the audience of the 2020–21 versions, as an unintended but eloquent evocation of Alex Chow Tsz-lok's 周梓樂 death. Chow was a student activist who suffered a fatal fall in a Hong Kong car park in November 2019, during the protests. An onscreen intertitle in the 2020 version that reads "I am falling I am falling" 我發現自己開始下墮 seems to confirm this cross-mnemonic subtext.[61]

FIGURE 4. An archival photograph of the 1989 Tiananmen Square democracy movement featured in *The Interrupted Dream: Chinois Dream at Château de Versailles*, 2019. Courtesy of Zuni Icosahedron.

FIGURE 5. *Kunqu* actor Shen Yili (right) performs *Peony Pavilion* in *The Interrupted Dream: Chinois Dream at Château de Versailles*, 2019. Courtesy of Zuni Icosahedron.

On an endless, cursed journey through history is also the ghostly figure of a deranged court lady, played by Shen Yili, who performs *Peony Pavilion* in the central scenes set in Versailles (fig. 5). Like the black-clad dreamers on the stage and the young Chinese men in the Tiananmen Square video, this tragic figure is a reflection of Liniang's transhistorical persona. Centuries earlier, she was cast into an eternal spell while learning the "Jingmeng" scene of *Peony Pavilion*. Forever singing the aria "Shanpoyang" 山坡羊 (Lamb on the Hill, aka Lamb on the Mountain Slope), in which Liniang laments her fate, she has traveled across centuries "to seek the spring" 尋春, only to encounter endless mirror images of herself "pursuing dreams" 尋夢 "under the hero's monument" 英雄碑下[62] and on "the stage of the present" 當下的舞台.[63] In Versailles the ghostly Liniang double performs a duet with Didik Nini Thowok in the role of another court lady. The Javanese dancer wears a Medusa mask and responds to Shen's classic *kunqu* rendition of the scene with a newly devised Indonesian version (fig. 6). Like Liniang, the figure of Medusa suggests a feminine rebellion against traditional morality and sexual taboos. Thus a reinterpretation of the Ming-dynasty heroine through the combined lens of Javanese court dance and Greek mythology offers not only a cross-gender and cross-cultural doubling of Tang's character but also a feminist reaffirmation of her identity.[64]

Another court lady stands at the back, her face hidden behind a grotesquely deformed white mask, as if forever petrified in an eternal scream. Like a ghostly apparition, she watches the reveries and rebellions unfolding before her eyes—a

FIGURE 6. Javanese classical dancer Didik Nini Thowok (right) in *The Interrupted Dream: Chinois Dream at Château de Versailles*, 2019. Courtesy of Zuni Icosahedron.

timeless witness to the endless, spectral return of interrupted dreams throughout history. More and more performers dressed as court ladies join in the frenzied fantasy of exotic dances taking place in the imaginary living museum and projection of the European orientalist gaze at Versailles. The spectacle of cultural appropriation reenacted by an ensemble of classical Asian performers, mostly from former European colonies, carries a critique of the historical legacy of colonization to the postcolonial stages of Hong Kong, Singapore, and Indonesia, where versions of the series have toured.[65] At the same time, the mediated and embodied evocations of 1989 Beijing and 2019 Hong Kong reconfigure the young men on-screen and those onstage as spectators and inheritors of myriad imaginations of China across eras and localities (fig. 7). Projected texts and voice-over announcements during the Versailles scenes frame the French craze for all things Chinese as the origin of "the centuries-old China Dream" 幾個世紀前已經亮相 的中國夢.[66] The seventeenth-century French court's "fantasies about a utopia four hundred years in the future" 他們在幻想四百年之後的理想國[67] overlap with twenty-first-century visions of "the Chinese Dream of the great rejuvenation of the Chinese nation" 中華民族偉大復興的中國夢,[68] linking the ostentatious illusions of Louis XIV's palace with the ambitions of China's current leadership.

Interrupted Hong Kong Dreams in Pandemic Times

The 2020–21 digital updates expand the web of dreamscapes and memoryscapes of the original live version, turning the series into a virtual channel for the circu-

FIGURE 7. Past and present Chinese dreams intersect in *The Interrupted Dream: Chinois Dream at Château de Versailles*, 2019. Courtesy of Zuni Icosahedron.

lation of mediated memories and metadreams across the Sinosphere. The opening intertitles of the 2020 production read:

> Dreams are almost like virtual theatre.
> The stage presentation is the reflection of a dream.
> Are the consciousness and subconsciousness involved in the practices of dreaming and theatre making considered a way of escaping the virtuality or seeking the truth?
> *The Interrupted Geng Zi Dream* transited from theatre to video
> critiquing the documentation of consciousness and subconsciousness in the year of Geng Zi.

> 夢本來就如虛擬劇場
> 錄像藝術演繹更令舞台呈現如夢的倒影
> 做夢及創作的意識和潛意識是逃避跨越假象還是追尋跨越真相
> 庚子驚夢由劇場過渡錄像
> 評議庚子年意識和潛意識記錄[69]

The *gengzi* 庚子 year is the thirty-seventh in a sixty-year cycle in the Chinese lunar calendar and is often associated with turbulence, crisis, and calamities. *Gengzi* years include 1900, the year of the Boxer Rebellion; 1960, a year in the Great Famine; and 2020, a year of pandemic and protest.[70] As the opening intertitles explain, "the public sphere in the Gengzi year" 庚子年公共空間 entered a phase of pestilence, death, violence, and destruction.[71] The pandemic year marked a "crisis chronotope,"[72] which was exacerbated in Hong Kong by the promulgation of the National Security Law in June 2020. In such circumstances, the pandemic condition provided "a complex *connective metaphor*, in the realm of individual and collective memory."[73] Similarly, *Peony Pavilion* offered "significant room for imagination" 隨意及想像空間 in a year of crisis: "Among the variety of symbols and narratives, we went with the flow to look for individual and collective imaginative space" 我們在眾多符號及敘事的空間中各自找到個人及集體的隨意及想象.[74] The suspension of the protests and of performances—that is, of mobility on the streets and on the stage—created an opportunity for distant connection and collective memory sharing in isolation. The pandemic enabled a virtual affective structure of "*mnemonic mobility* whereby subjects and objects establish a shared spatiotemporal economy of encoding, effacing, remembering and representation which is metaphoric, metonymic and mutable in quality."[75] The streaming version recasts *Peony Pavilion* as a protest narrative in the global context of 2020. Remote technology channeled a (not so) "secret discontent"[76] for the dual disciplinary regime of social distancing and political silencing, defying the forced interruption of the embodied time-spaces of sociopolitical life by generating virtual *lieux de mémoire* across online digital spaces.

The first year of the pandemic also saw important anniversaries such as the May Fourth Movement (1919), the founding of the People's Republic of China (1949), and the Tiananmen Square demonstrations (1989), which mark a succession of Chinese dreams since the modern era. They also resonate with the multiple connotations of *meng* (dream) as "transformation," "nostalgia," "ideals and aspirations," "illusions," and a traditional designation for "the darker side of palace politics."[77] Mnemonic traces of historical and current events inform the two pandemic versions, with associations between the literary dream regime of *Peony Pavilion* and the nightmarish governmental regime of surveillance enforced during and after the protests—only alluded to in the 2019 live version—becoming explicit. Hong Kong actors replaced the pan-Asian ensemble. This recasting may partly be attributed to the inability of the original cast members to travel due to the outbreak of the pandemic, but it also signals a shift from a transnational to a local focus, with unmistakable references to the protests—not least because the age of the actors onstage roughly matches that of the activist "dreamers" in the anti-ELAB movement.

In a program note, Yung asks of the 1989 demonstrators shown in the opening Tiananmen Square video, "Where are these students today?" 到了今天，這批同學們都在那裏?[78] The production seems to suggest that, thirty years later, the spirit of those "heroes on the heroes' monument" 英雄碑上的英雄, as an intertitle reads,[79] roams the streets of Hong Kong. The "anticipatory trauma"[80] that haunted pre-handover Hong Kong after 1989 seems to have become a traumatic reality, or a bad dream, in 2020. The ensemble of black-clad performers lying under oppressive tables and confining chairs, the bodies covered in white sheets, and the soundtrack of rallying voices evoke familiar scenes that circulated in the global media during the 2019–20 events. So do intertitles and voice-overs that adapt lines from *Peony Pavilion* to foreground tropes of springtime awakening and frustration with reality after "waking from a dream,"[81] while harking back to 1989. The online version lends itself to what Freda Chapple calls "a *digital reading*, in the sense of alerting the audience perception to the unseen texts and the layering of interpretation available behind the surface presentation."[82] The media components in the production provide "*hyperlinks*" that viewers must "activate in their minds by *making connections* to the unseen text behind the intermedial text."[83]

A video introduced in the 2020 version, "Xunzhao xin Zhongguo" 尋找新中國 (In Search of New China), by Yung and John Wong 黃志偉, reinforces the clustering of historical ghosts and the layering of haunted memories of old and new political dreams. Screened intermittently in the background of the livestreamed performance, the black-and-white footage shows scenes from a street march. Some of the marchers are wearing face coverings, which is replicated by the black-clad performers on the stage who hide their faces behind masks and balaclavas (fig. 8). These images seem to evoke the collective memory of the mass demonstration of June 16, 2019, when 2 million black-clad Hong Kongers streamed through the city center in the aftermath of the police's violent response to the activists' occupation of the Legislative Council building a few days earlier.[84] The street scenes alternate with shots of surging sea waves, recalling Bruce Lee's 李小龍 (1940–73) dictum and the slogan of the anti-ELAB movement: "Be water" (fig. 9). Textual and visual references to biometric identification and facial recognition systems are also recurrent reminders of the state of Hong Kong in the *gengzi* year. In the video, rapidly multiplying red frames are matched to the faces of the marching crowds and float over the seashore images until the entire screen is submerged in a solid expanse of red (fig. 10). In other sequences, projections and intertitles allude to technologies of "recognition" (*shibie* 識別), discipline, and surveillance (fig. 11).

In Zuni's digital reinterpretation of the Ming Dynasty narrative, the garden becomes a scene of protest, with the usual 1T2C set representing "the railings lined with tree peonies"[85] where the young lovers share their passion in the original scene. The theater (*juchang* 劇場) becomes a public square (*guangchang* 廣場)[86] for the staging of the "choreopolitics"[87] of resistance of today's young dreamers. The performers' monologues and voice-overs resonate with Liniang's "thoughts of passion [that] will not subside,"[88] and a projected text warning against visiting the (protest) site (*xianchang* 現場) echoes the prohibition against wandering in the forbidden garden. For example, the following sequence adapts Liniang's line:

FIGURE 8. Embodied evocations of the Hong Kong protests in *The Interrupted Geng Zi Dream*, 2020. Courtesy of Zuni Icosahedron.

FIGURE 9. A visual allusion to the Hong Kong "Be Water" movement in *The Interrupted Geng Zi Dream*, 2020. Courtesy of Zuni Icosahedron.

FIGURE 10. Multiplying red frames allude to facial recognition technology in *Two or Three Things about Interrupted Dream*, 2021. Courtesy of Zuni Icosahedron.

FIGURE 11. A reference to recognition technologies and the chair as a material signifier of authority in *Two or Three Things about Interrupted Dream*, 2021. Courtesy of Zuni Icosahedron.

"Without visiting this garden, how could I ever have realized this splendor of spring!"[89]

> If we did not come to the garden
> how should we know the splendour of spring
> If we did not come to the theatre
> how should we know the splendour of spring
> If we did not come to the outside
> how should we know the recognition was there

> 不到園林怎知春色如許
> 不到劇場怎知春色如許
> 不到場外怎知識別如許[90]

The script also references the slang of the anti-ELAB activists, particularly the use of coded allusions to dreaming (*fameng* 發夢) to exchange information about illegal activities during the protests:

> I was at the riot or was I not there or where.
> Is this your dream or my nightmare or theirs.
> Where am I and why is there so much tear gas.[91]

The following intertitle provides another example:

> I smelled lots of smoke
> I was in your dream
> I turned around and saw you
> Am I still dreaming
> I found myself in a garden
> I could not find the exit.

> 我聞到很多煙霧
> 我在你的夢中
> 我轉頭又看到你們
> 我是不是還在做夢
> 我發現自己在一個花園裡
> 我看不到花園有出口。[92]

Such an allusive strategy echoes Tina Lu's observation that in *Peony Pavilion* "dreaming, identity, and culpability are tightly bound together. Dream stands in for a subject unbounded by bodily limitations, yet a person is not considered guilty of actions committed in dream."[93] An equally allusive soundtrack combines the *kunqu* aria "Lamb on the Hill" from *Peony Pavilion*'s "Jingmeng" scene with somber classical music (Beethoven's Symphony no. 3 in E-flat Major plays over the street march and sea waves footage) and popular hits from the 1960s: Nancy Sinatra's "Bang Bang (My Baby Shot Me Down)" in the 2020 version and Carrie Koo Mei's "Meng" 夢 (Dream) in the 2021 version. While the former evokes armed violence and the activist subtext, the latter resonates with the *Peony Pavilion* themes of the ephemerality of youth and the blurring of boundaries between life and dream.

The 2021 version further amplifies the series' ghosting strategies by incorporating references to "In Praise of the Portrait" (the central scene in *Freud*) in the narrative of "Jingmeng." As is typical of Yung, essential elements of a classic scene are extracted and recontextualized in a new setting: in this case, the motifs of the mirror and the portrait, and Liu Mengmei's recognition of the face in the painting as the woman in his dreams. The transfiguration of the painted image as a medium for examining reality through modern technologies such as photography, reality TV, and screen-based media echoes tropes of "idolatry" 偶像崇拜,[94] as Yung notes, and the contemporary surveillance apparatus. It also prompts a reconsideration of the form and function of the theater as a communicative frame that is simultaneously enriched and challenged by technology and mediatization in times of virality and heightened virtuality. As a projected text summarizes: "To peep or be peeped, to monitor or be monitored, is the essence of our reflection on theatre making" 偷窺被偷窺，情慾監控被監控，本來就是思考劇場一而再的事.[95] The dualism of seeing and being seen and procedures of recognition, identification, monitoring, mirroring, gazing, and watching are foregrounded. The back of the stage and the stage floor are used as screening surfaces, and performers are often seen reading texts or looking at images on the back screen with their backs to the audience while simultaneously being watched by the same audience. At other moments, they inspect theater masks and stare at the palms of their hands as if examining a portrait, like Liu Mengmei, reflecting themselves in a mirror, like Du Liniang, or watching digital screens and mobile displays, like today's media consumers. In contrast to the feminine/feminist perspective of 2019 and 2020, various sequences in the 2021 version center on the activities of male dreamers, combining Du's and Liu's storylines to depict political passions and repressed visions of freedom. For example:

> He visited the back garden
> Later on in a dream he met his mate
> . . . .
> They made love
> When he woke up he was lovesick and died
> His last wish was to be buried in the garden
> His self-portrait was buried under the willow.

他終於一步踏入了後庭
然後他做了遇見他的夢
……
他們在花神包圍中造愛
他醒了就得到了單思病
他臨終前要求葬在後庭
埋柳樹下是他的自畫像。[96]

Ling Hon Lam's 林凌瀚 observations on "Xiezhen" 寫真 (The Portrait; scene 14), wherein Liniang immortalizes her youthful image before dying, effectively capture the combination of embodied and mediatized dreamers' portrayals, the mediated dynamics of seeing and being seen, and the proliferation of dreams and dreamers' identities in the series "as one of the effects of the transmutation of the dreamscape into theatricality."[97] Lam writes that "what this image production empathetically relies on is an interaction of mediums . . . in which the spectator's body is an integral part of the media environment. In this context, spectatorship entails not passive recipients but an assemblage of mediated relationships to the self and others through the production, distribution, and exchange of assorted images."[98]

The techno-oneiricism of the series' digital reincarnations, their ghosted channeling of dreams of resistance amid the nightmares of a global pandemic, the blurring of spatiotemporal dimensions through participatory online environments and recurring allusions to tropes of truth, illusion, doubling, and recognition (also frequent in *Peony Pavilion*)[99] reinforce the dialectics of virtuality and reality and the interlinks between history and the present that are central to the production concept[100] as well as, more generally, to Yung's 2.0 brand of expanded classicism.

Conclusion

The Interrupted Dream encapsulates the key dimensions of 2.0 outlined above, namely, as upgrading and updating through intermedial, intergeneric, and intercultural expansion; as versioning, serialization, and doubling/ghosting; and as participatory collaboration and networked interactivity. It does so by interlocking classical performance and new technologies, unfolding through several interconnected installments—conspicuously repurposing texts, media elements, and material properties—and relying on physical and virtual mnemonic participation. Additionally, the series resonates with Yung's method of expanded minimalism, or maximalism by subtraction, in that the selective repurposing of essential textual and performance elements from the classical canon magnifies the theatrical effect.

One might argue that both *2* and *0* carry meaning in the definition of *xiqu* 2.0, and both might be seen as corresponding to distinct mathematical operations that illuminate distinct approaches to *xiqu* classicism in Zuni's expanded *xiqu*. On the one hand, 2 signifies addition (+) and multiplication (×), hence maximization of the classical form through technology and strategies of doubling. On the other hand, *o* signifies subtraction (−) and division (÷) (i.e., separation), hence minimization of the form's orientalist traces through a form of minimalist critique. The interplay of these operational approaches is integral to the multimodal effect of aesthetic, epistemic, and semantic expansion that *xiqu* 2.0 achieves in shaping new forms of expanded Chinese opera in digital times.

ROSSELLA FERRARI is professor of Chinese studies at the University of Vienna, Austria. Her research and publications focus on the contemporary performance cultures of China and the Chinese-speaking region. She is the author of *Pop Goes the Avant-Garde: Experimental Theatre in Contemporary China* (2012), *Transnational Chinese Theatres: Intercultural Performance Networks in East Asia* (2020), and *Asian City Crossings: Pathways of Performance through Hong Kong and Singapore* (coedited with Ashley Thorpe, 2021).

///////////////////////////////

Notes

1   Yang, "Sinophone Classicism."
2   By *heritage genres*, I refer to the indigenous Asian performing arts inscribed on UNESCO's Representative List of the Intangible Cultural Heritage of Humanity. Within the *xiqu* 戲曲 (opera) category, *kunqu* 昆曲 (Kun opera) was proclaimed intangible cultural heritage in 2001 and inscribed in 2008, *yueju* 粵劇 (Cantonese opera) in 2009, and *jingju* 京劇 (Beijing opera) in 2010.
3   Woo, *Rong Nianzeng*, 36. The English translation quoted here is from the original bilingual publication.
4   Eckersall, Grehan, and Scheer, *New Media Dramaturgy*, 5. For an analysis of Zuni's technical innovation through the lens of new media dramaturgy, see Mansbridge, "Choreographing the Nonhuman."
5   See Eckersall, "Expanded Dramaturgical Practice."
6   Fischer-Lichte, "Introduction."
7   Yeung, "Danny Yung," 126.
8   Eckersall, "Expanded Dramaturgical Practice," 295.
9   See Ferrari, *Transnational Chinese Theatres*.
10 These works are part of an experimental *xiqu* trilogy also including *Tiao huache* 挑滑車 (The Outcast General, 2005). See B. Yung, "Deconstructing Peking Opera."
11 Mansbridge, "Choreographing the Nonhuman," 91–92.
12 See Alivizatou-Barakou et al., "Intangible Cultural Heritage and New Technologies."
13 D. Yung, "Experimenting China," 107.
14 Carlson, *Haunted Stage*, 7.
15 Ibid., 8–11.
16 Ibid., 2.
17 Ibid., 11.
18 Ibid., 14.
19 Schechner, *Performance Theory*, 324.

20 Blau, *Eye of Prey*, 173, cited in Carlson, *Haunted Stage*, 1.

21 Tang, *Peony Pavilion*, 42.

22 Ibid., 47.

23 Carlson, *Haunted Stage*, 79.

24 On *Freud* see Ferrari, "Tang Our Contemporary," and Yeung, "Danny Yung."

25 Causey, "Screen Test of the Double," 385.

26 Chapple, "Digital Opera," 84.

27 Causey, "Screen Test of the Double," 390.

28 See Ferrari, *Transnational Chinese Theatres*.

29 Carlson, *Haunted Stage*, 112.

30 The Theatre Practice and Emergency Stairs in Singapore and Za-Koenji Public Theatre in Tokyo, among others, have adopted 1T2C.

31 Ferrari, "Asian Theatre as Method." On Yung's dialectical approach see Ng, "Dialectics as Creative Process."

32 In 2021 Yung and director Liu Xiaoyi 劉曉義 hosted the online dialogue series *Shiri tan* 十日談 (The Decameron). Each dialogue addressed a specific (un)building block of Yung's decalogue for deconstructing and critiquing theater: "body" (*shenti* 身體), "sound and music" (*shiting* 視聽), "space" (*kongjian* 空間), "technology" (*keji* 科技), "symbol" (*fuhao* 符號), "structure" (*jiegou* 結構), "ideogram" (*yitu* 意圖), "narrative" (*gushi* 故事), "question/problem" (*wenti* 問題), and "morphology" (*cifa* 詞法).

33 D. Yung, "Experimenting China," 106.

34 B. Yung, "Deconstructing Peking Opera."

35 D. Yung, "Letter to Shi Xiaomei," 41.

36 On the concept of hegemonic intercultural theater, see Lei, "Interruption, Intervention, Interculturalism." See also the critique of Robert Wilson's "incomplete deconstruction of *jingju*" in the 2009 Taiwanese production of *Orlando*, which Lei views as the result of an intercultural partnership "based on postcolonial status inequalities" (Lei, *Alternative Chinese Opera*, 21).

37 On the downside of categorizing classical performance systems as intangible cultural heritage, see also a statement by the chairperson of the UNESCO International Jury, Juan Goytisolo, quoted in Lei, *Alternative Chinese Opera*, 107: "We must avoid the trap of *museumising* them and turning ourselves into anthropologists who, as a Mexican intellectual said, 'see peoples as cultural fossils.'"

38 Like *The Interrupted Dream*, *Heavenly Palace* has had several iterations. See Mansbridge, "Choreographing the Nonhuman," on a 2018 telematic performance version resulting from a collaboration with Zurich University of the Arts.

39 D. Yung, "Interrupted Dream."

40 D. Yung, "Experimenting China," 106.

41 Diamond, introduction, 2.

42 Lam, *Spatiality of Emotion*, 5.

43 Ibid., 7.

44 Bans on *Peony Pavilion* were issued during the Ming (1368–1644) and Qing (1644–1911). Zuni's *Wanli shiwu nian* 萬曆十五年 (1587, a Year of No Significance), directed by Woo in 2006, addresses the banning of the play and Tang's demotion under the Wanli 萬曆 Emperor (1563–1620). See Ferrari, "Tang Our Contemporary."

45 The title of the latter alludes to *Xianggang er san shi* 香港二三事 (Two or Three Things You Want to Know about Hong Kong), part of a 1993–95 series that Zuni developed in response to Hong Kong's handover. In September 2022 an additional installment of the

Interrupted Dream series (not examined in this essay) was presented as the opening performance of InlanDimensions at the Grotowski Institute's Bakery Centre for Performing Arts in Wrocław, Poland, and at the Gdánsk Shakespeare Theatre.

46   Rochebrune, Sourisseau, and Bastien, *China at Versailles*.
47   Witchard, "'Beautiful, Baleful Absurdity,'" 117–18.
48   Smith, "Interrupted Dream."
49   An example is Su, "Dreams of a Red Emperor."
50   Leung, "Youxian de longzi."
51   Tina Lu (*Persons, Roles, and Minds*, 33–34) observes that "there are multiple versions of Du Liniang" in *Peony Pavilion* and that her fragmented identity, "split among the corpse, the ghost, and the figure in the painting," is key to understanding the text.
52   D. Yung, "Jingmeng 2019 (biji)." Here and throughout, translations from this text are by the author.
53   D. Yung, *Jingmeng er san shi*. This and other quotations from *The Interrupted Dream* production scripts and recordings (including onstage text projections, onscreen intertitles, and voice-overs) are originally bilingual. The English and Chinese texts do occasionally differ and are reproduced here as they appear in the original source.
54   D. Yung, "Jingmeng 2019 (biji)."
55   Tang, *Peony Pavilion*, 42, 47.
56   D. Yung, *Gengzi jingmeng*. These intertitles are shown in English only.
57   Tang, *Peony Pavilion*, 42.
58   Ibid., 46.
59   Golley, Hillman, and Jaivin, "Introduction," xii.
60   D. Yung, *Gengzi jingmeng*. This intertitle is shown in English only.
61   Ibid.
62   Ibid. "Xunmeng" (Pursuing the Dream) is the title of scene 12 of *Peony Pavilion*.
63   D. Yung, "Jingmeng 2019 (biji)."
64   For a classic feminist interpretation of the Medusa myth, see Cixous, "Laugh of the Medusa."
65   The colonial reference is made explicit in the Singapore version when a performer watches over the scene posing as a statue of Sir Stamford Raffles (1781–1826), the founder of modern Singapore as a British colony.
66   D. Yung, *Jingmeng: Fan'ersaigong de jiushi*.
67   Ibid.
68   Xi, "Zai qingzhu." The English translation provided is the official and most widespread translation of Xi's slogan.
69   D. Yung, *Gengzi jingmeng*.
70   Penny, "2020—A *Gengzi* 庚子 Year," xi.
71   D. Yung, *Gengzi jingmeng*.
72   Parui and Raj, "COVID-19 *Crisis Chronotope*."
73   Ibid., 1432.
74   D. Yung, *Jingmeng er san shi*.
75   Parui and Raj, "COVID-19 *Crisis Chronotope*," 1434.
76   Tang, *Peony Pavilion*, 47.
77   Golley, Hillman, and Jaivin, "Introduction," xi.
78   D. Yung, "Zai du *Gengzi jingmeng*." Translation by the author.
79   D. Yung, *Gengzi jingmeng*.
80   Berry, *History of Pain*, 12.

81 "Waking from a Dream" is a common English-language translation for the *kunqu* performance extract (*zhezixi* 折子戲) of scene 10 in Tang's play.

82 Chapple, "Digital Opera," 98.

83 Ibid., 97.

84 See Dapiran, "Hong Kong's Reckoning," 53.

85 Tang, *Peony Pavilion*, 51.

86 D. Yung, *Gengzi jingmeng*.

87 Lepecki, "Choreopolice and Choreopolitics."

88 This is a quotation from "Lamb on the Hill" as translated in the 2020 bilingual script: "I know not why, thoughts of passion will not subside" 沒亂裡春情難遣 (D. Yung, *Gengzi jingmeng*). This version features a recording of Shen Yili's *kunqu* performance of the aria, which is sung live in the 2019 version.

89 Tang, *Peony Pavilion*, 44.

90 D. Yung, *Jingmeng er san shi*.

91 D. Yung, *Gengzi jingmeng*. This intertitle is shown in English only.

92 Ibid.

93 Lu, *Persons, Roles, and Minds*, 66.

94 D. Yung, "Rong Nianzeng shiyan juchang."

95 D. Yung, *Jingmeng er san shi*.

96 Ibid.

97 Lam, *Spatiality of Emotion*, 40.

98 Ibid.

99 On tropes of "identification," "recognition," and "proof" in *Peony Pavilion*, see Lu, *Persons, Roles, and Minds*.

100 D. Yung, "Rong Nianzeng shiyan juchang."

References

Alivizatou-Barakou, Marilena, et al. "Intangible Cultural Heritage and New Technologies: Challenges and Opportunities for Cultural Preservation and Development." In *Mixed Reality and Gamification for Cultural Heritage*, edited by Marinos Ioannides, Nadia Magnenat-Thalmann, and George Papagiannakis, 129–58. Cham: Springer, 2017.

Berry, Michael. *A History of Pain: Trauma in Modern Chinese Literature and Film*. New York: Columbia University Press, 2008.

Blau, Herbert. *The Eye of Prey: Subversions of the Postmodern*. Bloomington: Indiana University Press, 1987.

Carlson, Marvin. *The Haunted Stage: The Theatre as Memory Machine*. Ann Arbor: University of Michigan Press, 2001.

Causey, Matthew. "The Screen Test of the Double: The Uncanny Performer in the Space of Technology." *Theatre Journal* 51, no. 4 (1999): 383–94.

Chapple, Freda. "Digital Opera: Intermediality, Remediation, and Education." In *Intermediality in Theatre and Performance*, edited by Freda Chapple and Chiel Kattenbelt, 81–100. Amsterdam: Rodopi, 2006.

Cixous, Hélène. "The Laugh of the Medusa." *Signs* 1, no. 4 (1976): 875–93.

Dapiran, Antony. "Hong Kong's Reckoning." In *China Dreams*, edited by Jane Golley, Linda Jaivin, Ben Hillman, and Sharon Strange, 50–67. Canberra: ANU, 2020.

Diamond, Elin. Introduction to *Performance and Cultural Politics*, edited by Elin Diamond, 1–12. London: Routledge, 1996.

Eckersall, Peter. "Towards an Expanded Dramaturgical Practice: A Report on 'The Drama-turgy and Cultural Intervention Project.'" *Theatre Research International* 31, no. 3 (2006): 283–97.

Eckersall, Peter, Helena Grehan, and Edward Scheer. *New Media Dramaturgy: Performance, Media, and New-Materialism*. Basingstoke, UK: Palgrave Macmillan, 2017.

Ferrari, Rossella. "Asian Theatre as Method: The Toki Experimental Project and Sino-Japanese Transnationalism in Performance." *TDR: The Drama Review* 61, no. 3 (2017): 141–64.

———. "Tang Our Contemporary: Twenty-First Century Adaptations of *Peony Pavilion*." In *Passion, Romance, and* Qing: *The World of Emotions and States of Mind in* Peony Pavil-ion, vol. 3, edited by Paolo Santangelo and Tian Yuan Tan, 1482–518. Leiden: Brill, 2014.

———. *Transnational Chinese Theatres: Intercultural Performance Networks in East Asia*. Basingstoke, UK: Palgrave Macmillan, 2020.

Fischer-Lichte, Erika. "Introduction: Interweaving Performance Cultures—Rethinking 'Intercultural Theatre': Toward an Experience and Theory of Performance beyond Post-colonialism." In *The Politics of Interweaving Performance Cultures: Beyond Postcolonial-ism*, edited by Erika Fischer-Lichte, Torsten Jost, and Saskya Iris Jain, 1–21. London: Routledge, 2014.

Golley, Jane, Ben Hillman, and Linda Jaivin, eds. "Introduction: Dream On." In *China Dreams*, viii–xvii. Canberra: ANU, 2020.

Lam, Ling Hon. *The Spatiality of Emotion in Early Modern China: From Dreamscapes to Theatricality*. New York: Columbia University Press, 2018.

Lei, Daphne P. *Alternative Chinese Opera in the Age of Globalization: Performing Zero*. Basingstoke, UK: Palgrave Macmillan, 2011.

———. "Interruption, Intervention, Interculturalism: Robert Wilson's HIT Productions in Taiwan." *Theatre Journal* 63, no. 4 (2011): 571–86.

Lepecki, André. "Choreopolice and Choreopolitics; or, The Task of the Dancer." *TDR: The Drama Review* 57, no. 4 (2013): 13–27.

Leung Tong 梁栋. "Youxian de longzi, wuxian de bianzheng—guan *Tiangong* yu *Jingmeng*" 有限的笼子，无限的辩证—观《天宫》与《惊梦》[Limited Cage, Infinite Dialectics: Watching *Heavenly Palace* and *The Interrupted Dream*]. *As I Am, So I See*, February 12, 2019. www.leungtong.com/1055.html.

Lu, Tina. *Persons, Roles, and Minds: Identity in* Peony Pavilion *and* Peach Blossom Fan. Stanford, CA: Stanford University Press, 2001.

Mansbridge, Joanna Gwen. "Choreographing the Nonhuman: Cross-cultural Entanglements and Technologies of Capture in Zuni Icosahedron's and Zurich University of the Arts' Z/Z Twin Lab." *International Journal of Performance Arts and Digital Media* 16, no. 1 (2020): 88–103.

Ng, How Wee. "Dialectics as Creative Process and Decentring China: Zuni Icosahedron and Drama Box's *One Hundred Years of Solitude 10.0: Cultural Revolution*." In *Asian City Crossings: Pathways of Performance through Hong Kong and Singapore*, edited by Rossella Ferrari and Ashley Thorpe, 69–91. London: Routledge, 2021.

Parui, Avishek, and Merin Simi Raj. "The COVID-19 *Crisis Chronotope*: The Pandemic as Matter, Metaphor, and Memory." *Memory Studies* 14, no. 6 (2021): 1431–44.

Penny, Benjamin. "2020—A *Gengzi* 庚子 Year." In *Crisis*, edited by Jane Golley, Linda Jaivin, and Sharon Strange, xi. Canberra: ANU, 2021.

Rochebrune, Marie-Laure de, Anne-Cécile Sourisseau, and Vincent Bastien, eds. *China at Versailles: Art and Diplomacy in the Eighteenth Century*. Paris: Somogy Éditions d'Art, 2014.

Schechner, Richard. *Performance Theory*. London: Routledge, 2003.

Smith, Ken. "The Interrupted Dream at the Hong Kong Cultural Centre—Where Cultures Collide, and Collude." *Financial Times*, September 16, 2019. www.ft.com/content/7c75ff88-d867-11e9-9c26-419d783e10e8.

Su, Alice. "Dreams of a Red Emperor: The Relentless Rise of Xi Jinping." *Los Angeles Times*, October 22, 2020. www.latimes.com/world-nation/story/2020-10-22/china-xi-jinping-mao-zedong-communist-party.

Tang Xianzu. *The Peony Pavilion: Mudan ting*. Translated by Cyril Birch. Bloomington: Indiana University Press, 1980.

Witchard, Anne. "'Beautiful, Baleful Absurdity': Chinoiserie and Modernist Ballet." In *British Modernism and Chinoiserie*, edited by Anne Witchard, 108–32. Edinburgh: Edinburgh University Press, 2015.

Woo, Mathias 胡恩威, ed. *Rong Nianzeng: Shiyan Zhongguo shixian juchang* 榮念曾：實驗中國實現劇場 / *Danny Yung: Experimenting China, Realizing Theatre*. Bilingual ed. Hong Kong: Zuni Icosahedron E+E, 2010.

Xi Jinping 习近平. "Zai qingzhu Zhonghua renmin gongheguo chengli 70 zhounian dahui shang de jianghua" 在庆祝中华人民共和国成立70周年大会上的讲话 [Speech at the Celebration of the Seventieth Anniversary of the Founding of the People's Republic of China]. *Xinhua*, October 1, 2019. www.xinhuanet.com/politics/2019-10/01/c_1125065799.htm.

Yang, Zhiyi. "Sinophone Classicism: Chineseness as Temporal and Mnemonic Experience in the Digital Era." *Journal of Asian Studies* 81, no. 4 (2022): 657–71.

Yeung, Jessica. "Danny Yung in Search of Hybrid Matter and Mind: His Experimental *Xiqu* for Zuni Icosahedron." *Visual Anthropology* 24, nos. 1–2 (2011): 124–38.

Yung, Bell. "Deconstructing Peking Opera: *Tears of Barren Hill* on the Contemporary Stage." *CHINOPERL Papers* 28, no. 1 (2008–9): 1–11.

Yung, Danny 榮念曾. "Experimenting China—Realizing Traditions." In Woo, *Rong Nianzeng*, 106–14.

———. "A Letter to Shi Xiaomei." In Woo, *Rong Nianzeng*, 41.

———. "The Interrupted Dream: Chinois Dream at Château de Versailles—2019." Zuni Icosahedron Experimental Theatre Arts Archive. archive.zuni.org.hk/#/search-result/details/177 (accessed May 29, 2023).

———. "Jingmeng 2019 (biji) Rong Nianzeng 2019/10/2" 驚夢 2019（筆記）榮念曾 2019/10/2 [The Interrupted Dream 2019 (Notes) Danny Yung 2019/10/2]. 劇讀*thea.preter*, November 11, 2019. theatre-reviews.blogspot.com/2019/11/blog-post.html.

———. *Jingmeng: Fan'ersaigong de jiushi* 驚夢：凡爾賽宮的舊事 [The Interrupted Dream: Chinois Dream at Château de Versailles]. 2019. Zuni Icosahedron Archive, Hong Kong.

———. *Gengzi jingmeng* 庚子驚夢 [The Interrupted Geng Zi Dream]. 2020. Zuni Icosahedron Archive, Hong Kong.

———. *Jingmeng er san shi* 驚夢二三事 [*Two or Three Things about* Interrupted Dream]. 2021. Zuni Icosahedron Archive, Hong Kong.

———. "Rong Nianzeng shiyan juchang—*Jingmeng er san shi*" 榮念曾實驗劇場—驚夢二三事 [Danny Yung Experimental Theater—*Two or Three Things about* Interrupted Dream]. Zuni Icosahedron. zuniseason.org.hk/programme/2_or_3_things_about_interrupted_dream/ (accessed May 29, 2023).

———. "Zai du *Gengzi jingmeng* daoyan de hua" 再讀《庚子驚夢》導演的話 [Revisiting the Director's Notes to *The Interrupted Geng Zi Dream*]. Zuni Icosahedron. zuniseason.org.hk/z-live/revisit-the-interrupted-gengzi-dream-directors-note/ (accessed May 15, 2022).

FANGDAI CHEN

Avant-Garde Anachronism
Dream of the Red Chamber in the Forty-Ninth Century

ABSTRACT This article examines Chen Chuncheng, an up-and-coming mainland Chinese novelist emerging from the internet, as a representative case of a renewed manifestation of literary avant-gardism in the contemporary Sinosphere. It is an avant-gardism that challenges the status quo of the avant-garde's radical revolutionism and shields itself under a more sophisticated and adaptable aestheticism. In engaging with China's classical past, particularly in his imagined history of *Dream of the Red Chamber* in a fictitious forty-ninth century where futuristic digital motifs abound, the young novelist invokes the radical belief in the power of *wen* 文 (letters) to intervene in sociopolitical crises. It is a belief that aligns with the avant-garde's core spirit of coming to the rescue of a society through aesthetic means. In deconstructing the temporality and materiality of literary texts, Chen also enacts a meta-reflection on the existential condition of literature in cyberspace, where digital technologies make it possible for literary productions to take alternative forms, to roam around, and to dissolve when the exigency of socio-historical circumstances necessitates. The digital world therefore constitutes the most ideal site to host literature's omni-presence and omni-absence—two concepts that form the dialectical kernel of Chen Chuncheng's neo-avant-gardism.

KEYWORDS Chen Chuncheng, *Dream of the Red Chamber*, avant-garde, Sinophone classicism, digitality and materiality

Avant-garde literature (*xianfengwenxue* 先鋒文學) seems to have become a bygone era in the history of Chinese literature. In the 1980s, a group of seminal writers like Can Xue 殘雪 (b. 1953), Yu Hua 余華 (b. 1960), and Su Tong 蘇童 (b. 1963) emerged and churned out fictional works that boldly challenged both the aesthetic and the political conceptions of literary writing in the Chinese tradition. They experimented with linguistic conventions and narrative structures in ways that completely overthrew the system of socialist realism, which had dominated the literary sphere in China for the previous decades. These writers took the liberty to turn toward the medium of literature itself and tested its innovative limits. This common ethos earned them the collective label "avant-garde school" (*xianfengpai* 先鋒派), although they held individual agendas and never formed an organized coterie like the European historical avant-garde—Dadaism, Surrealism, Futurism, just to name a few.

PRISM: THEORY AND MODERN CHINESE LITERATURE • 20:2 • SEPTEMBER 2023
DOI 10.1215/25783491-10992730 • © 2023 LINGNAN UNIVERSITY

The aesthetic experimentation of the avant-garde school writers had a conspicuous political objective: it was a ferocious revenge on grand historical narratives that had inhibited the heterogeneity of individual memories under a decade of turmoil until Mao Zedong's 毛澤東 (1893–1976) demise. While subverting ideologically driven historical narratives with their radical literary experimentation, the avant-garde writers also resuscitated the realm of allegory and (re-) integrated the emphasis on subjective experience into Chinese literature. In other words, these writers in the 1980s epitomized the most radical cultural intervention in a time of sociopolitical upheavals.[1] Their avant-garde activism, however, did not last long with the advent of the social turmoil in the late 1980s. In addition, a rapidly growing market economy, as a result of Chairman Deng Xiaoping's 鄧小平 (1904–97) economic reform and open-door policy, gave rise to an emerging mass culture in the 1990s that also besieged pure literature (chunwenxue 純文學), of which works produced by the avant-garde writers were regarded the most representative. The heyday of literary avant-gardism in China therefore seemed to have come to an abrupt end.[2] The majority of the writers turned to writing "new historical novels" (xinlishixiaoshuo 新曆史小說) as the specter of realism made its powerful comeback in the Chinese literary sphere at the turn of the twenty-first century.[3]

While the avant-garde is commonly discussed as a past event in Chinese cultural and literary studies today, I contend that the defeat or the death of literary avant-gardism in the Chinese context has been announced prematurely. Far from a complete annihilation, the avant-garde finds a renewed manifestation in the contemporary Sinosphere, where the once rigid geopolitical definition of China has been expansively contested to address global Chinese diasporas and the rapidly growing cyberspace that stretches the demarcation of China as a polity. Michel Hockx, for one, makes a case for the continuous avant-garde intervention of the internet writer Chen Cun 陳村 (b. 1954), whose pre-internet writing was also associated with avant-garde literary innovations.[4] While I corroborate Hockx's acknowledgment of avant-garde literature's undiminished presence in China in the new millennium, I must contend with the conventional understanding of the avant-garde as a pronouncedly radical and progressive literary project, which Hockx argues is represented by Chen Cun's antimarket and antiestablishment internet writing.[5] Rather, in today's Chinese cyberspace, I observe a kind of literary avant-gardism that no longer outwardly promotes radical revolutionism but shields itself behind a more sophisticated and adaptable aestheticism. This aestheticism is nevertheless highly rebellious—against not only sociopolitical monoliths but also the stale perception of the avant-garde as a future-oriented progressive scheme; to borrow Zhiyi Yang's words about the relevant concept of "avant-garde classicism," it "rejects relentless progressivism and 'revolutions' as another status quo."[6]

The focus of this article, Chen Chuncheng 陳春成 (b. 1990), an up-and-coming mainland Chinese novelist who began as an amateur internet writer, best epitomizes this metamorphosed insurgence of the literary avant-garde in today's Sinophone world. I argue that underneath his highly praised refined language and ingenious literary imagination exudes a radical belief in literature's potential to contest, subvert, and even outlive established authorities. It is a belief that aligns with the avant-garde's core spirit of coming to the rescue of a society enmeshed in crises.

The Neo-Avant-Garde from China's Cyberspace

An engineering-major graduate working at a state-owned botanical garden in southern China, Chen Chuncheng began posting essays and novellas in 2017 on Douban 豆瓣, the most popular Chinese social networking platform among literature and film enthusiasts. His works, filled with refreshing imagination and written in an extremely refined language, quickly caught the attention of publishing professionals. In 2020 Chen Chuncheng's first collected works, *Yewan de qianshuiting* 夜晚的潛水艇 (The Submarine at Night), was published and includes many of the pieces previously posted online. It became one of the best-selling books of the year and won numerous major commercial literary prizes in China and the larger Sinosphere, including being selected as one of the top-ten fictional works of 2020 by the Hong Kong–based journal *Yazhou zhoukan* 亞洲周刊 (Asia Weekly).

What made Chen stand out is his ingenious literary imagination, which transcends boundaries of history, tradition, and space. The namesake story "Yewan de qianshuiting" portrays the unbelievable encounter between a blue submarine built in a Chinese teenager's imagination and a submarine employed by an Australian tycoon to search for a coin tossed by Jorge Luis Borges (1899–1986) into Uruguay's deep ocean. The lost Borges coin is paralleled by a five-hundred-year-old Chinese stone tablet, mysteriously concealed during the Chinese Cultural Revolution in "Zhufengsi" 竹峰寺 (Bamboo Teak Temple). "Chibo" 尺波 and "Niangjiushi" 釀酒師 (The Wine Maker) trace the eerie and yet enticing legends of sword craftsmanship and winemaking that end up devouring the artisans themselves. The obsession with historical knowledge possesses the protagonist in "Caiyunji" 裁雲記 (The Tale of Cloud Tailoring), who works for the absurd national Cloud Management Bureau. "Yinyuejia" 音樂家 (The Musician) records the birth and the evaporation of an exceptional musical piece on a rainy night in Leningrad in 1957.

The highly imaginative nature of Chen's literary writing, while garnering popularity among readers and many critics, has also received harsh criticism; some think Chen's writing epitomizes the increasingly common phenomenon of China's younger generations' evasion of social reality and their subsequent refuge seeking in fictitious worlds.[7] In defense of the writer, Chen Peihao 陳培浩 argues that, in a society where drastic sociopolitical transformations are no longer an urgent matter and therefore literature no longer plays the role of the cultural vanguard, "the avant-gardeness of literature inevitably retreats into the realm of imagination."[8] In other words, Chen Peihao believes that, rather than a direct intervention in societal affairs, literary avant-gardism preserves itself as "a seed" (*zhongzi* 種子) when a society has overcome its crises and entered a state of stability. This "seed" takes the form of "aesthetic revolution" (*meixuebiange* 美學變革) to maintain literature's power of resistance in the "post-avant-garde era" (*houxianfengshidai* 後先鋒時代). While I agree with Chen Peihao's endorsement of Chen Chuncheng's works as aesthetic revolutions that continue to demonstrate the resistant potential of literary writing, I take issue with his contextualization of the "post-avant-garde era" for two reasons. First, the present conditions of the contemporary Sinosphere still call for perceptive and ingenious cultural representations and interventions. Second, Chen Chuncheng's aesthetic revolution is hardly as innocent as it seems, as I will demonstrate shortly.

Certainly, today's China has modernized itself to a great extent, especially economically, and has evidently overcome its status of national humiliation that began with foreign powers' invasion in the middle of the nineteenth century. Its state of existence, nonetheless, remains haunted by the specters of its historical collision with the West. For instance, the unabating ideological confrontations between China and the United States loom large in the landscape of international politics. Meanwhile, domestically, as younger generations grapple with the increasingly aggressive competition for decent social status and financial security against the risk of falling prey to the mental malaise of modern life, it almost seems inevitable that a "culture of avoidance" (*taobiwenhua* 逃避文化), for which Chen Chuncheng's fiction has been condemned as a sinful advocate, becomes all the more prevalent. The external precarity and internal distress constitute proof that the larger Chinese society necessitates the coming of new cultural vanguards to represent and intervene in its current state of affairs, just as the emergence of the avant-garde writers did back in the 1980s. The question remains: How can today's literary avant-garde lead the wrestling with these multifarious sociopolitical circumstances by means of aesthetic tools?

Whereas socialist realism continues to be the state-authorized mode of literary writing, alternative agitational literary exercises started to make a curious appearance, especially in cyberspace, past the turn of the millennium. By 2016 the online Chinese literature community had grown to encompass 297 million members, which make up 43.1 percent of China's internet users.[9] In this expansive cyberspace, Guobin Yang observes that literary sites fare particularly well.[10] The wide range of literary productions, from grassroot poetry to Chen Chuncheng's imaginative fiction, substantiates cyberspace's capacity to host cultural representations beyond any single hegemonic mode.

The earliest Chinese internet literary works can be dated back to 1991, when an online journal called *Huaxiawenzhai* 華夏文摘 (China News Digest) began to publish prose, poetry, and fiction.[11] Curiously, this inception of Chinese internet literature was diasporic and transcultural in nature, as the journal's main contributors were Chinese students in the United States who wrote to "express their feelings of homesickness by writing and reading articles in Chinese." These Chinese students also accessed the journal to "[get] news from China because it republished articles from Chinese newspapers and magazines."[12] In other words, the emergence of Chinese internet literature testifies to cyberspace's distinctive capacity to disseminate textual information and composition across the otherwise rigid geopolitical borders of China. It also surfaced as a digital and digitized manifestation of the pressing yearning for an affirmative experience of "Chineseness" and the subsequent reconnection with and re-creation of "Chinese identity" among diasporic Sinophone communities.

Another considerable feature of internet writing is its low barriers to participation, expression, and transmission. Indeed, Chen Chuncheng benefits greatly from this participatory culture as an amateur writer without any former association with the commercial publishing industry.[13] The editor of *Yewan de qianshuiting*, Luo Danni 羅丹妮, one of the most successful junior publishing professionals in mainland China today, confesses that she first encountered Chen's writing on Douban by a friend's recommendation. From there she solicited the writer for manuscripts of what he considered his best works so far.[14] Chen Chuncheng's experience conforms to that of many internet literature writers in China who transitioned their online popularity into successful careers in print literature.[15] However, what distinguishes Chen from others is the peculiar condition that all the works included in the print book were—and remained for months after print publication—available gratis on his Douban account. In a private conversation that I had with the writer, Chen admitted that he made almost no revision when these stories that he started posting from 2017 went into print. In other words, all the while readers could access Chen's writing for free online, his print book still sold exceedingly well. Intriguingly, the popular circulation of Chen's works across the online-offline and therefore digital-material boundaries becomes a meta-demonstration of the writer's conception of literature's existential condition, which will be explored in the second half of this article.

The Classical and the Modern

I attribute the popularity of Chen's writing among today's Chinese readers to its philosophical inquiries into the latest conditions of modern life. And it does so through maximizing literature's imaginative and expressive potential. Many of his works address the dialectics of *cang* 藏 (concealment) and *chuan* 傳 (dissemination) in a world where rapidly changing external circumstances furthers the yearning for and the impossibility of certitude and reliability. But Chen suggests that perhaps to conceal is to disseminate. In "Zhufengsi" the protagonist hides his old house key under the stone tablet where it has been concealed since the Cultural Revolution. The exclusive knowledge of the little object's concealment provides him with a tremendous amount of peace in this tumultuous world. The protagonist takes peace in knowing that his key would be passed down secretly in history until the moment that it is called to reveal itself, only to inspire another gesture of concealment just like the stone tablet did for the protagonist. Chen Chuncheng's philosophy of *cang* is worthy of an extensive discussion.[16] But for the purpose of this article, I shall turn my attention toward another crucial aspect of his writing, namely, its engagement with the Chinese classical tradition.

Indeed, Chen Chuncheng's works represent world literature, as they take the world as a subject of interlocution and imagination. The young writer never shies away from expressing his appreciation of writers and works from outside the Chinese tradition; some of them, such as Borges, become specific intercultural and intertextual references in his writing.[17] However, Chen's wild imagination of the world is simultaneously grounded by his remarkably exquisite literary language. It conveys a lyrical elegance that reminds one of classical Chinese poetry. It is not surprising that Chen holds a deep admiration for Wang Zengqi 汪曾祺 (1920–97), a monumental Chinese essay and short story writer known for his mastery of the Chinese language. Chen champions his predecessor's idea that to write fiction is very much to write language; language is not a vehicle for the content but an essential part of what one's writing tries to convey.[18] The coexistent turning out toward the world as an infinite source of imagination and the turning in toward the classicist tradition of Chinese language forms a refreshing encounter between modernism and anachronism in Chen Chuncheng's works. It is in this constant oscillation between the modern(ist) and the classicist that he probes the temporal, spatial, and linguistic limits of literary imagination. In doing so, Chen's works manage to find a way out of the realist trend of Chinese literature that remains prevalent under state campaigns. Ultimately, he provides a rejuvenating response to the literary avant-garde's renewed challenge: What can literature do to cope with and even overcome our current state of affairs?

Modernism's intertextual engagement with the classics is not without precedence. In the Anglo-European tradition, James Joyce (1882–1941) famously transformed the Homeric epic *Odyssey* into a chronicle of an ordinary day in twentieth-century Dublin (*Ulysses*, 1920); T. S. Eliot's (1888–1965) *Waste Land* (1922) abounds with classical allusions from Ovid, Dante, and Shakespeare to Buddhism. In the Chinese context, Lu Xun 魯迅 (1881–1936) invokes mythologies, legends, and personal accounts of ancient Chinese philosophers (*Gushi xinbian* 故事新編 [Old Stories Retold], 1936) while carrying out his agenda of seeking a cultural modernity that would provoke the Chinese people's paralyzed spirit; more recently, in 2006 the former avant-garde writer Su Tong contributed a modernized tale about Mengjiangnü 孟姜女 (Lady Meng Jiang), titled *Binu: Mengjiangnü ku Changcheng de chuanshuo* 碧奴：孟姜女哭長城的傳說 (Binu and the Great Wall), to the Canongate Myth Series, a world literature project conceived in 1999 by the namesake independent Scottish publisher to revive ancient myths from diverse cultures.[19]

Lu Xun's and Su Tong's practices, in retrospect, exemplify the perpetual interplay between the classical and the modern in the long quest for Chinese modernity. At crucial historical junctures in which China had to negotiate domestic sociopolitical reshuffling and international repositioning, both writers turned to China's classical past as if it best captured the "structure of feeling" of the modern.[20] They are not isolated cases. In fact, more recent literary and artistic practices led Zhiyi Yang to announce the increasingly prevalent and popular phenomenon of "Sinophone classicism," which she tentatively defines as "the appropriation, redeployment, and reconfiguration of cultural memories harking back to Chinese aesthetic and intellectual traditions for local, contemporary, and vernacular uses."[21] Chen Chuncheng's writing certainly participates in this undertaking. Besides the lyrical elegance that reminds one of classical Chinese poetry, Chen's work frequently travels back to the historical, but more oftentimes the fictional, past of Chinese literary and intellectual traditions. The most evident example is his summoning of the eighteenth-century novel *Hongloumeng* 紅樓夢 (Dream of the Red Chamber, 1791) in his novella "*Hongloumeng* misa" 《紅樓夢》彌撒 (A Mass for *Dream of the Red Chamber*). Similarly, "Chuancaibi" alludes to the tale of poet Jiang Yan's 江淹 (444–505) magic pen (*caibi* 彩筆) recorded in *Nanshi* 南史 (History of the Southern Dynasties, 659 CE). "Chibo" and "Niangjiushi" reimagine the mythologies of swordmaking and wine-making craftsmanship in ancient China, whereas "Zhufengsi" presents, with impressive details, a completely fictional Ming-dynasty text titled *Fuchuanshanfang suibi* 覆船山房隨筆 (Jottings from the Upturned Boat Mountain Lodge).

Chen Chuncheng's classicist engagement, however, stands out, as it demonstrates an uncommon radicalism through the author's reconstruction of the historical temporality of a literary text and all its cultural and political associations. In particular, his allegorical imagination of *Dream of the Red Chamber*'s fate in a fictitious forty-ninth century performs a drastic revision of the historical perception of time that has governed Chinese national and literary histories. In returning to China's classical past, Chen is not simply evoking a mnemonic experience or seeking a resolution for the present and the future in the past. Instead, the writer conflates the past, the future, the past of the future, and the future of the past of the classic novel to propose a new answer to the question: What does it mean for literary writing to "exist"? In doing so, he instigates an anachronism that reveals the multiple temporalities belonging to and made possible by literary writing. It is in this anachronism that Chen reveals his potential as a literary avant-garde who holds an unyielding belief in literature's transcendental power.

This anachronism pertains to the existential condition of literature, which the novelist starts exploring in "Chuancaibi," the writer-protagonist of which was gifted a magic pen one day. The pen enabled him to compose the greatest literary works in the world. The reference of the magic pen, as aforementioned, dates to *Nanshi*. The eighty-volume history book includes a record of Jiang Yan, a poet who reportedly lost all his literary talent and could no longer write poetry after returning his pen to a mysterious figure in his dream. In Chen's short story, the dilemma of owning the magic pen transforms into a more paradoxical condition: any work written with this pen would become the most incomparable piece of literature in history, but under the condition that only the writer himself has access to it. In other words, the protagonist's paramount literary achievement would remain unknown to the rest of the world. The pen therefore connotes both a blessing and a curse. More important, this condition calls into question the physicality of literature. At the end of the story, the protagonist takes out his notebook only to find blank pages. However, he knows that the words he has written down will reveal themselves once the notebook is closed and concealed from human eyes. "In darkness, [the words] simply glow. I put the notebook under my pillow and caress it before bed. I lie on the entire universe that I almost came to possess, and then I fall asleep into the trivial dreams that I have every day" 黑暗中，它們自顧自地璀璨。我把本子放在枕下，臨睡前摩挲一番，枕著我幾乎就要擁有的整個宇宙，然後墜入日常的，瑣碎的夢中.[22] Is the existence of literature—its formation, revelation, and dissemination—subject to the preservation of its materiality? Can it not outlive its physical presentation by alternative mnemonics? The pen and the writing that the protagonist composed with it have perished, but its phantasmal remnants continue to sustain a formidable cosmos in the protagonist's life and to symbolize the possibility of transcending the mediocracy and the impasse of the everyday.

This suggestive proposal of literature's transcendental survival finds a more radical iteration in "A Mass for *Dream of the Red Chamber*." One of the best-known classic Chinese novels, the voluminous *Dream of the Red Chamber* depicts the decline of the once prosperous aristocratic Jia clan in imperial China and the concurrent downfall of the indeterminate dynasty during which it existed. Chen takes advantage of the genre of science fiction to situate the classic novel in the fictional future of the forty-ninth century. In imagining the classic novel's future, Chen's work revisits—and revises—its historical past, which turns out to be deeply intertwined with the cultural and political landscapes of every passing moment. However, more than a simple nostalgia toward the past and an eager revision of the present, Chen propounds an anachronistic presence of literature that refuses to be pinned down by any specific historical juncture and therefore acquires a mobility against the confinement of historical time—a mobility that makes possible the omni-presence and omni-absence of literature across all times.

In Chen Chuncheng's forty-ninth century, the entire planet earth has come to be ruled by one autocrat, namely, Global President Jiao Datong (Huanqiudazongtong Jiao Datong 寰球大總統焦大同). The peculiar name immediately brings to mind the concept of *datong* 大同 (great unity), established in classical Chinese philosophy as a utopian vision of a world in which everyone and everything coexists peacefully. This concept has been invoked many times by major historical figures in modern and contemporary China to convey their political ideals, including the late Qing reformist Kang Youwei 康有為 (1858–1927), the first leader of the Chinese Nationalist Party Sun Yat-sen 孫中山 (1866–1925), as well as Mao Zedong. One cannot but wonder if this seemingly Sinocentric imagination of the global future is highly suggestive with regard to China's increasingly prominent global presence. Meanwhile, the first two characters of the global president's name also allude to a minor character, Jiao Da 焦大, in *Dream of the Red Chamber*. Despite his extremely brief appearance, Jiao Da plays a crucial role in the classic novel. As one of the most senior servants in the Jia clan, he once saved the life of the clan's great master during a war. However, the master's descendants treated the senior servant maliciously, leading Jiao Da to make one of the earliest announcements of the clan's eventual downfall in the story. In other words, besides the grandiose ambition of global unity, the name *Jiao Datong* also contradictorily connotates a prophesy of nemesis and ruination. The writer proceeds to reveal to us what the dialectical existence of these two underlying meanings entails.

In Chen's story, it turns out that the global president's *datong* entails the restoration of *Dream of the Red Chamber*, which, by all accounts, began to disappear from physical records and people's memories around the first "Star War." For this scheme, President Jiao's regime hunts down the protagonist, Chen Xuanshi 陳玄石, who, as the oldest human being on planet Earth born in the era before the novel began to vanish, has read it in its entirety. Meanwhile, a nongovernmental organization also covertly chases after the protagonist, and it is none other than the Redology Society (Hongxuehui 紅學會, literally: Society for the Study of *Dream of the Red Chamber*), consisting of enthusiasts who worship the text as a sacred scripture.[23] The global president's government and the society's mania for *Dream of the Red Chamber* cannot be better summarized than as a type of "textual fundamentalism," or the rigid or even literalist attachment to the letters and the dogmas of scriptures underpinning many religious practices. In other words, Chen's fictionalized account of the Chinese classic novel forms a parallel with the biblical tradition in the West, where a text as *Logos* dictates the ultimate truth of all things.

The protagonist, having hibernated for thousands of years after accidentally imbibing an unusual alcohol, wakes up to an investigation by the president's government officials and learns the cause behind their textual fundamentalism: "According to some evidence, a theory, a formula, or a dictum may be hidden in *Dream of the Red Chamber*. Some believe that it could unleash an invincible power when applied to political governance, economic development, and scientific advancement" 有一定證據指出，《紅樓夢》中可能隱藏著一套理論、一條公式或一句至理名言，有人認為，如果把它運用到治國理政、經濟建設和科技發展中去，也許能發揮出戰無不勝的奇效。[24] The current global regime's aspiration to restore the original text carries another political agenda: to adapt it so it could reflect "the positive energy of the new era" 注入新時代的正能量—a familiar slogan of state propaganda—and subsequently boost President Jiao's approval rating. Their scheme, however, falls through when the protagonist recalls that the central theme of the text is "to reveal the inevitable extinction of the rotten feudal society" 揭示了腐朽的封建社會必然滅亡的命運, an alarming prediction of the future of President Jiao's regime from the past. For this reason, the regime decides to adopt a new strategy, that is, to destroy the original text and prevent any of the society's attempts at its restoration.

It is not a coincidence that President Jiao's battle with the society's revival of *Dream of the Red Chamber* frequently involves modern digital systems such as the use of avatars and algorithms. Given Chen Chuncheng's personal interest in gaming (as hinted at by the young monk Benpei's 本培 obsession with soccer video games in "Zhufengsi"), he readily integrates game imagination into the fictitious world in his writing. In fact, President Jiao's global regime, with all its digital qualities, seems to resemble a gigantic arena where game motifs abound. Not only does the main headquarters of the global regime where the protagonist was once imprisoned and interrogated turn out to be a titanic spacecraft, but the insurgent society's depot also unveils itself as a subterranean ship in the guise of a temple whenever it resurfaces above ground. This aerial and underground face-off reminds one of a typical setup of a team-oriented and competition-based video game. Moreover, to suppress the society's members, President Jiao's security officers adopt a type of avatar called Blue Birds (*Qingniao* 青鸟), essentially bird-shaped robots capable of firing shots from their steel-made mouths at the owner's command. The security team has also developed an algorithm used for brainwashing the society's members, whom they wish to turn into one of their own; the brainwashed member's brain is left with nothing but the tenets of President Jiao's official army.

Against the high technology of President Jiao's regime, the society builds its fetish for the classic novel on a radically classicist reimagination of the novel's historical past:

> They believe that *Dream of the Red Chamber* is the meaning of the universe. According to the society's doctrine, there is an unseen thread that weaves together everyone's fates. It is initiated in the chaos before the formation of the universe, discreetly wreathes all events and all objects, and extends throughout the ages. It is kindled at its incipient moment, and the spark continuously pushes forward through every dynasty and every generation until the moment when *Dream of the Red Chamber* is completed (they call this moment the "red point"). And then, kaboom! The universe reaches its most glorious acme. After that there is only the long downhill and the slow downfall: *Dream of the Red Chamber* begins to perish on its completion, and when it completely disappears, the universe will also vanish accordingly.
>
> 他們相信宇宙的意義就是《紅樓夢》。教義宣稱，冥冥中有一條引線，由所有人的命運共同編織而成，它從天地開闢前的混沌中發端，隱秘地盤繞在萬事萬物之間，千秋萬載地延伸。創始之初它就被點燃，火星不斷向前推進，穿過歷朝歷代，一直燒到《紅樓夢》完成的那一刻(他們稱之為紅點)，然後，轟隆，宇宙達到最輝煌燦爛的頂點。此後就是漫長的下坡、緩慢的衰亡：《紅樓夢》一完成便開始流逝，到它徹底消失時，宇宙亦將隨之泯滅。[25]

At first sight, the society's consecration of the novel seems to exemplify an extreme version of textual fundamentalism that interprets the universe as a Sinocentric establishment of *datong*. However, on a closer look, we see the paradox embedded in this textual fundamentalism. It is first of all premised on the continuous evolvement of the novel; however, the novel itself is evolving only to come to its complete obliteration. One could argue that the society's ultimate commitment to *Dream of the Red Chamber* takes the form of a resolute nihilism toward the future of humankind and the universe. But I argue that this life-death paradox in fact divulges the most radical part of Chen Chuncheng's anachronistic view of literature and literary history: *Dream of the Red Chamber* obtains its omnipresent and eternal life in the dissolution and obliteration of its physical existence.

As a matter of fact, the title already gives away Chen's double entendre behind the use of the word *mass*: "'Mass' in the title refers to the most lofty ritual in Catholicism. It is also a genre of religious music. I take this novella as a dedication or an ode to *Dream of the Red Chamber*. . . . Later I learned that '*missa*' (the Latin original) also means 'to dissolve, to depart,' so it happens to echo the vanishing of *Dream of the Red Chamber*" 我想把這篇小說當成向《紅樓夢》的一次獻禮，或一曲頌歌 . . . . . . 後來知道彌撒(missa)一詞原意是 '解散，離開'，和《紅樓夢》的消逝剛巧吻合。[26] In other words, through the society, the author conveys the message that the ultimate worship of the novel takes the form of an affirmative acknowledgment of its materiality's decomposition. This dissolution in fact becomes an emancipation because in divesting itself of the physical evidence of its existence, literature turns against history's endeavor to canonize it, interpret it, translate it, and demand its service for any specific juncture and agents other than literature itself. In dissolving, Chen Chuncheng's *Dream of the Red Chamber* testifies to the Frankfurt School philosopher Herbert Marcuse's (1898–1979) provocative observation in 1977 that "the radical qualities of art . . . are grounded precisely in the dimensions where art transcends its social determination and emancipates itself from the given universe of discourse and behavior while preserving its overwhelming presence."[27] In the case of *Dream of the Red Chamber*, its overwhelming presence becomes all the more overwhelming as it loses its corporeal existence. This counterintuitive logic also corroborates Chen Chuncheng's dialectical reflection on concealment and dissemination, namely, to conceal is to disseminate. In "Zhufengsi," the key that is hidden under the stone tablet, which represents "the eternal beauty of art," becomes "literature's secretive victory against modernity."[28] In other words, the concealment of the key enables its autonomous and exclusive preservation against the ticking clock of the modern era and against the irreversible ruination that the progressive agenda of modernity brings about.

Chen Chuncheng furthers the dialectical metaphor of life and death pertaining to the novel in the society members' reiteration of their doctrine. The president of the society, a mysterious one-eyed man called Hong Yiku 洪一窟, interprets the novel's return to "a vast expanse of whiteness" 白茫茫大地 in the end as a subtle analogy of "the disappearance of words" 文字的消失: "*Dream of the Red Chamber* surged from the inside of everything and it will eventually disperse into all things on earth because all feasts come to an end"《紅樓夢》從一切的內部奔湧而來，也終將彌散入萬物。因為盛宴必散，他說.[29] Both the name of the Redology Society's president and the expression of "a vast expanse of whiteness" allude to the fifth chapter of *Dream of the Red Chamber*, which records the male protagonist Jia Baoyu's 賈寶玉 trip to the Illusory Land of Great Void (*taixuhuanjing* 太虛幻境).[30] In the Illusory Land, Jia Baoyu drinks a tea called *qianhongyiku* 千紅一窟, noted by the author as a pun on *qianhongyiku* 千紅一哭. Meanwhile, the expression of "a vast expanse of whiteness" appears at the very end of a song performed for Jia Baoyu in the Illusory Land as a description of the fate of a once prosperous family. Both allusions from this Illusory Land episode serve as precursors to the eventual downfall of the aristocratic Jia clan and the perishing of the material abundance that once served as proof of the clan's wealth and fame. Chen Chuncheng adopts the disbandment of the Jia clan as a symbolic parallel of the fate of the very text that witnesses such a disbandment. The fact that all the global regime's and the society's attempts at restoring the text have been of no avail seems to testify to the similarly inevitable death of the text and subsequently of the entire universe.

However, a minor school within the society questions that the society's dominant doctrine may have had it wrong the entire time. Instead of an ultimate death, the text's disintegration and dispersion are only part of a cycle of life that is not subjugated to historical time and to literature's physical medium: "*Dream of the Red Chamber* is a *qi*-like matter, which roams over the world, converges into words, and then gradually dissolves into all things on Earth again"《紅樓夢》是一種氣一樣的物質，它遊蕩在世間，匯聚成文字，然後又逐漸分解，融入萬物.[31] *Qi* 氣, as a fundamental concept in Chinese medicine and philosophy, refers to a life force, a vital energy that circulates. In this interpretation, the novel becomes an ethereal being that periodically manifests in the corporeal form of words. The vision finds its confirmation when fragments of *Dream of the Red Chamber* come to be discerned everywhere on Earth, carved inside a jade stone, uttered by a panda, sitting at the bottom of the Mariana Trench of the Pacific Ocean, hidden in the pattern of a butterfly's wing and in the rosy clouds of dawn. The dissolving and reemerging of the text embodies what the nineteenth-century German dramatist Georg Büchner (1813–37) describes as "an infinite beauty that passes from form to form, eternally changed and revealed afresh."[32]

The most intense corporeal embodiment of the novel, however, is the protagonist himself. It is also at this last moment of the novella that Chen Chuncheng reveals the most disturbing and yet redeeming effect that literature can have on its reader. Chen Xuanshi, after surviving both the global regime's internment and the society's tragic disbandment, comes to "read" over and over in his brain the entirety of *Dream of the Red Chamber*, resuscitating the novel through his memory until it has fully occupied his consciousness. Eventually, the protagonist dies peacefully, knowing that he has experienced the best of what the novel has to offer and that the novel will continue to live, as he has passed down its title to the narrator, who stumbles on Chen Xuanshi in his final moments: "The title is also part of the novel" 標題也是小說的一部分.[33] The very last line of the story lists more discoveries of the novel's fragments, demonstrating that the novel has yet to disappear completely. Whether its final obliteration will eventually take place and lead to the destruction of the universe remains unknown. But Chen Chuncheng has had the reader of this novella bear witness to the ever-present and ubiquitous existence of literature as Chen Xuanshi does throughout his life. We then come to realize that the most radical aspect of his forty-ninth-century *Dream of the Red Chamber* lies not in the conflation of its historical past and imaginative future but in the reconceptualization of its temporality as one that cannot be pinned down by the passing of historical time. In its cycles of birth and rebirth, the classic text symbolizes literature's overcoming of time and of its binding responsibility to any concrete historical moment and to its prescribed cultural and sociopolitical functions.

The protagonist's corporeal embodiment of *Dream of the Red Chamber*, as an extreme manifestation of the obsession with the classic novel portrayed in the novella, epitomizes the vehement experience of cultural remembrance: "turning your body into a repository of cultural mnememes that connect you to an affective past—and an imagined community."[34] Along this line, Chen Chuncheng's work reveals a globalized and futuristic version of Sinophone classicism in which the obsessive impulses surrounding *Dream of the Red Chamber* as cultural mnememes are tangled up with the illusion of retrieving a lost past of future promises. In other words, the kernel of the impulse to "re-member" *Dream of the Red Chamber*, as exemplified by all parties in the story (the global president, the Redology Society, as well as the protagonist), is contingent on an inexorable reimagination of the classic novel. After all, their attempts at retrieving the memory of its textual existence take on the rather literal meaning of "re-membering," that is, to recompose, to stitch together once again the fragments and traces of the classic novel. With it comes renewed historical significance and future prospects promised by the very title of *Dream of the Red Chamber*, as the protagonist reminds us: "The title is also part of the novel."[35] The simultaneous process of remembrance and reimagination is carried out not only by characters in the novella but also metatextually by Chen Chuncheng himself as his entire novella reimagines the classic novel with no less intensity. However, Chen Chuncheng's reimagination of the classic novel not only practices Sinophone classicism but also enacts a metatextual meditation on such a practice. By portraying the extreme to which his characters are willing to go to "re-member" the classic novel and their repetitive failure at recomposing and repurposing the text for their own agenda, he reflects on the potential perilousness of cultural remembrance and meditates on the nature of the practice of Sinophone classicism. Doing so, Chen further upholds his proposal of literature's transcendental aptitude—besides overcoming material and temporal bindings, it is capable of introspecting about its precarious condition of being cultural mnememes that could easily be romanticized and politicized.

Chen Chuncheng's exploration of a literary text's transcendental temporality, however, should not be mistaken as an insistence of the autonomy of art and its separation from social praxis, an observation and criticism made by Peter Bürger with regard to the American and European neo-avant-garde in the 1960s–70s.[36] Rather, Chen's project demonstrates a mobility of literature, in dissolving and regrouping, to constantly adjust its distance to the social and political realms and the decreed historical temporality. In fact, this mobility, as proof of the unexhausted potential of contemporary Chinese literature, becomes a renewed strategy of the literary avant-garde's contestation with realism's dominance over the symbolic representation of China both domestically and globally. In an idiosyncratic variation of "telling a good China story" 講好中國故事, Chen Chuncheng tells a good story about Chinese literature. In doing so, he inherits the classicist belief in the sovereignty of *wen* (letters) and builds an unbound republic of literary mnemonics that defy all geopolitical demarcations. It is not a coincidence that cyberspace serves as the genesis and the nexus of this unbound literary republic: the internet has become a vitally important alternative platform where literary traces disseminate as "a *qi*-like matter" that takes concrete forms when the time calls for it, and then dissolves when the moment of crisis passes but never fully disappears. It continues to live in spirit and will arise again when the exigency of another historical juncture summons it.

It is unclear how widely Chen Chuncheng's avant-garde impulse has been detected by the reader who simply enjoys his imaginative narratives. However, the revolutionary thrust concealed within—and therefore simultaneously disseminated by Chen's anachronistic aestheticism—is already at work, as corroborated by Marcuse's words: "Against all fetishism of the productive forces, against the continued enslavement of individuals by the objective conditions (which remain those of domination), art represents the ultimate goal of all revolutions: the freedom and happiness of the individual."[37]

FANGDAI CHEN holds a PhD degree in comparative literature from Harvard University and is currently an assistant professor in the Department of Chinese at Lingnan University, Hong Kong. Her ongoing research on Chinese and Sinophone modernisms in global and comparative contexts has appeared and is forthcoming in journals such as *Modern Chinese Literature and Culture*, *Prism*, and *Modernism/modernity*.

///////////////////////////////////

Notes

1 For more on the avant-garde school in the context of post-Mao cultural and literary productions, see Braester, *Witness against History*, 177–91; Cai, *Subject in Crisis*; B. Wang, *Illuminations from the Past*, 93–178; D. Wang, *Monster That Is History*, 262–91; Knight, *Heart of Time*, 191–221; Huang, *Contemporary Chinese Literature*; Berry, *History of Pain*, 253–97; L. Chen, *Great Leap Backward*.

2 For more on the rise of mass consumerism and its impact on literary productions in China, see Chen P., "Jin bainian Zhongguo jingyingwenhua de shiluo"; McGrath, *Postsocialist Modernity*; Rojas, "Authorial Afterlives and Apocrypha."

3 For more on the emergence of "new historical novels" in 1990s China, see Kinkley, *Visions of Dystopia*.

4 Hockx, *Internet Literature in China*, 21.

5 Ibid., 72.

6 Z. Yang, "Sinophone Classicism," 662.

7 Li, "'Neixiangxing xiezuo' de meijie youshi yu kunjing."

8 Chen P., "Xiangxiangli: Tongwang gongtongti yuyan tuzhong," 100.

9 Feng and Literat, "Redefining Relations," 2584.

10 G. Yang, "Chinese Internet Literature," 338–39.

11 J. Chen, "Refashioning Print Literature," 540.

12 Ibid.

13 For more on internet literature as participatory culture, see Feng and Literat, "Redefining Relations," 2595.

14 Dandu, "Zai kanbujian xiaoyan de shenghuo li." Luo Danni was also the editor of the debut print books of Shuang Xuetao 雙雪濤 (b. 1983) and Ban Yu 班宇 (b. 1986), two of the most commercially successful novelists in mainland China in recent years.

15 For detailed analysis of this phenomenon, see Feng and Literat, "Redefining Relations," 2598–600.

16 For more on the issue of *cang*, see D. Wang, "Yinxiu yu qiancang"; and Fan, "Zai huanghun yu heiye de fengxi zhong cangni."

17 For more on Chen Chuncheng's reading experience, see my interview with him: Chen F., "Duihua Chen Chuncheng."

18 Luo, "Chen Chuncheng."

19 Here I use the official title of Su Tong's book in English translation, published by Knopf Canada in 2008.

20 The term *structure of feeling* was coined and developed by Raymond Williams (1921–88) in the 1950s–60s to refer to "the different ways of thinking vying to emerge at any one time in history. It appears in the gap between the official discourse of policy and regulations, the popular response to official discourse and its appropriation in literary and other cultural texts" (Buchanan, "Structure of Feeling").

21 Z. Yang, "Sinophone Classicism," 658.

22 Chen C., *Yewan de qianshuiting*, 67.

23 An organization called the Chinese Society of Dream of the Red Chamber (Zhongguo Hongloumeng xuehui 中國紅樓夢學會) in fact exists as an auxiliary to the Chinese National Academy of Arts. The society was founded in 1980 and reportedly has more than three hundred members today.

24 Chen C., *Yewan de qianshuiting*, 102.

25 Ibid., 111.

26 Quoted from the epilogue included in the novella's original online publication on Douban in 2018: Chen C., "*Hongloumeng* misa." For the second meaning of *missa*, Chen Chuncheng is likely referring to the feminine conjugation of *missus*, which is the perfect passive participle of the Latin verb *mittō*, meaning "to send"; *missus* then could mean "sent," "let go," "dismissed," or "put to an end."

27 Marcuse, *Aesthetic Dimension*, 6.

28 Li, "'Neixiangxing xiezuo' de meijie youshi yu kunjing," 40.

29 Chen C., *Yewan de qianshuiting*, 112.

30 Cao, *Hongloumeng*, ch. 5.

31 Chen C., *Yewan de qianshuiting*, 112.

32 Büchner, *Sämtliche Werke und Briefe*, 87. Translated and quoted in Marcuse, *Aesthetic Dimension*, 65.

33 Chen C., *Yewan de qianshuiting*, 124.

34 Z. Yang, "Sinophone Classicism," 667. *Mnememes*, for Yang, are "the most elementary components of cultural memory" (667).

35 Chen C., *Yewan de qianshuiting*, 124.

36 Bürger, *Theory of the Avant-Garde*. In this work originally published in German in 1974, Bürger announces that the early twentieth-century European avant-garde, or the historical avant-garde in his own terms, rebelled against the institution of art and

tried to reintegrate art into life praxis but failed. However, the neo-avant-garde—a collective coinage for a wave of post–World War II art movements based mostly in America such as abstract expressionism, pop art, and neo-Dada—merely replicated the historical avant-garde's aesthetic gesture while completely losing this social agenda. This failure of the neo-avant-garde described by Bürger contributed to the popular discussion on the death of the avant-garde in American and European cultural criticism in the 1960s–70s.

37 Marcuse, *Aesthetic Dimension*, 69.

References

Berry, Michael. *A History of Pain: Trauma in Modern Chinese Literature and Film*. New York: Columbia University Press, 2008.

Braester, Yomi. *Witness against History: Literature, Film, and Public Discourse in Twentieth-Century China*. Stanford, CA: Stanford University Press, 2003.

Buchanan, Ian. "Structure of Feeling." In *A Dictionary of Critical Theory*. Oxford: Oxford University Press, 2010. https://www.oxfordreference.com/display/10.1093/oi/authority .20110803100538488;jsessionid=9536556CC11D1347A26C45498570E8B5.

Büchner, Georg. *Sämtliche Werke und Briefe* [The Complete Works and Letters]. Munich: Carl Hanser, 1974.

Bürger, Peter. *Theory of the Avant-Garde*. Translated by Michael Shaw. Minneapolis: University of Minnesota Press, 1984.

Cai, Rong. *The Subject in Crisis in Contemporary Chinese Literature*. Honolulu: University of Hawai'i Press, 2004.

Cao Xueqin 曹雪芹. *Hongloumeng* 紅樓夢 [Dream of the Red Chamber]. Taipei: Nangang-shan wenshi gongzuofang, 2017.

Chen Chuncheng 陳春成. "Hongloumeng misa"《紅樓夢》彌撒 [A Mass for *Dream of the Red Chamber*]. Douban 豆瓣, March 13, 2018. https://www.douban.com/note/660733197 /?type=rec&start=90.

——. *Yewan de qianshuiting* 夜晚的潛水艇 [The Submarine at Night]. Shanghai: Shanghai sanlian chubanshe, 2020.

Chen Fangdai 陳芳代. "Duihua Chen Chuncheng: Suoyou xiaoshuo dou laiyuan yu xiang-xiang" 對話陳 春成：所有小說都來源於想象 [In Conversation with Chen Chuncheng: All Fiction Comes from Imagination]. *Tongdairen* 同代人, September 23, 2021. https:// mp.weixin.qq.com/s/TV8XN5DJM1GnPr1fT9ZtFA.

Chen, Jing. "Refashioning Print Literature: Internet Literature in China." *Comparative Literature Studies* 49, no. 4 (2012): 537–46.

Chen, Lingchei Letty. *The Great Leap Backward: Forgetting and Representing the Mao Years*. Amherst, NY: Cambria, 2020.

Chen Peihao 陳培浩. "Xiangxiangli: Tongwang gongtongti yuyan tuzhong—du Chen Chuncheng xiaoshuoji Yewan de qianshuiting" 想象力：通往共同體語言途中——讀 陳春成小說集《夜晚的潛水艇》[Imagination: Toward a Language of Community—Reading Chen Chuncheng's Collection *The Submarine at Night*]. *Nanfang wentan* 南方 文壇, no. 6 (2021): 98–100.

Chen Pingyuan 陳平原. "Jin bainian Zhongguo jingyingwenhua de shiluo" 近百年中國精英 文化 的失落 [Chinese Elite Culture's Sense of Loss in the Past Century]. *Ershiyi shiji* 二 十一世紀, no. 17 (1993): 11–22.

Dandu 單讀. "Zai kanbujian xiaoyan de shenghuo li, zheben shu neng daigei ni anning" 在看不見 硝煙的生活裡，這本書能帶給你安寧 [In the Life of Invisible Fumes, This

Book Can Bring You Peace]. Douban 豆瓣, October 12, 2020. https://book.douban.com /review/12909258/.

Fan Yingchun 樊迎春. "Zai huanghun yu heiye de fengxi zhong cangni—Chen Chuncheng de wenyi qihuan yu xiandai dongxue" 在黃昏與黑夜的縫隙中藏匿——陳春成的文藝奇幻與現代洞穴 [Hidden in the Seam between Dusk and Dark Night: Chen Chuncheng's Literary Fantasy and the Modern Cave]. *Changjiang wenyi* 長江文藝, no. 9 (2021): 111–14.

Feng, Yuyan, and Ioana Literat. "Redefining Relations between Creators and Audiences in the Digital Age: The Social Production and Consumption of Chinese Internet Literature." *International Journal of Communication*, no. 11 (2017): 2584–604.

Hockx, Michel. *Internet Literature in China*. New York: Columbia University Press, 2015.

Huang, Yibing. *Contemporary Chinese Literature: From the Cultural Revolution to the Future*. New York: Palgrave Macmillan, 2007.

Kinkley, Jeffrey. *Visions of Dystopia in China's New Historical Novels*. New York: Columbia University Press, 2015.

Knight, Sabina. *The Heart of Time: Moral Agency in Twentieth-Century Chinese Fiction*. Cambridge, MA: Harvard University Asia Center, 2006.

Li Jing 李靜. "'Neixiangxing xiezuo' de meijie youshi yu kunjing—yi Chen Chuncheng Yewan de qianshuiting wei ge'an" "內向型" 寫作的媒介優勢與困境——以陳春成《夜晚的潛水艇》為個案 [The Advantages and Dilemmas of 'Introversive Writing' as a Medium—Chen Chuncheng's *Submarine at Night* as an Example]. *Zhongguo xiandai wenxue yanjiu congkan* 中國現代文學研究叢刊, no. 8 (2022): 34–53.

Luo Xin 羅昕. "Chen Chuncheng: Xugou shi wo zui jiejin ziyou yu kuanghuan de yangshi" 陳春成：虛構是我最接近自由與狂歡的樣式 [Chen Chuncheng: Fiction Is My Closest Resemblance of Freedom and Festivity]. *Pengpai xinwen* 澎湃新聞, October 28, 2020. https://mp.weixin.qq.com/s/lNWlwEz8EYDOCIqVPkY3Zg.

Marcuse, Hebert. *The Aesthetic Dimension: Toward a Critique of Marxist Aesthetics*. London: Macmillan, 1979.

McGrath, Jason. *Postsocialist Modernity: Chinese Cinema, Literature, and Criticism in the Market Age*. Stanford, CA: Stanford University Press, 2008.

Rojas, Carlos. "Authorial Afterlives and Apocrypha in 1990s Chinese Fiction." In *Rethinking Chinese Popular Culture: Cannibalizations of the Canon*, edited by Carlos Rojas and Eileen Cheng-yin Chow, 262–82. London: Routledge, 2009.

Wang, Ban. *Illuminations from the Past: Trauma, Memory, and History in Modern China*. Stanford, CA: Stanford University Press, 2004.

Wang, David Der-wei. *The Monster That Is History: History, Violence, and Fictional Writing in Twentieth-Century China*. Berkeley: University of California Press, 2004.

———. *Why Fiction Matters in Contemporary China*. Waltham, MA: Brandeis University Press, 2020.

———. 王德威. "Yinxiu yu qiancang—Chen Chuncheng yewan de qianshuiting" 隱秀與潛藏——陳春成《夜晚的潛水艇》[Hidden Elegance and Implications: Chen Chuncheng's *Submarine at Night*]. *Xiaoshuo pinglun* 小說評論, no. 1 (2022): 33–37.

Yang, Guobin. "Chinese Internet Literature and the Changing Field of Print Culture." In *From Woodblocks to the Internet: Chinese Publishing and Print Culture in Transition, circa 1800 to 2008*, edited by Cynthia Brokaw and Christopher Reed, 333–52. Leiden: Brill, 2010.

Yang, Zhiyi. "Sinophone Classicism: Chineseness as a Temporal and Mnemonic Experience in the Digital Era." *Journal of Asian Studies* 81, no. 4 (2022): 657–72.

XIAOFEI TIAN

The Thrill of Becoming
Writing Poetry in Digital Times

A near-sighted sensei watches the grassroots.

近視先生看草根

—Qi Gong 啓功

ABSTRACT What is the politics of form in the changing political climate? How does the writing of old-style poetry (*jiuti shi*) and new-style or modern vernacular poetry (*xin shi*) fare in digital times? As the internet, computers, smartphones, and Chinese internet poetry continue to evolve, how do these ongoing manifestations and technological transformations impact the landscape of poetry writing, and how do researchers answer these new challenges? This essay sketches the trajectory of change of modern old-style poetry and new-style poetry in response to the changing times and to each other, discusses how these changes embody larger cultural shifts, and addresses the role played by scholars and critics in the process. It argues that the gap between old-style poetry and new-style poetry is closing in interesting ways, and that scholarship on modern poetry is not about deciding the literary canon or predicting what comes next, but about constantly adjusting our understanding in the eternal process of becoming and realizing that the past is also changing owing to the changing perspective of the present.

KEYWORDS modern Chinese poetry, modern classical poetry (*xiandai jiuti shi*), internet poetry, WeChat poetry, Chinese poetry on social media

The title of this essay materialized through contemplating the exciting transformations that have been taking place in modern Chinese poetry in both "old" and "new" forms and that have necessitated constant adjustments of critical and scholarly perspectives. None of these transformations happened in a vacuum. Rather, they are intimately bound with changes in society and thus are the manifestations of larger shifts of culture. They are also born from the pressures that these forms exerted, either overtly or implicitly, on each other. This essay reviews these ongoing changes in poetry writing in digital times, with an emphasis on the changes wrought by technology and the economy in the past two decades. While it takes the continuing evolution of old-style poetry (*jiuti shi* 舊體詩) as its focal

PRISM: THEORY AND MODERN CHINESE LITERATURE • 20:2 • SEPTEMBER 2023
DOI 10.1215/25783491-10992740 • © 2023 LINGNAN UNIVERSITY

point, the present essay by necessity also considers "new poems" (*xin shi* 新詩), which gave birth to "old poetry" in the first place, and whose presence on the scene has been undergoing a metamorphosis caused by the same economic and technological revolutions in the social sphere.

In sketching the trajectory of change in the meaning and significance of the writing of *jiuti shi* and *xin shi* in response to the changing times and to each other, this essay asks how these changes embody larger cultural shifts and addresses the role played by scholars and critics in the process. What is the politics of these forms in the changing political climate? How do we as scholars carry on our work critically and avoid becoming inadvertent advocates of nationalism complicit in a new form of imperialism? Is there a line between a researcher and an agent, and how do we draw that line? As both the internet and Chinese digital poetry continue to evolve, how do these ongoing manifestations and technological transformations impact the landscape of poetry writing, and how do researchers answer these new challenges?

The questions put forth by this essay dictate the adoption of a macro view of the playing field of poetry rather than focusing on any individual poet (*jia* 家), style (*ti* 體), or "school" (*pai* 派). Indeed, this is one of the most notable changes brought about by digital media in dealing with the contemporary poetic landscape: traditional literary historical narrative, rooted in and contributing to the belief in literary history as nothing but a hall of fame, is made up of "great writers" towering above a sea of scribbling obscurants; but the contemporary poetic landscape, infinitely expanded in digital media, draws more attention to poems than to their writers and compels us to think more of poetry than of poets, which is perhaps the only way not to lose sight of the big picture.

A Closing of the Gap?

I will begin with a poem by the famous modern poet Gu Cheng 顧城 (1956–1993):

> The setting sun,
> bathed in steam,
> the great river melts
>   lead and tin.
> Two and three
>   white gulls fall,
> tens of thousands of fire sparks
>   arise.[1]

The poem presents a nicely handled patterning of contrasts: rise and fall, white and red, steam and metal, dissolution and the moment of last splendor. It is a short exercise, though not unworthy of a poet like Gu Cheng, who is well-known for his simple, clean, and hauntingly beautiful imagery. This poem, however, is not written in modern vernacular; it is an old-style poem, a quatrain in five-syllable line. Apart from alerting us to the intriguing fact that Gu Cheng, a giant figure in modern vernacular poetry and a representative "misty poet" (*menglong shiren* 朦朧詩人), has left a sizable collection of old-style poems that to date almost no critic ever discusses, reading this poem in English poses a question: What, if any, is the difference between old-style poems and new-style poems when they appear in English translation?

In the case of Gu Cheng's poem cited above, there seems to be very little, and the poem would be equally charming were it translated back into modern vernacular Chinese. There is a distinctive possibility that, to a casual reader in English, the formal difference between old-style and new-style poems is barely perceptible. Would it be fair, then, to say that the politics of form, largely an event occurring in the Chinese language, is a linguistic internal affair (*yuyan de neizheng* 語言的內政)?

Perhaps not quite, for these forms have undeniably different representational habits, and the weight of the past is also quite different: unbearably heavy for one, and exhilaratingly light for another. Nevertheless, this is a good question to ponder, for it leads to the consideration of a host of issues that matter to both old-style and new-style poems: Why does form continue to be important long after having served the immediate political purpose of the May Fourth generation and after new-style poetry has become well established? What are those differences in representational habits, and, more important, what differences can account for the fact that old-style poetry, after it was declared "dead" so many times in the last century, not only still endures but is also flourishing and attracts numerous practitioners today?

I will not attempt to answer these complex questions in one essay, but they are worth contemplating, and we must begin somewhere. One can begin small, with titles and titular material. Old-style poems have occasion-based titles that one rarely, if ever, sees in new-style poems, such as "Having a Party at Pipa Garden Seeing Elder Brother Mei Off to Take Up a Job in Chengdu," or "In the Afternoon I Read in the News That Some Buddhist Temple in Jinling Made Offerings to Japanese War Criminals of the Nanjing Massacre."[2] If a new-style poem about smog is simply entitled "Smog," an old-style poem may sport a title that reads like a news story: "Twenty-Five Provinces Encounter Smog and the Middle Schools and Elementary Schools at Nanjing Suspended Classes in Emergency."[3] A *ci* lyric to the tune title of "Spring in Qin Garden" 沁園春 (Qinyuan chun) has a rambling preface:

> I have been living for two and a half years in Rhode Island in the Eastern US and got through the major phases of the American pandemic safe and sound. Then, as soon as I flew to San Francisco in the Western US to meet with my friends,

I contracted COVID. Nobody at the banquet was spared. At first my symptoms were like those of a common cold; only after self-testing did I find out I had been hit! It was merely coughing, nose running, et cetera, with no fever. Henceforth I stayed at home and convalesced in peace and quiet. Facing the empty mountain, listening to birds' talk, and enjoying mountain flowers, I slept, drank liquid, and sun-bathed. After a full eight days, I recovered without having to see a doctor. Thereupon I composed the following piece to give an account of my experience.[4]

余在美東羅德島二年半，經歷了美國疫情的主要階段皆安然無恙，飛來美西舊金山與友人聚，當即染疫，席上無一幸免。症狀初似感冒，自測方知中招，無非咳嗽流鼻涕等，然不發燒，遂居家靜養。對空山，聞鳥語，賞山花，睡覺、喝水、曬太陽，前後8日，未就醫即自愈也。因賦此闋以紀之。

Such elaborate contextualization anchors a poem in the reality of a poet's personal life and that of a public time-space. At a basic level, poems like this collectively constitute the picture of an age that are refracted through the lens of individuals. The everydayness located in a precise time and space of the lyrical subject is an act of self-historicization, which sets a sharp contrast with the attempt on the part of a new-style poet to remain an intense, but anonymous, voice.[5] Take, for example, Gu Cheng's Lorca-esque "Elegy" 挽歌 (Wan ge) written in 1982:[6]

A small potato under the moon
A small potato under the moon
Coming up, a dog
Sniffs
A small potato under the moon

月亮下的小土豆
月亮下的小土豆
走來一隻狗
嗅
月亮下的小土豆

The mystique of the poem in no small part owes to the disembodied poetic voice devoid of any context. I once described new-style poetry as "the poet's poetry" and the old-style as "everyone's poetry" or "everyone else's poetry."[7] Although the statement, just like any comparison between two complex entities or phenomena, risks the criticism of generalization, that does not render it untrue.

Here, however, is the interesting twist: in the past two decades, new-style poetry has been shifting in a noteworthy direction, closing the gap between the two forms in one critical aspect. That is, new-style poetry has achieved an earthiness, an accessibility, and along with it a general acceptance by a mass audience that it had declared as its raison d'être at its point of origin in the early twenti-eth century but, ironically, never quite accomplished until now—and all this has happened while old-style poetry opens up a crack for modern, and modernist, expressions to get into the age-old forms, which will be explored more deeply in the third section of this essay. This, I argue, is largely thanks to the internet, used via computers and, in recent years, increasingly via smartphones—even though smartphone users and social media users may not be aware that they are using the internet.[8] The internet has done several things for contemporary poetry: it allows a prominent visibility of the coexistence of old-style and new-style poetry in the virtual space; it creates a community for poetry writers and readers that, forego-ing the inconvenience of the logistics and expenses of physical space, transcends the local or even the national by crossing geographic and political boundaries; it facilitates and enables the emergence of the voices of ordinary people in a wider, more public sphere, as people can now compose, read, and share poems without going through print media, and they can do so even more easily on their smart-phones, which are more portable and mobile, and more prevalently embedded in people's daily lives, than the lightest laptops or tablets. The story of a peasant with a disability whose poems had first become popular on WeChat and only later were "discovered" and published in print media is a representative example of the grassroots nature of poetry writing in the digital age.[9]

The impact of the last point is particularly acute for new-style poetry, an orig-inally elite form created and advocated by Chinese intelligentsia despite its ver-nacular medium. To that end, all the poems that have gone viral for good or bad reasons, poems justly or unjustly derided as "vulgar" and denounced as "vul-garization," poems dubbed "pear-blossom style" (*lihua ti* 梨花體), "lamb style" (*yanggao ti* 羊羔體), "dark blue (or bruise) style" (*wuqing ti* 烏青體), or "shallow-shallow style" (*qianqian ti* 淺淺體), are all useful components from the broader perspective, for they have contributed to an unprecedented saturation of new-style poetry among the masses.[10] What are regarded as disastrous consequences caused by the "mediocritization" of contemporary new-style poetry, namely, the fact that poetry writing has become too easy and that poetic language is no differ-ent from colloquial speech, may be the best thing that has ever happened to new-style poetry since its birth, for accessibility and pervasiveness constitute exactly the kind of background and atmosphere for a literary form to develop—the his-tory of *ci* poetry is a good precedent.[11]

Old-style poetry has been transformed in the new ecosystem as much as the new-style, but it takes a different trajectory.

The Trajectory of Change in the Last Century

Looking back at the composition of old-style poetry in the past hundred years, we see a clear trajectory of change. Much of this trajectory has only begun to emerge into full view in recent years, because new-style poetry had principally dominated the interest of critics and scholars in the twentieth century and the writing of old-style poetry was considered a fringe activity outside a literary historian's proper sphere of attention. But despite the success of new-style poetry, old-style poetry had never disappeared; on the contrary, it was composed in large numbers by cultural conservatives and increasingly by the advocates of new-style poetry as well. A statistical study shows that many writers who were eager experimenters of new-style poetry turned to old-style in the 1930s and especially 1940s.[12] The flourishing of old-style poetry in the 1940s led some scholars to conclude that there was a revival (*fuxing* 復興). The term is debatable because "revival" is accurate only in regard to a changed aesthetic judgment, but not so much if we consider the enormous quantity of old-style poems produced in the Republican Era.[13]

Social occasions call for the composition of old-style poetry rather than new-style, and the need for socializing and networking remains as intense as ever throughout wars and civil unrest. Apart from the social need for old-style poetry, however, a strong political call was issued for "old forms" (*jiu xingshi* 舊形式), "ethnic forms" (*minzu xingshi* 民族形式), and "Chinese styles and Chinese manners" (*Zhongguo zuofeng and Zhongguo qipai* 中國作風和中國氣派).[14] That this call came at a time when many writers turned to old-style poetry may not have been a pure coincidence.

A turning point in old-style poetry writing occurred during the socialist period of the 1960s and 1970s when social circumstances and personal predilection became the cooperative components in the molding of a new creation in the hands of Nie Gannu 聶紺弩 (1903–86). Nie Gannu went from a fervent participant in the New Culture movement and a writer of new-style poems to a devoted practitioner of old-style poetry, writing about his experience as a Rightist working in the cold wilderness of the Northeast.[15] If the biggest problem suffered by a vast number of old-style poems (or new-style, for that matter) is the absence of a distinctive voice, then Nie Gannu is an exception. His old-style poems are marked by a singular mixture of pain and humor, poignancy and playfulness, impressive imagery and memorable wit. Choosing to write about his predicament in the demanding style of regulated verse (*lüshi* 律詩), he manages to embed modern vernacular and socialist lingo in well-crafted parallel couplets, achieving a complex balance of sincerity and irony, deep feelings and gentle mockery. It turns out to be a fiercely modern old-style poetry that faithfully adheres to and yet transcends its classical form, widely recognized as "Gannu style" (*Gannu ti* 紺弩體).

One could say that Nie Gannu's poems were politically motivated, even though their content is exactly the opposite of what the state might expect from something contained in such a pure "Chinese ethnic form." Old-style poetry became a voice of quiet resistance or loud protest, and the latter found its most concentrated expression in poetry posted on Tiananmen Square during the April 5

Tiananmen Incident in 1976. Large masses of people spontaneously gathered at Tiananmen Square to mourn the deceased premier Zhou Enlai 周恩來 (1898–1976) and express their discontent with the Cultural Revolution and Mao's policies by laying wreaths and banners with "mourning couplets" (*wanlian* 挽聯) and poems around the Monument to the People's Heroes. Many were arrested, and the gathering was labeled counterrevolutionary in its immediate aftermath; but the verdict was repealed at the third Plenary of the Eleventh Central Committee two years later, and the poems, having first circulated as handwritten copies and in mimeographed editions, were put in print by Beijing's well-known publishing house, People's Literature Press.[16] Of the nearly 600 poems included in this volume, 515 are in old style and only 59—one tenth of the total—in new style.[17]

As the Cultural Revolution era came to an end, the aging Nie Gannu, now famous for his old-style poetry, expressed his hope that the younger generation would no longer practice the form, since he regarded his own old-style poems as the products of a traumatic age.[18] But old-style poetry did not die with him. Ten years after his passing, an anthology was published, which in many ways may be considered an illustrative specimen of old-style poetry before the advent of the internet. It certainly regards itself as a collection of "the best of the best." Titled *A Collection of the Refined Talents of Ocean and Alp* 海嶽風華集 (Haiyue fenghua ji), the anthology was compiled by Xiong Shengyuan 熊盛元 (b. 1949) and Mao Gufeng 毛谷風 (b. 1945), two practitioners who both had academic affiliations and are generously represented in the anthology.[19] The first edition was published in 1996 and included 33 authors and 631 poems, of which 372 are *shi* poems and 259 are *ci* lyrics. It appeared as a stitch-bound volume contained in a case. Two years later, a revised, enlarged edition with computer typeset was printed, which includes 52 authors and 1,191 poems, of which 787 are *shi* poems and 404 are *ci* lyrics.

It helps us place things in perspective to compare this anthology with the Tiananmen Square poems, on the one hand, and with the poems published in some of the contemporary old-style poetry journals, on the other. The Square poems are gritty and emotionally charged; the poems in poetry journals are more polished but sport all kinds of earthy topics from everyday life, such as this gem: "On the Night of October 5, 1980, I Received a Long-Distance Call from [My Son] Guang'er Asking for a Tape Recorder under the Pretext of Studying Foreign Language, and I Wrote This to Admonish Him."[20] One cannot find anything of this sort in *Haiyue fenghua ji*. The diction and imagery therein are both refined and hackneyed, often recycled directly from premodern poetry; most pieces are about innocuous occasions such as gazing at the moon, appreciating flowers, visiting a scenic site, staying overnight at a temple, reading a book, inscribing a painting, corresponding with a friend, and so on and so forth. These activities could happen in any day and age and are also among the most conventional poetic topics in the tradition. Ironically, one of a small number of titles that manage to convey the temporality of the poems is "Power Cut" (*tingdian* 停電), which is a negative indication of the modern era by its very failure and cessation.[21] In a word, the anthology is by and large filled with elegant but utterly faceless verses that, if placed in the collection of a late imperial literatus, would have been wholly indistinguishable, and *that* is precisely the problem of this kind of old-style poetry, which resembles a well-oiled, but unplugged, machine. If *ci* lyrics had started out in history as pop songs and acquired dynamism through a juxtaposition of high poetic imagery and the simulation of colloquial speech, then there is hardly any contemporary colloquialism in the present anthology.

The title of the anthology, *A Collection of the Refined Talents of Ocean and Alp*, was modeled on *A Collection of the Finest Souls of River and Alp* 河嶽英靈集 (Heyue yingling ji), a poetic anthology made by Yin Fan 殷璠 (fl. 753) in the High Tang that lay claim to an unbiased position regarding "new sounds" (*xinsheng* 新聲) and "old styles" (*guti* 古體). Yin Fan's was a countercultural anthology set against the courtly style of the capital poets, and he deliberately promoted "talented men in lowly official positions."[22] That, however, is hardly the case with the present anthology, because a preponderance of the authors were literature professors or journal editors and belonged to the cultural establishment.[23] Even those outside the establishment were active members of a poetry society. More important, the compilers take pains to demonstrate in the biographical notes that these poets all have a lineage: that is, their poetic styles are described as inheriting the legacy of some premodern master or school, and in most cases a poet is introduced as a disciple of a certain senior poet, either one of the preface writers or an older poet included in the anthology. Quite a few poems were presented to one another or composed together during an outing. This, we realize, is a close-knit and self-enclosed community. These poets were not outsiders to a capital elite like most of the *Heyue yingling ji* poets had been; instead, they themselves constituted the cultural elite. The only forces that the *Ocean and Alp* poets opposed, delicately alluded to by the compilers in the afterword of the 1996 edition, would be those who had, ironically, "gone into the ocean" (*xiahai* 下海), that is, people who took advantage of the economic growth in 1980s and 1990s China and became wealthy through commercial ventures. Not the *Ocean and Alp* poets, who observe the ocean from the beach: the compilers proudly announce that they consider "propagating our motherland's cultural essence and reviving the Huaxia poetic enterprise" as a more noble pursuit than getting rich.[24]

The anthology is ordered by seniority, from old to young. In the 1998 edition, thirty-one poets were born in the 1940s, twelve poets in the 1950s, five in the 1960s, and four in the 1970s; they certainly do not fit the stereotype that most people writing old-style poetry in the 1980s and 1990s were "retired cadres" who sported the so-called old-cadre style (*laogan ti* 老幹體). Seen from one perspective, it shows continuity; from another, however, it shows a continuous dwindling. But even more noteworthy is the fact that the few authors who would not be considered members of the intelligentsia, such as the customs officer, the transformer factory worker, and the air force pilots, were almost all from the last pages of the volume—that is, from the younger generation. This is open to interpretation, but one thing is for sure: outside the anthology, capitalism and technology were gradually changing the cultural and social order; ultimately, it would be up to the Chinese internet to loosen the iron hold of the establishment.

"A Near-Sighted Sensei Watches the Grassroots": The Digital Age

In an essay on world poetry published in 2003, Stephen Owen writes, "What has changed since 1990 is, of course, the remarkable expansion of the Web. . . . Poetry has taken a new and strange life there."[25] He comments on "the proliferation of centers located in e-space" and says at the end of the essay, "We will see, someday, how this all plays out and where poetry, in our new century, is."[26] Now, twenty years later, even though we still have much of the century ahead of us, we can at least make some observations.

As mentioned earlier, one of the most impactful consequences of the internet—and by the internet I refer, throughout this essay, to the "broader internet" that many smartphone users are unaware is enabling them to access social media platforms, apps, and browsers—is that old-style poetry has acquired a visibility that can no longer be ignored by scholars, critics, or any casual observer of the poetry scene. We can see this easily by running a keyword search in the China Academic Journal Database. If we type in the keyword *jiuti shi*, we get about one thousand titles beginning in 1978 and going all the way up to mid-2022. Of these titles, about six hundred were produced in a thirty-one-year span between 1978 and 2009. Then, between 2010 and mid-2022, in barely thirteen years, we have about 450 articles, which counts for nearly half of the total. This is just a rough estimate, but it gives us a good idea of the changing amount of attention that old-style poetry has been receiving over the years. Also, if earlier articles tend to focus on the old-style poems written by literary luminaries such as Lu Xun 鲁迅 (1881–1936), Yu Dafu 郁達夫 (1896–1945), Zhou Zuoren 周作人 (1885–1967), and so on, then toward the end of the first decade of the new century, we begin to see articles that discuss *jiuti shi* writing as a general phenomenon.[27] In English-language scholarship there has been a similar trend.[28]

More important than the visibility of the continuous prosperity of old-style poetry, the internet has led to the diminishment of the monopolizing influence of the cultural establishment represented by journals, presses, and universities. It opens the venue of publication to virtually anyone who has access to a computer or, in more recent years, a smartphone. In the early days, even people who could not afford a personal computer could easily go online in a Web bar (*wangba*

網吧) for a modest fee. The internet has infinitely expanded the sphere of reading, copying, downloading, critiquing, and discussing poetry. Netizens (*wangyou* 網友) have diverse voices and are a powerful force in all kinds of cocreation; their likes and dislikes, preferences and clicks, are independent from the establishment and can override the establishment, so much so that print media—newspapers, journals, and publishing houses—are more often influenced by what has gone viral on the internet than the other way around. We also have the problem of textual losses: if one does not engage in active preservation of the fluid material on the Web, texts can vanish without a trace with shocking speed. The digital ecosystem evokes the manuscript culture of the medieval world; what we have is medievalism in a digital age.[29]

In a conventional Chinese literary historical account, one goes to the poets to look for their poems; but on the internet one looks at poems, which may be attached to a name but are not necessarily attached to a person. That is, readers often do not know the real person behind the screen name, which can be deliberately or inadvertently misleading about the identity of the real person; just as important, they often do not care so much about knowing, at least not until an author posts enough pieces and develops a reputation and a following. Furthermore, many netizens who write and post poetry do not consider themselves "poets" (*shiren* 詩人), and they may post just one poem or a few poems and subsequently disappear or never post poems again. An internet reader could read a thousand poems and find only one good piece—or zero—by a random netizen. This is an important point because it changes how we think of literary history or canonization.

There is pushback, as the establishment attempts to assert or reassert authority. There are efforts to enforce metrical rules—even though there had been no such rules in early classical poetry—or to prescribe what kind of modern colloquialism can or cannot enter old-style poetry. There are also outcries that the internet lacks standards and is a massive mess. But the internet is not standardless: rather, it has numerous standards, for each user—or each niche community online—has their own standard and threshold. If one does not like something one sees, one has options: one could leave a negative comment or go somewhere else, or both. Unless one prefers a single standard and "unified thought" (*tongyi sixiang* 統一思想), the internet provides an ideal playing field for all tastes. More than the limiting lens of any newspaper, journal, collection, or anthology in print media—all the conventional venues through which contemporary literature is known—the internet in its totality indiscriminately, promiscuously, presents us with "what is out there."[30] And poetry grows from all that is out there.

The most striking phenomenon in the world of internet poetry is the transformation of old-style poetry in the hands of a small number of practitioners who have nevertheless received more critical attention than is proportionate to their relative size. One of the representative authors in this regard is the Jiangxi-born Hunan poet Lizilizilizi 李子梨子栗子 (Zeng Shaoli 曾少立, b. 1964). Introducing him to Western academic readers in 2009, I have described his poetry as a new kind of old-style poetry that belongs to the twenty-first century, as he liberally uses contemporary vocabulary and imagery in his works, even making allusions to well-known new-style poetry.[31] Lizi, however, is far from an isolated case. Noteworthy cyberpoets writing in a distinctive "new-old" style (*xinjiuti* 新舊體) include, among many others, Xutang 噓堂 (Duan Xiaosong 段曉松, b. 1970), Dugu shiroushou 獨孤食肉獸 (Zeng Zheng 曾崢, b. 1970), and Jinyu 金魚 or Jinzhengyu 金正魚 (Peng Mo 彭莫, b. 1983).[32] Jinyu has some remarkable long narrative poems, and his shorter *shi* poems and *ci* lyrics are hybrid creatures of classical forms and contemporary language. One five-syllable-line poem reads:

Night

Like memorial monuments, the streetlamps stand erect,
the shadows hinting at the scars of the night.
Thought has been gradually diluted;
souls are being added up.

Scraps of paper fly up to the sky;
on street corners crows alight.
A traveler quietly passes by,
roses in his hand.

夜

如碑路燈立，影射夜傷疤。思想漸稀釋，靈魂在累加。
天空飛紙屑，街角落烏鴉。有客悄然過，手中玫瑰花。[33]

In this poem, *xishi* 稀釋 (dilute) and *leijia* 累加 (add up) are both modern technical terms. In the third couplet there is an implicit contrast of white (color of paper) and black (color of crow). Roses might be red. These hidden colors, repressed by the poet, contribute to the oppressive atmosphere of the poem.

A *ci* lyric by Jinyu to the tune of "Abridged Magnolia" 減蘭 (Jian lan) might pass for a "thing poem" (*yongwu shi* 詠物詩), a special subgenre of classical poetry, but it is an unusual thing—a rotten apple whose "corpse" attracts hordes of ants—with a surprise ending:[34]

An apple, so ripe it's rotten:
putrid smell, sour juice, its skin half clinging.
The ants all go crazy,
lining up in a circle to gaze at the red sun.

Who gives it a kick?
This world is suddenly clean again.
It's got nothing to do with me;
I only sing softly "Abbreviated Magnolia."

爛熟蘋果，腐氣酸汁皮半裹。螞蟻瘋狂，列隊圍觀紅太陽。
誰飛一脚，世界瞬間清净了。與我無關，我只溫柔唱減蘭。

Some of the poems by Shusheng bawang 書生霸王 (Zhao Que 趙缺, b. 1977)
offer lively vignettes of modern urban life. One is titled "A Woman Scavenger's
Young Son" 拾荒女人幼子 (Shihuang nüren youzi):

Having a great time in the brick shed—
there's no need to bother Mum.
Tearing up a piece of yellow cardboard,
he cut it into a small gun.
"Bang bang"—he shouted in a low voice,
glaring around proudly, with a scowl.
When by chance seeing a kid up on a balcony,
he took distant aim at his chest.

得意磚棚下，何須擾阿娘。撕開黃紙板，剪作小機槍。
突突低聲叫，昂昂怒目張。偶逢樓上子，瞄遠對胸膛。[35]

There is something poignant about the young boy who, living in poverty, plays
with a self-made toy from cardboard. The fifth line, that the boy "yelled in a *low
voice*" (emphasis added), is the key: he does not want to be a nuisance to his
mother; he is trying to quietly entertain himself. The maturity, mixed with the
innocence, is vividly and touchingly represented.

Another poem, "An Imported Bathtub" 進口浴缸 (Jinkou yugang), moves
from a thing to the poet himself and finally to people in the larger world; it is a
Du Fu move:

Made with porcelain, an exotic thing,
traveling ten thousand miles, washed in wind and dust.
Before containing the water of the Splendid and Pure Pool,
it first invites in the rich and famous.
I am shocked to find out the price of one
is my salary of ten years.
But I am by no means a poor person—
there are the refugees at River Huai.

陶瓷舶來品，萬里沐風塵。未蓄華清水，先邀富貴人。
驚他一缸價，是我十年薪。我亦非貧者，淮河有難民。[36]

But Shusheng bawang can also write poems in a different tenor, poems that return from the outside back to the self, such as this quatrain, "Valentine's Day" 情人節 (Qingren jie):

> Alone I sit by the west window,
> my coffee already half cold.
> The sweet memories of all my life—
> just like chewing gum.

獨坐西窗下，咖啡已半涼。平生甜蜜事，恰似口香糖。[37]

The first word of the poem makes it clear that his romantic life has been a failure. As the hot coffee is losing its heat, the sweet memories are losing their sweet flavor like the chewed gum.

Many poems capture interesting moments in life.

A Glance from the Car Passing by the Northern Peak

By Hengdaozi

> In this remote land, clouds hang low,
>   mountain and river oozing out;
> a slanting wind blows rain,
>   ruffling spring banners.
> A flock of sheep all bend over endless grass;
> one looks up, having something on its mind.

車過北嶺一瞥 (橫道子)
地迴雲低山水滋，斜風吹雨亂春旗。
群羊俯就無邊草，一隻擡頭有所思。[38]

Seeing Someone Off at the West Station in the Seventh Month of the Jiashen Year

By Shutong

> A traveler myself, I am seeing off a southbound traveler.
> The splendid light of the station floats in the night.
> We promised each other
>   not to be sappy like kids;
> then, just as I turned my head,
>   I saw you turn yours.

甲申年七月西站送客 (殊同)

客中送客更南游，一站華光入夜浮。
說好不爲兒女態，我回頭見你回頭。[39]

What Happened in Twilight, No. 2

By Zimoxiangxue

A cicada on a tall tree sounds breathless,
sitting alone in the shade toward sunset.
A bee, how so very flirtatious!
Right over there by the fence, I saw him
    give a kiss to the white rose.

黃昏即事之二 (紫陌香雪)

蟬聲高樹氣微微，獨坐濃蔭向夕暉。
一隻蜜蜂輕薄甚，籬邊吻了白薔薇。[40]

The phrase in the third line in Shutong's poem, "*shuohao*" 說好 (make a promise to each other), or the last line of Zimoxiangxue's poem, 籬邊吻了白薔薇, are as modern and vernacular as can be. In the poem by Hengdaozi, the immensely resonant classical poetic phrase "*yousuosi*" 有所思 (thinking of something/longing for someone) is hilariously embedded after the much more colloquial "*taitou*" 擡頭 ("look up," as opposed to its more literary synonyms such as *jushou* 舉首, *jiaoshou* 矯首, or *angshou* 昂首), all governed by the subject *yizhi*, the measure word for an animal. None of these poems reads like anything from the *Ocean and Alp* anthology or from a late imperial collection.

The incorporation of contemporary colloquialisms and modern expressions calls to mind a wry remark of Lizi: "If one keeps sliding on this road [i.e., writing old-style poems in this manner], it'd become 'new poetry' :)."[41] Indeed, some of the old-style poems by Lizi and some other poets discussed in this special issue push the very boundary of the representational habits of old-style poetry, even though—and this is important for us to bear in mind—whether an old-style poem is experimental and modernist is, in and of itself, not a measure of good old-style poetry. That is to say, if a poet writes ultra-modernist verse in an age-old form, that itself does not make the poem good or bad. This statement, simple as it is, enables us to direct our attention to something much more important, namely, the fact that the gap can close between old-style and new-style poems demonstrates the degree of freedom that contemporary writers of poetry have acquired from the tyranny of conventional representational habits of the two forms. To any poetry watcher, this is an exhilarating development.

Nevertheless, one of the keys to the attraction of successful contemporary old-style poetry is juxtaposition. In other words, it is neither the ancient form nor the modern vocabulary alone, but rather their *conjunction* and, in that conjunction, the *disjunction* of modern vocabulary and the classical form that are responsible for their success. Most Chinese readers are familiar with the classical poetic form, not only thanks to the increased number of classical poems included in Chinese textbooks for every grade of elementary schools across the mainland, or to many Chinese parents' indefatigable efforts to instill some famous Tang poems in their children, but also owing to children's ballads (*erge* 兒歌), which are always rhymed and typically in three-, five-, or seven-syllable lines.[42] As Brian Boyd demonstrates in his evolutionary literary criticism informed by cognitive science, rhyme and rhythm go deeper than any element of a cultural tradition in building a biological response in human beings.[43] When a poet, touched by a fleeting moment in life, manages to wed living language, imagery, and moods with rhyme and rhythm in a resonant tried-and-true literary form, they will have achieved an impressive feat.

In a somewhat reversed mirror image of the old-style poems that experiment with a modernist suffusion, many new-style poems are increasingly leaning toward an earthy everydayness. The call for everydayness went back to the 1990s, as a reaction against the pretentiousness and sentimentalism that one finds in many of the "misty poems" of the previous decade. The change in new-style poetry, as I argue earlier in this essay, would not have been accomplished without the popularizing forces of the internet, either. That people can write/post poems on the internet like a diary entry without having to go through the filtering process of the establishment has led to profound transformations in the poetic landscape, not the least of which is the de-mystification, even trivialization, of the very act of poetry writing.

Some years ago, doing research for a conference presentation, I came across a series of poems by an author named "Xiaonüsheng aiyuwen" 小女生愛語文 ("A Girl Student Who Loves Chinese"). Some of the poems are delightful but wholly unremarkable; some are basically pieces of uninspired prose divided into lines. The topics range from "testing" her boyfriend by not responding to his text messages to criticizing a couplet (*duilian* 對聯) cited by President Xi Jinping. The author clearly did not aspire to be regarded as a poet (*shiren* 詩人), and the avatar has long since vanished from the websites after some intense activities lasting a few months. Nonetheless, those poems, ordinary as they are, constitute the very "voices of the people" that the Chinese poetic tradition had always prized. Such verses anticipate the poem cited below, which was first posted by the author in her "friends' circle" on WeChat and made the initial round at the 2022 Global Chinese-Language College Students Short Poems Competition. The background of the poem is the state's ban on college students' leaving school grounds "unless it is absolutely necessary" during the COVID-19 pandemic.

Unnecessarily Leaving Campus

By Zhu Haoyue

Internship; making a medical appointment; IELTS classes—these, I suppose,
    are necessary.
Then how about crouching over there to watch a cloud above the soaring eaves?
How about bringing back a bag of chestnuts?
How about soaking hair wet with fallen leaves?
How about sitting in a sleepy school bus for two hours to hold hands
    with the other half?
Just in case this photograph becomes a classic?
Just in case this bag of chestnuts is shared with a fellow student
    on the edge of a break-down?
Just in case the soaked head is that of a poet?
Just in case in this life he is the One?
The pandemic makes everything into a Necessity that sits so solemnly upright.
But heck, this human world is composed of numerous unnecessary things. . . .

非必要離校

朱皓月
實習 掛號 雅思課 算是必要的吧
那 蹲守一朵飛檐上的雲呢
捂回一袋板栗呢
被落葉淋上頭髮呢
坐兩個小時昏昏欲睡的校車 去牽另一半的手呢
萬一 這張照片被傳成經典呢
萬一 這袋板栗分給了一個瀕臨崩潰的同學呢
萬一 淋濕的是一個詩人呢
萬一 這輩子就是他呢
疫情讓這一切都變成了正襟危坐的必要
誒 人間是由無數個非必要組成的呀[44]

Still largely absent from new-style poems are the kind of rambling titles such as admonishing one's son for wanting a tape recorder or the kind of rambling preface about contracting COVID; however, the seemingly irreconcilable separation of old-style and new-style poems we saw in the 1980s and earlier is being bridged in some of the poems we see today.

The Thrill of Becoming

The old-style poems cited in the preceding section are but a notable fraction of the vast landscape of digital poetry. Much of old-style poetry remains largely indistinguishable from (bad) late imperial poetry except perhaps in terms of their lack of classical erudition. But change has been undeniably taking place, both inside poetry itself and outside.

When I was writing "Muffled Dialect Spoken by Green Fruit: An Alternative History of Modern Chinese Poetry" in 2006, there had been very little English publication about old-style internet poetry. That article calls for a new kind of literary history that includes modern old-style poetry, departing from the mainstream literary historical accounts that present "new poetry" (*xin shi*) as the unquestioned victor over *jiushi shi*. At the time it still met with much opposition, as one of the anonymous reviewers of the article considered it "reactionary" for simply trying to put old-style poetry on the map. Over time, however, that resistance has proven outworn, and old-style poetry has become an increasingly hot topic of research. The question is, now what?

One thing we can do is to remain sensitive to ongoing change both inside and outside literature. It is noteworthy that the last poem cited in the preceding section went viral online but did not make the final round of the poetry competition. Not only that, but it was disappeared from the social media platform on which it was first publicized, along with poems about contemporary social problems such as human trafficking, abuse of women and the mentally ill, and the Wuhan doctor known as the pandemic whistle-blower.[45] The judges of the poetry competition must be commended for having chosen these poems in the first place, but they were ultimately overruled.

There has been an intensification of the state's nation-building agenda in the past decade. In mainland China, old-style poetry has been aggressively promoted, sponsored, and funded by the state. It is regarded as the culturally authentic "ethnic form" with a uniquely Chinese character, uncontaminated by foreign influences. In response to the "instruction" issued by the People's Republic of China leadership to "be a faithful transmitter of the excellent traditional Chinese culture,"[46] there have been numerous regional, national, and international poetry competitions either exclusively for old-style poetry or including both old-style and new, and many scholars and writers are roped in as judges.[47] Thinking back to Nie Gannu and the 1976 Square poems, we can see how old-style poetry can easily turn from a progressive means of resistance into a hijacked form of belligerent conservatism.

Meanwhile, one faces the increased policing of the internet. Under the current conditions, it would be delusional to believe that the Chinese internet is open and free. One question we should constantly ask ourselves is: What role are we as scholars and critics playing in all this? Like anthropologists whose very presence in a social group they study may change the object of their study, scholars and critics are active participants in these large cultural shifts, and overseas sinology plays a particularly influential part because it represents "international recognition" to many contemporary Chinese writers. Might we inadvertently become complicit in the nationalistic project of the state through our enthusiasm for contemporary old-style poetry? And how do we avoid it?

One answer is that, instead of fans, promoters, and agents, we act as self-conscious observers and commentators, reflecting on the larger cultural phenomenon even as we analyze individual texts. Another answer is to discard, as many already have, the notion that old-style and new-style poetry are enemies or competitors and that scholars must side with one or the other and, even more importantly, recognize that the discursive segregation of the two forms is not to our advantage in considering the continuing evolution of Chinese poetry. In an essay titled "New Poetry and Modern Poetry," I argue for a spatialized view of modern Chinese poetry instead of a temporalized view; that is, we should envision modern Chinese poetry as "a space marked by multipolarity and hybridity" (一個以多元與雜糅為特點的空間). In other words, we reject the evolutionary narrative of transitioning from premodern to modern and equating modern poetry (*xiandai shi* 現代詩) with new-style poetry (*xin shi* 新詩) or vice versa, but instead regard Chinese poetry in its totality and recognize that the modernity of modern Chinese poetry lies in the very conjunction of the two forms. For that reason, I contend that, quite apart from the question of whether this form can still be aesthetically creative and productive, modern old-style poetry has a theoretical significance for modern poetry watchers and researchers.[48] In practice, we should integrate the study of a poet's old-style poetry with that of their new-style poetry when they have both, like in Gu Cheng's case.

In the past decade, Chinese internet users have increasingly turned to WeChat to live life and, among many other things, share poetry.[49] By virtue of a function created on WeChat, known in Chinese as "friends' circle" (*pengyou quan* 朋友圈), launched in April 2012, users can access and share accepted WeChat friends' information, creating a semi-closed micro-community that is more private than websites are. The consequences of such a shift are complex. If anything, it brings more challenges to researchers who intend to collect and preserve data, and it certainly makes drawing any general conclusions about internet poetry on WeChat in a responsible manner virtually impossible, since no one can join all the WeChat groups, let alone follow them for several years, unless one were the ever-watchful Chinese state with its immense capabilities for surveillance. These challenges could drive a researcher to go for the already-known quantities on the WeChat platform and become severely limited in her or his view of what is going on, which is a danger posed by any over-exaggerated attention to WeChat.

If, however, we consider the consequences of WeChat for internet poetry or poetry in general, then they are arguably minimal. WeChat users still visit websites, and poems that go viral in WeChat circles can, as demonstrated by several examples cited in this essay, still get disseminated to a wider public. In other words, there is always a leakage and a fluidity regarding these "friends' circles." More important, we can gain a better perspective if we adopt a historical point of view; that is to say, "friends' circles" are, for one thing, a more extreme manifestation of internet communities where like-minded internet users congregate, and many BBS (bulletin board system) forums on the Web can be just as restrictive;[50] for another, they represent a contemporary digital re-creation of premodern Chinese literati elite's social networking mechanisms such as poetry societies or social gatherings, with the most significant difference being the changed social identities of participants. The compositions of those local poetry societies did not always circulate widely or nationally, and many simply disappeared in the course of time, which is not necessarily a bad thing for the authors or the future readers. The English name for *pengyou quan*, Moments, precisely captures the ephemeral nature of these posts and exchanges that create an avalanche of information consuming individuals and the society at large to a worrying degree, as testified to by many studies in recent years. Like the poems recited, sung, copied on paper or on the walls of post-stations, taverns, temples, or brothels in the age of manuscript culture, poems posted on Moments in WeChat come and go, and thankfully not all will be preserved or need to be. Instead of becoming fixated on a few known authors or groups, we would do better to set our sights on the big picture: namely, how poetry writing, and poetry in both old and new styles, are being transformed, powerfully and positively, in the twenty-first century by social and technological changes.

Indeed, viewing the contemporary digital poetryscape and reading netizens' responses to poems, I have never felt so optimistic about Chinese poetry, after a long twentieth century when both forms were constantly plagued by a sense of disorientation and loss. Now the reading public no longer merely treats poetry with either reverence or ridicule, which in truth are no more than two sides of the same coin; instead, they sometimes talk about how touched they are by poems in old or new style. This is not the last word because we live in an ongoing present and the future is not set, and it is thrilling to be part of this never-ending becoming. Scholarship is not about deciding what the literary canon is or predicting what comes next, but about constantly adjusting our understanding in the eternal process and, in doing so, realizing that the past is also changing owing to the changing perspective of the present.

XIAOFEI TIAN is professor of Chinese literature at Harvard University. She is the author of many books in Chinese and English, including *Tao Yuanming and Manuscript Culture: The Record of a Dusty Table* (2005), *Beacon Fire and Shooting Star: The Literary Culture of the Liang (502–557)* (2007), *Visionary Journeys: Travel Writings from Early Medieval and Nineteenth-Century China* (2011), *The Halberd at Red Cliff: Jian'an and the Three Kingdoms* (2018), *Qiushuitang lun Jin ping mei* 秋水堂論金瓶梅 (2003; rev. ed. 2019), and *Yingzi yu shuiwen: Qiushuitang zixuanji* 影子與水文：秋水堂自選集 (2020).

Acknowledgments

The draft of the article was presented at the symposium "Classicism in Digital Times" organized by David Wang and Zhiyi Yang in June 2022. I am indebted to the organizers, participants, and audience for their questions and comments. I thank Frank Kraushaar for his feedback on an earlier draft, and Hu Xiaoming of Huadong Normal University and Zang Di of Peking University for their generous assistance during the writing of the paper.

Notes

1   The title of the poem is "The Big River at Twilight" 大河夕時 (Dahe xishi). The original text reads: 夕陽浴水氣, 大河溶鉛錫. 三兩白鷗落, 萬千火星起. Gu Cheng, *Gu Cheng shi*, 1:99. All translations in this essay are mine unless otherwise noted.

2   "枇杷園宴梅兄成都赴任," bbs.tianya.cn/post-n002-589067-1.shtml (webpage defunct); "午後讀新聞金陵某寺院供奉南京大屠殺倭寇戰犯牌位." bbs.tianya.cn/post-n002-588512-1.shtml (webpage defunct). Accessed August 6, 2022.

3   That is, "霧霾" vs. "25省份遭遇霧霾天氣南京中小學緊急停課." Cited in Tian, "'Du Fu Is Busy!'"

4   The author's name is Liu Haibin 劉海彬, who had worked in China's National Audit Office before retirement. I thank my colleague Jie Li for providing me with this *ci* lyric.

5   It is interesting to observe that poetry recitation to an audience consisting of strangers is a modern phenomenon. In premodern times the poet almost always addressed a community of friends and acquaintances. Classical poems were of course read and copied by strangers as well, but usually the poet would not address them in his poetry or recite his poems to a roomful of strangers. For discussion of modern poetry recitation practice, see Admussen, *Recite and Refuse*.

6   The translation is by Stephen Haven and Wang Shouyi, with slight modification. Haven, *Trees Grow Lively*, 82–83. For composition date, see Gu Cheng, *Gu Cheng shi*, 1:806–7.

7   Tian, "Ershi shiji Zhongguo shige."

8   As a Pew Research Center study reports, many smartphone users do not know that they are also internet users. The confusion stems from two sources: first, "many people who use smartphones are unaware that the apps and browsers on their devices involve using the internet," and second, "apart from a lack of awareness that smartphones and feature phones connect to the internet, many people who use social media and messaging apps appear unaware that the platforms themselves are part of the broader internet" (Silver and Smith, "In Some Countries"). Although there is a difference between posting/reading poems on a social media platform such as WeChat and doing so on a "traditional" website, to which we will return at the end of this essay, it is important to understand that WeChat users are going online and "are part of the broader internet," and that digital poetry and internet poetry are interchangeable terms.

9   I am referring to the story of Li Songshan 李松山, a Henan peasant who writes poems while tending sheep. See Yang, Niu, and Liu, "Fangyang shiren."

10   "Pear-blossom" (*lihua*) puns on the name of the woman poet and painter Zhao Lihua 趙麗華 (b. 1964). "Lamb," *yanggao*, puns on the name of Che Yangao 車延高 (b. 1956), a Wuhan poet who was awarded the Fifth Lu Xun Literature Prize in 2010. "Bruise style," aka "crap style" [as in "cut the crap"]" 廢話體, is named after the poetry of Wuqing, the penname of Zheng Gongyu 鄭功宇 (b. 1978). Qianqian ("shallow-shallow") is named after Jia Qianqian 賈淺淺 (b. 1979), poet and scholar who is the daughter of the famous

writer Jia Pingwa 賈平凹 (b. 1952). All the poets are widely ridiculed for their "non-poetic" poems and have received a strong backlash online.

11 For a depiction of these "disastrous consequences," see Liao and Li, "Panghuang yu zhengzha," 111. Yet another consequence delineated by the authors is the loss of standard of judgment. The statement implies there exists or should exist a uniform standard of judgment among readers, which is, of course, a flawed premise.

12 Zeng, "Ershishiji."

13 See Hu, "Lun kangzhan." Also see Hu, *Minguo jiuti shi*. An early monograph by Zhu Wenhua on modern old-style poetry traces the lifelessness of old-style poetry to the premodern period and considers the twentieth century as a period of its resurrection. See Zhu, *Fengsao yuyun*.

14 The last phrase is quoted from Mao Zedong's talk delivered at the Sixth Plenary Session of the Six Central Committee in 1938, in which Mao states: "Foreign platitudes must be dismissed, empty abstract tune sung less, and dogmatism put to rest. Instead, they shall be replaced by new, fresh, and lively Chinese styles and Chinese manners in which the common people of China find delight" 洋八股必須廢止，空洞抽象的調頭必須少唱，教條主義必須休息，而代之以新鮮活潑的、為中國老百姓所喜聞樂見的中國作風和中國氣派. Mao, "On a New Phase" 論新階段 (Lun xinjieduan), in *Mao Zedong xuanji*, 534. This talk was quickly followed by a series of articles focusing on "old forms" and "ethnic forms" by heavyweight CCP theorists Chen Boda 陳伯達 (1904–1989) Zhou Yang 周揚 (1908–1989), and Ai Siqi 艾思奇 (1910–1966), and further rippled to more discussions and essays in Yan'an, Chongqing, and Hong Kong. See Shi, "Cong 'jiu xingshi.'"

15 For a comprehensive evaluation of Nie Gannu's old-style poetry in relation to the evolution of modern Chinese poetry, see Tian, "'Each Has Its Moment.'"

16 For an annotated translation of the poems, see Goodman, *Beijing Street Voices*.

17 See *Tiananmen shichao* 天安門詩抄.

18 See his letter to his good friend and famous writer Shu Wu 舒蕪 (1922–2009), dated October 25, 1982. Nie Gannu, *Nie Gannu shi*, 488. Shu Wu gives an insightful elucidation of Nie's position in his "Yifen baijuan," 47–48.

19 Xiong and Mao, *Haiyue fenghua ji*. Xiong was an editor of *Jiangxi shici*, a regional magazine of old-style poetry, and affiliated with Jiangxi Social Sciences Academy. Mao was a professor at Zhejiang University before retirement.

20 The Chinese title reads: 1980年10月5日夜光兒來長途電話以學外語爲由索錄音機書以訓之. See *Dangdai shici*, 42.

21 Xiong and Mao, *Haiyue fenghua ji*, 85, 194.

22 Chen et al., *Literary Information*, 215–23.

23 Only a handful worked outside the cultural professions: two financiers, two air-force pilots, one airport customs officer (with a master's degree in literature), and one worker in a transformer factory. There were also one engineer and one biologist, but both would count as "high-level intelligentsia" *gaozhi* or *gaoji zhishifenzi* in Chinese terms.

24 "弘揚祖國文化精粹、振興華夏詩詞事業." See the editors' afterword, Xiong and Gufeng, *Haiyue fenghua ji*, 146.

25 Owen, "Stepping Forward," 540. A side note about the poetic line cited in the section title and used as the epigraph for this essay: The line is from a *ci* lyric, "Taking a Bus" 乘公交車, to the tune title "Partridge Sky" 鷓鴣天, written by the Manchu poet and calligrapher Qi Gong 啓功 (1912–2005), about his experience of being bumped by a big fellow and falling off from a crowded bus in Beijing (https://www.aisixiang.com/data

/85338.html). Qi Gong is another notable poet of old-style poems from Nie Gannu's generation. For a discussion of his poems, see Wang Yichuan, "Jiuti wenxue chuantong."

26 Ibid., 548.

27 Li, "Zhongguo xiandangdai," 5–14.

28 In "Muffled Dialect Spoken by Green Fruit: An Alternative History of Modern Chinese Poetry," published in 2009, I call attention to modern old-style poems including those on the internet and advocate the rewriting of the history of modern Chinese poetry by including modern old-style poetry. This article also appeared in Chinese later that year (see Tian, "'Yinyue yipo qingguo jiangfangyan'"). The 2010s saw the publication of two monographs dedicated to modern old-style poetry by Shengqing Wu and Yang Hao-sheng as well as several articles by Zhiyi Yang. Frank Kraushaar has also written extensively on internet old-style poetry (Kraushaar, *Fern von Geschichte und verheißungsvollen Tagen*).

29 Regarding the textual fluidity and lack of center and authority common to manuscript culture and digital culture, see Tian, *Tao Yuanming and Manuscript Culture*, 21–22, and 223–25.

30 The exception is political intervention, which I will discuss below.

31 "Muffled Dialect," 36. Lizi subsequently received much attention in Western academia. A monograph focusing on his poetry has just been published in German, Kraushaar, *Fern von Geschichte und verheißungsvollen Tagen*.

32 According to an online interview, Jinyu's real name is Peng Mo 彭莫, a piano teacher who lives in Shenyang (zhuanlan.zhihu.com/p/633103150). Many of his online fans, however, do not know for sure who he is or what he is like, which shows that the knowledge of Jinyu's real-life name, birthplace, and experience does not have much, if any, impact on how the poems attached to this name are received online. For a demonstration of this point, see a discussion of his poems on this forum: www.zhihu.com/question/61262575/answer/594833442.

33 See Jinyu, *Chishui ji* 尺水集, which I translate as *A Puddle Collection*. This poem and the ones cited below are all from this source.

34 "Jianlan" is the abbreviation of the tune title, "Jianzi mulanhua" 減字木蘭花.

35 Shusheng bawang, "Shihuang nüren youzi."

36 Shusheng bawang, "Jinkou yugang."

37 Shusheng bawang, "Qingren jie."

38 Hengdaozi, "Cheguo Beiling yipie." bbs.tianya.cn/post-n002-547631-1.shtml#12_3940664.

39 Shutong, "Seeing Someone Off at the West Station." The *jiashen* year would be 2004. The poem has a variant title, "Beijing xizhan songke" ("Seeing Someone Off at Beijing's West Station").

40 Zimoxiangxue, "Huanghun jishi zhier."

41 "這一路再滑下去就是新詩了:)." Lizilizilzi, "Quanji."

42 See, for instance, a collection of nearly two hundred children's ballads called *Caitu jingdian erge daquan*.

43 Boyd, *Why Lyrics Last*.

44 Zhu Haoyue, "Fei biyao lixiao."

45 Ibid.

46 See "Erling yiwu."

47 Just to list a few: Shici Zhongguo chuantong shici chuangzuo dasai 詩詞中國傳統詩詞創作大賽 (Shici China Traditional Shi and Ci Writing Competition); Wangluo shici chuangzuo dasai 網絡詩詞創作大賽 (Internet Shi and Ci Writing Competi-

tion); Huayaobei quanguo shici dasai 華耀杯全國詩詞大賽 (Huayao Cup National Shi and Ci Competition); Nie Gannu bei 聶紺弩杯 (Nie Gannu Cup); Fuxing bei 復興杯 (Revival Cup); Shisheng bei 詩聖杯 (Poetry Sage Cup); Hanjian bei 韓建杯 (Hanjian Cup); Fengshan bei 鳳山杯 (Fengshan cup); Suxian bei 蘇仙杯 (Su the Immortal Cup); Zhonghua bei quan Mei shici dasai 中華杯全美詩詞大賽 (China Cup United States Shi and Ci Competition); Zhongguo shici dahui 中國詩詞大會 (China Shi and Ci Assembly; i.e., the CCTV game show); and so on.

48 Tian, "Xin shi," 75–80.

49 According to a Statista report, "As at the end of March 2023, the Chinese multifunctional social media platform had over 1.3 billion monthly active users." See Thomala, "Number of Active WeChat Messenger Accounts."

50 This is especially true if the theme of a forum is on a sensitive topic. While I undertook research on slash fan fiction on the internet, I discovered that some BBS forums require an elaborate registration process and that "one's acceptance into the forums is subject to the approval of the forum manager(s). Sometimes, even after one is accepted into the forum, the novice needs to accumulate enough points through posting to gain access to certain restricted content on the forum." Tian, "Slashing Three Kingdoms," 229.

References

Admussen, Nick. *Recite and Refuse: Modern Chinese Prose Poetry*. Honolulu: University of Hawaii Press, 2016.

Boyd, Brian. *Why Lyrics Last: Evolution, Cognition, and Shakespeare's Sonnets*. Cambridge, MA: Harvard University Press, 2012.

Caitu jingdian erge daquan 彩圖經典兒歌大全 [Complete Classic Children's Ballads with Colored Illustrations]. Changchun: Jilin meishu chubanshe, 2006.

Chen, Jack W., Anatoly Detwyler, Xiao Liu, Christopher M. B. Nugent, and Bruce Rusk, eds. *Literary Information in China: A History*. New York: Columbia University Press, 2021.

Dangdai shici 當代詩詞 [Contemporary Shi and Ci Poetry]. Guangzhou: Huacheng chubanshe, 1984.

"Erling yiwu 'Gandong Zhongguo' quanguo shici dasai zhenggao tongzhi 2015" 感動中國 全國詩詞大賽徵稿通知 [2015 "Moving China" *Shi* and *Ci* Poetry National Competition: Call for Submissions]. sirmuellera37.rssing.com/chan-18864847/all_p3.html (accessed August 14, 2022).

Goodman, David S. G. *Beijing Street Voices: The Poetry and Politics of China's Democratic Movement*. London: Marion Boyars, 1981.

Gu Cheng 顧城. *Gu Cheng shi quanji* 顧城詩全集 [Complete Collection of Gu Cheng's Poems]. Edited by Gu Xiang 顧鄉, 2 vols. Nanjing: Jiangsu wenyi chubanshe, 2010.

Haven, Stephen, Jin Zhong, Li Yongyi, and Wang Shouyi, trans. *Trees Grow Lively on Snowy Fields: Poems from Contemporary China*. Dual-Language Edition. Sherman, IL: Twelve Winters, 2021.

Hengdaozi 橫道子. "Cheguo Beiling yipie" 車過北嶺一瞥 [A Glance from the Car Passing by the Northern Peak]. zhuanlan.zhihu.com/p/25717005 (accessed August 11, 2022).

Hu Yingjian 胡迎建. "Lun kangzhan shiqi jiuti shige de fuxing" 論抗戰時期舊體詩歌的復興 [On the Revival of Old-Style Poetry during the Sino-Japanese War Period]. *Jinyang xuekan* 晉陽學刊 [Academic Journal of Jinyang] 4 (2000): 56–64.

Hu Yingjian 胡迎建. *Minguo jiuti shi shigao* 民國舊體詩史稿 [A History of the Old-Style Poetry in the Republican Period]. Nanchang: Jiangxi renmin chubanshe, 2005.

Jinyu 金魚. *Chishui ji* 尺水集 [A Puddle Collection]. <github.com/wwj718/forum-poetry/Jinyu (accessed August 1, 2022).

Kraushaar, Frank. *Fern von Geschichte und verheißungsvollen Tagen. Neoklassizistische Cyberlyrik im ChinaNetz und der Stil des Lizilizilizi (2000–2020)* [Far from History and Hopeful Days: Neoclassical Cyberpoetry on the Chinese Web and the Style of Lizilizilizi (2000–2020)]. Bochum/Freiburg: Projektverlag, 2022.

Li Yuchun 李遇春. "Zhongguo xiandangdai jiuti shici pingyi" 中國現當代舊體詩詞平議 [A Discussion of Modern and Contemporary Chinese Old-Style *Shi* and *Ci* Poetry]. *Chuangzuo yu pinglun* 創作與評論 [Writing and Criticism] 10 (2014): 5–14.

Liao Deming 廖德明, and Li Jiayuan 李佳源. "Panghuang yu zhengzha: Zhongguo dangdai shi mianlin de kunjing yu chulu" 彷徨與掙扎：中國當代詩面臨的困境與出路 [Wandering and Struggle: The Trap and Way Out for Contemporary Chinese Poetry]. *Changchun gongye daxue xuebao* 長春工業大學學報 [Changchun Industrial University Journal] 19, no. 1 (2007): 109–11.

Lizilizilizi 李子梨子栗子. "Quanji 108 pian" [Complete Collection in 108 Pieces]. Posted September 13, 2002. wo.5ilog.com/cgi-bin/sys/link/home.aspx?logname=lizilizi (accessed August 10, 2022).

Mao Zedong 毛澤東. *Mao Zedong xuanji* 毛澤東選集 [Selections of Mao Zedong's Works]. Vol. 2. Beijing: Renmin chubanshe, 1991.

Nie Gannu 聶紺弩. *Nie Gannu shi quanbian (zengbu ben)* 聶紺弩詩全編 (增補本) [Complete Collection of Nie Gannu's Poems (Supplemented Edition)]. Edited by Luo Fu 羅孚. Shanghai: Xuelin chubanshe, 1999.

Ouzhai 藕齋. "Ouzhai fangtan lu zhi Jinyu pian" 藕齋訪談錄之金魚篇 [Ouzhai's Interviews: Jin Yu]. zhuanlan.zhihu.com/p/633103150/ (accessed June 30, 2023).

Owen, Stephen. "Stepping Forward and Back: Issues and Possibilities for 'World' Poetry." *Modern Philology* 100, no. 4 (2003): 532–48.

Shi Fengzhen 石鳳珍. "Cong 'jiu xingshi' dao 'minzu xingshi': Wenyi 'minzu xingshi' yundong faqi guocheng tanle" 從 "舊形式" 到 "民族形式"：文藝 "民族形式" 運動發起過程探略 [From "Old Forms" to "Ethnic Forms": A Study of the Process of Launching the "Ethnic Forms" Movement in Literature and Arts]. *Xi'nan minzu daxue xuebao* 西南民族大學學報 [Southwest Minzu University Journal] 1 (2007): 45–50.

Shu Wu 舒蕪. "Yifen baijuan: Guanyu Nie Gannu de *Beihuang cao*" 一份白卷：關於聶紺弩的北荒草 [A Blank Examination Paper: About Nie Gannu's *Beihuang cao*]. *Du shu* 讀書 [Reading] 4 (1988): 47–51.

Shusheng bawang 書生霸王 (Zhao Que 趙缺). "Jinkou yugang" 進口浴缸 [An Imported Bathtub]. bbs.tianya.cn/post-funinfo-1387687-1.shtml (accessed August 11, 2022).

———. "Qingren jie" 情人節 [Valentine's Day]. zhuanlan.zhihu.com/p/25717005 (accessed August 11, 2022).

———. "Shihuang nüren youzi" 拾荒女人幼子 [A Woman Scavenger's Young Son], and "Jinkou yugang" 進口浴缸 [An Imported Bathtub]. bbs.tianya.cn/post-funinfo -1387687-1.shtml (accessed August 11, 2022).

Shutong 殊同. "Jiashen nian qiyue xizhan songke" 甲申年七月西站送客 [Seeing Someone Off at the West Station in the Seventh Month of the Jiashen Year]. bbs.tianya.cn/post -n002-547631-1.shtml#12_3940664 (webpage defunct; accessed August 11, 2022).

Silver, Laura, and Aaron Smith. "In Some Countries, Many Use the Internet without Realizing It." Pew Research Center, May 2, 2019. www.pewresearch.org/short-reads/2019/05/02 /in-some-countries-many-use-the-internet-without-realizing-it/

Thomala, Lai Lin. "Number of Active WeChat Messenger Accounts Q2 2011–Q1 2023." Statista, May 22, 2023. www.statista.com/statistics/255778/number-of-active-wechat-messenger-accounts/.

Tian, Xiaofei 田曉菲. "'Du Fu Is Busy!' Classical Poetry on the Chinese Internet." Paper presented at the Annual Convention of the Modern Language Association, Chicago, January 10, 2014. *PMLA* 128, no. 5 (2013): 1176.

———. "'Each Has Its Moment': Nie Gannu and Modern Chinese Poetry." *Frontiers of Literary Studies in China* 12, no. 3 (2018): 485–525.

———. "Ershi shiji Zhongguo shige de chongxin faming" 二十世紀中國詩歌的重新發明 [The Reinvention of Chinese Poetry in the Twentieth Century]. *Wenhua yanjiu* 文化研究 [Cultural Studies] 6 (2006): 189–204. Reprinted in Tian, *Liubai: Qiushuitang wenhua suibi* 留白：秋水堂文化隨筆 [Blank: Cultural Essays from the Hall of Autumn Flood], 64–93. Beijing: Lixiangguo, 2019. Citation is for the 2006 publication.

———. "Muffled Dialect Spoken by Green Fruit: An Alternative History of Modern Chinese Poetry." *Modern Chinese Literature and Culture* 21, no. 1 (2009): 1–44.

———. *Tao Yuanming and Manuscript Culture: The Record of a Dusty Table*. Seattle: University of Washington Press, 2005.

———. "Xin shi yu xiandai shi" 新詩與現代詩 [New Poetry and Modern Poetry]. *Xinshi pinglun* 新詩評論 2 (2010): 75–80.

———. "'Yinyue yipo qingguo jiangfangyan': Xiandai Hanshi de linglei lishi" 隱約一坡青果講方言：現代漢詩的另類歷史 [Muffled Dialect Spoken by Green Fruit: An Alternative History of Modern Chinese Poetry]. Translated by Song Zijiang 宋子江 and Zhang Xiaohong 張曉紅. *Nanfang wentan* 南方文壇 [Southern Cultural Forum] 6 (2009): 12–20.

Tiananmen shichao 天安門詩抄 [Poems from Tiananmen Square]. Beijing: Renmin wenxue chubanshe, 1978.

Wang Yichuan 王一川. "Jiuti wenxue chuantong de xiandaixing shengcheng: Qi Gong de jiuti shi yu Hanyu xianxiang yanjiu" 舊體文學傳統的現代性生成：啓功的舊體詩與漢語研究 [The Modern Formation of the Tradition of Old-Style Literature: Qi Gong's Old-Style Poetry and Chinese Language Study]. *Chuantong wenhua yu xiandaihua* 傳統文化與現代化 [Traditional Culture and Modernization] 2 (1998): 56–68.

Xiong Shengyuan 熊盛元, and Mao Gufeng 毛谷風, eds. *Haiyue fenghua ji* 海嶽風華集 [A Collection of the Refined Talents of Ocean and Alp]. Expanded ed. Zhejiang: Zhejiang wenyi chubanshe, 1998.

Yang Dekun 楊德坤, Niu Mingyuan 牛明遠, and Liu Lei 劉磊. "Fangyang shiren Li Songshan" 放羊詩人李松山 [The Shepherd Poet Li Songshan]. *CRNews*. journal.crnews.net/nmwz/2019n/2019nd6q/xjyh/928336_20190604033349.html (accessed August 7, 2022).

Zeng Yan 曾艷. "Ershishiji sishiniandai xinwenxuejia jiuti shi fuxing jiqi chengyin" 二十世紀四十年代新文學家舊體詩復興及其成因 [The Revival of Old-Style Poetry among Writers of New Literature in the 1940s and Its Reasons]. *Changjiang shifan xueyuan xuebao* 長江師範學院學報 [Academic Journal of Changjiang Normal University] 25, no. 4 (2009): 57–62.

Zhu Haoyue 朱皓月. "Fei biyao lixiao" 非必要離校 [Unnecessarily Leaving Campus]. Wikipedia. zh.m.wikipedia.org/zh-hans/2022全球华语大学生短诗大赛 (accessed August 14, 2022).

Zhu Wenhua 朱文華. *Fengsao yuyun lun: Zhongguo xiandai wenxue beijing xiade jiuti shi* 風騷餘韻論：中國現代文學背景下的舊體詩 [On the Lingering Notes of *Feng* and *Sao*:

Old-Style Poetry against the Background of Modern Chinese Literature]. Shanghai: Fudan daxue chubanshe, 1998.

Zimoxiangxue 紫陌香雪. "Huanghun jishi zhier" 黄昏即事之二 [What Happened in Twilight, No. 2]. www.zhtanyuan.com/forum.php?mod=viewthread&tid=160394&page=1 (accessed August 14, 2022).

ZHIYI YANG

Writing in the Digital Sand
Technological Transformation and Classicist Poetry Writing in China's Fluid Cyberspace

ABSTRACT This article examines the interface, power structure, and media technology of the digital platforms that have enabled the production and dissemination of Chinese internet classicist poetry, born in the late 1990s, as well as the impact that technological evolution bears on its aesthetics, economics, and ecosystem. The rapid transformations of Chinese cyberspace make it a digital sand beach in which the poets write. This situation creates a curious paradox: while the internet is supposed to "remember forever" words indifferently, the death of platforms and digital censorship can also erase words thoroughly and forever. On the digital sands thus arises a phantasm of literary immortality, which, in ways unprecedented in human history, is conjured by capital, technology, and political authority.

KEYWORDS internet poetry, digital literature, lyric classicism, Chinese censorship, social media

The digital age is not unkind to poets. In 2015 a little-known young Canadian of Punjabi-Sikh descent gained attention on Instagram with her controversial photography, which in turn boosted the sales of her self-published poetry anthology. Suddenly, a social-media-powered literary industry was born. Today, Rupi Kaur, born in 1992, has 4 million Instagram followers. Her three poetry collections have sold more than 10 million copies worldwide and have been translated into more than forty-two languages. These airport-novel-size successes make her the best-selling poet alive.[1] Kaur and her fellow "Instapoets"—poets who first publish their works on popular social media platforms like Instagram, X (formerly Twitter), Tumblr, or TikTok—have arguably defeated, once again, the tired prophecy that poetry is dead. While some critics lament how "collectively, to differing degrees, they lean to aphoristic, confessional and inspirational verse, often brief enough to fit into a tweet, or to be overlaid on a photo or an illustration like Kaur's own eye-catching line drawings,"[2] others welcome the "fresh feel" as well as the non-traditional readership that new media technology has brought to poetry.[3]

The flourishing of "Instapoetry" shows the power as well as the limits of digital media in the global market of literature. On the one hand, digital platforms

PRISM: THEORY AND MODERN CHINESE LITERATURE • 20:2 • SEPTEMBER 2023
DOI 10.1215/25783491-10992750 • © 2023 LINGNAN UNIVERSITY

weaken the authority enjoyed by guardians of traditional publication and lower the entry barrier for aspiring authors and casual readers (cultural consumers) alike. On the other, virtual fame still needs to be consolidated by hard copies and translated into cash through old-fashioned book sales and readings. The situation may change anytime. And if it does, it will most likely tilt toward the further empowerment of digital publication. Kaur may, for instance, turn her illustrated poems into NFTs (non-fungible tokens), thereby further breaking down the boundary separating visual and literary arts. Digital media open new possibilities not only for poetry to interact with its audience as text, as sound, and as image, but also for poets to reinvent their agency in the cultural industry.

Instapoetry also highlights the imbalance of linguistic power in a new, worldwide reading bazaar. Born in India, it is through the hegemonic English language that Kaur has found a global and multilingual readership. In contrast, "ethnic" literary sites publishing in other languages may be accessible globally, but their readership remains mostly limited to their respective native speakers. Translation software, which works well for marketing pop music and TV shows in other languages, performs poorly in rendering poetry. The geographic "global" does not readily translate into the cultural and literary "global." The latter remains a hegemonic, even colonial, space. Technological advancement, especially in artificial intelligence technology, however, remains a crucial ally for the task of decolonializing "world literature."

Mainland Chinese internet today hosts one of the major "ethnic" digital bookshelves. Owing to its (in)famous "great firewall" and its population size, China may be the only country where domestic companies confidently compete with American giants in terms of capital, technological innovation, and customer outreach. Its digital cultural entrepreneurship thus breeds a unique flora and fauna, in which virtual literary success is differently defined. The poet Yu Xiuhua 余秀華, for instance, burst onto the literary scene after her poetry was published by *Shikan* 詩刊 (Poetry Journal), first in print and then on its WeChat public account (*weixin gongzhonghao* 微信公眾號) in November 2014. Most public attention, however, was paid to the tension between her bold articulation of female desire and her identity as a poverty-stricken farmer suffering from cerebral palsy. Her feisty retorts against online vitriol were relished by her polite readership. The sales of her poetry anthology, however, are unimpressive in a general ranking of best sellers.[4] But China is a global leader in digital commerce and payment technology. WeChat, for instance, is a super app that combines functions of messaging, social media, publishing, and payment in one digital ecosystem. It has a bonus (*dashang* 打賞) function, which allows readers to reward the author directly and is activated once the reader clicks the "Like the Author" (*xihan zuozhe* 稀罕作者) button below a post. Using the same app, readers can also share a post in their social circles—"GroupChat" (*qunliao* 群聊) or "Moments" (*pengyouquan* 朋友圈)—to further its viral circulation. The minimum "bonus" is 5 yuan (ca. US$0.70). Theoretically, therefore, popular authors like Yu, who regularly receives hundreds of contributions from readers per post (the number of the contributions, though not the total amount, is displayed below the post), can live on their WeChat income alone. After she became famous, Yu was also recruited into the local Municipal Writers' Association as its vice chair, a salaried position.[5] She thus benefits from the traditionally socialist state-sponsored literary institutions, the capitalist print market, and the new digital media.

The monetary benefit from the new digital media, however, comes with strings attached. To take advantage of the bonus function, content creators must not let WeChat ban their public accounts or censor their posts. For instance, on February 27, 2022, three days after the Russian invasion of Ukraine, Yu Xiuhua published a poem "A Prayer" (*Daogao ci* 禱告詞) on her WeChat public account, in which she wrote:

I beg that a poem may withstand a tank;	我乞求詩歌能 夠阻擋一輛坦克
One that is full of tears, a little more so.	蓄滿眼 淚 的詩歌阻擋的多一些

It went viral and received bonuses from nearly two thousand readers before it was censored,[6] possibly because of its sympathy for Ukraine, which went against China's pro-Russia diplomacy, and its allusion to the Tiananmen "Tank Man." Since WeChat bonuses are paid to the author only after seven days, a post deleted within seven days will receive no money, and the bonuses will be returned to their donors. After all, a printed page may last forever in a dusty library corner, while the instant search-ability of the internet also means universal censor-ability. The unique ecosystem of digital China thus fosters another kind of precarious existence for texts: they are written in the digital sand, a slate easily wiped clean by those who control the means of digital reproduction. Erasure is the result either of the political sensitivity of the content or, in some cases, of the rapid evolution and consolidation of cyberspace.

This article is about neither Rupi Kaur nor Yu Xiuhua. Rather, it is about the encounter between digital media and Chinese classicist poetry around the turn of the millennium, a new kind of lyric aesthetics generated by this encounter, and the innovations and challenges brought about by the transformation of media technology. Nonetheless, this preamble through some better-known sights of digital poetry helps outline an unfamiliar landscape, where algorithms have replaced traditional gatekeepers. The communicative network linking authors to their readers, too, has become much more interactive, instantaneous, proliferative, and rhizomatic. Most importantly, classicist poetry has developed a new kind of aesthetics in response to the digital age, one that we may term "avant-garde classicist poetry." This development is significant perhaps even in the long history of classical-style Chinese poetry and represents the zenith of the post-revolutionary classicist revival in mainland China. Since this proverbial digital "sand" is still transforming, my article will not reach a definitive conclusion but will end with preliminary summaries and cautious projections.

Out of the Maoist Shadows

Internet literature in China, as Michel Hockx defines it, means "Chinese-language writing, either in established literary genres or in innovative literary forms, written especially for publication in an interactive online context and meant to be read on-screen."[7] He argues that the years from 2000 to 2013 have seen "the rise, climax, and gradual demise of a unique form of Chinese-language cultural creativity."[8] Both the definition and the judgment apply to the case of China's internet classicist poetry, even though, since the completion of Hockx's monograph, the Chinese internet has seen a dramatic transformation brought on by the dominance of smartphones as the primary medium for consuming digital content. Thus arguably, "classicist internet poetry" (*wangluo shici* 網絡詩詞 in Chinese)[9] existed as an ecological system separate from traditional print media only for a short period of time. It began in the late 1990s, with the advent of the personal computer era, and ended in the early 2010s, when the ubiquity of smartphones enabled the predominant majority of classicist poetry to be first published and primarily circulated online, thereby rendering the modifier "internet" nearly obsolete. Even though more literature across all genres is being published first online, the dominance of online publication in the field of classicist poetry seems to be more total than in the case of "new poetry," as the latter continues to enjoy institutional support from the literary establishment, a support often articulated in print publication. The significance of this technological transformation merits further investigation. For one thing, personal computers of the late 1990s were mostly available in public or semipublic spaces, such as offices, internet bars, and university computer centers. Their users thus must break out of the confines of their private space to place themselves in the surroundings of others to "surf" online. Reading on a smartphone, however, is a highly private and intimate act. In a social situation, it often leads to the erosion of social communication when the public space is fragmentized into respective distances between eyes and screens. While the former enabled a virtual public space for debates and exchanges, the latter facilitates consumption and empowers sharing. Second, in the last decade, China has pioneered the technology of digital censorship, making digital totalitarianism no longer a remote paranoia. The interaction between anonymized authors and readers in the early phase of online classicist poetry writing has thus been greatly restricted and reshaped in the smartphone era. This, among other subtle but important transformations, divides the digital era of classicist poetry writing into two distinct stages, with different aesthetic orientations.

This article further argues that early internet classicist poets like Lizi, Xutang, and Dugu represent the high point of the postrevolutionary classicist revival in mainland China. They see themselves as the heirs of a once-glorious living tradition, the norms of which were mostly established a millennium ago despite continuous transformation. This is not to say that classicist poetry has ever "died" in China. Since the 1917 New Culture movement, classical-style Chinese poetry had become a marginalized genre that seldom entered literary history or received institutional recognition. Yet it has never ceased to be written and read. Even in the iconoclast Maoist era, given Mao's personal literary tastes, his and his literary lieutenants' classicist poems were canonized as the new red classics.[10] Thus, at a time when traditional culture was uprooted and ancient books burned, the People's Republic of China's (PRC) "court poetry" remained strangely classicist. The classicism of Maoist lyrics, however, was heavily corrupted by revolutionary dictions and served ideological purposes. Meanwhile, intellectuals prosecuted by the regime also turned to the lyric tradition for courage and for satire, as the coded classical poetic language granted them some breathing space of freedom in thought and in expression. The writing and circulation of their poetry, however, remained covert.[11]

When the Red Terror ended and the ideological grip loosened, regional shici poetry societies (*shici xiehui* 詩詞協會) sprang up across China. They led to the foundation of a national organization: the state-sponsored Chinese Shici Poetry Society 中華詩詞學會.[12] Its opening ceremony was held on May 31, 1987, in the National Political Consultative Hall, a symbolic location that showed the importance of this organization for the state's outreach to senior intellectuals in China and beyond. It is a branch of the China Writers Association, which is again subordinate to the Propaganda Department of the Chinese Communist Party Central Committee. The foundation of the Chinese Shici Poetry Society was a milestone in the institutionalization of research into and writing of modern classicist poetry. Before its foundation, at least twenty-one regional classicist poetry societies had been founded; since then, more than a thousand of such societies, civil and official, had been founded by 1990, with over fifty thousand registered members.[13] By 2004 there were no fewer than two thousand registered classicist poetry societies in China.[14]

As a curious phenomenon, despite the institutional dominance of the "new poetry" for almost a century, classicist poetry continues to enjoy competitive popularity among readers. The *Poetry Journal* (*Shikan* 詩刊, est. 1957), the most authoritative poetry journal in China, has a column dedicated to classicist poetry, a tradition established by its publication of Mao Zedong's poetry in its first issue. *Contemporary Shici Poetry* (*Dangdai shici* 當代詩詞, est. 1981), the first influential classicist poetry journal founded in mainland China after 1949, had a first print run of 36,000 copies and a second run of 33,600 copies—as Stephen Owen notes, "enough to make any publisher of a journal of contemporary poetry envious."[15] The periodical *Chinese Shici Poetry* (*Zhonghua shici* 中華詩詞, est. 1994), published by the Chinese Shici Poetry Society, reached a print run of ten thousand copies per issue in the first year and thirty thousand prints per issue in 2003.[16] Its frequency of publication also changed from quarterly to bimonthly (1997–2003) and then to monthly (since 2003). Now it continues to be published in print but also curates a WeChat public account. Regional classicist poetry societies similarly publish their own poetry journals, suggesting an enormous network of active authorship and readership.

And yet the general quality of poems produced by these officially sanctioned classicist poetry societies is questionable, and they tend to ideologically conform to the taste of the political establishment. Aiming at broadening their influence, these societies are eager to recruit members with established positions in the government or in academia. A great percentage of works published in their journals, at least well into recent years, are colloquial in language, straightforward in expression, and crude in prosody, a feature resulting from their authors' upbringing in the culturally iconoclast Maoist era. Many poems have been produced as "occasion poetry" to celebrate political events. The December 2014 issue of *Chinese Shici Poetry*, for instance, contains poems about the 2014 Asia-Pacific Economic Cooperation meeting in Beijing, the *Communique* of the Fourth Plenary Session of the Eighteenth Central Committee of the CPC, Chairman Xi Jinping's 2014 speech on the arts conclave, and so forth. In May 2022 its public account set up a special column for poems that "welcome the Twentieth National Congress of the Chinese Communist Party." These poems succeed the propagandist poetry tradition of Maoist China. Since they reflect the literary taste of established interests in a hierarchical political order largely inherited from the Mao era, this style is colloquially known in China as "old cadre style" (*laoganti* 老幹體).

Certainly, age or job alone does not make a poet "old cadre," as it is more of a derogatory epithet implying a certain aesthetic value judgment than a description of the poet's identity. The poet Liu Mengfu 劉夢芙 (b. 1951), for instance, belongs to the same generation of "old cadres," but he proposes a thorough cultural and aesthetic conservatism, which amounts to a radical reaction against the iconoclastic Maoist classicism.[17] He and his fellow senior poets thus subscribe to the traditionalist aesthetics once "in exile" in the Maoist era. Their poetry preludes the traditionalist school rising in recent years that is becoming the mainstream of classicist poetry writing in mainland China. The highly aesthetic and ornamental style of their poetry, however, often epitomizes a dissociation from reality or any pressing concerns of the time.

The stunning rise of internet poetry in the late 1990s, therefore, was the first major breach of the institutional dominance of the societies of senior poets and of the aesthetic dominance of the Maoist classicism (or traditionalism). Since digital literacy was rare in those years, and private ownership of computers even rarer, this poetry sprang up on campuses and in internet bars. Suddenly, isolated young classicists discovered their peers in university BBS,[18] QQ[19] chatrooms, and literary internet forums. Many tried to write just like their medieval precursors, but some ventured to experiment with fresh language and imageries.

Digital Poetry and Avant-Garde Classicism

In the winter of 1999, Zeng Shaoli 曾少立 (b. 1964), a concrete materials engineer who had spent a few years "drifting" through various jobs in Beijing, found a six-month job in Haikou selling refrigerating fluid. In social isolation, he whiled away days and nights in internet bars that newly sprang up along the shore of this tropical town. He was trying out QQ and, per chance, wandered into a chatroom where people were exchanging original poetry in classical styles. Zeng had previously learned the basic rules of writing classical-style poetry but had never truly practiced this art. Now, with a community easily accessible at his fingertips, he suddenly discovered a new passion.[20] Writing under the sobriquet Lizilizilizi 李子栗子梨子 (Plum Chestnut Pear), he quickly distinguished himself in this online community by developing a unique poetic voice.

Around the same time, Duan Xiaosong 段小松 (b. 1970),[21] a former 1989 student protest leader who had been in prison, had become a monk, had left the order, and had edited a Buddhist journal in Beijing, returned to his hometown Hefei to work for an advertising agency. In the intellectual starvation of this secular provincial life, he found excitement when a tech-savvy coworker told him about Rongshuxia 榕樹下 (Under the Banyan Tree; 1997–2020), a fledging literary website. He began using his office computer to peruse the site and quickly discovered a forum dedicated to classical-style poetry writing. He coined a sobriquet for himself too: Xutang 噓堂, or Hall of Vital Breath, a name alluding to his former religious training.[22]

In 2000 Zeng Zheng 曾崢 (b. 1970), a finance major who got a job as lecturer and administrator at Wuhan University, began to use his office computer to access the internet. Addicted, in the evening he used the university phone number to dial in from home. Sometimes he went to internet bars, paying 2 yuan per hour, when he wanted to disguise his IP address in voicing risky political opinions.[23] Though he was writing classicist poetry since high school, his poetry acquired a radical avant-gardist voice only around the time he began to publish online. His poems were published in Poetry Commune (Shigongshe 詩公社) and easily garnered more than five hundred views per post, a strong incentive for him to keep experimenting. He adopted the sobriquet Dugu-shiroushou 獨孤食肉獸 (Lone Carnivore; hereafter Dugu), for his love of meat.

This generation of poets was mostly born during or shortly after the Maoist era. Though some had had the chance of receiving a traditional education owing to their family or special circumstances, to them the literary tradition was not holy but a new infatuation. The poet Pei Tao 裴濤 (sobriquet Su Wuming 蘇無名; b. 1978), for instance, told me in an interview that he first learned to write classical-style poetry and calligraphy from an old neighbor; only afterward did he realize that his own grandfather was proficient in this art. Throughout the Maoist decades, his grandfather neither wrote nor thought of transmitting poetry.[24] Most other classicist poets, however, learned to write by reading old poems and improved their skills by talking to and debating with others online. In the nascent Chinese cyberspace, a peer group quickly took shape. In stories like Lizi's, Xutang's, and Dugu's, the recent accessibility of cheap internet and the novel excitement of social media culture were crucial elements in the narrative. The development of user-friendly Chinese input systems, including Zhineng 智能 ABC (invented in 1993) and Wubi 五筆 Method (invented in 1986; improved in 1998), empowered the popularity of digital writing among a relatively tech-savvy crowd. More importantly, even though all three poets had been "outsiders" with regard to literary circles, they quickly gained the self-awareness that they were participating in a literary experiment that, on one hand, reforms traditional Chinese lyric language and aesthetics and, on the other, retains some essential formal features (such as strict prosodic prescriptions) that make lyric classicism instantly recognizable. They became the vanguards of a generation of classicist internet poets, who have revived and reinvented medieval Chinese lyric prosody while featuring an aesthetic that may be called avant-garde.[25]

Perhaps owing to their iconoclast upbringing, the young internet poets dared to venture into new domains of expression unimagined by the ancients. And given the limited access to internet facilities, these poets grouped around urban centers, and their poetry naturally chronicled daily lives in China's booming metropolises. And yet, to distinguish themselves from the Maoist classicists, whose unrefined verses regularly received public mockery, most successful internet poets abided by traditional prosodic rules. The nature of internet fame also helped innovative verses, which would have been suppressed by traditional print media, to attract attention. Their styles are thus innovative in language and aesthetics and conservative in prosody. In a way, they foreshadowed the rise of Chinese nationalist cultural conservatism of the next decade; though, coming of age in the 1980s, most first-generation internet poets subscribe to political liberalism and intellectual cosmopolitanism.

Take, for instance, the following poems by Dugu: "To 'The Charm of Niannu': Last Imageries before the New Millennium" 念奴嬌·千禧年最後的意象 (1999), a lyric song in which the poet transforms the vertically observed city into surrealist reverse mirror images. The first stanza is translated below:

Inside a matchbox	火柴盒裡
I gaze at the opposite Tower B	看對面 B 座
With deep dark glass walls.	玻璃深窈
Winter rain: gouache paint streams down the riverside city;	冬雨江城流水粉
Tinted leaves and human figurines stand in mirror reflection.	樹色人形顛倒
Salvador Dali and Zhuang Zhou	達利莊周
Both seem to be me	恍然皆我
In the three milliseconds of a midday dream.	午夢三微秒
Blood splatters on the pomegranate blossoms	石榴血濺
Where butterflies shriek.	花間蝴蝶尖叫[26]

In the second line, the roman letter *B* should be pronounced in a level tone to fit the prosodic prescription of this tune; its matter-of-factness accentuates the colloquial parlance of office workers. This stanza, however, quickly progresses from the mundane to the fantastical. The poet's daydream relates him both to Salvador Dali's repeated painting of butterflies in landscapes and to Zhuangzi's famous dream of becoming one with a butterfly. The reference to the butterfly again introduces the image of pomegranate blossoms, tainted red with the blood of butterflies, whose otherwise inaudible elegy of death is here rendered as a sharp cry. The pomegranate dream may also be inspired by Dali's painting *Dream Caused by the Flight of a Bee around a Pomegranate a Second before Awakening* (1944), in which an exploding pomegranate shoots out of a fish; from the mouth of the monstrous fish two tigers leap forward to devour a seemingly sleeping naked woman, the painter's wife, Gala. The poet lingers in this reverie of symbolic violence. The absurdist shriek of butterflies finally breaks the silence in the "matchbox."

The poet's fondness for surrealism is also shown in an ekphrastic lyric song on Dali's 2003 exhibition in Wuhan, titled "The Dead Sea: Eternal Memories" (*Sihai: Yongheng de jiyi* 死海： 永恆的記憶) and written to "Washing Creek Sands" (*Huanxisha* 浣溪沙):

A clock on back, a skinny horse knocks at a frosty fortress gate;	羸馬馱鐘叩冷關
The night sky lowers its blue cheeks, pockmarked by stars;	夜垂藍靨蝕星瘢
And a forgotten lamp silently waits for an ancient boat.	遺燈默待古航船
From the taste of the Dead Sea I know that fish tears are bitter;	死海味知魚 淚 苦
The shimmering pearls reflect the coldness in a clam's heart;	珍珠光鑒蚌心寒
Upon the boundless and timeless sands, a rock-like moon.	恆沙無際月如磐[27]

In this poem, the reader recognizes many typical Dali elements, such as Don Quixote's skinny horse, a deformed clock, a lamp, sand, and so forth. But the poet does not limit himself to visual description. The "bitter" taste of fish tears and the "cold" heart of the clam are synesthetic associations inspired by the images of the Dead Sea and shiny pearls. It may remind the reader of a famous couplet by the Tang poet Li Shangyin 李商隱 (813–ca. 858):

Upon a vast ocean shines a bright moon—pearls   滄海月明珠有淚
     contain tears;
On the Blue Field hangs the warm sun—jade   藍田日暖玉生煙[28]
     breathes mist.

In Dugu's poem, Li Shangyin's "oceans" and "pearls" are reintegrated into their native contexts. Now the generic "oceans" become the specific (and foreign) "Dead Sea," which is again associated with fish tears, salty from sterile brine. The "pearls" under the moon are returned to a clam, and their cold shimmer is attributed to the coldness of the latter's heart. Li Shangyin's strange couplet becomes stranger, heightened in intensity and by synesthesia. What Dugu re-creates, however, is not just a Tang dynasty poet's imaginary landscape but also a pictorial space in an urban gallery conjured up by the art of a Spanish painter. The surrealist exegetical dimension that has always underlain Li Shangyin's lines as potentials is hereby actualized. In this way, global artistic modernism is brought into a surprising dialog with Chinese lyric traditions, expanding the latter's exegetical horizon.

Dugu now lives in Melissia, Greece, a country for which he nurtured a cultural nostalgia due to the Greek mythology he devoured as a child. To him, Chinese is an accidental mother tongue, and he yearns to be a poet of no home by deliberately resisting and rejecting Chineseness. He confesses to be against practically everything Chinese: cuisine, aesthetics, philosophy, medicine, and social norm.[29] The only Chineseness that Dugu permits himself to embody is being a poet, who delves into the depths of his mother tongue to find signifiers that accommodate the signified—his destiny. The advantage of being an internet poet, however, is that he remains just as present in the Chinese classicist poetry scene as ever. In a certain sense, Dugu has become a digital literary nomad.

The avant-garde aesthetics of this generation of classicist poets did embed a gesture of ideological resistance—against the state-sanctioned ideology the "old cadre" style represented, against the traditionalism the old rebels of the Maoist era championed, and against the brutal capitalist force Deng Xiaoping's famous black-cat-white-cat pragmatism unleashed. Many took part in, or were at least sympathetic to, the 1989 student protests. They fully embrace modernist aesthetics and liberal values, but, in a postrevolutionary and postmodern twist, they argue that a full integration of horizons is possible only by being thoroughly rooted in Chinese lyric traditions.

Xutang's archaism, for instance, embodies such literary resistance. A poem written on June 4, 2003, the anniversary of the Tiananmen massacre, and entitled "Song of Souls" (Lingge 靈歌), is striking for its interlacing of profanity and archaic elegance. The repetition of the carrier sound *hey* (*xi* 兮) at the end of every odd-numbered line emulates the most prominent stylistic feature of the ancient "Songs of the South" (*Chuci* 楚辭), anthologized in the second century. The poem similarly evokes the shamanistic voice in "Songs of the South":

Time can never reverse, *hey*,	時不可復兮
like soiled undergarment.	如骯髒內衣
The stains of love-making remain, *hey*,	遺交歡之污漬兮
on branches and petals of the roses.	在玫瑰干支
What's the point: to lament and to wail, *hey*,	何嗚呼哀哉兮
to tremble and to shiver?	戰戰而兢兢
There comes a team of chariots of the souls, *hey*,	爰有靈之車隊兮
its banners white yaks' tails.	白旄而素旌
I list the names of the gods, *hey*,	列衆神之名字兮
and murmur them on the street.	喃喃於街區
The whip of the summer is raised, *hey*,	夏日之鞭已揚兮
melting nests of glass.	融玻璃之巢居
I gather the luminous lights in a grain, *hey*,	斂光華於米粒兮
and attach it to an illusion—the evergreen.	附幻象輒長青
Now this land is not my land: *hey*,	我土今不在茲兮
what remains are voices suppressed.	餘克制之音聲
Now this land is not my land: *hey*,	我土今不在茲兮
perhaps even time no longer exists.	時光或罔存
The chariots of souls are slowly dispersed; *hey*,	靈車漸已渙散兮
in darkness stand palace gates of scarlet red.	並暗峙之朱門
I squeeze the fatherland in my fist, *hey*,	攥祖國於拳兮
and pierce it with long nails.	復貫之以長釘
If the dead can again rise, *hey*,	死者其能復現兮
just like that the blind will again see.	猶盲者之復明[30]

In Xutang's poem, the fatherland manifests itself as a social and ideological predicament, in which the lyrical subject fails to find a sense of belonging. This song is an elegy mourning the victims of the fatherland. It starts with an existential condition: the irreversibility of time. Soiled undergarments are their wearers' secrets. Hardly visible on the petals of roses are stains of lust. The noble and the sordid, the romantic and the bestial, coexist, if they are not one and the same. The next few couplets depict mourning. The gods, to whom the poet prays, are perhaps dead too. The reader is encouraged to associate the image of murmuring the gods' names on the street with idols of liberty and democracy that the student protesters of 1989 rallied around. A ten-meter-tall statue, the Goddess of Democracy and Freedom, was literally erected on Tiananmen Square. Made of foam and papier-mâché, the statue was fragile, an ominous sign for the protestors. The "nests of glass" may stand for greenhouses, as students at elite Chinese universities are often compared to greenhouse flowers, now crushed under the whip of a harsh god of summer. The luminous light, shrunk to the size of a grain, represents hope. But the poet readily admits that it is perhaps only a wistful illusion to keep hope evergreen. He then declares his unbelongingness to "this land," where voices are mute and where time, no longer moving forward, might just as well not exist. The "gates" may be the most explicit reference to Tiananmen Square, on whose northern side stand the palace gates of the Forbidden City, a symbol of imperial power dyed red by blood. The poem ends with putting a curse on the fatherland—a terrible beast that devours its children.

This poem innovatively blends modern everyday vernacular such as *neiyi* 內衣 (undergarment), *jiequ* 街區 (street block), and *zuguo* 祖國 (fatherland) with the archaic lyric form. It further evokes the shamanic tradition of *Chuci*, especially the "summoning of the souls" (*zhaohun* 招魂) cycle of poems, to call the victims of the massacre to return and haunt the present. Xutang wrote many poems commemorating the Tiananmen massacre. The fact that they continue to circulate online attests to the power of classicist poetry to defy censorship. Since internet censors routinely depend on automated screening of so-called sensitive words (*minganci* 敏感詞), a classicist poem may employ a plethora of images and archaic terms to construct meaning without using any "sensitive words" and thereby avoid alerting the censor. Even if a well-known poet and ex-activist like Xutang might merit the privilege of actually being read by a human censor, the textual difficulty and imagistic ambiguity could give the author plausible grounds for denial regarding any one specific reading. As a matter of fact, Xutang never endorses any readings of his poems. The interpretation above, therefore, is entirely mine.

The Poetry of Digital Flaneurs

The early 2000s could well be described as the age of China's digital "gold rush." All kinds of domestic and foreign capital were injected into the market, and servers were set up and closed overnight. The development was nearly anarchic, at least by the Chinese standard, since the state was lagging behind in comprehending the new technology and designing ways to control it. Regulative authorities were divided and were slow to react to the emerging media landscape. It led to a euphoric claim by US president Bill Clinton, on March 8, 2000, that the internet represented the triumph of liberty around the world and that China's fledging efforts to restrain online speech were like "trying to nail Jello to the wall."[31]

The most important classicist poetry websites in that era included the following:

Qingyun 清韻 (www.qingyun.net), founded in February 1998 by an Australian Chinese, was first meant to provide a forum for overseas Chinese interested in traditional culture. In 1999 its headquarters moved to Xi'an, and a sub-forum dedicated to classicist poetry, Shiyun yaju 詩韻雅聚, was created. Due to a server error in 2002, all historical posts disappeared. In 2009 the website was entirely shut down.

Shici-bixing 詩詞比興, hosted by Tianya Club (bbs.tianya.cn/list-n002-1.shtml) (hereafter SCBX), was created in November 1999, or eight months after the foundation of the Tianya Club. In its heyday, Tianya Club had more than 80 million registered accounts (back then, one user could open many accounts), arguably the biggest public internet space for global Sinophone netizens. With its many sub-forums, it was well-known for its multifaceted content ranging from politics to history to literature and to gossips. One sub-forum could have many moderators, known as *banzhu* 版主 (often written homophonically as *banzhu* 斑竹, or "spotted bamboo"). The most famous moderator to preside over SCBX in its heyday was Feng Xiaoshen 馮小申 (sobriquet Zhongtao-daoren 種桃道人, or "peach-planting Daoist"; 1959–2018). Given the importance of this forum, it will be further investigated below. On April 1, 2023, Tianya Club turned off its server, purportedly only for maintenance; as of May 23, 2023, its server is yet to be switched on again, and all contents remain inaccessible. It might have just become another fallen giant unceremoniously buried in the great digital graveyard.

Juzhai 菊齋 (www.juzhai.com) was founded in 2001 and moderated by the poet Juzhai. In 2002 the poet Meng Yiyi 孟依依 joined as a cohost and attracted many admirers, making the forum a major salon for classicist poets. The forum was closed in 2018. An eponymous WeChat public account is now managed by both poets. Juzhai also presides over a private academy for traditional Chinese culture. The forum was closed in March 2020 and all data was deleted in December 2021.

Xiakedao 俠客島 (www.xiakedao.com; later www.guoxue.com/island) was founded in 2000 for the purpose of publishing both classicist and new poetry. Because of the conflict between the two factions, however, the classicists abandoned the original website in 2001 and regrouped under a new host website, Guoxue-wang 國學網 (National Learning). The moderator was Jin Hui 靳暉 (sobriquet Xiangpi 象皮, or "Elephant Skin"; b. after 1970). The first website address is now used by a tourist company. The second address is still owned by guoxue.com, but its content is currently not accessible.

As of late May 2023, none of these websites, which were crucial for the development of internet classicist poetry, are operative. The reason is multifaceted. On one hand, market forces and networking effects conspire to reduce cyber biodiversity, a worldwide trend. On the other, in a uniquely Chinese situation, the state encourages consolidation, as it is easier to regulate a few big players than an unruly mass. Stricter licensing requirements were introduced in 2011, leading to a consolidation of the market.[32] Since the National Library of China has so far declined to keep a general archive of Chinese websites, most of their contents are irrevocably lost when the sites are closed down. Some websites are partially archived by the Internet Archive Wayback Machine (web.archive.org, hereafter IAWM), but, especially for the early 2000s, documentation has been sporadic.

Since classicist internet poetry was born together with China's internet literature, poets were often internet novelists too. Yanleisheng 燕壘生 (real name Zhang Jian 張健), a famous internet martial arts novelist, was and remains a classicist poet. Such genre crossovers were facilitated by the fact that all the major literary sites, such as Rongshuxia, had different pages dedicated to different genres, and it took only one click for an author or a reader to jump to another page and join a different circle. Most classicist poets-cum-novelists write fantasy or martial arts fiction, perhaps because the latter tends to inherit certain linguistic and formal features from the classical Chinese popular fiction tradition. Another feature is that most Chinese internet writers, and virtually all classicist poets, use sobriquets, which are in sometimes highly eccentric. It undoubtedly is related to China's classical literary tradition: a literatus normally had a polite name (*zi* 字), given to him when he came of age, and a minimum of one style name (*hao* 號), created by himself often to encode aspects of his character, interests, or life experience. Sobriquets of classicist internet poets, however, were first and foremost introduced as avatars or sock puppets (*majia* 馬甲) used to disguise the poet's identity online, either out of convention or to create split identities for debates or self-promotion. Over the years, many classicist internet poets have disappeared without a physical trace, once they stopped publishing under a certain sobriquet. In these cases, "authorship" must be reconceptualized, as it cannot be tied to a biological author but can only be perceived as an imagined persona constructed around a group of works and a sobriquet.

Most poets posted in multiple forums and wandered around the virtual literary landscape until they found circles to their taste. They were the flaneurs of this early digital world. As Walter Benjamin notes, nineteenth-century Parisian flaneurs were connoisseurs of the street. As a lifestyle, their act of idle strolling was architecturally enabled by the construction of arcades, which turned the city into a landscape and a room. The poet Charles Baudelaire was a quintessential flaneur. In his alienated gaze, the crowd becomes the veil "through which the familiar city beckons to the flaneur as phantasmagoria—now a landscape, now a room."[33] Tianya Club, in its heyday, was such a digital urban landscape. Aside from its millions of registered users, unregistered visitors could roam the website freely too, though they could not post or comment. When users visited Tianya, they saw a list of the forums on the right-hand panel and might decide to visit one of them based on their interest or pure curiosity—or if they were fans of Yanleisheng's martial arts novels, they could well follow him into other forums like SCBX. Once they wandered into SCBX, they would see dozens of posts listed in a spread-out design, their rankings constantly refreshed, updated by new posts or comments. Posts deemed by the moderator as "outstanding" were marked in red (*jiajing* 加精), and some received the rare honor of being placed at the top of the page (*zhiding* 置頂) for a period of time. Our digital flaneur therefore could immediately jump into the most heated debate, based on the number of comments following a post, or get a taste of the newest critical standards and fashionable trends, based on the recommendations. A visitor to Tianya thus typically hopped into a few forums to check out the newest updates or debates, very much like a Parisian flaneur went from coffee shop to coffee shop.

Lizi's trip to and experience of SCBX illustrate the appeal of, as well as the kind of communicative actions enabled by, this digital space. Soon after he began writing poetry in a QQ chatroom, he found Xiakedao to be where better poets gathered. Publishing there quickly brought him to the core of the online classicist circle. Then he ventured into other forums, including Sina, 163.com, Shuimu Tsinghua 水木清華 (Tsinghua University BBS), and eventually more dedicated sites like Rongshuxia, Qingyun, and Tianya SCBX. In 1999 Rongshuxia began hosting a competition for internet literature. In 2000 a poetry prize was set up, which for the first and only time accepted both vernacular and classicist submissions. Lizi, who so far had written only a dozen poems, submitted five or six of them. The poetry prize was awarded to ten poets, of whom three were classicist, and, to Lizi's surprise, he was one of the laureates.[34] He was emboldened to find his own lyrical voice, which he developed further through interaction with other poets and readers, in particular on SCBX.

As Xiaofei Tian points out, "Lizi is a true Internet poet: he not only composes his poems on the Web but also discusses them with readers online, and his revisions are often based on readers' feedback and suggestions. In this way, the Chinese Web has re-created the traditional poetry community in which authors, readers, and critics are often one and the same."[35] Thanks to the fact that SCBX stayed operative when I was conducting research for this article, traces of this collective deliberation have been preserved. Take, for instance, the following lyric song "To 'Wind Entering the Pine'" (Fengrusong 風入松). The first version was published in SCBX on June 20, 2005:[36]

Catalpa trees on top of the hill, mulberries planted by the house;	坡頭木梓屋邊桑
Crispy laughter circles around the mountain ridge.	脆笑繞山梁
Green branches swayed by rosy tender hands:	青枝搖曳紅酥手
Collecting lumps of clouds	把雲朵
Into the chambers of the heart.	采入心房

Sparrows run away from jewels;	麻雀遠離珠寶
Mountain blossoms fill the sunrays.	山花開滿陽光
Tobacco pipes, stone walls;	旱煙桿子石頭墻
On small stools sit pa and ma.	小凳坐爹娘
The iron pot turns red hot for a ten-thousandth time;	鐵鍋萬次燒紅了
On the backside of the mountain,	後山上
Ancestral tombs peacefully rest.	祖墓安詳
A plane casts its shadow,	一架飛機投影
Through the middle of the old village.	行經老寨中央

The original post was published at 19:17, and within four hours it had gathered fourteen comments. The critics pointed out, among other things, that the image of "rosy tender hands" alludes to aristocratic ladies and seems ill-fitted for countryside labor;[37] the images of "sparrows" and "jewels" are hard to relate; and the plane in the last lines feels dangerous.

Lizi took all valid criticisms to heart. He subsequently revised the poem multiple times, all posted below the original post for others to comment on. The final version of the poem, as it stands today, reads:

The cooking smoke sways; the small river extends;	炊煙搖曳小河長
A stack of firewood weighs on the coldness of the wind.	柴垛壓風涼
Talking about the moon and witchcraft:	有關月亮和巫術
Machetes that hack open the mountain	砍山刀
Gather on the hillside grain-airing ground.	聚在山場
Sparrows run away from treasures;	麻雀遠離財寶
Mountain blossoms fill the sunrays.	山花開滿陽光
Tobacco pipes, grain baskets;	旱菸杆子穀籮筐
On low stools sit pa and ma.	矮凳坐爹娘
The iron pot and lumps of clouds have all turned red;	鐵鍋雲朵都紅了
On the backside of the mountain,	後山上
Ancestral tombs peacefully rest.	祖墓安祥
Months and years grow on the old tree's branches;	老樹枝頭歲月
Below a coarse ceramic bowl sleeps a hamlet.	粗瓷碗底村莊

Rosy tender hands is replaced by witchcraft, which conjures stories of Hakka shamanism that the poet heard as a child—and with this change, gone is the only allusion to classical Chinese literature. Jewels is replaced by treasures, which for sparrows can simply mean golden grains drying in the sunshine, an association further integrating this image into the previous and the next lines, making the poem more holistic. The last couplet is a stroke of genius. Though the shadow of a plane imposed on an ancient village is an interesting image, it is also ominous, suggesting an intrusion of modernity into the peaceful countryside—even menacing, if it is about to crash. The new ending couplet continues the mood of peace and nostalgia of the poem. Time grows on an old tree like fruits, an image suggesting plenitude and eternity; a hamlet is juxtaposed to a bowl, a line that uses distorted proportionality to create a sense of country life sheltered from external forces. Furthermore, the two lines are now in perfect parallelism, increasing the poem's structural stability. The history of the poem's revision illustrates the "workshop" nature of forums in the early stage of the development of classicist internet poetry.

Soon after the birth of classicist internet poetry, compilation and appreciative criticism, usually by practitioners themselves, began. It could be seen as a self-conscious effort at canonization. The earliest print collection was *Three Hundred Classicist Internet Poems*.[38] The actual editor was Jin Hui ("Elephant Skin"). The term *three hundred poems* derives from the *Analects* and originally refers to the number of odes included in the *Book of Odes*. The most popular anthology of Tang dynasty poems is also called *Three Hundred Tang Poems* 唐詩三百首, compiled and published in the eighteenth century. Selecting three hundred contemporary internet poems for publication, therefore, shows the editor's literary historiographical ambition. Subsequent physical publications, such as one anthology compiled by Lu Qingshan 盧青山 (sobriquet Pengbi zhaizhu 碰壁齋主, or "Against the Walls") and another by Tan Zuowen 檀作文 (sobriquet Zhou Muwang 周穆王, or "King Mu of Zhou"), showed further attempts to increase the prestige and influence of classicist internet poetry among traditional readers.[39] A broadly circulated piece of appreciative criticism was the "Registry of 108 Stars of Internet Classicist Poetry," written by Su Wuming first in 2008 in elegant classical prose, which compares the leading poets to the 108 "stars of destiny" in the late imperial novel *Outlaws of the Marsh*.[40] Since late Ming and especially the late Qing period, the "registry of 108 Stars" (*dianjianglu* 點將錄) has become a well-established genre of appreciative criticism used in particular to rank one's contemporaries or near-contemporaries.[41] Applying this genre to online poets emerging only in the last decade is a gesture of literary historical confidence shared by this group of poets.

In the late 2000s, such innovative classicist internet poetry, especially that of Lizi, first began to attract broader scholarly attention beyond the practitioners' circle. Tan Zuowen's article in 2003 represents one of the earliest attempts to locate Lizi's style in literary history.[42] Xiaofei Tian, one of the most celebrated scholars of classical Chinese poetry today, went on to introduce him to the English-language academia as the worthy progeny of Huang Zunxian 黃遵憲 (1848–1905), the nineteenth-century reformer of poetry, and of Nie Gannu 聶紺弩 (1903–86), whose classicist poems were humorous responses to political prosecution during the Cultural Revolution.[43] Since then, classicist internet poetry has finally begun to gain traction among polite circles. Today no fewer than three doctoral dissertations and a dozen master of arts theses have been written in China on this topic, though a substantial monograph is still outstanding.[44] Outside China, Frank Kraushaar's German monograph on Lizi's poetry is the first of its kind in any major academic language.[45] At the University of New South Wales, Australia, Haizhi Luo is completing a doctoral dissertation that also includes a discussion of Lizi's poetry.

And yet the drive toward experimentation suddenly came to a halt with the advent of the smartphone era, partially caused by the change of media platform, and partially by the rise of cultural nationalism and conservatism that continues to haunt Chinese literature today.

Social Media and Its Discontents

In 2009 Tencent closed the QQ chatroom service, purportedly for its being an anarchic space hard to manage. In its stead, WeChat was launched in 2011. It was a multipurpose messaging, social media, and mobile payment app—in short, a "super app" that created an ecosystem of its own. The smartphone cyberspace built around WeChat began to siphon a tremendous amount of Web traffic from all other services. Longer-standing (and desktop-based) literary websites, BBS, and social media saw active users migrating to WeChat en masse. The gravitational pull of smartphone-based services has proved unstoppable. When people increasingly read from their pocket devices, "public accounts" began to supersede older sites to become the major venue of poetry publication. On August 25, 2020, five years after it was acquired by Tencent, Rongshuxia, once the largest Chinese online literature website, shut down its server, purportedly for maintenance, and it was never switched back on again.[46] Niche websites dedicated to classicist poetry had begun to disappear even earlier. With the advent of the WeChat age, the internet became pervasive, and the term *classicist internet poetry* is no longer a meaningful description—*digital poetry* even less so, given that digitality is now baked into every step in the writing and publication processes, starting from a poem's conception.

In contrast to the flaneurs of the BBS age, WeChat is a closed system of absolute and total digital control. As researchers point out, "WeChat divides information dissemination and communication about common interests into an instant messenger, similar to WhatsApp, called GroupChat, and a Facebook wall called Moments. In both communication environments, communication is organized around users, with information dissemination second."[47] For a long time, WeChat even forbade hyperlinks to other platforms, meaning that only links created by public WeChat accounts, certain online websites, or mainstream media accounts could be forwarded within WeChat. This ban has only loosened since September 2021. In short, unlike its Western counterparts such as Facebook, X, or Instagram, information dissemination and discussion are highly restricted on WeChat, and the level of digital surveillance and censorship is much greater. With WeChat and other developments in digital surveillance technologies, the Chinese state seems to have succeeded in "nailing Jello to the wall" after all.

Certain features of WeChat publications create unique challenges to classicist poets accustomed to the former "flaneurial" digital culture. A WeChat public account has "followers," who subscribe to passively receive updates. If an update is not read or saved in time, it is quickly buried in a constant flow of new content. The evolution of this kind of social media thus leads to increasing top-down authoritarian control. A QQ chatroom was egalitarian and cacophonic, where everyone had the equal right to speak, though the moderator could have stopped an account from posting further commentary. A BBS forum had moderators, but their power was limited. Everyone still posted and commented freely. The moderator rarely issued a warning, deleted a post, or, in extreme cases, deleted an account. When enough visitors revolted or boycotted a moderator, he or she might even be expelled. A WeChat public account, on the other hand, is curated by an editor or an editorial team. Its control structure thus rather resembles a traditional print medium than a forum. In a QQ chatroom or BBS, the readers' comments were presented in the same visual format as the author's original post, creating a sense of dialog. Often, the author accepted criticism and revised the poem, posted in the same thread of conversation. Technology thus created an egalitarian space for the writing and discussion of poetry. When a poem is published in a WeChat public account, however, the readers' comments are posted in a small font below the main article, implying a hierarchy. It also makes revisions much harder and conversations much more difficult to have and follow. A WeChat poet may choose to post in Moments, but then again only common friends will see each other's comments. A debate among strangers, let alone with anonymous random visitors, is entirely impossible.

Last but not least, since any e-mail address can be used to register for an account on a BBS, censorship is often futile and sometimes backfires, as a banned user can simply register a new account and even begin a verbal war with the moderator, cheered on by bystanders. WeChat, however, was founded right around the time when China promulgated the "real-name system" in 2011. Starting in 2012, its users must register with official identification credentials and legal names (and bank information, if one wishes to use the payment function), a requirement that empowers censors and severely limits freedom of speech. A poet can still post under a sobriquet, but Tencent knows exactly who you are and is watching you. Once a WeChat account is taken down, opening a new account is time-consuming and expensive. This situation makes self-censorship much more frequent and thorough.

The mechanism of publication, sharing, and commercialization of WeChat poetry is thus very different from that of Instapoetry. As mentioned earlier, a "public account" may receive bonuses from readers, but this only applies when the account is curated by an individual (based in mainland China) and the content is original (at least purportedly). Authors cannot activate, or even apply to activate, the "receiving bonus" function, but must patiently wait for an invitation issued by the WeChat management team. The selection criteria are opaque. Normally, a public account must be continuously updated at least for a few months, regularly interact with its readers, and have never been reported by its readers for any violations (either due to plagiarism or to political activism), before it may attract the attention of the WeChat management team (most likely based on algorithmic recommendations) and be awarded the badge of an "original content" (*yuanchuang* 原創) producer. And only afterward, it may eventually be invited to open the coveted "receiving bonus" function, displayed as a large red "Like the author" button below the post. For most content creators, the bonus function is like Godot.

This system is not favorable to classicist poets, as most of them do not write fast enough or long enough to receive the attention of the algorithms. A poet like Lizi, who regularly sees his content censored (normally because it was flagged by readers), could not expect WeChat to award him the bonus function either, though his public account Shici-guoxue 詩詞國學 is doing well in attracting traffic. Almost all other successful classicist poetry public accounts publish collections by established or aspiring authors. Two leading accounts are Yuanshan-xingji 遠山星際 and Yuefu-zhifei-xisheihe 樂府之妃豨誰和. Though their posts do not always contain original content created by the accounts' owners, they do enjoy the privilege of receiving bonuses. Hardly any of their posts, however, receive monetary contributions, perhaps owing exactly to the lack of direct connection between the actual author and the readers. Some popular public accounts, like Juzhai 菊齋, seem to profit from advertisements selling online classes or peddling items associated with a classicist lifestyle, like calligraphy brushes or Hanfu (Han-ethnic clothing) clothing and accessories. Though the precise profit margins are unknown to me, such posts are probably more profitable than original classicist poetry: Juzhai barely posts any original poetry nowadays. Of course, there are always official accounts, like the one curated by the Chinese Shici Poetry Society, which do not need to worry about income. They continue to post propagandist poetry very much in the old-cadre style. This twisted ecosystem is a constant force of erosion corrupting the quality of classicist poetry today.

In Lieu of Conclusions

In 1978 WordStar became the first commercially successful word processor. The half century since then has seen digital writing technology eventually replacing typewriters and handwriting by and large to become the dominating method of textual creation. In the five-thousand-year history of human writing technologies, digital writing so far represents only a blip in time. Just like the appearance of parchment, printing, and the modern press, however, it has fundamentally changed the way we create and access literature. It has fostered new genres of writing, such as e-mails, blog posts, chats, and tweets. But perhaps more significantly, it has greatly expanded the pool of writers who create, instead of just copying, texts.[45] It may be safe to assert that, without the digital community as well as the opportunities of exchange and appreciation that it affords, many leading avant-garde classicist poets in China today would not have started writing poetry, or at least not in the way that they do now. It is therefore crucial to understand that digital technology is not only a tool—it has become an active partner in our literary imagination and production, changing how literature is conceptualized, inspired, composed, exchanged, and understood.

While digital writing and especially the appearance of internet literature have enabled anyone to become an author, the self-regulating desire to reestablish rules and aesthetics may explain the renaissance of formalism and archaism among internet classicists around the millennium, whose style distinguishes themselves not only from their "old cadre" fathers but also from other internet-based creative writers. It is perhaps the same dynamism, coupled with the highly controlled and curated nature of WeChat publications, that has led to the rise of aesthetic conservatism among new lyric classicists in the last few years. Some features of avant-gardism pioneered by the generation of fin de siècle classicists have become more broadly accepted, such as the description of contemporary life and the use of vernacular terms, but the radical, shocking, and provocative energy is gone.

Another noteworthy phenomenon is the real-time versified commentary on contemporary social or political events, such as the outbreak of the COVID-19 pandemic in Wuhan, the Russian invasion of Ukraine, the lockdown of Shanghai in April 2022, and human tragedies caused by China's draconian anti-pandemic methods throughout summer 2022. Many poets post their poems de jour in WeChat Moments, some of which may be later collected and published by public accounts like Yuanshan or Yuefu. Quick talents like Lu Qijie 陆奇捷 (sobriquet "luq"), who moonlights as a financial service entrepreneur, have emerged as "poet-historians" of the digital age. Since they use historical allusions and classical language to comment on contemporary events, they are less likely to be censored than vernacular-language poems or essays. On the other hand, posts on Moments can be viewed only by people who have already added the poet as a "friend." Does this channel with targeted exposure change the concept of publication? How does the mechanism of instant feedback, primarily in the reductionist form of the number of likes (with the thumb-up button) instead of written comments, impact the writing? What makes poems different from other texts, when they are arranged in an indifferent stream of postings? Since WeChat posts are mostly visual (posting only texts without images is possible but not intuitive), how does it change the relationship between a poem and an image? While all these questions merit long-term and evidence-based research, such research runs the risks of quickly becoming obsolete owing to the availability of new features, updates, and apps.

Whither does classicist Chinese internet poetry go? For now, I have no answer to this question, aside from predicting that, as a living tradition, it will continue to transform. Consistent observation and diligent archiving, however, are necessary, before these texts as fluid cybernetic data disappear into the digital sand. The task of academic researchers, therefore, is all the more urgent, as well as treacherous: through archiving, appraisal, criticism, and translation, we play an active role in the remembrance, canonization, and globalization of this poetry. How do we know that our "choices" are right? To which degree are our choices swayed by the technological means of textual dissemination and algorithmic preselection? Have we been vigilant enough in preserving underestimated voices, so as to leave enough heuristic opportunities for future readers to rewrite history? Scholars of classicist internet poetry, just like their poets, are thus confronted with the impossible task of untangling the intertwining temporalities, which grow on the digital sand like vines, continuously bringing "pastness" back to the new sunlight.

ZHIYI YANG is professor of Sinology at University of Frankfurt. Her research investigates how Chinese classical lyric traditions engage with aesthetics (of nature and art) and with ethics (of private and public life). She is the author of *Dialectics of Spontaneity: The Aesthetics and Ethics of Su Shi (1037–1101) in Poetry* (2015) and *Poetry, History, Memory: Wang Jingwei and China in Dark Times* (2023). She is currently writing a monograph on avant-garde classicist poetry in the Sinophone cyberspace and collaborating with scholars on an interdisciplinary project of global Sinophone classicisms.

/////////////////////////////////////

Acknowledgments
I thank all poets mentioned or cited in this article who have maintained contact with me over the years, generously accepting my interviews and sharing their poems with me. All poems cited in this article have been approved by the poets. Since many Chinese internet pages cited in this article are no longer accessible, I have archived them in a Google folder, identified by the note in which they're referred (drive.google.com/drive/folders /1EkRrU1q8ROKI41SWG4xAPvvoMTvEK5sy?usp=sharing).

Notes
1   See RupiKaur.com; Kassam, "Rupi Kaur."
2   Wilson, "Why Rupi Kaur."
3   McElwee, "Instapoetry."
4   Yu's first anthology sold one-hundred thousand copies by April 2015, according to a report by *People's Daily* (April 7, 2015). It has arguably been the best-selling poetry anthology in mainland China for decades. A sales ranking of Chinese books with concrete numbers is strangely hard to find. According to an industrial

report published in 2016 ("2015中國圖書產業發展報告"), however, at least 66 titles sold more than 1 million copies each in 2015. Both reports are no longer accessible online but are archived in a Google folder (drive.google.com/drive/folders /1EkRrU1q8ROKI41SWG4xAPvvoMTvEK5sy?usp=sharing).

5   She was expelled in August 2022 (see "Yu Xiuhua's response") but remains a member of the National Writers' Association (see "New members").

6   See the screenshot embedded in an anti-Yu blog post, which accuses Yu of "cashing in" on political dissension; see "Ten thousand for a Poem."

7   Hockx, *Internet Literature*, 4.

8   Ibid.

9   According to the poets interviewed for this article, this term was first used by Tan Zuowen 檀作文 around 2001, but no original posts can be found today.

10 For the case of the poet and scholar Guo Moruo 郭沫若, see, e.g., H. Yang, *Modernity*, 147–82.

11 An example is the case of Nie Gannu 聶紺弩; see H. Yang, *Modernity*, 183–231; Tian, "'Each Has Its Moment.'"

12 The official English name of this society is simply Chinese Poetry Society, but it may lead to confusion, as it implies coverage of all genres of premodern and modern Chinese poetry. I thus add the *Shici* modifier to the names of all such publications and societies.

13 Dai, "*Zhonghua shici*," 41–43.

14 See Wu, *Ershi shiji*, 1009.

15 Owen, "Stepping Forward and Back," 545. Technically speaking, the first classicist poetry journal in the PRC was *Shici jikan* 詩詞集刊, founded seven months earlier than *Dang-dai shici*. For more on this journal, see Dai, "*Zhonghua shici*," 128–30.

16 See the journal's Baidu Baike entry; baike.baidu.com/item/中华诗词/3990474 (accessed May 24, 2023).

17 Liu, *Jinbainian mingjia*, 577.

18 Bulletin board system. In mainland China, this term is normally used to refer to BBS maintained by university servers and are accessible primarily via Telnet. In this article, I use *BBS* to refer to all forums accessible from a dial-up modem, Telnet, or the internet.

19 An instant messaging software and Web portal released by Tencent in February 1999.

20 I met the poet in person twice and maintained contact with him via WeChat over the years. A more in-depth interview, on which most of the biographical information here is based, was conducted on October 20, 2020.

21 This is his legal name. His preferred written form for his name is Duan Xiaosong 段曉松.

22 I met the poet once in Nanjing in the summer of 2019 and have similarly remained in contact over the years. An in-depth interview was conducted on October 20, 2020.

23 By his own account, he was the first person in China who began to call the PRC "heavenly dynasty" (*tianchao* 天朝), by writing a broadly circulated post "Big Talks about the Heavenly Dynasty" (*Dahua tianchao* 大話天朝). WeChat interview, May 29, 2022. We maintained contact over the years, and an in-depth interview was conducted over WeChat on September 7, 2020.

24 WeChat audio interview on October 30, 2020.

25 See Z. Yang and Ma, "Classicism 2.0."

26 Dugu, "Self-Selected Anthology," 10.

27 Ibid., 17.

28 Li Shangyin, "*Jinse*" 錦瑟, in *Li Shangyin shiji shuzhu*, 1. Blue Field, or Lantian, is a county in Shaanxi famous for its jade production.

29 A lyric song that articulates this radically iconoclastic attitude toward the cultural tradition is "Jiepeiling: Dugu shiroushu zihuaxiang" 解佩令‧獨孤食肉獸自畫像 (To Jiepeiling: The Self-Portrait of a Lone Carnivore; 2009); see Dugu, "Self-Selected Anthology," 29–30.

30 Xutang, "Self-Selected Anthology of Experimental Wenyan Poetry," 2.

31 For a clip of this speech, see Clinton, "User Clip: Clinton on Firewall and Jello."

32 Creemers, "Cyber China," 91, 95.

33 Benjamin, "Paris," 40.

34 Rongshuxia abruptly turned off its server in August 2020, and only a limited portion of its historical archives can be accessed via IAWM, which has crawled the website eight times in 2000 but has archived only the call for the competition. I did verify Lizi's claim at the time of the interview by finding a list of the winners on Chinawriter.com.cn, but regrettably I forgot to archive the page, which is now no longer accessible. Recently Rongshuxia.com, now a subsidiary of the conglomerate China Literature Group, is again accessible, but it only features web novels, no poetry, and historical announcements can no longer be found.

35 Tian, "Muffled Dialect," 29.

36 See the archived page in the Google folder (drive.google.com/drive/folders/1EkRrU1q8ROKI41SWG4xAPvvoMTvEK5sy?usp=sharing).

37 It comes from a lyric song by the Southern Song poet Lu You 陸游 (1125–1210) to his ex-wife, whom he was forced to divorce; see Lu You, "Chaitou feng" 釵頭鳳, in *Fangweng ci*, 1.

38 Chen, *Wangluo shi*.

39 See Lu Qingshan, *Chunbingji*; Tan, *Wangluo shici*.

40 Pei, "Wangluo shitan."

41 The famous scholar Qian Zhonglian 錢仲聯 (1908–2003), for instance, wrote a *dianjianglu* for *shi* and *ci* poets since the late Qing; see Qian, "Jin bainian citan dianjianglu" 近百年詞壇點將錄 (Registry of Prominent Ci Poets in the Last Century) and "Jin bainian shitan dianjianglu" 近百年詩壇點將錄 (Registry of Prominent Shi Poets in the Last Century), in *Dangdai xuezhe zixuan wenku Qian Zhonglian juan*.

42 Tan, "Dianfu yu tuwei."

43 Tian, "Muffled Dialect." Lizi admitted to me that he read Nie Gannu only after Tian's article came out.

44 There are a few monographs on twentieth-century classicist poetry, but none on contemporary classicist internet poetry.

45 Kraushaar, *Fern von Geschichte*.

46 For an overview of its history of ownership, see "End of Rongshuxia."

47 Stockmann, Luo, and Shen, "Designing Authoritarian Deliberation," 246–47.

48 See Baron, *Better Pencil*, 139, 159, 164.

References

Baron, Dennis E. *A Better Pencil: Readers, Writers, and the Digital Revolution*. Oxford: Oxford University Press, 2009.

Benjamin, Walter. "Paris, the Capital of the Nineteenth Century." In *Selected Writings*, vol. 3, translated by Edmund Jephcott and Howard Eiland, 32–49. Cambridge, MA: The Belknap Press of Harvard University Press, 2002.

Chen Cun 陳村, ed. *Wangluo shi sanbai* 網絡詩三百 [Three Hundred Internet Classicist Poems]. Zhengzhou: Daxiang chubanshe, 2002.

Clinton, Bill. "User Clip: Clinton on Firewall and Jello." C-span, March 9, 2000. www.c-span.org/video/?c4893404/user-clip-clinton-firewall-jello (accessed May 24, 2023).

Creemers, Rogier. "Cyber China: Upgrading Propaganda, Public Opinion Work, and Social Management for the Twenty-First Century." *Journal of Contemporary China* 26, no. 103 (2017): 85–100.

Dai Yong 戴勇. "*Zhonghua shici* yu xinshidai jiuti shici de chuanbo yu chuangzuo yanjiu" 《中華詩詞》與新時代舊體詩詞的傳播與創作研究 [Chinese Shici and the Dissemination and Production of Old-Style Shici in the New Age]. PhD diss., Central China Normal University, 2015.

Dugu 獨孤食肉獸 (pen name of Zeng Zheng 曾崢). "Self-Selected Anthology 1985–2020." https://drive.google.com/open?id=1Isjbal6tf2MIeGJ2enAiButI-YHBjxCc&usp=drive_fs.

"End of Rongshuxia." https://www.163.com/dy/article/FPL4QNUH05148UNS.html (accessed January 25, 2024)

Hockx, Michel. *Internet Literature in China*. New York: Columbia University Press, 2015.

Kassam, Ashifa. "Rupi Kaur: 'There Was No Market for Poetry about Trauma, Abuse, and Healing.'" *Guardian*, August 26, 2016. www.theguardian.com/books/2016/aug/26/rupi-kaur-poetry-canada-instagram-banned-photo.

Kraushaar, Frank. *Fern von Geschichte und Verheißungsvollen Tagen. Neoklassizistische Cyberlyrik im ChinaNetz und die Schreibweise des Lizilizilizi (2000–2020)* [Far from History and Days of Promise: Neoclassical Cyber Poetry in the ChinaNet and the Writing Style of Lizilizilizi (2000–2020)]. Bochum: Projektverlag, 2022.

Li Shangyin 李商隱. *Li Shangyin shiji shuzhu* 李商隱詩集疏注 [Annotated Poetry of Li Shangyin]. Commentated by Ye Congqi 葉聰奇. Beijing: Renmin wenxue chubanshe, 1998.

Liu Mengfu 劉夢芙. *Jinbainian mingjia jiuti shici ji qi liubian yanjiu* 近百年名家舊體詩詞及其流變研究 [Old-Style Poetry and Its Transformations in the Last Century]. Vol. 2. Beijing: Xueyuan chubanshe, 2003.

Lu Qingshan 盧青山, ed. *Chunbingji: Wangluo shici shiwujia* 春冰集：網絡詩詞十五家 [Spring Ice: Fifteen Internet Shici Poets]. Shijiazhuang: Hebei jiaoyu chubanshe, 2005.

Lu You 陸游. *Fangweng ci biannian jianzhu* 放翁詞編年箋註 [Chronicled and Annotated Lyric Songs of Lu You]. Commentated by Xia Chengtao 夏承燾 and Wu Xionghe 吳熊和. Shanghai: Shanghai guji chubanshe, 1981.

McElwee, Molly. "Instapoetry: The Age of Scrolling Literature." *Gibraltar Magazine*, October 25, 2017. https://www.scribd.com/document/558361443/INSTAPOETRY-The-age-of-scrolling-literature-Molly (accessed January 25, 2024).

"New members." http://m.news.cn/book/2017-08/10/c_129676796.htm (accessed January 25, 2024).

Owen, Stephen. "Stepping Forward and Back: Issues and Possibilities for 'World' Poetry." *Modern Philology* 100, no. 4 (2003): 532–48.

Pei Tao 裴濤 (aka Su Wuming 蘇無名). "Wangluo shitan dianjianglu" 網絡詩壇點將錄 [Registry of Prominent Internet Classicist Poets]. In *Kexingji* 客行集 [Wanderer's Records], 54–86. Shanghai: Shanghai shehui kexueyuan chubanshe, 2019.

Qian Zhonglian 錢仲聯. *Dangdai xuezhe zixuan wenku Qian Zhonglian juan* 當代學者自選文庫·錢仲聯卷 [Self-Selected Anthology of Contemporary Scholars: Qian Zhonglian]. Hefei: Anhui jiaoyu chubanshe, 1999.

Stockmann, Daniela, Ting Luo, and Mingming Shen. "Designing Authoritarian Deliberation: How Social Media Platforms Influence Political Talk in China." *Democratization* 27, no. 2 (2019): 243–64.

Tan Zuowen 檀作文. "Dianfu yu tuwei: Lizi ti chuyi" 顛覆與突圍：李子體芻議 [Reversal and Resistance: A Preliminary Analysis of Lizi-Style]. *Zhongguo shige yanjiu tongxun* 中國詩歌研究通訊 [Bulletin of Research on Chinese Poetry] (2003): 27–35.

———, ed. *Wangluo shici nianxuan* 網絡詩詞年選 [Annual Selection of Internet Shici Poetry]. Beijing: Shoudu shifan daxue chubanshe, 2006.

"Ten Thousand for a Poem." http://www.360doc.com/content/22/0302/11 /65730069_1019638249.shtml (accessed January 25,2024)

Tian, Xiaofei. "'Each Has Its Moment': Nie Gannu and Modern Chinese Poetry." *Frontiers of Literary Studies in China* 12, no. 3 (2018): 485–524.

———. "Muffled Dialect Spoken by Green Fruit: An Alternative History of Modern Chinese Poetry." *Modern Chinese Literature and Culture* 21, no. 1 (2009): 1–45.

Wilson, Carl. "Why Rupi Kaur and Her Peers Are the Most Popular Poets in the World." *New York Times Book Review*, December 15, 2017. https://www.nytimes.com/2017/12 /15/books/review/rupi-kaur-instapoets.html.

Wu Haifa 吳海發. *Ershi shiji Zhongguo shici shigao* 二十世紀中國詩詞史稿 [A History of Twentieth-Century Chinese Shici Poetry]. Beijing: Zhongguo wenshi chubanshe, 2004.

Xutang 噓堂 (pen name of Duan Xiaosong 段小松). "Self-Selected Anthology of Experimental wenyan Poetry." https://drive.google.com/open?id=1IvzKip -CaUraOW920SBQGpmKQ_KEYqCj&usp=drive_fs

Yang, Haosheng. *A Modernity Set to a Pre-modern Tune: Classical-Style Poetry of Modern Chinese Writers*. Leiden: Brill, 2016.

Yang, Zhiyi, and Dayong Ma. "Classicism 2.0: The Vitality of Classicist Poetry Online in Contemporary China." *Frontiers of Literary Studies in China* 12, no. 3 (2018): 526–57.

"Yu Xiuhua's response." https://www.163.com/dy/article/HFAOF2S30553256M .html;%20last%20access%20May%2024,%202023 (accessed January 25, 2024)

MICHAEL O'KRENT

Gaming Sinographs beyond the Ludic
Word Game and the Digital Sinophone

ABSTRACT This article rethinks the notion of the Sinophone through digital technology by using the Taiwanese videogame *Word Game* (*Wenzi youxi*, Team9, 2022) as a case study. The digital Sinophone sees Chineseness as an act of positive identification claimed by engaging with digital artifacts; it defines a single mass audience coterminous with the Sinophone cultural sphere. *Word Game* constructs a two-dimensional space in which all objects are composed of sinographs, requiring the player to possess extensive knowledge of the construction of and relationship between sinographs according to Chinese grammatical and semiotic uses in order to progress in the game. Contrary to the internationalizing tendencies of the videogame market and the long history of tension between sinographic writing and the typographical technologies of technological modernity, the result is a uniquely Sinophone videogame. In *Word Game*, the logic of gameplay mechanics consists not of mathematical universals but culturally determined relationships between sinographs. The article concludes by examining the implications for the interdisciplinary study of videogames. Whereas contemporary videogame studies seeks to situate video gaming in broader cultural discourses, a culturalist view of videogames sees game mechanics as cocreators of culture rather than a mirror of culture.

KEYWORDS video games, Sinophone, digital, Taiwan, writing systems

> According to *Bartlett's Quotations*, "a picture is worth 10,000 words" is a Chinese proverb. On inquiry, we find that the Chinese seem not to have heard of it.
>
> —Jill H. Larkin and Herbert A. Simon, "Why a Diagram Is (Sometimes) Worth Ten Thousand Words"

In the official preview for *Word Game* (文字游戲),[1] a 2022 personal computer (PC) game by the Taipei-based digital art collective and game design studio Team9, the Chinese character *wo* 我 moves across the screen until it reaches an obstacle: another character, *men* 門. A speaker of any Chinese language will recognize that these characters mean "I" and "door," respectively. When 我 approaches 門, the 門 appears to "swing" open, and the 我 passes through it and disappears. That is, 門 functions not only as the sinograph that means "door," but also as a door. Thus for the entire game: all objects in the game are composed of sinographs, and player input advances the game by manipulating the location, appearance, composition, meaning, and syntax of sinographs. A wall might consist of a line

PRISM: THEORY AND MODERN CHINESE LITERATURE • 20:2 • SEPTEMBER 2023
DOI 10.1215/25783491-10992760 • © 2023 LINGNAN UNIVERSITY

of *qiang* 墙 characters; and the game's main enemy is a dragon, itself made of *long* 龍 (dragon) characters, that opens its mouth to show *ya* 牙 (tooth) characters and spit *huo* 火 (fire) characters. Sinographs are usually set against negative space. They sometimes change color for aesthetic effect or to demonstrate which ones cannot be modified. The only other graphical elements are fully filled-in squares the size of one sinograph, used only occasionally to create pixelated images; four directional arrows to indicate player movement or the need to press the down arrow key to cue the game to print the next line of instructions; and seven animations to show either the success or failure of one of the game's four core mechanics (deleting a character, pushing or pulling a character, splitting a character into two, or merging two characters into one).[2]

The goal of the game is comically simple. An evil dragon has kidnapped the kingdom's beloved princess, and the player must become the "character-recognizing hero" (*shizi yongzhe* 識字勇者) in order to save her. Habitual videogamers will recognize two things: first, that "saving the princess" is the goal in Nintendo's classic series of *Super Mario* games, and as such that *Word Game* alludes to the history of its own medium. In combination with the title, this framing of the game's story foregrounds its mediality. Second, its graphic arsenal is extremely sparse, and this choice is made to simplify the developer's job in the cutthroat business of videogames. Though *Word Game* was backed by an extremely successful crowdfunding project,[3] the continued existence of the Team9 studio (and guaranteed employment for its members) hinges on *Word Game* generating sufficient revenue at the lowest possible cost to leave the studio with the liquidity to fund future products. The development of stable computer systems to execute a game's mechanics and the creation of digital models to stand in for its graphical components are enormously difficult and time-consuming tasks. Every successful videogame studio must either invest a massive amount of resources—in-studio computing power, developer time, and the money required to fund both—to overcome these hurdles or find technical innovations that simplify the process. *Word Game* accomplishes the latter by removing the need to create realistic two- or three-dimensional models of every object in the game, instead opting for pixelated sinographs. Every sinograph in *Word Game* consists of an eleven-by-eleven grid, resulting in a font that evokes the text-only programming environments that characterized computing prior to the widespread adoption of graphical user interfaces in the 1980s. Each square of the grid is not a single pixel but rather a square box meant to look how a single pixel on older hardware would appear. Though many of the sinographs in the game are animated, animating an object of 121 squares (that scale flawlessly to resolution) is astronomically easier than designing and animating an object that would need to be represented in multiple resolutions ranging up to potentially hundreds of thousands of pixels.

This deliberately primitive stylization is partially a self-aware concession that a game developed by an independent studio such as Team9 will lack the sophisticated graphics and systems of most big-budget "AAA" games, but it is also a clever lie that conceals a functioning graphical rendering system that is deliberately made to look simpler than it is. At play is also the supposed primitiveness of mere Chinese text compared to the advanced technology of videogames, which is associated with alphabetic writing systems. *Word Game* problematizes the notion that writing technologies advance in a linear fashion. Text and sinographs do not belong to the past; rather, they push the boundaries of what can be done in digital artwork.

How does such a game construct its audience? By and large, videogame distribution is built on an internationalizing framework in which the ubiquity of translation effaces its presence for players. We speak not of games "translated" into another language as we might of a novel, nor of "subtitled" or "dubbed" works as we might say of a film or TV show, but rather simply of "language support" and "localization." When the textual components of videogames are translated, the logical system of their mechanics does not change. That is, no matter the language used to read instructions, the rules, goals, and methods of gameplay remain the same. Digital gameplay is governed by a piece of software, which is a system of formal logic whose internal relationships depend not on natural language but on binary code that represents logical operations. The mathematical nature of computer logic makes it universally valid, and this feature of computing language is often scaled up to propose that videogame mechanics are culturally universal. Videogame theorist Espen Aarseth writes, "Unlike in music, where a national anthem played on electric guitar takes on a whole new meaning, the value system of a game is strictly internal, determined unambivalently by the rules."[4] This article will refute this claim.

Mainland China is one of the world's fastest growing videogame markets. On Steam, the largest digital distribution platform for PC games, 9 percent of users[5] had selected Simplified Chinese as their primary language (i.e., the language for Steam's user interface) in 2017.[6] By 2022 that number was up to nearly 25 percent.[7] But as the global lingua franca, English still rules supreme: more than one-third of Steam users select English as their primary language, and fully half of games on the platform only support English.[8] Anecdotally, game developers suggest that more players actually play games in their English-language versions than use English as their primary language, though hard data on this point remains scarce.[9] This suggests that players for whom English is a second or third language will use English to engage with a game when their native language is not supported or the localization is of poor quality. While Chinese-speaking game studios don't need to translate their games into English to find commercial and critical success, the ability to distribute worldwide in English is generally a sign of a respectable, well-established studio. Though Team9 was only founded in 2018,[10] *Word Game* is well designed and well produced. From a marketing standpoint, one would expect to see an English localization of such a game. *Word Game* supports both simplified and traditional Chinese characters, but the game has not been localized to non-Sinophone markets. This is not an oversight on the developer's part but rather the centerpiece of its design.

By mostly restricting itself to an audience capable of understanding the Chinese-language wordplay that constitutes the game's mechanics, *Word Game* seeks to define a set of Sinophone videogame players. The manner in which this audience is constituted prompts a reconsideration of commonalities between otherwise diverse Sinophone populations in the use of digital media. In *Sound and Script in Chinese Diaspora*, Jing Tsu describes "literary governance" as "the tactics of collaboration across different occasions of Chinese-language writing. Governance, in this sense, means less a control from the top down than the ways in which linguistic alliances and literary production organize themselves around incentives of recognition and power."[11] My previous work has argued that videogames attempt to gain the form of recognition that Pierre Bourdieu named "cultural capital" as a way to differentiate themselves as carriers of cultural prestige, rather than merely marketable products.[12] *Word Game* uses a form of Sinophone literary governance to accomplish this. It is literary because it speaks to contested criteria for aestheticized language, and it is governance because the game is engaged in defining a limited audience that can be seen as coterminous with the Sinophone cultural sphere. Team9 seeks recognition that *Word Game* is a worthwhile artistic work because it aestheticizes the sinographic script that is taken as a common point of comprehension among its audience. In this Sinophone context, the purpose of aestheticizing the Sinographic script is to "mobilize the currency of national and cultural prestige to gain a greater foothold in the literary world rather than to express something like Chineseness in the spirit of repatriation or even defiance,"[13] in which "literary world" can be understood as the set of actors whose interventions determine the distribution of cultural capital in the field of artistic creation.

Word Game is neither an attempt to reclaim membership in a mainland-oriented concept of China nor an attempt to further develop a uniquely Taiwanese identity. Instead, by hybridizing an exploration-oriented role-playing game (RPG) and text adventure, *Word Game* creates a set of game mechanics whose functions must be understood through sinographs. This is not to say that *Word Game* is untranslatable per se; rather, *Word Game* shows us that there is a Sinophone way of thinking about game design. Emily Apter's *Against World Literature* sees the untranslatable not as "pure difference in opposition to the always translatable . . . but as a linguistic form of creative failure with homeopathic uses."[14] Though the best rejoinder to the accusation of untranslatability is "never say never" (after all, who knows what an extremely creative translator might be capa ble of?), Apter's notion of untranslatability as an interpretive framework whose deployment leads to analytical insight rather than prohibitive diktat fits *Word Game* well. In the case of *Word Game*, a translator would also need to act as a videogame designer, as its mechanical systems depend on the language used to give instructions. Notably, there is a Japanese-language translation in progress, and Team9 has acknowledged that making the game comprehensible in Japanese requires altering the design of gameplay challenges. Toward its conclusion, this article will examine the Japanese translation to make the point that changes in gameplay design because of translation resemble changes in linguistic quality and texture that occur when a literary text is translated.

In this article, the logic underlying the unique design of *Word Game* will be termed the *digital Sinophone*. The digital Sinophone demonstrates that there is a transnational, culturally Chinese approach to computing technology defined by shared access to Sinographic script, counter to the assumption that digital technology seamlessly crosses cultural boundaries. On the other hand, the digital Sinophone shows that ways of constructing transnational Chinese identity through digital technology differ substantially from the forms of Sinophone culture that characterize the field's existing emphasis on written literature and film, as a virtual community of players can be called into being through the highly internationalized distribution mechanisms of videogames.

The theme of this special issue, "Sinophone Classicism in Digital Times," appears to take to juxtapose the digital as an emblem of novelty against the belatedness of the classic. Zhiyi Yang defines Sinophone classicism as "the appropriation, redeployment, and reconfiguration of cultural memories harking back to Chinese aesthetic and intellectual traditions for local, contemporary, and vernacular uses."[15] But the past that gives rise to the notion of "classicism" need not appear only as the *Chinese* past—*Word Game* also derives its visual style from the past of digital technology. In this history, Chinese characters have long been seen as marginal to an alphabet-centric linguistic modernity whose technologies accommodate sinographs only with great difficulty. Indeed, for much of the twentieth century, many Chinese intellectuals pushed to abandon sinographic writing in favor of alphabetization.[16] Thomas S. Mullaney's 2017 history *The Chinese Typewriter* details the numerous, often tortured, iterations of typographical technologies that Chinese engineers experimented with in order to adapt Western typography to the Sinographic script, underwritten by the still-present suspicion that sinographs are "incompatible with modernity."[17] The Sinophone logic of *Word Game* is a way of reclaiming digital modernity as Chinese, not in the name of the ancientness of sinographs but as a matter of their continued use.

Playing off the Chinese-language convention of referring to the narrative persona of a first-person story as "我" when discussing the story, the player's avatar is the character 我. When the player uses the arrow keys or WASD to move this 我 character around the screen, the hooked *gou* 鈎 elements at the bottom of the *shugou* 豎鈎 stroke (on the left) and the *xiegou* 斜鈎 stroke (on the right) move up and down, as if they were feet on which the 我 walks. This description hints toward what is classicist about the way *Word Game* treats sinographs: careful attention to all components of characters and their functions, satirically mapped on to an antiquated eight-bit graphical style. Zhiyi Yang also notes that classicism consists of "aesthetic principles such as formal precision, adherence to tradition, artistic conservatism, simplicity, and restraint"[18]—all associated with a past understood as the formative ground of aesthetic traditions. *Word Game* presents sinographs as digital heirs to the tradition of sinography worthy of classicist aesthetic admiration.

As technological emblems of global modernity, computing technology and typography originated in the West and spread outward. China was seen as a latecomer. As a result, these technologies were designed to be uniquely responsive to alphabetic scripts and hostile to other writing systems. Essentially all widely used "high-level"[19] software languages represent logical operations through keywords drawn from English, with a few exceptions that tend to be relegated to the status of curiosity. Why is it that these supposed mathematical universals are almost always expressed in English? As Tara McPherson has argued, the development of computer systems reflects the same undergirding assumptions that govern their sociotemporal context.[20] The hegemony of English in software languages can thus be seen as yet another symptom of the Anglocentrism that permeates globalization by positioning English-speaking countries as the global center[21]—and this is the same hegemony that gives rise to the impetus to study world literature by including texts that originated in a text other than English.

Word Game playfully critiques digital Anglocentrism. The game conflates Sinophone culture with digital nostalgia to suggest that sinography is not a latecomer to digital technology but part and parcel of its history. Many of the game's keystone elements are named phonetically as sinographical representations of common English computing terms. The player visits Clippy Village (Kelipi Cun 克理皮村, named for Microsoft Word's former digital assistant); Qwerty Village (Kuerdi Cun 庫爾堤村), and the Kingdom of Windows (Wenduosi Wangguo 溫鐸斯王國). The player's greatest ally is named "Ctrl+S" (Kangzhuo Aisi 康卓艾斯). One of the recurring enemies in the game are toxic "slimes" that the player dies on touching. But they are represented by different sinographs throughout the game, and the player must connect their phonetic similarity to the English word *slime* to realize that they are the same thing. At first they are called *sīláimǔ* 斯萊姆; by the game's fifth chapter (of eight) they are called *shǐláimǔ* 史萊姆, and in chapter 6 they are called *shīláimǔ* 濕萊姆. The player's greatest weapon is the "backspace sword" (*beikesibeisi jian* 貝克斯貝斯劍), which allows them to delete characters. Team9 knows that they can expect their audience to know at least a little bit of English because both widely used computing terminology and the logical operators of programming languages inevitably originate in English, even while at the same time they know their game is completely inaccessible to players who do not speak and read Mandarin Chinese. The game thus repackages English words in a way that is accessible only to Mandarin speakers as an acknowledgment of the peculiar status of a Mandarin user base within a technological sphere that is otherwise Anglocentric.

Just as world literature offers a remedy for Anglocentrism by encouraging the study of texts that do not originate in English, *Word Game* is a sort of "world literature" for computing language—not because it is written in one of those elusive software languages that does not draw on English, but because the game's approach to its medium relies on the logic of Sinographic writing. The next section will expand the medium-oriented analysis of *Word Game* by showing how the game challenges the distinction between text and graphics in videogames by blending the RPG and text adventure videogame genres. The following section argues that the Sinophone design paradigm emerges in *Word Game* because only a *pleremic* script—one such as Chinese in which individual components of words signify meanings as well as pronunciation—can systematically and comprehensively use text as graphics. The notion of the digital Sinophone accounts for this essentializing use of Sinographs as a collective identity marker in the construction of a videogame's audience. The article will conclude by discussing the implications for future directions in the field of videogame studies. Videogame studies finds itself refreshed by the introduction of the Sinophone, and vice versa: both fields can come to see videogames as active participants in, rather than merely products of, the ongoing evolution of cultures.

Text, Graphics, Genre

Videogames generally distinguish between graphical and textual signification. *Word Game* draws on this distinction in order to challenge it. Graphics represent objects, whereas text represents information. This text-graphics distinction is necessary to distinguish between videogames and other digital literary forms that consist merely in the computerized manipulation of text, such as hypertext novels. This distinction corresponds to that between graphical and textual representation of digital systems in software engineering.[22] Graphics are a non-symbolic form of visual signification. Graphics convey multiple pieces of information that can be processed in parallel, whereas text conveys information through symbols whose relationships must be processed linearly. Likewise, videogame objects constitute a space that adheres to the rules of a simulated physics, whereas text is said to exist outside it.

As a matter of medium, poems and novels are texts. Conversely, video-games contain texts, but they are not themselves texts. Rather, they are virtual spaces. Space is usually made available to the player by the presence of a virtual camera that allows them to see the space and movement within it on a screen. This is as opposed to a hypertext novel, which allows its audience to move through a somewhat indeterminate path of text but does not present the player's choices as spatial navigation. Likewise, *Word Game* is not a text but, rather, a space made of text, in turn made possible by features of the Sinographic writing system.

The text adventure genre of videogames eschews graphical signification in favor of completely textual signification. But text adventures still ought to be considered videogames to the extent that they describe a virtual space and the player's interactions with it. They are also among the oldest of videogame genres because the basic text processing required to operate a text adventure requires relatively little computing power; sophisticated graphics came about only with later advances in semiconductors. Perhaps the most famous example is William Crowther's *Adventure* (1975; aka *Colossal Cave Adventure*). *Adventure* is a digital representation of sections of the Mammoth Caves in the US state of Kentucky, through which a player can navigate by entering one- or two-word instructions into a command prompt.[23] The game then feeds back information about where the player is, such as: "YOU ARE IN A ROOM WHOSE WALLS RESEMBLE SWISS CHEESE. OBVIOUS PASSAGES GO WEST, EAST, NE, AND NW. PART OF THE ROOM IS OCCUPIED BY A LARGE BEDROCK BLOCK."[24] *Adventure* uses evocative textual descriptions for the purpose of implying a space. The text adventure and the RPG both treat exploration of a space as a key component of gameplay, though they differ in how they communicate information about that space. In adventure-genre videogames that run on hardware more advanced than *Adventure*'s 1970s Fortran, the communication of spatial logic tends to rely much more on graphics than text. But in a game such as *Adventure*, text does all the heavy lifting. Though one must reason about the nature of a space described by the text, that space remains permanently behind the words, through a screen that requires an act of interpretation to penetrate. Objects contained within that space exist, but only at a distance.

A simple example: one ordinarily recognizes a door in a videogame because it looks similar to doors the player has walked through in their own life and in other videogames. But in *Word Game*, passing through the door prompts the game to load the next level. Software is being executed that tells the computer to do this, but videogames generally rely only on graphical signification to communicate to the player that they should expect to enter the next level or a new room. The character 門 functions simultaneously as a textual instruction, as in, "This is a door; move here to enter a new room," and as the graphical object.

The conceit of the videogame is that modifying sinographs has material effects on the world because description and instruction are not separate from objects. A 門 character in a line of narrative description can function mechanically as a door (i.e., a gateway to the next level) whether it is printed in a line of narrative text or when it is surrounded by *lou* 樓 or *fang* 坊 characters to form the image of a building. Multiple puzzles in the game feature the self-doubting hero saying something along the lines of "I can't do this!" and solving the puzzle by deleting *can't* (*bu* 不). The game simulates a space governed by the linguistic logic of the written words that make up its narrative, as opposed to the text adventure's system of words governed by spatial logic. At one point in the game, the four-character-wide body of a snake demon splits into moving pieces that consist of four-character phrases, each of which now acts as its teeth. If caught between them, the player will "die" and be forced to restart the puzzle. But if the player finds the right phrase of which to make 我 the grammatical subject by moving into the correct physical position, the snake will be defeated (figs. 1–4).[25] In a fully graphical mode of representation, an animation would be necessary to show this change in perspective: the camera has gone from a side view to a front view of the snake, or the snake has rotated ninety degrees relative to the player. Not so here, as there is no virtual camera. The words that make up the snake demon constitute whatever spatial function the narrative requires.

Word Game takes an axe to the text-graphics distinction by simultaneously treating every sinograph as both a graphical element of a videogame and a semiotic element of linguistic expression. It is a Taiwanese videogame that successfully crosses this boundary because such a blurring of graphics and textuality cannot occur in a language with an alphabetic or syllabic script. Sinographs are by far the most widely used writing system whose components correspond to units of meaning rather than solely to units of speech. The next section will explore why this game could only have been made using the Chinese writing system.

Whose Virtual Words? The Need for the Digital Sinophone

Word Game is a culturally Chinese videogame whose target audience is delineated by their command of Mandarin. This is in stark contrast to the highly internationalized tendencies of the videogame market. The platforms on which videogames are sold and distributed are usually available worldwide and in many languages. The developers of *Word Game* have chosen a market strategy that sacrifices its international audience in exchange for a shared experience of insider knowledge among its target audience. This is a case of targeting a smaller market with an eye toward greater penetration, rather than aiming for low penetration among a broader market.

Existing frameworks for Sinophone studies depend on a narrow set of relationships between linguistic community and nationhood that are determined

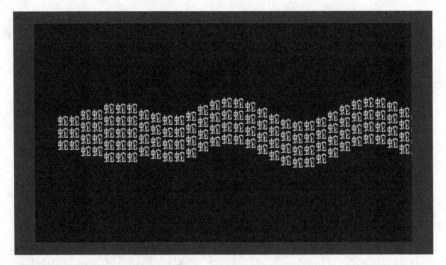

FIGURE 1. Snake demon, bird's-eye view.

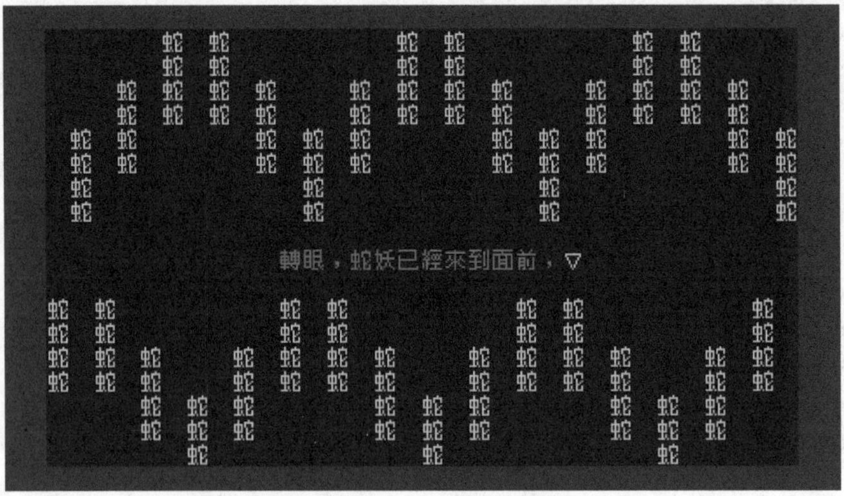

轉眼，蛇妖已經來到面前，▽

FIGURE 2. The snake's body has become teeth, with narrative text printed in between.

by the conditions of circulation that characterize written literature and film. The Sinophone as presently understood participates in a deconstruction of older assumptions regarding the existence of national literature and its counterpart national cinema, proposing instead the multiplicity of Sinophone cultural production as a destabilizing riposte to both the national literature of mainland China and the emerging national literatures of the various decolonizing locales that contain substantial overseas Chinese communities. On the other hand, the digital Sinophone is not "differentially articulated to the timespace conjunctions in particular Sinophone locales"[26] but instead posits a "shared visual economy of

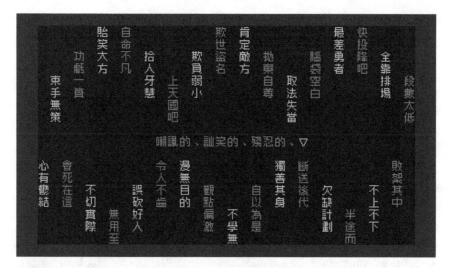

FIGURE 3. The four-character teeth transform into linguistic puzzle pieces.

FIGURE 4. Failure state; 我 is about to be caught between gnashing teeth.

the Sinograph"[27] that comes into being only during the moment of access to digital technology.

The digital Sinophone is not a Sinophone digital diaspora. *Digital diaspora* refers to a diasporic experience that is felt and shared through the use of digital communications, such that a diasporic community is said to exist online. Michel S. Laguerre defines *digital diaspora* as "an immigrant group or descendant of an immigrant population that uses IT connectivity to participate in virtual networks of contacts for a variety of political, economic, social, religious, and communicational purposes that, for the most part, may concern either the homeland, the host land, or both."[28] Digital diaspora thus preserves the link to a lost homeland as a major axis of identification that the Sinophone militates against.

Digital art and communications displace diaspora from the (sometimes negative) central position it has held in multiple definitions of the Sinophone. Shu-mei Shih writes that "the Sinophone foregrounds not the ethnicity or race of the person but the languages he or she speaks in either vibrant or vanishing communities of those languages. Instead of the perpetual bind to nationality, the Sinophone may be inherently transnational and global and includes wherever various Sinitic languages are spoken."[29] The digital Sinophone constitutes an ongoing, vibrant virtual community, not necessarily "in the process of disappearance as soon as it undergoes the process of becoming."[30] A growing digital Sinophone community can emerge from multiple physical Sinophone communities, each in the process of disappearing (should one agree with Shih's assessment that this is the fate of Sinophone communities outside mainland China). The digital Sinophone, on the other hand, enables one to think Chineseness independently of geography, as the extreme penetration of digital technology into global markets creates the possibility for a singular Sinophone audience that draws members from both within and outside diasporic communities and does not anchor the audience to the specificity of their physical location. The digital Sinophone rather functions as a virtual location that hosts cultural self-identification. A player located in almost any country can buy *Word Game* on Steam's digital platform, but only someone who can understand the game's use of sinographs would bother to do so.

Word Game is unique because, as its title implies, its gameplay mechanics are also linguistic mechanics, that is, the grammatical, syntactical, and lexical rules of Mandarin Chinese. When looking at *Word Game* as a piece of Sinophone culture, one cannot avoid the question of why it relies solely on script as a way to access the Chinese language. For all its wordplay, the game has no spoken words to accompany the script at any point in the game. This is a contrarian design choice, considering videogame audiences' demands for increasingly realistic and immersive environments. Why would Team9 eschew the spoken word in favor of the written?

A key principle for the cultural analysis of videogames is that every successful design choice will be supported by coinciding aesthetic and pragmatic reasons. Here the pragmatic reasons are simple: voice acting is expensive, requires additional steps to prepare the audio for production, and does not substitute for text. A look at the promotional materials and crowdfunding website for *Word Game* shows that Team9 invested quite a bit of resources in their Foley artists, who perform and record custom audio for ambient sounds such as footsteps, fire crackling, water flowing, or the sound of a sword being drawn.[31] Foley artists are among the most invisible in media industries—film, TV, and game studios rarely show off this type of audio, instead intending it to be forgotten as it blends seamlessly into the presentation of a scene. The sparse graphic arsenal of *Word Game* means that the Foley artists have largely carried the burden of building absorbing and comprehensive scenes, hence the need to invest heavily and advertise the quality of their work. There was likely neither money nor labor hours left to include the human voice.

The aesthetic reasons are thornier. In *Word Game*, the dual graphical-textual function of Sinographs erases topolect in the service of defining a single mass audience. If spoken language were to enter the scene, the game would be tied to the local pronunciation of its narrators. This would position some of the game's players closer to the game by virtue of shared (likely standard) pronunciation and relegate others to marginal status because they pronounce these sinographs differently in a way that marks them as dialect against a prestige language's claim to universality. The digital Sinophone resists such localization, instead preferring to create a single audience defined by a bright-line threshold of familiarity with Chinese grammatical and semiotic usage of sinographs. A player who reads only, say, Japanese, or who has an advanced knowledge of Korean mixed script, might be able to solve some of *Word Game*'s puzzles but would most likely be unable to complete the game without the aid of a dictionary or walkthrough. For example, several puzzles require the player to create a phrase by selecting the correct character in reverse order from a randomly scrambled word bank, building a phrase from back to front. The approximate knowledge of Mandarin sinograph usage given by knowledge of a proximate language likely would not suffice, since the player must anticipate the correct syntax. But varying pronunciations and topolects within the Chinese cultural sphere would not stop a player from solving these puzzles as long as they can access the formal written language (*shumian yu* 書面語).

Against the backdrop of digital technology's historical association with alphabetic scripts—English in particular—*Word Game* presents sinography as a singular form of digital difference by leaning into the *pleremic* characteristics of the Chinese writing system, as opposed to the *cenemic* nature of alphabetic scripts. While the pleremic-cenemic distinction has a long history in linguistics,[32] a useful gloss comes from Mullaney's *Chinese Typewriter*, which defines cenemic script as "a writing system in which graphemes represent meaningless, phonetic elements" (i.e., alphabets and syllabaries) and pleremic script as "writing systems like Chinese in which graphemes represent meaningful segments of language."[33] *Graphemes* refer to the smallest intelligible components of writing systems. For alphabetic scripts, a grapheme is an individual letter. In the case of Chinese languages, graphemes include individual simple characters, as well as both radical and phonetic character components. The core of the pleremic-cenemic distinction is that letters, words, and texts written in alphabets and syllabaries are visually unconnected to their semantic meanings, whereas pleremic scripts feature a

FIGURE 5. The helmet that confers on the player the power to split sinographs into their components, one of three "sagely artifacts" (*shengqi* 聖器) wielded by the player. Note the glow surrounding each filled-in white box.

systematic correspondence between visual units (i.e., graphemes) and semiotic units (i.e., morphemes), though the relationship is not necessarily one of visual resemblance.[34] Because *Word Game* takes pleremic script as the essential characteristic of sinography, the sinographic writing system must also be presented as the essential characteristic of a broadly understood category of Chinese identity defined by access to the script. There are three ways *Word Game* takes advantages of pleremic characteristics of Sinographic script to break down the text-graphics distinction in a way that is accessible only to its particular audience.

First, the game uses an abundance of Chinese characters to create visual phenomena similar to what Tong King Lee calls "spectacles of the sinograph." The game uses the repetition of characters and the shock of color and filled-in boxes against the uniformity of sinographs written as text to create impressive displays of artwork (figs. 5–7). Another useful comparison is to Chinese calligraphy. Like calligraphy, *Word Game* allots a fixed and identical amount of space for each character and positions them in a grid. That grid is then aestheticized—for calligraphy, by the beauty of the calligrapher's strokes, and for *Word Game*, by the spectacular repetition of sinographs. Such spectacles "resemiotize the Chinese character into the uncanny—the familiar yet unidentifiable—triggering a politics of recognition that destabilizes the visual organicity of Language (as an institution)."[35] These spectacles create a moment of recognition based on shared access to dual semiotic and visual functions of each character.

Second, the treatment of sinographs in *Word Game* seems to resemble the attitude taken toward the mediality of sinographs by some works of concrete poetry. Since at least the Sixteen Kingdoms period (304–439 CE), Chinese poets have written poems whose textual representation takes on an evocative shape. Styles include

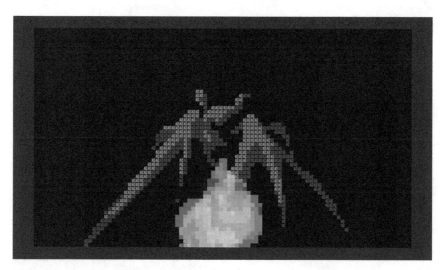

FIGURE 6. The menacing dragon blows a puff of smoke.

huiwen 回文, or poems that can be read as palindromes, often presented in the shape of a circle; pagoda-shaped poetry, in which each line consists of two more characters than the previous, creating the stepped triangular slope visually associated with pagoda roofs; and the exceptional example of the wife of a Tang dynasty general who composed a poem hoping for her husband's return from the frontier and presented it in the shape of a tortoise.[36] In the twentieth century, concrete poetry gained cultural capital as an edge case in literary writing that might push the boundaries of textual and graphical signification in a manner similar to that of *Word Game.* As Andrea Bachner writes, "In order to become an object, rather than remaining an instrument of signification, the concrete poem has to court other art forms and thereby deterritorialize written signs into graphic materiality and spoken language into sonic force. This emphasis on the poem's materiality . . . allows poetry in its new form to circulate globally, as its material concretion endows it with aesthetic energy beyond linguistic specificity."[37] In *Word Game,* both the shape in which characters are presented (see fig. 7) and the shape of individual characters such as *men* 門 that do visually resemble their meanings contribute to this materializing of the language. But the consequences are the opposite of what Bachner suggests for concrete poetry—*Word Game* dangles the universal signification of videogame graphics and the mathematical universalism of game mechanics but denies both by replacing them with the cultural-linguistic logic of sinographs.

Third, various forms of semiotic and material Sinophone wordplay constitute an allographic tradition that "emphasizes hybridity and difference at the heart of the sinograph" in the work of writers such as Taiwanese poet Chen Li 陳黎 and Malaysian novelist Ng Kim Chew 黃錦樹.[38] Bachner claims that allographic practices reveal the "multiplicity and thus strangeness within one script tradition"[39] by

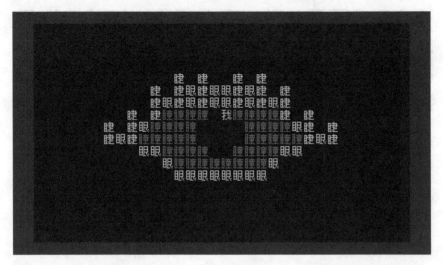

FIGURE 7. The player stands before the dragon; the 我 becomes the glimmer in the dragon's eye to emphasize its enormous size.

permuting characters in alternative forms whose relation to the original graph is determined by the cultural logic of script. A number of *Word Game*'s mechanics accomplish this. For example, a *shou* 獸 character representing a menacing wild beast can be converted into a *shou* 瘦 character, meaning "frail" or "skinny," when the player approaches and presses the space bar, thereby defeating this particular enemy by rendering it less than terrifying. One need not read these characters as *shou* to solve the puzzle, but one must know that these two characters are pronounced the same way.

John Marney argues that the *fanqie* 反切 technique of "splitting the pronunciation of two other graphs respectively into initial and final consonant and vowel values and combining the product" is "metathesis, the phonetic equivalent of the graphic anagram."[40] The videogame mechanics of splitting characters into radicals and phonetic components and recombining them is a derivation of *fanqie*, and the allographic way *Word Game* treats sinographs is highly anagrammatic as a result. At one point in *Word Game*, the player must build a bridge across a river, not by assembling in-game objects such as wood or steel but rather by looking at the game's description of a riverbank: "A stream blocks the way forward. The tree next to it is very sturdy. I think it should be able to help" 一條溪水阻擋前路。旁邊的喬木很結實，我感覺應該幫得上忙. This description looks much like what one might see in *Adventure*—if not for the more numerous mechanical options given to the player thanks to the intervening half-century of technological advances, and the fact that one can also see objects made from characters: a tree with a trunk made from the character *mu* 木 and a canopy made from the character *shu* 樹, and a river made out of *xi* 溪 characters, with each row of characters moving in a wavelike fashion while each *dian* 點 stroke within the phonetic

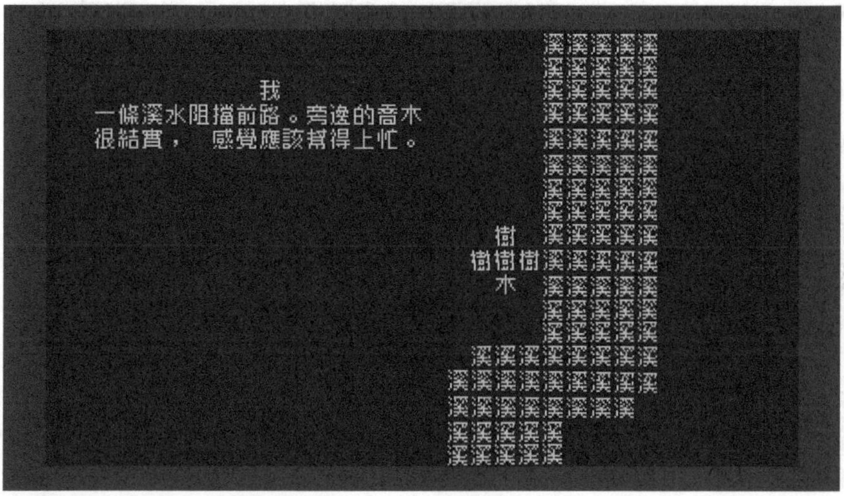

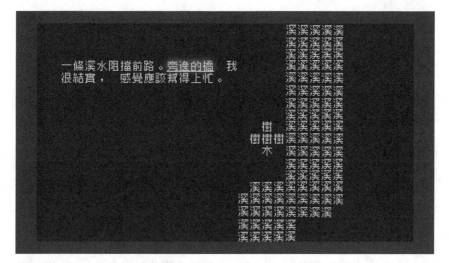

FIGURE 8. 喬 and 木 form a compound word.

FIGURE 9. 喬 and 木 form the compound sinograph 橋.

xi 奚 component sways within the character to represent the flow of water. The player must then move the 我 to push the *qiao* 喬 and *mu* 木 characters together (fig. 8). When this happens, 木 becomes a radical rather than a character, and the two combine to form *qiao* 橋 (fig. 9). Then the tree next to the river is replaced by a bridge over the river (fig. 10).

Bachner presents two paths that an anagrammatic text might follow:

> With their emphasis on the basic building blocks of language they can cement linguistic othering by discovering that what lies beneath language simply

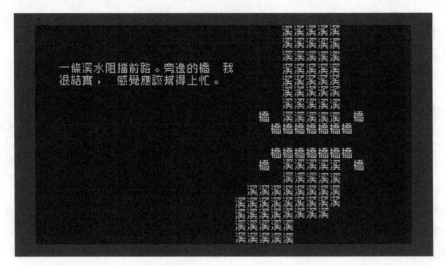

FIGURE 10. A bridge appears over the river.

replicates our preconceived notion of (our own or another's) language.... And yet, since these practices push the possibilities of linguistic creation to their limits and open up a dimension of language below language, they can also render a language other to itself by putting into play the basic units of language and its basic rules of combination.[41]

Sinophone studies as conceived thus far can more easily accommodate the second path. Bachner's study of Chen Li, for example, notes that "his poems effectively open up the category of Chineseness to include its margins"[42] by satirizing characters used to define ethno-national categories such as country (*guo* 國) and barbarian (*hu* 胡).

Word Game lacks a similar thematic gesture. Instead, *Word Game* reproduces precisely the "univocal link between such an unyielding script system and cultural identity" that writers familiar to Sinophone studies such as Chen and Ng repudiate.[43] The presence of a mass audience for the videogame repositions the player as the agent executing the deconstructive self-othering of the sinograph, a function that proceeds from the assumption of the player's prior familiarity with all the degrees of difference contained within the sinograph. This comprehensive knowledge of the language—the expertise of a "native speaker," as Jing Tsu puts it—becomes the locus of commonality. Tsu argues that "linguistic nativity propels both the quest for literary prestige and the various challenges to its institutionalization."[44] *Word Game* challenges the currently defined boundaries of Sinophone literary prestige by borrowing from previously recognized calligraphic, concrete, and allographic literary practices to show that videogames can implicate a literary treatment of language through interactive descriptions of space. *Word Game* distinguishes itself from other forms of Sinophone literary practice by returning the self-othering of sinographic script to the prior understanding of a singular language. By reducing the constant "othering" or "deconstruction" of language to a function of gameplay mechanics, these forms of linguistic uncertainty are rendered tame by the player's assumed knowledge of a reified form of standard Mandarin. The game participates in that reification of Mandarin in the service of imagining a Sinophone community that exists only digitally as the audience of the game.

For most videogames, rules and mechanics are easily representable in any target language, since natural language serves as a receptacle for the culturally universal, mathematical-logical functioning of the software behind the game. Here, not so. Contrary to the notion of mathematical and logical operators as universally valid across cultures—a mathematical universalism captured in the very dismissal of alphabetic universalism implied by the Anglocentrism of both programming languages and the global videogame market—sinographs constitute a logical system whose operation is contingent on implicit knowledge of the relationship between concepts, that is, knowledge of a culture. If videogame mechanics are the mere execution of logical operations represented by software code, then translating a videogame would distort linguistic and narrative elements, but not its mechanics. But when mechanics are linguistic, translation requires mechanical alterations. Case in point: Team9's 2023 announcement of a Japanese version of *Word Game* goes to great lengths to explain that the game is being re-created while trying to preserve its spirit, and that translation alone will not suffice to make the game playable in Japanese:

> A Japanese version of *Word Game* is confirmed to be in development!
> Everyone knows that "written characters" are the core element of this work.
> Therefore, releasing *Word Game* in a different language has always been part of *Team9*'s plan.
> But, do you think this is only translation? Oh, it's not so simple.
> In addition to translating, we must also develop new concepts while keeping the spirit of the game. Many a person has come up short.
> Finally! There! A true translation hero has appeared—the Japanese game publisher Flyhigh Works.
> All scenes, characters, and obstacles will be meticulously created and refined by Flyhigh Works. We look forward to this journey and making lots of progress together!

＼《文字遊戲》日文版銳意開發中！／
大家都知道「文字」就是這款作品的核心元素，
因此，推出不同語言的《文字遊戲》一直是 Team9 計畫之一。
但，你以為只是翻譯而已嗎？喔，才沒那麼簡單。

翻譯的同時要發揮創意又要保有遊戲精神，好一堆人早鎩羽而歸。

終！於！真正的翻譯勇者現身了—日本遊戲發行商 Flyhigh Works

所有的場景、角色、關卡都是 Flyhigh Works 精心雕琢與製作的結晶，已經很期待接下來一起前進的旅程！[45]

Team9's announcement stresses that the game will be redesigned; while some of its mechanics (for example, deleting or merging sinographs) remain the same, the actual puzzles have to be re-crafted and go through the painstaking design process once again. The Japanese "version" (*ban* 版) of the game (note that Team9 avoids the terms *localization* or *translation*) works because Japanese writing also uses sinographs, and the sinographic mechanics can be reinterpreted for Japanese usage. The trailer shows no evidence that Japanese *kana* can be modified as part of gameplay.

The reception and potential translation of *Word Game* can be thought of as a series of concentric circles. The original *Word Game* belongs to a singularly defined digital Sinophone audience; this is the inner circle. With some redesign work, the game can be made available to speakers of other languages within the Sinographic "scriptworld,"[46] who have access to the game at a slightly greater distance. An outer circle could well encompass a possible approximate alphabetic translation of *Word Game*, but the translator would be forced to find cenemic approximations for mechanical operations that depend on pleremic script. It would be much harder to "keep the spirit of the game" in an alphabetic script. Broadly speaking, translation translates meaning. But no similar process exists to translate the formal linguistic features of writing systems. Explanations of individual examples such as those in this article may provide the best possible access to a work such as *Word Game* for someone who cannot read sinographs in any language in which they are used. Pascale Casanova, for example, understands translation as "the movement of a text from one language into another."[47] But let us recall that videogames are not texts, but contain texts. For most videogames, mechanics transfer seamlessly between cultural and linguistic contexts, requiring only the textual components to be moved from one language to another. But *Word Game*'s non-textual components depend on the textual logic of sinographs. *Word Game* is thus not a Sinophone text but rather a Sinophone videogame. Understanding the distinction between text and videogame here requires Sinophone studies to expand the universe of ways Chinese identity can be contested and reconstituted across media.

The Digital Sinophone contra the Ludic

This article has examined how *Word Game* might give rise to a new, more medium-aware form of Sinophone studies. But how can videogame studies benefit from dialog with Sinophone studies? This article aims to help remedy a tendency in videogame studies to see gameplay as an independent cultural activity that, at most, instantiates cultural phenomena that exist in a broader sphere. The digital Sinophone emerges from a culturalist critique of what I call the ludic paradigm in videogame studies. The word *ludic*, from the Latin *ludere* ("to play"), denotes an approach to videogames that centers the act of playing a videogame, in contrast to an analysis of videogames as participants in cultural discourses. The ludic approach to videogames seeks to distinguish the act of gameplay from acts of narration, storytelling, and meaning making connected with the outside world. The ludic approach originates with functionalist readings of historian Johan Huizinga's argument that play has a unique role in human culture because games constitute a "magic circle" outside the sphere of normal sociocultural activity.[48]

More than twenty years ago, videogame scholars began debating between narratological and ludological approaches to videogames. Henry Jenkins describes "a blood feud . . . between the self-proclaimed ludologists, who wanted to see the focus shift onto the mechanics of game play, and the narratologists, who were interested in studying games alongside other storytelling media."[49] This early approach to videogames is a representative case of what Marsha Kinder calls "cyberstructuralism," which "privileges formalism while ignoring the ideological implications of structural choices."[50] To some extent, the debate is still going on,[51] even though commentaries on its stagnation have their own history, now also approaching twenty years in length.[52] That is, the ludology-narratology debate has been stale for almost its entire existence, but videogame studies seems unable to fully move past it or describe what is gained by continuing to use its frame of reference. While other approaches to videogames have since developed that emphasize their visuality, didacticism, and the practical functioning of the videogame industry, the ludology-narratology debate remains a touchstone citation because of the ongoing fascination with "play" as a distinct category of activity.[53]

In this vein, Tara Fickle speaks of a more recent "second wave" of videogame studies that does not formally distinguish between narrative and ludicity and is more attuned to the sociopolitical context in which gaming takes place.[54] The implicitly outmoded "first wave" would be scholarship that divided itself along the lines of the ludology-narratology debate, with its embedded assumption that one can cogently speak about the systems of a game's mechanics without reference to its narrative content and vice versa. Second-wave videogame scholarship participates in the broader conversation over representation (in particular, how often and in what ways women, racial minorities, and queer sexuality are represented).

This is a first step toward a more holistic approach to videogames, but even second-wave videogame scholarship remains embedded within the ludic paradigm. Second-wave scholarship asks how videogames reflect broader cultural discourses around race, gender, sexuality, and so on but too often stops short of asking how videogames can change the way we think about those discourses. Because second-wave videogame studies still treats gameplay as a discrete category of analysis, it is natural to situate videogames in the broader culture by arguing that they are subject to the same trends and questions as those of other domains of cultural and sociological analysis. Scholars therefore argue that preexisting ideas about representation are "reinforced,"[55] "imported,"[56] or "facilitated"[57] by videogames. Adrienne Shaw writes that "games are not the only contemporary texts that demonstrate how and when representation comes to matter,"[58] exemplifying the tendency to treat videogames in parallel with literature, film, and so on. It is one thing to critique a videogame's manner of representing, for example, racial difference, because it resembles a state of affairs familiar from other domains of culture and society; it would be another altogether to find in a videogame a novel way to think about race. Videogame scholarship still seeks to understand what videogames are and what videogames do, so far stopping short of taking the approach common in literary and film studies of asking how videogames can help us think through questions of scholarly and cultural import. Critics working within the ludic paradigm critique videogames, but they have not yet sought to make videogames a tool available to criticism rather than mere objects of study.

My work seeks to push videogame scholarship further by drawing attention to the ways in which videogames are actively involved in the construction, modification, and evolution of cultural ideas. A culturalist approach recognizes that play is not the only relevant aspect of videogames. Videogame studies need not hesitate to say that videogames can indeed change the way we think about race, sexuality, gender, ethnicity, nationality, environment, or any other question that is of interest to scholars. In *Word Game*, not only do we see the politics of sinographic writing influence game design choices, but we also see the designers of *Word Game* creating a new set of politics for sinographs. The game does not simply instantiate the discourses of linguistic nativity, diaspora, cultural hybridity, and mutual identification seen elsewhere in Sinophone culture; it also speaks back to those discourses and demands that our notion of the Sinophone expand and change as well.

At first glance, the culturalist approach for which this article advocates might seem to resemble narratology. This is false. Though *Word Game* contains a strong narrative element—and as argued above, narrative necessity dictates the presence of physical space in the game—this article is not substantively engaged in an analysis of the meaning or structure of that narrative. No close reading or narratological typology is necessary for understanding how *Word Game* functions not only as form but also as culture. One need only look at what this article has so far failed to mention: *Word Game*'s shocking twist ending. In the game's final chapter, the player is said to "become the author" (*chengwei zuozhe* 成爲作

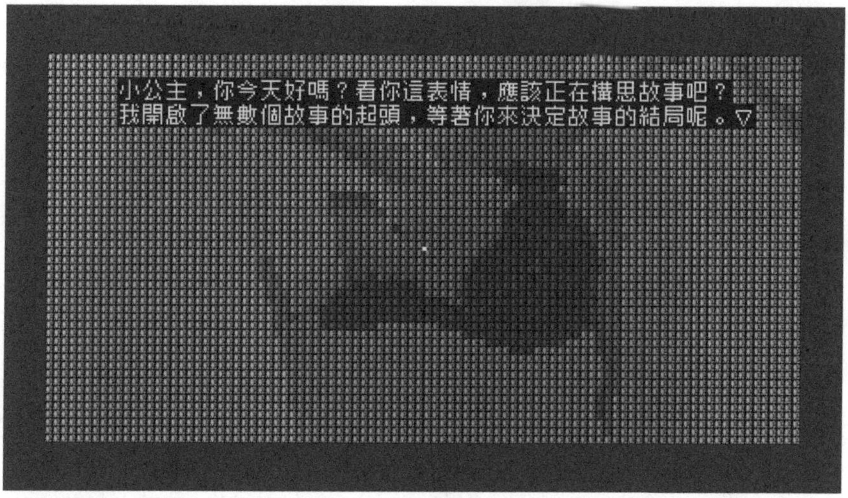

FIGURE 11. The daughter's face. Note the center reticle that marks the transition to three-dimensional space.

者), and then moves from the two-dimensional space of most of the game to the three-dimensional space of the apartment of the man who has written the story of *Word Game*. By examining objects in his living space, the player learns that the author is deeply depressed because his daughter has fallen terminally ill and been placed in a cryogenic coma until the technology to save her can be invented. He writes heroic adventure stories as a way of reliving the happier days of his daughter's childhood but leaves all of them—including *Word Game*—unfinished, as his sadness at the loss of his daughter and guilt over his inability to save her causes him to doubt himself as a writer. The melancholic tone that characterizes this final section and its reframing of the game itself deserve further analysis. For one thing, the presence of doubt and authorial instability recalls key techniques of Taiwanese modernist literature by authors such as Qiu Miaojin 邱妙津 and Zhu Tianxin 朱天心. Another angle might seek to read the father-daughter relationship allegorically as an inversion of the "lost father" trope of post-1949 Taiwanese literature. These types of analysis would implicate (though not be reducible to) the tools of narratology, but neither is directly at issue here. What is more important is how the use of language modifies ongoing debates regarding the boundaries of the Sinophone. In other words, for the present analysis, it is less important that the game ends with an image of the daughter's face than that her "face" is in fact skin-tone colored *cang* 艙 sinographs repeated many times (fig. 11), representing the cryogenic chamber in which she is held.

The study of videogames is beginning to benefit from being repositioned in context other than new media. Visual studies scholar Soraya Murray's recent work has been exemplary in this area. Her 2018 monograph *On Video Games: The Visual Politics of Race, Gender, and Space* asks, "How do games not only powerfully mirror, but also engender, a certain sense of how the world is—as well as the capacities for our relations within it?"[59] This is the right question, and this article has argued that scholarly domains, including Sinophone studies, that focus on literature or film are well-equipped to ask it. Scholars who study only videogames or place videogames in the context of new media may struggle to push past the boundaries of the ludic paradigm. Videogames should be studied in comparative disciplinary contexts beyond new media. A more recent article by Soraya Murray indeed attempts to do this by addressing a situation in which "both games studies and the history of art/visual studies are intellectually uninterested in one another."[60] A similar failure to engage exists at the intersection of videogame studies and literary studies that this article seeks to address by positioning culture as a remedy to ludic myopia. The multilinguistic study of literature positions narrative and language within conversations about the nature of culture and its differential operationalization across the globe. This article's proposal of the digital Sinophone demonstrates that videogames can speak to these questions. The ludic viewpoint severely restricts the potential for such scholarship regarding videogames. A videogame such as *Word Game* demonstrates what is to be gained by jettisoning the ludic viewpoint of videogames in favor of an analysis of how videogames are not only embedded in but also contribute to cultural discourses.

MICHAEL O'KRENT is a PhD candidate in comparative literature at Harvard University. He studies contemporary Chinese-language science fiction.

///////////////////////////////////

Acknowledgments
Many scholars have encouraged me to continue undertaking literary studies of videogames, especially in Harvard University's Department of Comparative Literature. I would like to thank David Damrosch, Verena Conley, Karen Thornber, Stephanie Burt, and Delia Ungureanu for their support, as well as special issue editors David Der-wei Wang and Zhiyi Yang for seeing a place for videogame studies in broader context. I would also like to thank the two anonymous peer reviewers; the overview of videogame studies at the end of the article was completely rewritten after a small comment from one of them made me rethink how to present that history.

Notes
1   Team9, "*Wenzi youxi* guanfang xuanchuan pian."
2   There are seven, rather than eight, because the last mechanic on the list—merging two characters—does not result in a visual cue when it fails. That the two characters stay the same suffices to communicate to the player that they cannot be merged.
3   Team9, "Zeze! Shoukuan quan yi wenzi zucheng de jiemi RPG."
4   Aarseth, "Genre Trouble," 48.
5   As many game commentators have pointed out, the proportion of Steam users who live in mainland China is likely even higher. This is because the available statistics refer only to Steam's *global* platform, which is difficult to impossible to access in the PRC without a VPN

(see Crosali, "What Languages Should I Consider Localizing"). To comply with mainland Chinese censorship laws, Steam offers an alternative PRC-specific platform, whose users are not included in the monthly surveys Steam uses to produce these numbers.

6   Yoccoz, "What Languages to Localize"
7   Clement, "Most Common Main Languages."
8   Crosali, "What Languages Should I Consider Localizing"
9   u/sergeiklimov, "We Sold 30K on Steam in Twelve Languages."
10 Team9, "About."
11 Tsu, *Sound and Script in Chinese Diaspora*, 12.
12 O'Krent, "Welcome."
13 Tsu, *Sound and Script in Chinese Diaspora*, 14.
14 Apter, *Against World Literature*, 20.
15 Yang, "Sinophone Classicism," 2.
16 See Zhong, *Chinese Grammatology*; Bachner, *Beyond Sinology*; Tsu, *Sound and Script in Chinese Diaspora*.
17 See Mullaney, *Chinese Typewriter*.
18 Yang, "Sinophone Classicism," 5.
19 That is, a language that a human programmer is capable of manipulating. A piece of software called the compiler translates high-level programming language into a binary code of zeroes and ones on which computers operate.
20 McPherson, "U.S. Operating Systems at Mid-century," 23–24; see also Philip, Irani, and Dourish, "Postcolonial Computing."
21 Mimiko, "Talking to Machines."
22 Moody, "'Physics' of Notations."
23 Chang, *Playing Nature*, 21–31.
24 Quoted in Chang, *Playing Nature*, 28.
25 All figures are screen captures of the game taken on the author's personal device.
26 Lee, "Spectacles," 104.
27 Ibid., 119.
28 Laguerre, "Digital Diaspora," 50.
29 Shih, *Visuality*, 30.
30 Ibid., 31–32.
31 Team9, "Zeze! Shoukuan quan yi wenzi zucheng de jiemi RPG."
32 First introduced by Hjelmslev, *Essais linguistiques*; first applied to sinographs by French, "Observations on the Chinese Script."
33 Mullaney, *Chinese Typewriter*, 11.
34 The notion of cenemic script is meant to supersede the notions that sinographs are logographic (visually resemble the objects they symbolize—absurd beyond the Oracle Bone script) or ideographic (each character represents one concept—false for many compound characters).
35 Lee, "Spectacles," 104.
36 Li, "Concrete Poetry in China," 37–39. *Gui* 龜, meaning "tortoise," is pronounced the same way as *gui* 歸, meaning "return."
37 Bachner, "Concretely Global," 157.
38 Bachner, *Beyond Sinology*, 133.
39 Ibid., 130.
40 Marney, *Chinese Anagrams and Anagram Verse*, 2.
41 Bachner, "Secrets of Language," 125–26.

42 Ibid., 121.
43 Bachner, *Beyond Sinology*, 164.
44 Tsu, *Sound and Script in Chinese Diaspora*, 14.
45 Team9, "*Wenzi youxi* riwen ban"; my translation.
46 Damrosch, "Scriptworlds"; Park, "Introduction."
47 Casanova, "Consecration and Accumulation," 407.
48 Huizinga, *Homo Ludens*.
49 Jenkins, "Architecture," 118.
50 Kinder, "Medium Specificity," 4.
51 See, e.g., Suter, Bauer, and Kocher, introduction; Kokonis, "Intermediality between Games and Fiction"; Koenitz et al., "Myth of 'Universal' Narrative Models."
52 See, e.g., Murray, "Last Word on Ludology versus Narratology in Game Studies"; Mateas and Stern, "Build It to Understand It."
53 Chang, *Playing Nature*, 24.
54 Fickle, *Race Card*; Kunzelman, *World Is Born from Zero*.
55 Fickle, *Race Card*, 3.
56 Kunzelman, *World Is Born from Zero*, 101.
57 Patterson, *Open World Empire*, 9.
58 Shaw, *Gaming at the Edge*, 2.
59 Murray, *On Video Games*, 2.
60 Murray, "Horizons Already Here," 43.

References

Aarseth, Espen. "Genre Trouble: Narrativism and the Art of Simulation." In *First Person: New Media as Story, Performance, and Game*, edited by Noah Wardrip-Fruin and Pat Harrigan, 45–55. Cambridge, MA: MIT Press, 2004.

Apter, Emily. *Against World Literature: On the Politics of Untranslatability*. London: Verso, 2013.

Bachner, Andrea. *Beyond Sinology: Chinese Writing and the Scripts of Culture*. New York: Columbia University Press, 2014.

——. "Concretely Global: Concrete Poetry against Translation." In *Globalizing Literary Genres: Literature, History, Modernity*, edited by Jernej Habjan and Fabienne Imlinger, 155–68. New York: Routledge, 2016.

——. "The Secrets of Language: Chen Li's Sinographic Anagrams." In *The Oxford Handbook of Modern Chinese Literature*, edited by Andrea Bachner and Carlos Rojas, 112–30. Oxford: Oxford University Press, 2016.

Casanova, Pascale. "Consecration and Accumulation of Literary Capital: Translation as Unequal Exchange." In *The Translation Studies Reader*, 4th ed., edited by Lawrence Venuti, 407–23. New York: Routledge, 2021.

Chang, Alenda Y. *Playing Nature: Ecology in Video Games*. Minneapolis: University of Minnesota Press, 2019.

Clement, J. "Most Common Main Languages of Steam Gaming Platform Users in July 2022." Statista, August 10, 2022. https://www.statista.com/statistics/957319/steam-user-language/ (accessed December 1, 2022).

Crosali, Giorgio. "What Languages Should I Consider Localizing My Steam Game to in 2022?" GameScribes, May 22, 2022. https://www.gamescribes.com/steam-games-popular-languages-localization-2022.

Damrosch, David. "Scriptworlds: Writing Systems and the Formation of World Literature." *Modern Language Quarterly* 68, no. 2 (2007): 195–219.

Fickle, Tara. *The Race Card: From Gaming Technologies to Model Minorities.* New York: New York University Press, 2019.

French, M. A. "Observations on the Chinese Script and the Classification of Writing-Systems." In *Writing without Letters*, edited by William Haas, 101–29. Manchester: Manchester University Press, 1976.

Hjelmslev, Louis. *Essais linguistiques.* Copenhagen: Nordisk Sprog-og Kulturforlag, 1959.

Huizinga, Johan. *Homo Ludens: A Study of the Play-Element in Culture.* London: Routledge & Kegan Paul, 1949.

Jenkins, Henry. "Game Design as Narrative Architecture." In *First Person: New Media as Story, Performance, and Game*, edited by Noah Wardrip-Fruin and Pat Harrigan, 118–30. Cambridge, MA: MIT Press, 2004.

Kinder, Marsha. "Medium Specificity and Productive Precursors: An Introduction." In *Transmedia Frictions: The Digital, the Arts, and the Humanities*, edited by Marsha Kinder and Tara McPherson, 3–19. Oakland: University of California Press, 2014.

Koenitz, Hartmut, Andrea Di Pastena, Dennis Jansen, Brian de Lint, and Amanda Moss. "The Myth of 'Universal' Narrative Models: Expanding the Design Space of Narrative Structures for Interactive Digital Narratives." In Interactive Storytelling: Eleventh International Conference on Interactive Digital Storytelling, ICIDS 2018, Dublin, Ireland, December 5–8, 2018. *Proceedings*, edited by Rebecca Rouse, Hartmut Koenitz, and Mads Haahr, 107–20. Lecture Notes in Computer Science. Cham: Springer, 2018.

Kokonis, Michalis. "Intermediality between Games and Fiction: The 'Ludology vs. Narratology' Debate in Computer Game Studies: A Response to Gonzalo Frasca." *Acta Universitatis Sapientiae, Film and Media Studies* 9, no. 1 (2014): 171–88.

Kunzelman, Cameron. *The World Is Born from Zero: Understanding Speculation and Video Games.* Berlin: De Gruyter Oldenbourg, 2022.

Laguerre, Michel S. "Digital Diaspora: Definition and Models." In *Diasporas in the New Media Age: Identity, Politics, and Community*, edited by Andoni Alonso and Pedro Oiarzabal, 49–64. Reno: University of Nevada Press, 2010.

Lee, Tong King. "Spectacles of the Sinograph in Chinese Literary and Art Productions." *Prism: Theory and Modern Chinese Literature* 19, no. 1 (2022): 102–24.

Li, Li. "Concrete Poetry in China: Form, Content, Theme, and Function." In *The Translation and Transmission of Concrete Poetry*, edited by John Corbett and Ting Huang, 36–55. New York: Routledge, 2020.

Marney, John. *Chinese Anagrams and Anagram Verse.* Taipei: Chinese Materials Center, 1993.

Mateas, Michael, and Andrew Stern. "Build It to Understand It: Ludology Meets Narratology in Game Design Space." In *Worlds in Play: International Perspectives on Digital Games Research*, edited by Suzanne de Castell and Jennifer Jenson, 267–81. New York: Peter Lang, 2007.

McPherson, Tara. "U.S. Operating Systems at Mid-Century: The Intertwining of Race and UNIX." In *Race after the Internet*, edited by Lisa Nakamura and Peter Chow-White, 21–37. London: Routledge, 2012.

Mimiko, Ejilayomi. "Talking to Machines: The Political Ascendance of the English Language in Computer Programming." MA thesis, Simon Fraser University, 2018.

Moody, D. "The 'Physics' of Notations: Toward a Scientific Basis for Constructing Visual Notations in Software Engineering." *IEEE Transactions on Software Engineering* 35, no. 6 (2009): 756–79.

Mullaney, Thomas S. *The Chinese Typewriter: A History.* Cambridge, MA: MIT Press, 2017.

Murray, Janet. "The Last Word on Ludology versus Narratology in Game Studies." Preface to keynote presented at the Digital Games Research Association, Vancouver, June 17, 2005.

Murray, Soraya. "Horizons Already Here: Video Games and Landscape." *Art Journal* 79, no. 2 (2020): 42–49.

———. *On Video Games: The Visual Politics of Race, Gender, and Space*. London: Tauris, 2018.

O'Krent, Michael. "Welcome to the Field: Cultural Capital for Videogames and the Ecofeminist Position-Taking of Horizon Zero Dawn." *Journal of World Literature* 6, no. 3 (2021): 430–48.

Park, Sowon S. "Introduction: Transnational Scriptworlds." *Journal of World Literature* 1, no. 2 (2016): 129–41.

Patterson, Christopher B. *Open World Empire: Race, Erotics, and the Rise of Global Video Games*. New York: New York University Press, 2020.

Philip, Kavita, Lilly Irani, and Paul Dourish. "Postcolonial Computing: A Tactical Survey." *Science, Technology, and Human Values* 37, no. 1 (2012): 3–29.

Shaw, Adrienne. *Gaming at the Edge: Gender at the Margins of Gamer Culture*. Minneapolis: University of Minnesota Press, 2015.

Shih, Shu-mei. *Visuality and Identity: Sinophone Articulations across the Pacific*. Berkeley: University of California Press, 2007.

Suter, Beat, René Bauer, and Mela Kocher. Introduction to *Narrative Mechanics: Strategies and Meanings in Games and Real Life*, edited by Beat Suter, René Bauer, and Mela Kocher, 9–16. Edition Medienwissenschaft 82. Bielefeld, Germany: Transcript, 2021.

Team9. "About." https://team9.co/about/ (accessed December 1, 2022).

———. "*Wenzi youxi*" 文字游戲 [Word Game]. Indienova. Steam. 2022.

———. "*Wenzi youxi* guanfang xuanchuan pian Word Game Official PV" 《文字遊戲》官方宣傳片 [*Word Game* Official Preview Video]. YouTube video, 1:56. November 18, 2020. https://www.youtube.com/watch?v=pBzFgfKJnPI.

———. "*Wenzi youxi* riwen ban diling zhang Teaser" 《文字遊戲》日文版第零章 Teaser [*Word Game* Chapter 0 Japanese Version Teaser]. Facebook video, 1:17, April 27, 2023. https://fb.watch/kDiRQI3SJO/.

———. "Zeze! Shoukuan quan yi wenzi zucheng de jiemi RPG-*Wenzi youxi*" 嘖嘖！首款全以文字組成的解謎 RPG-《文字遊戲》[Wow! The First Puzzle RPG Made Entirely of Written Words—*Word Game*]. Zeczec, November 18, 2018. https://www.zeczec.com/projects/wordgame.

Tsu, Jing. *Sound and Script in Chinese Diaspora*. Cambridge, MA: Harvard University Press, 2010.

u/sergeiklimov. "We Sold 30K on Steam in Twelve Languages, Which Languages Are Used the Most?" R/gamedev. Reddit, 2015. https://www.reddit.com/r/gamedev/comments/4kjaf6/we_sold_30k_on_steam_in_12_languages_which/.

Yang, Zhiyi. "Sinophone Classicism: Chineseness as Temporal and Mnemonic Experience in the Digital Era." *Journal of Asian Studies* 81, no. 4 (2022): 1–15.

Yoccoz, Damien. "What Languages to Localize Your Steam Game Into?" *Level Up Translation* (blog), October 11, 2017. https://www.leveluptranslation.com/single-post/what-languages-to-localize-your-steam-game-into.

Zhong, Yurou. *Chinese Grammatology: Script Revolution and Literary Modernity, 1916–1958*. New York: Columbia University Press, 2019.

YEDONG SH-CHEN

China in the Skin
In Search of a Chinese Video Game

ABSTRACT How do video games tell "the good China story"? In reviewing Chinese official media's months-long criticism of the mobile MOBA game, *Honor of Kings* (*Wangzhe rongyao* 王者榮耀), and the game's rounds of responses in 2017 and 2018, this article investigates a unique digital object that affords storytelling in video games: skin (*pifu* 皮膚). Neither a playable character per se nor a player's avatar, skin constitutes a special digital milieu where China stories are told, debated, and their "goodness" performed. It traverses various composing strata of video games and distributes narrative into a game's mechanics, procedure, representation, playing experience, and more. Skin, the author argues, is a yet-theorized differentiator that anchors "Chineseness" in the world of video gaming. It is a new site in a digital age in which the theoretical problem of Chineseness manifests different kinds of difficulty. The article ends with a discussion of the significance of researching skin to our understanding of what a *Chinese* video game is. The author calls for a new conceptualization of a Chinese video game that accounts for video game's medium specificity. Speaking to scholars of both Chinese studies and digital game studies, this article anticipates more scholarly interest in the intersection of the two fields.

KEYWORDS skin, *Honor of Kings*, China stories, Chinese video games, storytelling and game mechanics

On the morning of March 28, 2017, the *Guangming Daily* (*Guangming ribao* 光明日報) published an article titled "Mobile Games Must Not Overturn History," denouncing the mobile MOBA (multiplayer online battle arena) game *Honor of Kings* (*Wangzhe rongyao* 王者榮耀; Tencent Games, 2015; hereafter *HoK*) for falsifying Chinese history and miseducating the country's youth.[1] The article was soon reposted by the *People's Daily* (*Renmin ribao* 人民日報) on Weibo and went viral across the Chinese internet. As if a fuse were lighted, the Chinese official media over the following months unleashed an avalanche of castigation of *HoK*, with charges mounting daily in even harsher tones. The media crusade culminated in July, when the four most powerful Communist Party mouthpieces—Xinhua News Agency (Xinhuashe 新華社), *People's Daily*, *Guangming Daily*, and *People .cn* (*Renmin wang* 人民網)—churned out eleven broadsides against the game within only ten days. *HoK*, "the target of all arrows" (*zhong shi zhi di* 眾矢之的), as the *People's Daily* put it,[2] was eventually accused of hampering the national endeavor to "tell the good China story."[3]

PRISM: THEORY AND MODERN CHINESE LITERATURE • 20:2 • SEPTEMBER 2023
DOI 10.1215/25783491-10992770 • © 2023 LINGNAN UNIVERSITY

"Tell the good China story." So decreed Xi Jinping 習近平 (b. 1953) in August 2013 at the National Conference on Thought and Propaganda.[4] That year, mainland China had over 490 million video game players, and the number grew another 20 percent to 580 million in 2017.[5] Nearly half the population of the People's Republic of China (PRC) play video games, and almost one-third of them play *HoK*. In 2017, amid massive criticism, *HoK*'s registered users surpassed 200 million. It also became the world's most lucrative mobile game, grossing a yearly revenue of over US$1.9 billion.[6] The game is so popular that at a workshop organized by Tsinghua University and the magazine *Shouhuo* 收穫 (*Harvest*) on the "future of Chinese literature," the novelist Datou Ma 大頭馬 (b. 1989) declared that "the battlefield of contemporary Chinese literature has long relocated. Today's writers are competing with neither Mo Yan [莫言; b. 1955] nor Yu Hua [余華; b. 1960], nor even internet literature, but *Honor of Kings*."[7] Given such popularity, it is only natural that Xi's mandate to "tell the good China story," observed at "every level of Chinese society,"[8] comes to interpellate the realm of video gaming and demand *HoK*'s compliance.

But how do video games tell stories? Where in video games does storytelling happen?[9] If it is intuitive that role-playing games (RPGs) weave narratives as do novels and films, how does a MOBA game like *HoK* tell stories? Have scholars not long concluded that in MOBAs "narrative plays no role in actual gameplay"?[10] On a different note, how do video games tell "China stories"? Where can one locate any China story, good or bad, in video games? If the *problématique* of "tell the good China story" has been broached at the level of language in fiction, of picture in film, and of sound and voice in music, where should we start in the context of video gaming? The answers to these questions, I argue, are hidden in the dramatic series of events that took place around *HoK* in 2017 and 2018, which this article aims to unpack.

If storytelling, as Hannah Arendt argues, conjures up a public realm of the *polis* in which different positions clash and debate,[11] this article claims that video gaming, despite its short history, has become one of the hottest arenas where politics—political negotiations—takes place in mainland China at its most intense. In reviewing the rounds of official criticisms and *HoK*'s responses, I aim to accomplish three tasks in this article. First, I investigate a unique digital object known in video-game parlance as "skin" (*pifu* 皮膚), in which a video game's tangled relations with narrative, aesthetics, capital, and control are enfolded. Second, I show how negotiations about *good* China stories transpire in the digital milieu that skin constitutes. I pay special attention to how *HoK* performs what Zhiyi Yang calls "Sinophone classicism" in this milieu and demonstrate how "goodness" can be a matter of performativity.[12] Last, I discuss the potential of skin as a yet-theorized differentiator that anchors "Chineseness" in the world of video gaming. I end the article with a call for a new conceptualization of a Chinese video game that accounts for the video game's medium specificity.

Concerned with both skin and "China stories," this article also aims at widening the intersection between digital game studies and Chinese studies in the humanities and speak to scholars of both fields. For the former, I propose skin as an understudied subject of research, a unique digital object cutting across different strata of video gaming's complex structure from narrative to mechanics, procedure, playing experience, technology, and representation. For the latter, I pinpoint a new site of storytelling in the digital age in which China stories are told, debated, and performed: skin. In distilling the aesthetic, technological, and political intricacy of skin, I hope to shed light on its basic grammar of storytelling, to encourage more scholarly interests in this crossroads of the two fields and to anticipate more objects of critique found here.

China in the Skin

In November 2015 Tencent Games's subsidiary, TiMi Studio Group (Tianmei gonzuoshi qun 天美工作室群), released the first public version of *HoK*. The mobile MOBA game soon rose to be a smash hit in the domestic market. By the end of 2017 it had amassed over 200 million registered users, including 80 million daily active users (DAU) and 1.8 million new users added daily.[13] In November 2020 TiMi announced that *HoK*'s DAU had surpassed 100 million;[14] and according to Tencent's latest financial report, *HoK* remains the "highest-ranked [game] by total time spent *across the industry*" in 2022 with an estimated DAU of 160 million.[15] Such astonishing popularity comes with incredible capital gains. In 2017 *HoK* became the world's most lucrative mobile game, grossing approximately $1.9 billion in player spending.[16] The number jumped to a stunning $2.8 billion in 2021, making *HoK* the world's first mobile game to reach $10 billion of lifetime revenue.[17] Playing off the game's name, many jokingly call *HoK* "the drug of kings" (*wangzhe nongyao* 王者農藥) or "honor that kills people" (*wangzhe rongyao* 亡者榮耀), given how irresistibly captivating and addictive the game is. In a more positive light, many also agree that *HoK* is China's national game (*guomin youxi* 國民遊戲), as it is an all-time favorite of Chinese players. Proposed by the Chinese government, *HoK* was listed in 2021 as an official medal sport for the Asian Games. If nothing else, *HoK* tells a good story of China's prosperous gaming industry, advancement in mobile technology, rising economic prowess, and cultural ambitions worldwide.

In a round of *HoK*, usually lasting fifteen to twenty minutes, ten players form two teams and compete against each other on a square battlefield. Initially, each team occupies half the field (divided diagonally) and on each half locates a base structure (called a "crystal") in the corner and nine turrets lined radially from the crystal in three rows. Before a game starts, each player picks a "hero" (*yingxiong* 英雄) to control. With distinctive sets of abilities, these heroes attack enemies and assist teammates, aiming to knock down as many enemy structures as possible while protecting their own. The team that first reaches and destroys the opponent's crystal wins the game.

A "free-to-play" game, *HoK* owes most of its commercial success to one paid form of content: skin.[18] Neither a character as such nor a player's avatar, skin is a special digital object composed of three-dimensional modeling, animation, graphics, special visual and sound effects, voice-overs, background stories, and extra statistics for a given hero. If choosing a hero means choosing a predetermined set of statistics (e.g., attack speed, baseline health points, etc.) and abilities (e.g., to heal a teammate), choosing skin determines how the hero and their abilities look, sound, and feel[19] and what stories they can tell in the game. Players make both choices at the same time. A hero cannot exist without skin. A hero in its default status—without paid skin—is referred to as *yuanpi yingxiong* 原皮英雄 (hero in its original skin) in *HoK*. This well testifies that skin is how heroes exist; it is the sine qua non of a hero.

Contrary to popular notions that take skin merely as "cosmetic avatar adjustments" or "alternative appearances," this article argues that skin is a more complicated digital object than just the visual look of a hero.[20] Skin's existence traverses different composing strata of video gaming and constitutes a reticulated digital milieu where data, metadata schemes, representations of data, and the playing subject all connect.[21] In this digital milieu of relations, China stories are generated, told, debated, played, and experienced; and via this space of networks, narrative is transmitted and distributed to all interlinked composing parts of video gaming, including game mechanics, representation, playing experience, and more. To explain what I mean, I will lay out three series of skin as examples to demonstrate how skin exists and tells China stories at different composing strata of *HoK*. The series may intertwine, but they each underscore a different facet of how what Zhiyi Yang calls "Sinophone classicism"—the "appropriation, redeployment, and reconfiguration of cultural memories evoking Chinese aesthetic and intellectual traditions"—operates in *HoK*.[22] For convenience, I use *hero/skin* to mean a hero in its original skin, and *skin* to mean skin in general.

Many of *HoK*'s hero/skins are modeled on renowned figures from Chinese history, mythology, and literary classics.[23] Their looks, quotes (a hero/skin's remarks in the game), and abilities resemble those figures in the popular imagination, and such resemblance is immediately recognizable given these figures' popularity in cultural memory. For example, Daji 妲己, the consort of King Zhou of Shang (Shang zhou wang 商紂王), is a mage in *HoK*. She has vulpine features, particularly a fluffy tail from which she can shoot little pink hearts that "dizzy" her enemies and kill them instantly. An alluring but dangerous woman, Daji the *HoK* mage inherits this image from Chinese folktales and literary classics such as *Investiture of the Gods* (*Fengshen yanyi* 封神演義). Her famous quote—"My tail is not just for tickling"—highlights both her seductiveness and deadly power.

By the same token, Guan Yu 關羽 (d. 220), the Eastern Han general, is a warrior in *HoK*. In accordance with the popular imagination of the historical figure, the hero/skin always rides a horse in the game; he can charge at his enemies and shove them away. Di Renjie 狄仁傑 (630–700), the grand chancellor of Wu Zhou, is a marksman in the game. Dressed just like a Tang official, he uses *lingpai* 令牌 as his weapon, just as officials in dynastic China carried small tablets to signify identity and authority. The popular imagination of Chinese historical, mythological, and literary figures informs the design of hero/skins in the first series. Through such imagination embedded in cultural memory, these heroes' abilities—game mechanics otherwise usually considered unrelated to narrative—are imbued with narratorial meanings.[24]

Hero/skins of the second series hide "China stories" deeper in their design. If not steeped in Chinese classics, one may easily miss the cultural references. Gongsun Li 公孫離, for instance, is a markswoman in *HoK*. No official history has spilled ink on her, yet she can be found between the lines in Du Fu's 杜甫 (712–70) poem, "On Seeing a Student of Mistress Gongsun Dance the 'Sword Dance'" (觀公孫大娘弟子舞劍器行並序). In this poem Du relates his experience of meeting and marveling at a certain Mistress Li (Li shi'er niang 李十二娘) who dances the sword dance. Mistress Li tells Du that she is a student of Mistress Gongsun, whose dance Du once saw as a child and put him in total awe. "Once [Mistress Gongsun] danced the sword dance," Du writes, "she stirred the world around" (一舞劍器動四方); "she came like a peal of thunder withdrawing its rumbling rage, then stopped like clear rays fixed on the river and sea" (來如雷霆收震怒/罷如江海凝青光).[25] What is the name of this Mistress Gongsun? Du does not specify, but *HoK* names her Gongsun Li, and Du's verses become her most frequent in-game quotes. Another example is Zhuang Zhou 莊周 (fl. 4th c. BCE), a support in *HoK*. Referring to "Free and Easy Wandering" (逍遙遊), the hero/skin rides a big fish in the game; and citing "Discussion on Making All Things Equal" (齊物論), his most famous quote goes: "Heaven and earth were born at the same time I was, and the ten thousand things are one with me" (天地與我並生/萬物與我唯一).[26] More interestingly, Zhuang Zhou's passive ability—an ability affecting a hero/skin but not requiring the player's control—is to "naturally enter dreams" every six seconds and rid himself of any debuff (negative effects).[27] This ability embodies the Chinese philosopher's signature ideas such as "forgetting" (*wang* 忘) and "concern-free" (*wuyou* 無憂).[28] Not merely relying on popular imagination, hero/skins in the second series directly reference Chinese classical texts. To the extent players are familiar with these texts, their gaming experience is saturated with different depths of China stories. Like hidden bonuses, these narratives quietly await curious discoverers versed in the classics who bother to make a little effort. Skin in the second series encourages players to go beyond the game text and find the narratives that are hinted at; it tells China stories in this amplified playing experience, prompting players' explorations outside the game.

Besides corresponding one-to-one with classical figures, skin can also meld several stories together and tell them simultaneously. The Two Qiaos—Daqiao 大喬 and Xiaoqiao 小喬—are a salient case in point. In *HoK*, Daqiao is a support who can teleport her teammates, and Xiaoqiao a mage who throws a fan to attack enemies. They are still the loved ones of Sun Ce 孫策 and Zhou Yu 周瑜 as in history, who are themselves hero/skins in the game. Special voice-overs will be triggered when these hero/skins meet or interact. Xiaoqiao will call out Zhou's name when she dies ("Master Zhou Yu . . ."); Sun will say to Daqiao when meeting her, "Please allow me to bring you smiles for the rest of your life."

In March 2020 TiMi released two new skins for the Two Qiaos: "White Snake" and "Green Snake," modeled on none other than Bai Suzhen 白素貞 and Xiaoqing 小青 from the legend of the White Snake.[29] Now the snake sisters become skins of the Qiao sisters, and two narrative worlds blend into each other. When the two Qiao-snake sisters meet each other, special voiceovers like "sisters are bigger than the universe" (天大地大，姐妹最大) will be played—which sisters, one may wonder—and when meeting Zhou or Sun, their dialogues as Two Qiaos remain unchanged. In these moments, the universe of the Three Kingdoms and that of the legend of the White Snake are evoked at the same time. Skin offers a unique space for multiple China stories to wed and merge, and the resulting amalgam comes into being only through this special digital object that connects graphics, sound, narrative, mechanics (e.g., death in game), and players' actions (e.g., to make hero/skins meet) together.

Now we can draw a few conclusions about skin. First, neither a playable character per se nor an alternative look, skin is a complicated digital object that weaves together narrative, mechanics, game procedure, and playing experience. Second, skin affords storytelling; it offers a space, with its capacity and limits,[30] for China stories to be told in *HoK*. Third, via skin, narrative in *HoK* occurs at different composing strata of the game, including texts, graphics, sound, players' in-game interactions, their out-of-game discoveries, and more. These features of skin are key for us to grasp why the denunciations of *HoK* in 2017 and the game's rounds of responses all concentrated on skin, the site where issues about "good" China stories can be and indeed are contested.

Jing Ke Is a Woman

"Jing Ke [荊軻] is a woman, Li Bai [李白] is an assassin, and the renowned physician Bian Que [扁鵲] is a master of poisons. . . . Don't such mismatches shock you?" Spearheading the vehement media crusade against *HoK* in 2017, the *Guangming Daily*'s initial broadside by reporter Zhang Yuling 張玉玲 began with this question. Concerned not with how the game incorporates Chinese history and classics but with the historical discrepancies, Zhang charged that *HoK* falsifies Chinese history and misleads the nation's youth. This was no small matter for Zhang. At stake was whether we were to "forgo historical and cultural traditions," "sever the nation's cultural bloodline," and "cause our cultural development to lose directions and goals." "There should be bottom lines and rules," Zhang quoted a professor of cultural studies and continued: "No matter how we reinterpret history, we must not alter its real looks or change the conclusions we have drawn about it. Nor can we manipulate the national feelings congealed around it. We must not let the value skew or collapse."[31]

Dogmatic as it might seem, Zhang's article sent a ripple effect across China's media sphere and triggered a tsunami wave of public castigation of *HoK*.[32] It also provided the entire media campaign that ensued with two pivotal things: a primary charge and sensational imagery. The primary charge was that *HoK* "overturns history." This accusation was rehashed time and again in the ensuing months until *HoK* was criticized for hindering Xi's national project of telling "the good China story." For example, echoing Zhang, the *People's Daily* berated *HoK* for failing to construct a worldview in accord with "Chinese cultural background and contemporary social commonsense."[33] *People.cn* later condemned *HoK*'s fictional history for "distort[ing] the nation's sense of value," which verged on "murdering lives" (*xianhai rensheng* 陷害人生).[34] The Xinhua News Agency, concerned with *HoK*'s cultural impact worldwide, noted that *HoK* was "deceiving overseas players not familiar with China," and its fabricated history misguided them "at their first contact with Chinese culture."[35] The *Guangming Daily* declared in July 2017 that *HoK*'s problem was germane to whether one could "tell the good China story and promote Chinese culture abroad," an "urgent demand for enhancing our nation's cultural soft power and for winning out in the international competition of comprehensive national power."[36] Now that Xi's decree was invoked, no one could underestimate the gravity of *HoK*'s transgressions. The denunciations reached a crescendo.

Zhang's article also gave other commentators that followed in her shoes a sensational image to target their criticism at: a female Jing Ke. Catchy and polemical, the imagery ran through the entire media campaign like a meme; all the grandiloquent criticisms evoked it to keep their audience titillated and scandalized. In one of its earliest diatribes, the *People's Daily* created a cartoon based on this imagery to illustrate *HoK*'s offense (fig. 1).[37] In what is supposedly a family scene, the father is reading a book titled *Ci Qin* 刺秦 (To Assassinate the Qin Emperor) and is just about to remark on "the guy Jing Ke . . . ," when the boy child, playing a certain "online game" on a computer, corrects him: "It should be the gal Jing Ke." The boy's grandfather, sitting between the two, is shocked. The message is patent, comical but disconcerting: the children of our nation, miseducated by a video game, take Jing Ke for a woman.

FIGURE 1. Cartoon by Xu Pengfei in *People's Daily*, June 20, 2017.

Many a tacit assumption underlies the cartoon. Most salient of all: only men play and care about video games. Schoolboys play them; male adults care. No woman appears in the cartoon to discuss whether Jing Ke can or should be a woman. This is of course a false assumption. In 2017 more than 54 percent of *HoK*'s players were women, and only 3.5 percent of all players were under age fourteen.[38] In reality such conversation would statistically be more likely to occur between a female—old enough to know who Jing Ke is in history already—and her family. The cartoon may have succeeded in causing parents to lose sleep, but it failed to reflect *HoK*'s gender and age demographics.

Also noticeable is that the female hero/skin Jing Ke itself became a focus of criticism. In the article to which the cartoon is appended, the author Sun Jiashan wrote that "the society has not really grasped the daily profounder cultural significance [of online games]," and "this can be seen from *the controversy triggered by Honor of Kings setting Jing Ke as a female character*."[39] Sun boiled the whole issue of *HoK*'s "overturning history" down to the skin's gender transgression, whereas Zhang cited it only as a sensational example (if not an outright clickbait) to grab attention at the beginning of her *Guangming Daily* article.[40] The female hero/skin eventually became a convenient bugbear in the media campaign. *Wenyi Bao* 文藝報 exclaimed that Jing Ke being a female "is the most inconceivable adaptation" in *HoK*,[41] and the Xinhua News Agency cited a schoolboy's essay as evidence of

HoK's crime: "I'd always been knowing Jing Ke as a female, until my teacher told me the truth."[42] The female skin/hero was marked as the most notorious testimony of *HoK*'s outrage of "overturning history." Skin, accordingly, became the battlefield where "good" China stories are fought about.

At a press conference held in April 2017, a director of Tencent's public relations department responded to the series of criticisms by explaining that all *HoK*'s hero/skins were designed through "careful research." The design team knew very well who Jing Ke was, but in *HoK*'s universe, "it is an honorary title passed down in the assassin family Jing, and only the most talented assassin is qualified to inherit the title." "If one does not pay attention," added the director, "they may fail to notice this."[43] Apparently, *HoK* had its own China stories to tell.

Since its beta stage, *HoK* has been creating background stories for each hero/skin. Though short and fragmentary, these stories are parts of "a world system" that "will all connect in the future."[44] Jing Ke in *HoK*'s universe, for example, is a title of honor passed down in the Jing assassin family. After all other family members die in missions, only a brother and a sister are left, and the brother inherits the title first. Different from Sima Qian's 司馬遷 (145–86 BCE) narrative in *Shiji* 史記 (Records of the Grand Historian), in *HoK*'s story it is Fan Wuqi 樊於期 who commissions Jing Ke to assassinate the Qin emperor, while Crown Prince Dan (Taizi Dan 太子丹), jealous of Fan's reputation, commissions Jing Ke to assassinate Fan. Jing, as Fan's friend, rejects the prince's commission, which results in the murder of both him and Fan later by the prince. Now that the brother is dead, the sister needs to inherit the title "Ke"; hence the *HoK* hero/skin, the only assassin alive in the Jing family, hankers both to revenge her brother's death and to finish his incomplete mission of assassinating the Qin emperor. "Perhaps different from the Jing Ke in your memory, it is the same deadly assassin,"[45] so goes the last line of Jing Ke's story in *HoK*.

Now two Jing Ke stories clash. Skin is the site for debates and negotiation. There are many ways to interpret *HoK*'s female Jing Ke. The skin can be simply an example of the gender-bending trend popular in internet literature, animation, comics, and games across the 2010s. Or it can be what Robert A. Rosenstone calls "doing history," that is, a "serious attempt to make meaning of the past" by adapting or rewriting history.[46] (Notably, such practice owes its modern genealogy to the late Qing, when fictional adaptations of history flourished in the most imaginative manners. Particularly in the case of Jing Ke, the ancient assassin's story has inspired radically different responses, interpretations, and adaptations since as early as the Six Dynasties.)[47] There is also potential to interpret the female hero/skin as a feminist critique of male-dominated historical narratives that demands recognition and representation of women in history. But no matter how we interpret the hero/skin, we should acknowledge that skin has become the arena, a yet-claimed regime of truth in the digital age, in which different voices that claim to be true and good vie for the final say over what constitutes goodness.

Journey to a Good China Skin

The 2017 media campaign against *HoK* shook the entire video gaming landscape of the PRC. Appalled, game developers hurriedly X-rayed their own games and sieved out any suspect content. In an instant update, miHoYo (Mihayou 米哈遊) renamed all characters and armor sets related to Chinese history and classics in its then flagship game, *Honkai Impact 3rd* (2016). *Honkai*'s players were notified on the morning of January 2018 that their beloved Li Er (李爾)—a female armor skin (called "stigma" in the game) modeled on Laozi (老子)—was renamed Xiao Yun (蕭雲); Zhuge Kongming (諸葛孔明) became Delisha Guanxing (德麗莎·觀星, Theresa Apocalypse); and Shennong (神農) became Lianshan (連山), whose ability to *chang baicao* 嘗百草 (to try hundreds of herbs, as Shennong does in Chinese mythology) was changed to *fengrang* 豐壤 (to fertilize the earth).[48] In a twinkling, miHoYo rids China stories as if shedding a slough. Tencent, at the center of the storm, also renamed Jing Ke. On April 24, 2017, *HoK* announced that the hero/skin was renamed Ah Ke (阿珂).

Yet more than one name change would be needed to sever *HoK* from its built-in "Sinophone classicism." As I have demonstrated, the game has thickets of relations with Chinese history, mythology, and classical literature enfolded in the digital object skin, which distribute China stories in the game's texts, graphics, sound, mechanics, playing experience, and more. Renaming Jing Ke as Ah Ke, for many, caused nothing but a "cancer of awkwardness" (*ganga ai* 尷尬癌). "All who play know this is Jing Ke," commented one player. "Although the name is changed, we still make the connection."[49] Indeed, skin can be renamed, but what about Daji's vulpine figure? What about the dialogues between the Two Qiaos and their husbands? What about Zhuang Zhou's passive ability that embodies the ancient thinker's philosophy? Are all these to be redone or removed? A skin is not a name. It is a complex digital object that tells China stories through words, pictures, and sounds, evoking cultural memories, encouraging in-game interactions, and inciting out-game explorations. Effacing China stories for *HoK* cannot be as easy as changing a name. A different type of strategy—a different "art of being governed" to use Michael Szonyi's term—is in need.[50]

HoK decided to tell China stories better instead of erasing them. Over the two years following Zhang's initial critique, *HoK* launched projects and programs, parading its effort of good storytelling. In April 2017 *HoK* created a new webpage for each classics-based hero/skin titled "He/She in History" (*Lishishang de TA* 歷史上的 TA). Put next to the original "Hero's Story" (*Yingxiong gushi* 英雄故事), this new page was meant to tell the "real history" of hero/skins.[51] In May the game piloted an online show named "*Honor of Kings* History Lessons" (*Wangzhe lishi ke* 王者歷史課), inviting celebrities and history scholars to "interpret the background stories of historical figures from varied perspectives, and relate historical events in today's words."[52] If these efforts remain, to borrow New Criticism's terminology, extrinsic to the game text, then to intrinsically tell the good China story, *HoK* also strives to make "the good China skin." Key to the mission is to tap into those cultural founts undeniably good and undeniably "Chinese." *HoK* starts with the supreme murals on the stone walls of the Dunhuang Mogao Caves.

On October 28, 2018, *HoK*'s third anniversary, TiMi rolled out "Encounter Apsaras" (*Yujian feitian* 遇見飛天), a new skin for hero Yang Yuhuan 楊玉環. An eponymous song was also released—a collaboration of "the 'national singer' Han Hong [韓紅; b. 1971] and the 'Chinese style' lyricist Fang Wenshan [方文山; b. 1969]."[53] A documentary titled *Two Lives, the Same Perseverance* (两种人生，一种执着), which recorded the process of creating the skin, was later posted online. For the first time in *HoK*'s history, a skin launch became a pageant. An analysis of the documentary, the song, and the skin itself uncovers how, at this event of showy displays, *HoK* performed telling good China stories.

Well-orchestrated, the documentary begins with TiMi's young female art designer, Xu Yanyi, trying to draw a prototype for the new skin based on online pictures of apsaras at her home in Chengdu, "167 days prior to the skin's release." Next it cuts to the middle of a desert where Dunhuang Academy (Dunhuang Yanjiuyuan 敦煌研究院) is located and introduces Han Weimeng, a middle-aged male artist who has been arduously copying murals at the academy for over fifteen years. Back to Chengdu, all five of Xu's initial drafts fail; the color, the clothing, and especially the "feeling" of the apsaras she draws all remain only "on the surface without the real aura of Dunhuang." Then Xu and her team decide to journey west to Dunhuang, to learn from the field and from the masters at the academy. A plethora of shots ensue, showing Xu meticulously practicing mural copying under the instruction of master Han. She keeps drawing, time and again, honing her skills in ritualistic repetition, hoping she can, in Han's words, "reach the air and breath [*qixi* 氣息] of Tang . . . even without looking at what you are drawing." "The copying is a cultivation about faith," Xu later remarks; and people like Han are "cultural ascetics." Eventually, Xu and her team return to Chengdu. They now feel their design work treads on the right course. "After six months of dedicated smithing and thirty-seven versions of repeated drafting in total," reads an intertitle, the skin "is finalized, with authorized affirmation from Dunhuang experts." "Now I understand," concludes Xu, "the so-called cultural inheritance means not merely to inherit the craftsmanship but . . . a perseverant hold [*zhizhuo jianshou* 執著堅守] on our culture."[54]

An apprentice journeys west to learn from a master. The documentary is a bildungsroman as well as a modern *Journey to the West*. Its extravagant display of both Han's and Xu's diligent copying work screams but one message: what matters is not the holy scriptures fetched but the pilgrimage itself. The point is, as Xu discovers, being faithful, perseverant, and—even better still—being an "ascetic" (*kuxing seng* 苦行僧), a monk forever on a bitter journey. Yet the bitter journey can only be a prolonged lingering "before the law." An earnest artist lingers before Chinese culture as such, which is guarded by an authorized doorkeeper (who is himself lingering, even after more than fifteen years of copying and practicing) and which appears only by missing, in the "air and breath," best captured "without looking." Besides the doorkeeper's "authorized affirmation," the documentary never specifies what else Xu attains from the journey. Highlighted instead is "the one who waits for the law, sits before the door of the law, [who] attributes a certain force to the law for which one waits."[55] A "good" China story remains a mystery even where it promises itself. It is conjured and installed by the pilgrim's repeated acts of paying respect, anticipating, journeying, again and again. Such performativity of goodness manifests itself more saliently in the eponymous song, in which Han Hong sings: "To the west we go, a road of thousands of miles . . . my steadfast belief does not change for a thousand years . . . I am faithfully meditating. I am practicing nonstop." And still more pronounced in the hundreds of bullet comments left on the documentary—from different times and spaces, viewers on Bilibili salute the design team in one voice: "*Xinku le!*" 辛苦了, meaning, "You've done your hard work."[56]

The outcome of *HoK*'s bitter journey, "Encounter Apsaras" (fig. 2), is replete with the most minute aesthetic details borrowed from Dunhuang murals, so minute that players can barely see them all, given the size of a cell phone screen and the even smaller hero/skin. Notwithstanding, through a deluge of advertisements and news reports, *HoK* trumpets the following design elements: the shawl of the skin is inspired by women's clothes from the caves numbered 130, 295, and 431 and the hair style from caves 322 and 404; the color of the skin reproduces a particular blue and orange that is mostly used in the Dunhuang murals, exemplified by cave 423; and the skin's weapon, a string-less *pipa*, is specifically designed to embody a mythological trope, *buguziming* 不鼓自鳴 (to sound without being hit), which describes the majesty of heavenly instruments that function on their own—a trope, we are told, murals at cave 321 best depict.[57] No player can see the strings—or the stringless-ness—of the *pipa* in *HoK*, but the game ensures that its strenuous efforts are detailed and known. Telling the good China story for *HoK* is to show the performance, the "bitter journey," of storytelling itself.

"Encounter Apsaras" was well received and broadly acclaimed. On release, it ranked the second most used skin among over two hundred in *HoK*.[58] It was also selected by CCTV and the National Museum of China as an example of cultural-heritage preservation to feature in a documentary titled *2019 China Memory* (*2019 Zhongguo jiyi* 2019中國記憶).[59] If I have demonstrated that skin can be a space both to tell China stories and to debate what is "good," the case of "Encounter

FIGURE 2. "Encounter Apsaras."

Apsaras" shows that skin can also be a stage to perform storytelling itself. In the most ornate and excessive way, *HoK* via skin tells a story no less about Dunhuang and Chinese culture than about itself being able—and obliged—to tell stories and perform good storytelling.[60] The digital object of skin has become a site where China stories and the performance of telling them happen at the same time.

In Search of a Chinese Video Game

At this moment we should discuss why singling out skin as a subject of study is vital to researching Chinese video games. But before that, one pertinent question should be addressed: What is a Chinese video game? Almost fifteen years have passed since the publication of the first major research article in Anglophone academia calling for the study of digital gaming culture in the Asia-Pacific and in China.[61] In that time, game studies has moved away from the ludology-versus-narratology debate and refocused attention on the variations of player experience across races, classes, genders, and locations.[62] And Chinese studies in the humanities has also set out to grapple with the phenomenon of video gaming and its cultural impact. Yet, despite important work on translation and localization, addiction, gender, policy, gold farming, representation, and aesthetics,[63] at the intersection of the two fields, the core question—What is a Chinese video game?—remains unanswered.

In the popular lexicon *Chinese video game* often refers to games made by Chinese companies.[64] A similar term in Chinese is *guochan youxi* 國產遊戲 (domestically made games), used both in the PRC and in Taiwan, emphasizing a game's location of production. This notion binds "Chineseness" with geographic territories and fails to account for the global Sinophone space. It also fails, more importantly, to account for the global circulation of capital and labor that has long disseminated Chinese money and power to the farthest corners of the global video-gaming industry. Mainland China today is one of the world's biggest sources of games investment; it is also one of the largest centers for outsourcing programming. Dig deep enough and one will find that behind almost all the popular games in the world, there are traces of Chinese money, Chinese labor, and code written by Chinese hands.[65] These games are not included in the purview of "domestically made games." Games "made in China," like *Horizon: Zero Dawn* (Guerrilla Games, 2017), are not "domestically made games."

Chinese also indicates Chinese-style or "China wind" (*zhongguo feng* 中國風). The so-called China wind has been blowing through video-game design since at least the mid-1980s, when Konami published the arcade game *Yie Ar Kung-Fu* (*Yi'er gongfu* 一二功夫; 1984). It has then picked up, motivating generations of Chinese developers to create "China's own" games[66] and inspiring developers outside the Sinophone world to articulate their own versions of Chineseness in games. From the Three Kingdoms–themed real-time strategy games to the recently released trailer (June 2023) of *Assassin's Creed Codename Jade* (Ubisoft), the China wind boils Chineseness down to (usually orientalist) aesthetic elements (jade, flute, etc.), adaptable history and historical figures, and at times stereotypical cultural ideas. Certainly breaking away from the limitation of national borders, and perhaps also with a potential to "reflect the great linguistic and cultural variety in different Sinophone communities,"[67] the China wind nonetheless reduces a game to its visual and aural elements, equalizing games to "picture + music," no different from, say, film.

Some may also appeal to language for guaranteeing Chineseness, which soon proves similarly inadequate in the context of video gaming. Deep localization has made it the case that today, major game titles worldwide are released with their on-screen texts, speech recordings, and sometimes even in-game images and thematic elements translated into multiple languages. "Simplified Chinese" and "Traditional Chinese" are but two options among many alternative language settings. To further complicate the matter, games like *Mahjong Soul* (*Quehun* 雀魂; Cat Food Studio, 2018) and *Evony* (Top Games, 2009), though produced in mainland China by Chinese companies, are played almost solely in other countries (*Mahjong Soul* in Japan; *Evony*, the United States) and in other languages. The two games do not even hold a Chinese server. Then we have games like *Novel Containment* (Mike Ren, 2020) and *Journey* (Thatgamecompany, 2012), designed and programmed by people of Chinese ethnicity but with meager or no on-screen text. Language plays a negligible role in the former and is intentionally removed in the latter to create an experience of nonverbal communication. Above all, what is language to video games anyway? The on-screen Chinese script is but outputs of programming languages that govern actions of computing machines and ultimately the on and off switches of electric currents. How easily, if possible at all, can we claim any part of programming languages and machine codes as "Chinese"?

The "theoretical problem" of Chineseness,[68] if hitherto abundantly discussed in scholarship of modern Chinese literature, film, and arts, manifests still different kinds of difficulty when it enters the world of video gaming. Such difficulty, I argue, is precisely where video games' medium specificity lies. The importance of studying skin also resides here. Skin, as I have demonstrated in this article, is a new site in the digital age where Chineseness is anchored and debated, one that takes video games' medium specificity into consideration. As a digital object, skin marks a special digital milieu that connects narrative, mechanics, game procedure, and the player's playing experience. It is in this milieu that China stories are generated, told, played, and experienced. It is in this space that good China stories are debated and negotiated, and their goodness performed. Skin, I emphasize, is a yet-theorized differentiator that anchors Chineseness in the world of video gaming. It points to a new conceptualization of a "Chinese" video game with the medium's vocabulary and grammar in account.

Toward this new conceptualization, this article presents a case study of *HoK* and the China stories it tells or performs telling. In the rounds of criticisms and responses between Chinese official media and *HoK*, we see at least four layers of China stories. The first is Chinese history, mythology, and literary classics that inform the design of *HoK*'s skin. Sinophone classicism operates through skin, imbuing different component parts of video gaming with China stories. The second layer is the authoritatively good version of China stories. The umbrage against the female hero/skin Jing Ke betrays the gender-biased assumptions of these good China stories. Third, Chinese video games are in continuous negotiation with different powers of discipline and control. Skin bears an intimate relationship with regulation and censorship; institutions of punishment are enfolded in its wrinkles. Fourth is the story of goodness as performative acts. Through the case of "Encountering Apsaras," I show how skin not only tells stories but also performs the act of storytelling. *HoK*'s Chineseness reveals itself precisely in these four layers of China stories told through skin.

I shall end my article with another story about skin. On August 12, 2021, the Chinese Academy of History, the nation's official institute for historical research, published a long post on Weibo accusing the mobile game *Hundred Views of Jiangnan* (*Jiangnan baijin tu* 江南百景圖; Coconut Island Games, 2020) of "gaming with history" (*youxi lishi* 遊戲歷史). The charge zeroed in on one specific visual design of the game's hero/skin, Yue Fei 岳飛, who is standing by a sheep, half-naked. To its perplexed audience the academy explained that this skin illustrates a Chinese idiomatic phrase, *rou tan qian yang* 肉坦牽羊 (naked with a sheep), which can be traced back to a ritual of surrender first recorded in *Zuo Zhuan* 左傳. In addition, Yue Fei in the game is a *xianren* 閒人 (idler), meaning that at the level of game mechanics, he only aimlessly wanders on the map, doing nothing else. How can a warrior, a national hero, be linked to a ritual of surrender and just saunter around without doing anything? The academy bristled. Soon after, *Hundred Views of Jiangnan* posted its response: Yu Fei is designed so because he is born in a year of the goat; considering that he has devoted his lifetime to war, the game made him a *xianren*, hoping that he could peacefully live in the small *Jiang-nan* village the game builds. A negotiation about good China stories is again in the offing. Chinese classical texts, authoritatively good China stories, negotiations, and storytelling performance once more clash at the site of skin. As the academy writes in its long post: "Petty is the game; grave is its significance" (遊戲雖小，意義不小).[69] Video games and their skin are and will continue to be the hottest arena where politics takes place in mainland China at its most intense.

YEDONG SH-CHEN is a PhD candidate in East Asian languages and civilizations at Harvard University. His research focuses on media, media technology, and twentieth- and twenty-first-century Chinese media culture. He is now finishing his dissertation project, which traces the genesis and evolution of digital gaming in China and the broader Sinophone world. The dissertation offers not only a succinct historical overview of the transnational techno-cultural phenomenon but also keen insights into the politics of play and pleasure in contemporary China.

Acknowledgments
I thank David Der-wei Wang, Zhiyi Yang, and two anonymous reviewers for their careful reading and insightful comments on earlier drafts of the article. Special thanks to Jerry Shu for all his trust.

Notes
1   Zhang Y., "Shouji youxi buneng dianfu lishi." All translations in this article are mine unless otherwise noted.
2   Zhang H., "Shouji weihe chengle 'dianzi yapian.'"
3   Sun, "Wangluo youxi."
4   Xi Jinping, "Xionghuai daju."
5   See Zhongguo yinshuxie youxi gongwei, "2013 nian zhongguo youxi" and "2017 nian zhongguo youxi."
6   See Jiguang dashuju, "2017 nian 5 yue"; Wang Y., *Zhongguo youxi fengyun*, 531; Super-Data, "2017 Year in Review."
7   Fu, "Xin de wenxue liliang."
8   For a detailed study of the origins and consequences of Xi's national campaign, see D. D. Wang, *Why Fiction Matters*, 1–7.
9   For a structural understanding of digital games, see Juul, *Half-Real*, 23–54. For a survey of what a digital game is, see Heide, Tosca, and Egenfeldt-Nielsen, *Understanding Video Games*, 27–51.
10 Bembeneck, "Game, Narrative, and Storyworld," 44.
11 See Arendt, *Human Condition*, 50–58; and Jackson, *Politics of Storytelling*, 11–36.
12 See Yang, "Sinophone Classicism."

13 See Jiguang dashuju, "2017 nian 5 yue"; Wang, *Zhongguo youxi fengyun*, 531; and Shen, "Wangzhe rongyao qishilu."

14 "Ri huoyue yonghu."

15 Tencent, 2022 *Interim Report*, 6; Jinghaijun, "Rihuo yonghu 1 yi 6000 wan"; emphasis added.

16 SuperData, "2017 Year in Review."

17 Chapple, "Record-Breaking Eight Mobile Games Surpass $1 Billion in Global Player Spending."

18 Widely reported in mid-2017, a skin for hero Zhao Yun 趙雲 made Tencent over $25 million in a single day. See Ciweigongshe, "Yikuan pifu."

19 How skin modifies "game feel" is a crucial question but goes beyond this article's purview. For common players' views on this, see Zhihu discussions such as Limerence, "*Wangzhe rongyao*." For scholarship on "game feel," see Pichlmair and Johansen, "Designing Game Feel"; Swink, *Game Feel*.

20 "Cosmetic avatar adjustments" is from Jarrett, "Gaming the Gift," 103. The view of skin as "alterative appearances" is prevalent in popular discourse. See, for example, the League of Legends Wiki's introduction to "Champion Skin."

21 I borrow this understanding of a digital object from Yuk Hui, who argues that a digital object marks a digital milieu of relations and exists only through these relations. See Hui, *On the Existence of Digital Objects*, 109–49.

22 Yang, "Sinophone Classicism," 2.

23 By the end of 2017, sixty-three out of sixty-six hero/skins in *HoK* were based on Chinese (and Western) historical, mythological, or literary figures. See Xiang, "'Guangong' heyi zhan 'Qin Qiong,'" 119–20.

24 Long suspected of plagiarism, *HoK* borrows many ideas from *League of Legends* (Riot Games, 2009) in designing its heroes' abilities. Daji's ability to "dizzy" others, for instance, is similar to *League of Legends* champion Ahri's abilities. But while Ahri's abilities lack narratorial significance, Daji's are imbued with narrative referencing of Chinese folklore and classics. That is, by the special digital object skin, *HoK* infuses game mechanics with narrative.

25 Stephen Owen's translation in *The Poetry of Du Fu*, 335.

26 Burton Watson's translation in Zhuangzi, *Chuang Tzu*, 38.

27 "Zhuang Zhou."

28 See both "Dasheng" 達生 (Mastering Life) and "Shanxing" 繕性 (Correcting the Nature) in *Zhuangzi* 莊子.

29 For an extensive study of the history and various modern adaptations of the legend, see L. Luo, *Global White Snake*.

30 Meaningful story experience, as Emily Joy Bembeneck argues, does not inform some parts of MOBA games' game play. China stories cannot be held accountable for, say, why Zhuang Zhou is worth 120 golds per death, or why Xiaoqiao has only three abilities but not four. Narrative extends only as far as where skin carries it. Skin *affords* the telling of China stories. See Bembeneck, "Game, Narrative, and Storyworld."

31 Zhang Y., "Shouji youxi buneng dianfu lishi."

32 Besides "overturning history," *HoK* is also indicted for fueling and profiting from game addiction, misusing national intellectual property, lacking moral values, etc. The months-long media campaign caused Chinese video-game companies' stocks to plummet; it also compelled tech giants like Tencent and NetEase to launch various "health systems," both to limit players' (adults included) playing hours and to cap their in-game

spending. *HoK* set up its health system in July 2017. This foreshadowed the nationwide restriction of teenagers' online gaming time introduced by the PRC government in 2021.

33 Sun, "Chanye chenggong."

34 Liguan, "Renmingwang yi ping."

35 Ji, "Youxi lishi."

36 Sun, "Wangluo youxi."

37 Xu, "Manhua."

38 Jiguang dashuju, "2017 wangzhe baogao."

39 Sun, "Chanye chenggong"; emphasis added.

40 Evidence shows that *HoK*'s detractors may know little about the game. One factual error in the cartoon gives such ignorance away: *HoK* is a mobile game and cannot be played on a computer.

41 Li, "'Fanzhuan' de qizhi xingbie."

42 Ji, "Youxi lishi."

43 Youxiputao, "Tengxun shoudu huiying."

44 Liu, "Li Bai he Jing Ke."

45 "Jing Ke."

46 Rosenstone, *History on Film*, 17.

47 For a concise study of this history and how Jing Ke's story gains different meanings in different historical contexts, see Yang, "Memory of an Assassin," 42–49.

48 Benghuai3, "Youxi nei bufen shenghen."

49 17173, "Ganga ai yao fan le!"

50 See Szonyi, *Art of Being Governed*.

51 As of December 2022, no such "real history" has been attached to Ah Ke. TiMi apparently wants to dissociate the female hero/skin from the historical figure.

52 "Wangzhe lishi ke."

53 "Xianhuo qiannian Dunhuang."

54 Wangzherongyao, "Liangzhong rensheng, yizhong zhizhuo."

55 Butler, *Gender Trouble*, xiv. See also Derrida, "Before the Law."

56 Wangzherongyao, "Liangzhong rensheng, yizhong zhizhuo."

57 See website dedicated to this skin: https://pvp.qq.com/cp/a20180906dhtheme/meet .html (accessed October 9, 2022).

58 Luo S., "Xin wen chuang, xin zai na?"

59 "Zhongguo wenhua he ziran."

60 Two more Dunhuang-themed skins were released after "Encounter Apsaras." In July 2021 *HoK* also collaborated with the Three Gorges Museum and the Chongqin Baiheliang Underwater Museum, designing a new skin for Daqiao: "Goddess Baiheliang" (*Baiheliang nüshen* 白鶴梁女神).

61 See Hjorth, "Games@Neo-Regionalism."

62 For a general introduction to the history of digital game studies in the Anglophone world, see Jagoda, "Introduction: American Game Studies."

63 Representative scholarship includes Ng, "Street Fighter"; Golub and Lingley, "'Just like the Qing Empire'"; Lin, "Body, Space, and Gendered Gaming"; Liboriussen et al., "Ban on Gaming Consoles"; Tai and Hu, "Play between Love and Labor"; and Heather, *Games and Gaming in China*.

64 For example, see Chan, "Rise of Prestige Chinese Games."

65 Thomsen, "The Universe Has Been Outsourced."

66 One such example is Yao Zhuangxian 姚壯憲 (b. 1969), producer of *Legend of Sword and Fairy* (*Xianjian qixia zhuan* 仙劍奇俠傳; Softstar 1995). See Feng, "Yao Zhuangxian Atuzai."

67 Yang, "Sinophone Classicism," 8.

68 Chow, "Introduction: On Chineseness."

69 Zhongguo lishi yanjiuyuan, "Yue Fei 'rou tan qian yang.'"

References

17173. "Ganga ai yao fan le! *Wangzhe rongyao* jieshou piping Jing Ke gaiming A Ke" 尷尬癌要犯了！王者榮耀接受批評 荊軻改名阿珂 [Oh My Cancer of Awkwardness! *Honor of Kings* Accepts Criticisms and Renames Jing Ke Ah Ke]. *Sohu*, April 19, 2017. https://sports.sohu.com/20170419/n489410504.shtml.

Arendt, Hannah. *The Human Condition*. 2nd ed. Chicago: University of Chicago Press, 1998.

Bembeneck, Emily Joy. "Game, Narrative and Storyworld in League of Legends." In *The Play versus Story Divide in Game Studies: Critical Essays*, edited by Matthew Kapell, 41–56. Jefferson, NC: McFarland, 2016.

Benghuai3 崩壞3. "Youxi nei bufen shenghen mincheng tiaozheng shuoming" 遊戲內部分聖痕名稱調整說明 [Notes on Adjusting Some Stigmas' Names]. *Sohu*, January 5, 2018. https://www.sohu.com/a/218973354_632941.

Butler, Judith. *Gender Trouble: Feminism and the Subversion of Identity*. New York: Routledge, 2006.

CCTV. "Zhongguo wenhua he ziran yichan ri tebie Jiemu '2019 zhongguo jiyi'" 中國文化和自然遺產日特別節目「2019中國記憶」 [A Special Program for China's Cultural Heritage Day: "2019 China Memory"], June 4, 2019. tv.cctv.com/2019/06/04/ARTI5g6iFE12x L3xCJXCz7yG190604.shtml.

Chan, Khee Hoon. "The Rise of Prestige Chinese Games." *Polygon*, February 19, 2022. https://www.polygon.com/22893265/china-aaa-indie-video-games-genshin-impact-dyson-sphere-program.

Chapple, Craig. "Record-Breaking Eight Mobile Games Surpass $1 Billion in Global Player Spending during 2021." Sensor Tower, December 2021. https://sensortower.com/blog/billion-dollar-mobile-games-2021.

Chow, Rey. "Introduction: On Chineseness as a Theoretical Problem." *boundary 2* 25, no. 3 (1998): 1–24.

Ciweigongshe 刺猬公社. "Yikuan pifu yitian maichu 1.5 yi yuan" 一款皮膚一天賣出1.5億元 [A Skin Makes Over $25 Million a Day]. *Sina*, May 12, 2017. https://k.sina.cn/article_522 4196989_13762eb7d0190037g7.html.

Derrida, Jacques. "Before the Law." In *Acts of Literature*, edited by Derek Attridge, 181–220. New York: Routledge, 1992.

"Di Renjie" 狄仁傑.. Tencent Games. https://pvp.qq.com/web201605/herodetail/133.shtml (accessed October 9, 2022).

Du Fu. *The Poetry of Du Fu*. Translated and edited by Stephen Owen. Boston: De Gruyter, 2015.

Feng Yinjie 馮寅傑. "Yao Zhuangxian Atuzai de maoxian lücheng" 姚壯憲 阿土仔的冒險旅程 [Yao Zhuangxian, the Journey of a Atuzai]. *Nanfang renwu zhoukan* 南方人物周刊 [Southern People Weekly], no. 25 (2014): 84–87.

Fu Xiaoyue 付小悅. "Xin de wenxue liliang zhengzai qiaoran chengzhang" 新的文學力量正在悄然成長 [New Power of Literature Is Growing Quietly]. *Guangming ribao* 光明日報 [Guangming Daily], July 30, 2018.

Golub, Alex, and Kate Lingley. "'Just like the Qing Empire': Internet Addiction, MMOGs, and Moral Crisis in Contemporary China." *Games and Culture* 3, no. 1 (2008): 59–75.

Heather, Inwood, ed. *The British Journal of Chinese Studies: Games and Gaming in China and the Sinophone World* 12, no. 2: (2022).

Hjorth, Larissa. "Games@Neo-Regionalism: Locating Gaming in the Asia-Pacific." *Games and Culture* 3, no. 1 (2008): 3–12.

Hui, Yuk. *On the Existence of Digital Objects.* Minneapolis: University of Minnesota Press, 2016.

Jackson, Michael. *The Politics of Storytelling: Violence, Transgression, and Intersubjectivity.* Copenhagen: Museum Tusculanum, 2002.

Jagoda, Patrick, and Jennifer Malkowski. "Introduction: American Game Studies." *American Literature* 94, no. 1 (2022): 1–16.

Jarrett, Josh. "Gaming the Gift: The Affective Economy of League of Legends 'Fair' Free-to-Play Model." *Journal of Consumer Culture* 21, no. 1 (2021): 102–19.

Ji Xiaobo 季小波. "Shouyou bugai 'youxi' lishi" 手游不該 "遊戲 "歷史 [Mobile Games Should Not "Game" with History]. *Xinhua wang* 新華網 [Xinhua Net], July 10, 2017. http://www.xinhuanet.com//politics/2017-07/10/c_1121292493.htm.

Jiguang dashuju 極光大數據 [Aurora Mobile]. "2017 nian 5 yue wangzhe rongyao yanjiu baogao" 2017年5月王者榮耀研究報告 [Research Report of Honor of Kings in May 2017], June 2017.

"Jing Ke" 荊軻. Tencent Games. https://pvp.qq.com/web201510/hero-mod/jingke.shtml (accessed October 9, 2022).

Jinghaijun 靜海君. "Rihuo yonghu 1 yi 6000 wan, *Wangzhe rongyao* 6 yue jiaochu manyi dajuan" 日活用戶1億6000萬，王者榮耀6月交出滿意答卷 [DAU 160 Million, *Honor of Kings* Has a Satisfactory Report]. *Tengxun shouyou zhushou* 騰訊手游助手 [Tencent Mobile Game Helper], July 11, 2022. https://syzs.qq.com/blog/news /20220711A0CDTL00.

Juul, Jesper. *Half-Real: Video Games between Real Rules and Fictional Worlds.* Cambridge, MA: MIT Press, 2005.

League of Legends Wiki. "Champion Skin." Fandom. https://leagueoflegends.fandom.com /wiki/Champion_skin (accessed October 8, 2022).

Li Huichuan 李匯川. "'Fanzhuan' de qizhi shi xingbie?—Cong *Wangzhe rongyao* li de 'nv Jing Ke' tanqi" "翻轉" 的豈止是性別？——從「王者榮耀」裡的 "女荊軻" 談起 [Overturned Is Not Only the Gender: Female Jing Ke in *Honor of Kings* and More]. Zhongguo zuojia wang 中國作家網 [Website of Chinese Writers]. http://www .chinawriter.com.cn/n1/2017/0721/c405176-29418993.html (accessed October 9, 2022).

Liguan 理觀. "Renminwang yi ping *Wangzhe rongyao*: Shi yule dazhong haishi 'xianhai' rensheng" 人民網一評「王者榮耀」：是娛樂大眾還是 "陷害" 人生 [People.cn's First Opinion on *Honor of Kings*: Entertaining the Masses or Murdering Lives]. *Renmin wang* 人民網 [People.cn], July 3, 2017. http://opinion.people.com.cn/BIG5/n1/2017/0703/c1003 -29379751.html.

Limerence. "*Wangzhe rongyao* limian de pifu zhende cunzai shougan chayi ma?" 王者荣耀里面的皮肤真的存在手感差异吗? [Is There Really a Difference between Skins in *Honor of Kings*?]. *Zhihu*, August 9, 2020. https://www.zhihu.com/question/413103016.

Lin, Holin. "Body, Space, and Gendered Gaming Experiences: A Cultural Geography of Homes, Cybercafes, and Dormitories." In *Beyond Barbie and Mortal Kombat: New Perspectives on Gender and Gaming*, edited by Yasmin B. Kafai, Carrie Heeter, Jill Denner, and Jennifer Y. Sun, 54–67. Cambridge, MA: MIT Press, 2008.

Liu Shengjun 劉勝軍. "Li Bai he Jing Ke tongchang jingji de beihou, Wangzhe weihe zheme zaihu shijieguan?" 李白和荊軻同場競技的背後，王者榮耀為何這麼在乎世界觀? [Behind the Stage Where Li Bai Competes with Jing Ke, Why Does *Honor of Kings* Care So Much about Its World?]. *Donews*, May 10, 2017. https://www.donews.com/news/detail/3/2952687.html.

Luo, Liang. *The Global White Snake*. Ann Arbor: University of Michigan Press, 2021.

Luo Shixian 羅施賢. "Xin wen chuang, xin zai na? Chuang shenme? Ruhe chuang?" 新文創，新在哪？創什麼？如何創? [Neo-culture Creativity, What's New? What's to Create? How?]. Tencent Institute of Games. https://gameinstitute.qq.com/course/detail/10194 (accessed October 9, 2022).

Ng, Benjamin Wai-ming. "Street Fighter and the King of Fighters in Hong Kong: A Study of Cultural Consumption and Localization of Japanese Games in an Asian Context." *Game Studies* 6, no. 1 (2006). http://gamestudies.org/0601/articles/ng.

Pichlmair, Martin, and Mads Johansen. "Designing Game Feel: A Survey." *IEEE Transactions on Games* 14, no. 2 (2022): 138–52.

Rosenstone, Robert A. *History on Film/Film on History*. Harlow, UK: Longman/Pearson, 2006.

Shen Xing 申星. "*Wangzhe* rongyao qishilu" 王者榮耀啟示錄 [*Honor of Kings* Revelation]. *Qiye yanjiu* 企業研究 [*Business Research*], July 2017, 24–25.

Smith, Jonas Heide, Susana Pajares Tosca, and Simon Egenfeldt-Nielsen. *Understanding Video Games: The Essential Introduction*. 2nd ed. New York: Routledge, 2013.

Sun Jiashan 孫佳山. "Ba chanye chenggong zhuanhua wei wenhua chenggong" 把產業成功轉化為文化成功 [On Transforming the Industrial Success to a Cultural One]. *Remin ribao* 人民日報 [*People's Daily*], June 20, 2017.

———. "Wangluo youxi: Haowan gengyao you dandang" 網絡遊戲:好玩更要有擔當 [Online Games: Fun but Need to Be Responsible]. *Guangming ribao* 光明日報 [*Guangming Daily*], July 13, 2017.

SuperData. "2017 Year in Review: Digital Games and Interactive Media." SuperData Research Holdings, 2018.

Swink, Steve. *Game Feel: A Game Designer's Guide to Virtual Sensation*. Boston: Morgan Kaufman/Elsevier, 2009.

Szonyi, Michael. *The Art of Being Governed: Everyday Politics in Late Imperial China*. Princeton, NJ: Princeton University Press, 2017.

Tai, Zixue, and Fengbin Hu. "Play between Love and Labor: The Practice of Gold Farming in China." *New Media and Society* 20, no. 7 (2018): 2370–90.

Tencent Holdings Lid. "2022 Interim Report." Hong Kong, August 2022.

Thomsen, Michael. "The Universe Has Been Outsourced." *The Outline*, February 6, 2018. https://theoutline.com/post/3087/outsourcing-blockbuster-video-games-made-in-china-horizon-zero-dawn.

Wang, David Der-wei. *Why Fiction Matters in Contemporary China*. Waltham, MA: Brandeis University Press, 2020.

Wang Yahui 王亞暉. *Zhongguo youxi fengyun* 中國遊戲風雲 [History of Chinese Games]. Beijing: Zhongguo fazhan chubanshe, 2018.

Wangzherongyao 王者榮耀. "Liangzhong rensheng, yizhong zhizhuo" 兩種人生，一種執著 [Two Lives, the Same Perseverance]. Bilibili video, September 20, 2018. https://www.bilibili.com/video/BV1ZW41167MA/.

———. "Ri huoyue yonghu 1 yi! *Wangzhe rongyao* ganxie meiyige bukehuoque de ni!" 日活躍用戶日均1億！王者榮耀感謝每一個不可或缺的你! [DAU Over 100 Million! *Honor*

of Kings Thanks Each and Every One of You!], November 1, 2020. https://pvp.qq.com/m
/m201606/newCont.shtml?newCont.shtml?G_Biz=18&tid=488335.

———. "Xianhuo qiannian Dunhuang wenhua fuhao" 鮮活千年敦煌文化符號 [Enlivening
the Thousands-Year-Old Dunhuang's Cultural Signs], September 27, 2018. https://pvp
.qq.com/webplat/info/news_version3/15592/24091/24092/24094/m15241/201809/763057
.shtml.

———. "*Wangzhe* lishi ke daini huange zishi xue lishi" 王者歷史課 帶你換個姿勢學歷史
[*Honor of* Kings History Lessons Guide You to Learn History in a Different Way].
May 10, 2017. http://pvp.qq.com/webplat/info/news_version3/15592/24091/24092/24094
/m15241/201705/582861.shtml.

Xi Jinping. "*Xi Jinping*: Xionghuai daju bawo dashi zhuoyan dashi ba xuanchuan sixiang
gongzuo zuo genghao" 習近平：胸懷大局把握大勢著眼大事把宣傳思想工作做更好.
Xi Jinping zhongyao jianghua shujuku 習近平重要講話數據庫 [Database of Important
Talks by Xi Jinping]. *People.cn*, August 20, 2013. http://jhsjk.people.cn/article/22634049.

Xiang Lei 項蕾. "'Guangong' heyi zhan 'Qin Qiong': Cong yingxiong zhaohuan lei dianzi youxi
shuoqi" "關公" 何以戰 "秦瓊"：從英雄召喚類電子遊戲說起 [How Do Guangong
Fight with Qin Qiong: On Digital Games of the Hero-Summoning Genre]. *Wenyi lilun yu
piping* 文藝理論與批評 [Literary Theory and Criticism], no. 1 (2018): 117–25.

Xu Pengfei 徐鵬飛. "Manhua" 漫畫 [Cartoon]. *Remin ribao* 人民日報 [People's Daily], June
20, 2017.

Yang, Zhiyi. "The Memory of an Assassin and Problems of Legitimacy in the Wang Jingwei
Regime (1940–1945)." *Harvard Journal of Asiatic Studies* 80, no. 1 (2020): 37–83.

———. "Sinophone Classicism: Chineseness as Temporal and Mnemonic Experience in the
Digital Era." *Journal of Asian Studies* 81, no. 4 (2022): 1–15.

Youxiputao 遊戲葡萄. "Tengxun shoudu huiying Wangzhe rongyao waiqu lishi" 騰訊首度
回應「王者榮耀」歪曲歷史 [Tencent's First Response to HoK Overturning History].
Sohu, April 14, 2017. www.sohu.com/a/ 134068569_204824.

Zhang He 張賀. "Shouji weihe chengle 'dianzi yapian'" 手機為何成了 "電子鴉片" [Why
Have Mobile Phones Become "Digital Opium"?]. *Remin ribao* 人民日報 [People's
Daily], July 13, 2017.

Zhang Yuling 張玉玲. "Shouji youxi buneng dianfu lishi" 手機遊戲不能顛覆歷史 [Mobile
Games Must Not Overturn History]. *Guangming ribao* 光明日報 [Guangming Daily],
March 28, 2017.

Zhongguo lishi yanjiuyuan 中國歷史研究院. "Yue Fei 'rou tan qian yang'? Lishi buneng
'youxi'!" 岳飛 "肉坦牽羊" ？ 歷史不能 "遊戲" ！[Yue Fei Naked with a Sheep? History Cannot Be Gamed With]. *Weibo*, August 12, 2021.

Zhongguo yinshuxie youxi gongwei 中國音數協遊戲工委 [China Game Publishers Association Publications Committee]. "2013 nian zhongguo youxi chanye baogao" 2013年中國
遊戲產業報告 [2013 China Gaming Industry Report]. Youxi chanye wang 遊戲產業網
[China Game Industry Group Committee], August 18, 2022. www.cgigc.com.cn/details
.html?id=08da80fe-8383-4b5c-8ba0-bb5d5ff5ea71&tp=report.

———. "2017 nian zhongguo youxi chanye baogao" 2017年中國遊戲產業報告 [2017 China
Gaming Industry Report]. Youxi chanye wang, August 18, 2022. www.cgigc.com.cn
/details.html?id=08da8101-103c-4af9-8476-34f09cac2da0&tp=report.

"Zhuang Zhou" 莊周. Tencent Games. pvp.qq.com/web201605/herodetail/113.shtml
(accessed October 8, 2022).

Zhuangzi. *Chuang Tzu: Basic Writings*. Translated by Burton Watson. New York: Columbia
University Press, 1996.

MICHELLE YEH

Classicist Drama in Digital Times
Reimagining the Past in Chinese Cyberspace

ABSTRACT This article begins with an overview of the rise of internet drama, or web drama, in China in the past fifteen years. The new platform boasts several advantages, which accounts for its rapid development. Web drama has become so popular that it is replacing television drama series as the mainstream. The article then examines a major genre of web drama: stories set in traditional China. While costume drama or period drama, whether based on history or fiction, has always been popular, classicist web drama series in recent years stand out for their authenticity and creativity. Based on two case studies, the article explores two distinct themes. The first is *Royal Nirvana* (2019), a pseudo-historical drama that integrates Song-dynasty culture into the plot. In doing so, it beautifully demonstrates the appeal of "Chinese style" or "Asian aesthetics" in popular imagination. The second case study is *The Untamed* (2019), a fantasy martial arts tale that features two male protagonists who start out as diametrically opposed but end up as soul mates and loyal allies. The drama series skillfully transforms *danmei* or BL (boys' love) in the original story into a subtly titillating relationship between two men. The article concludes with a discussion of the new business model that web drama has successfully introduced into the entertainment industry in contemporary China.

KEYWORDS web drama, *Royal Nirvana*, *The Untamed*, Chinese style, *danmei*

This article studies the cultural form of classicist drama series on the internet in recent years. Classicist web drama refers to stories set in traditional China and overlaps with such subgenres as historical drama, period drama, and costume drama. Many television drama series in contemporary China are adaptations of classic novels (e.g., *The Water Margin* and *Journey to the West*), historically based contemporary fiction (e.g., the trilogy on the Qing Emperors Kangxi, Yongzheng, and Qianlong by Eryue He 二月河), and canonical martial arts sagas (e.g., works of Jin Yong 金庸). This is especially true from the 1980s to the early 2000s. In recent years, classicist drama tends to rely less on classics (whether traditional or modern) but more often than not is based on original stories by a younger generation of web writers. The phenomenon is inseparable from the fact that the internet is playing an increasingly significant role in cultural production in China today. The symbiosis of web fiction and web drama goes beyond the relation between original stories and television adaptations. In fact, it has given rise to a new business model. Through

PRISM: THEORY AND MODERN CHINESE LITERATURE • 20:2 • SEPTEMBER 2023
DOI 10.1215/25783491-10992780 • © 2023 LINGNAN UNIVERSITY

the two case studies, this article aims to highlight two distinctive cultural trends in contemporary China. *Royal Nirvana* (鶴唳華亭) illustrates the ever-popular "Chinese style" (中國風) or "Asian aesthetics" (東方美學), whereas *The Untamed* (陳情令) embodies the equally popular but more precarious *danmei* 耽美 (literally, "obsession with beauty") or BL (boys' love) phenomenon.

In what follows, I will first give a brief overview of the rise of web drama and then offer two in-depth analyses of two highly successful classicist drama series from 2019.

Web Drama in the Twenty-First Century

Since the 1990s, the internet has transformed the culture and society of mainland China. Most studies thus far have focused on the development and impact of internet literature. In the first English-language study of web fiction in China, Jin Feng examines web romances that are mostly written by female authors and read by female fans.[1] From a perspective that is broader in scope, Heather Inwood discusses the production and reception of contemporary poetry in new media spaces, including the internet.[2] The most comprehensive study of internet literature comes from Michel Hockx. In his overview of internet literature, he defines various genres—fiction, poetry, and nonfiction prose—as original writings, thus excluding digital reproductions of printed works.[3]

These and other studies of web literature have created a new subfield of literary and cultural studies of contemporary China.[4] It offers a valuable point of departure for understanding internet drama or web drama (網絡劇, 網劇), which originated in China in 2007. Whereas, prior to that, drama series were aired first on television and then made available online, web drama series are only available online. Despite its shorter history than web literature, web drama shares similar advantages and challenges, which I summarize below.

Lower Costs

Web drama costs less in production. This is especially true in the early years of its development; the investment in a drama series could be anywhere from under a million to ten million renimbi. On average, the cost of web series is one-fifth to one-third of television drama series. One reason for the low production cost is that, instead of casting much sought-after A-line or even B-line stars, production companies would hold open auditions, and young actors and actresses would be given opportunities to play roles that they might not be able to get in television drama or film. This is eminently true of the second case study in the article. The two protagonists of *The Untamed*, Xiao Zhan 肖戰 and Wang Yibo 王一博, had a modest reputation prior to the airing of the web drama: the first as a singer and member of the boy band X Nine (X玖); the other as a hip hop dancer, singer, and cohost of the popular show *Day Day Up* (天天向上) on Hunan TV

(湖南衛視). Although both men had had some prior acting experience, it was *The Untamed* that catapulted them to fame overnight and made them the top idols that they are today.

Web drama costs less not only in production but also in promotion. Both *The Untamed*, which premiered on June 27, 2019, and *Royal Nirvana*, on November 12 of the same year, did little promotion prior to their launch online. The situation has changed somewhat as the ecosystem of the entertainment industry has evolved in recent years. As web drama becomes more and more popular and profitable, understandably, production costs go up because increasingly it features A-line stars. While cost may not factor in as much as it used to, web drama still has other advantages.

24/7 Access

Wherever and whenever Wi-Fi is available, viewers can watch web drama on multiple devices and around the clock. This is an enormous advantage over television drama. One no longer needs to follow a program schedule or record a show for later viewing. The market-driven notion of "prime time" is rendered obsolete. Moreover, unlike television drama, web drama series can accumulate astronomical numbers of viewings in a narrow time frame. *The Untamed*, for example, first aired in June 2019; by April 2020, ten months later, it had been viewed almost an astounding 8 billion times. Around-the-clock availability also gives the production company more flexibility in airing a web drama series. Instead of airing as single weekly episodes, *Royal Nirvana* once showed five episodes in a single day.

Artistic Freedom

Besides 24/7 access, web drama enjoys a greater degree of creative freedom in subject matter. As we know, movies and television drama are subject to state censorship. Under the current name, the National Radio and Television Administration (NRTA, 國家廣播電視總局) reviews and preapproves scripts before they can go into production.[5] It is not uncommon for extensive changes to be made before a work can pass censorship. At least in the early years of its development, web drama evaded the scrutiny of the NRTA and was free to deal with some taboo subjects, such as horror, supernatural elements, and, most notably, *danmei*. The web movie *Like Love* (類似愛情) in 2014 and the drama series *Counter-Attack* (逆襲之愛上情敵) in 2015 are two early examples of *danmei*. *Addiction* (上癮) depicts homosexual love between two high school students played by the novices Huang Jingyu 黃景瑜 and Xu Weizhou 許魏洲 (fig. 1). Its first episode, aired on January 29, 2016, attracted more than 10 million hits, which broke the record for web drama. However, the phenomenal success also caught the attention of the NRTA. The drama series was abruptly taken off the internet on February 22 of the same year, after fifteen episodes. To this day, viewers have no idea how the story will end.

FIGURE 1. *Addiction.*

In recent years, the authorities have stepped up censorship of web-based entertainment. As early as 2014, the Cyberspace Administration of China (國家互聯網信息辦公室) was established. In February 2016 the NRTA proclaimed that "what cannot be aired on television cannot be aired on the internet either." More than a year later, on June 1, 2017, the NRTA announced their "Notice of Further Reinforcing the Management of Internet Audiovisual Program Creations and Broadcasts" (關於進一步加強網絡視聽節目創作播出管理的通知), which was followed, on June 30 of the same year, by the passing of the "General Regulations for Auditing Internet Audiovisual Program Contents" (網絡視聽節目內容審核通則).[6] The tightening of regulation took place alongside the launch of the "Clear Action" (清朗行動) campaign in 2016. The campaign is ongoing and shows no sign of letting up. One consequence of the above measures is that *danmei* web drama, best represented by *The Untamed*, is no longer possible in the foreseeable future.

Interactive Mode

Understandably, the 24/7 access and the relative diversity of subject matter appeal especially to young people, who are savvy users of digital technology. Young viewers are also more likely to make comments—in real time and off-the-cuff—through the "bullet screen" (彈幕) feature as they watch the show.[7] Thus the screen becomes an instantaneous communicative space and creates a virtual community among the viewers. In comparison, it is much slower for television drama to receive viewer responses by traditional means, such as letters, phone calls, and published reviews. The virtual community that revolves around a web drama facilitates the formation of fandom through shared identity. Instead of passive viewers, these fans play a much more active role; in some cases, their opinions even influence plot development of a drama series. For example, during the shooting of *The Untamed*, the leading female roles were given extra scenes. As a result of protests from the fans, those scenes were deleted. This may be seen as another example of the "affective alliance" that Shuyu Kong talks about in her study of web drama.[8] Another article posted on a Chinese website describes the interactive mode of viewer participation as a deconstructive "carnival."[9]

Global Reach

There is no denying that Chinese film and television drama reach beyond the Chinese-speaking world. However, there is inevitably a considerable time lag between the domestic launch and international exposure, and global circulation is premised on success in the domestic market. In other words, a big hit in China may eventually lead to distributions in other countries. In contrast, web drama has the option of being aired domestically and internationally at the same time. This is true of both web drama series under study. *The Untamed* claimed to be the first web drama to be launched in and outside China simultaneously. As a matter of fact, its initial circulation was limited to Southeast Asia (i.e., Thailand and Indonesia) and North America, but later it was aired in many other countries. In comparison, *Royal Nirvana* was truly global. Produced by Tencent, the drama series was launched in 240 countries simultaneously.[10] This is clearly a major advantage over traditional television drama.

Symbiosis of Digital Literature and Web Drama

As mentioned in the opening section, it is a long-standing practice for film and television drama to be adapted from fiction, and the same is true of web drama. However, there is a subtle difference. Typically, the original story on which a web drama is based has already enjoyed considerable popularity on the internet. In other words, it has a large fan base. Harking back to the advantage of saving on promotion costs, the fan base of web fiction provides built-in viewers for the dramatic adaptation, with or without any promotion. This is true of both case studies. It may seem similar to a scenario in which a film or television drama is based on a literary classic; but when we consider the shrinking market share of literature and the increasing marginalization of literature in school curricula today, it is usually the other way around: a successful film or television adaptation draws some viewers to the literary sources, not the other way around. The reverse is true for web drama. Both *The Untamed* and *Royal Nirvana* attracted viewers initially because the web novels had been enormously successful.

The success of web drama is the result of a combination of the advantages outlined above. Its rapid growth is supported by statistics. In 2007 there were fewer than thirty drama series. From 2007 to 2014, there were 374 in total, and 2015 alone saw the airing of 152 drama series. In subsequent years, the numbers have trended upward, hovering around 230 each year. For example, there were 268 drama series in 2020, and 266 in 2021.[11] Not surprisingly, popularity equals profitability. In the past few years, we have seen an enormous influx of capital into web drama. It has attracted the biggest names in digital technology and entertainment, including Tencent (騰訊), Youku (優酷, a subsidiary of the conglomerate Alibaba [阿里巴巴]), iQiyi (愛奇藝, a subsidiary of Baidu [百度]), Mango TV (芒果TV), and Billibilli (嗶哩嗶哩). Each of these companies has created a business chain that manages the production, promotion, and distribution of web drama.

Profit is not the only measure of success. As web drama goes mainstream, it has increasingly received recognition from the establishment in the entertainment industry. In 2020 the three major national awards for television—Golden Eagle (金鷹獎), Magnolia (白玉蘭獎), and Flying Apsaras (飛天獎)—all included web drama in their nominations for the first time. And this has become the norm since.

Case Study 1: *Royal Nirvana*

The first classicist web drama under analysis is *Royal Nirvana* (fig. 2). The drama series is based on a highly successful story on Jinjiang Literature City (晉江文學網), which, founded in August 2003, is one of the largest sites for web fiction in China. As of July 6, 2022, the story had 128,665,816 viewings.[12] Although the story is fictional, it is clearly modeled after Song culture, from architecture and décor to costumes and makeup, from etiquettes and rituals to the refined arts of poetry, painting, calligraphy, music, the tea ceremony, and aromatics. What distinguishes *Royal Nirvana* from the classicist dramas before is how classic culture is fully integrated into the plot and how deeply it is imbued with the grace and elegance of the past.

Classicism begins with the author's pseudonym: Xueman Liangyun 雪滿梁園, which means "snow fills the Liang Garden." The name is taken from a Regulated Verse by Yuan Kai 袁凱 (active 1370) of the early Ming dynasty:

白燕

故國飄零事已非，舊時王謝見應稀。
月明漢水初無影，雪滿梁園尚未歸。
柳絮池塘香入夢，梨花庭院冷侵衣。
趙家姊妹多相忌，莫向昭陽殿裡飛。

FIGURE 2. *Royal Nirvana.*

White Swallows

The fatherland has fallen apart, and everything has changed;
Swallows must be few in the yards of the prominent families of Wangs and Xies.
Moon is bright at the beginning, casting no shadow on the Han River;
Snow fills the Liang Garden, yet the man has not yet returned.
Willow catkins on the pond, their scent wafts into a dream;
In the garden, pear flowers send a chill that penetrates one's clothes.
The beautiful Zhao sisters vied with each other out of jealousy;
Swallows do not fly into the Zhaoyang Palace of the Han.[13]

Not much is known about Yuan Kai. His name is almost exclusively associated with this poem. Lamenting the fall of the Yuan to the Ming dynasty, "White Swallows" is full of historical and literary allusions that evoke the ideas of decline and impermanence. As the author of *Royal Nirvana*, Xueman Liangyuan takes her name from the fourth line of the poem, which is based on an older allusion. Liu Wu 劉武 (?–144 BCE), the Lord of Liang in the Western Han period, built the Liang Garden in his palatial mansion, and here he would gather eminent literati to drink and compose poetry. Centuries later, "Liang Garden" appeared in "Rhapsody on Snow" (雪賦) by Xie Huilian 謝惠連 (407–33) to connote the transience of worldly glory. Hence the author's name Xueman Liangyuan is itself a multifarious classical allusion.

Likewise, classical allusions abound in *Royal Nirvana*. To start off, the Chinese title of the story—literally, "Cranes Cry in Huating"—alludes to the tragic life of the poet and military general Lu Ji 陸機 (261–303). After the fall of the Kingdom of Wu and the founding of the Jin dynasty, Lu withdrew to Huating (ancient name of Songjiang, a suburb in today's Shanghai) and lived a life of reclusion. He returned to government service but was falsely accused of treason by his political nemesis. According to *A New Account of the Tales of the World* (世説新語), before he was executed, Lu lamented: "Is it possible for me to hear again the cranes' cry in Huating?"[14] (欲聞華亭鶴唳可復得乎). Thus the title of the web fiction suggests a peaceful life away from political intrigue. This idea is reinforced by the image of the crane, which symbolizes spiritual purity, integrity, and loyalty, qualities found not only in the crown prince Xiao Dingquan 蕭定權, the male protagonist, but also in his teacher, Minister Lu Shiyu 盧世瑜, who is like a father to him, and the righteous official Lu Ying 陸英, father of the female protagonist Lu Wenxi 陸文昔.[15] The English title, *Royal Nirvana*, based on the Buddhist notion of enlightenment, resonates with the Chinese title in suggesting freedom from the world of desires.

The web drama of sixty episodes aired from November 12, 2019, to January 5, 2020. The enigmatic conclusion—with the last words "To be waited for" (可待) on the black screen—left some loose ends and differed significantly from the original story. For these reasons, the drama received much criticism from viewers. However, the enigma was resolved on September 22, 2020, when the sequel was aired under the title *Farewell to Clouds*, literally, "Farewell to Yunjian" (辭雲間). Yunjian—meaning "amid the clouds"—is another name for Huating, thus making clear the continuity with *Royal Nirvana*.

There is yet another layer of allusiveness in the title of the sequel in that "Farewell to Clouds" is the name of a quatrain written by Xia Wanchun 夏完淳 (1631–47), the Ming loyalist who studied with Chen Zilong 陳子龍 (1608–47) and was executed for resisting the Manchus at the age of sixteen. The poem reads:

Farewell to Clouds

For three years, a wandering traveler,
Today, I am a prisoner in the south.
Tears for the mountains and rivers are ceaseless;
Who says it's wide between Heaven and Earth?
I know the road to the underworld is near;
It's hard to say goodbye to my hometown.
The day when the brave soul returns,
It will watch the battle flag flying high in the sky.

別雲間

三年羈旅客，今日又南冠。
無限山河淚，誰言天地寬!
已知泉路近，欲別故鄉難。
毅魄歸來日，靈旗空際看。

In borrowing the title of Xia's poem, the sequel to *Royal Nirvana* forebodes unfulfilled aspirations and death. The web drama ends with the crown prince's suicide, followed by Wenxi's suicide after she has given birth to a baby boy, who grows up to be the crown prince.

In my view, the re-creation of imperial culture in *Royal Nirvana* surpasses that of its predecessors, even as authenticity in historical representation in television drama has made great strides in recent years as a result of costly productions and viewers' expectations. A salient example is *The Story of Yanxi Palace* (延禧宮略), a mega hit in 2018 that was set during the reign of Emperor Qianlong 乾隆 (1711–99). Part of the appeal of the television drama series was the authenticity of Qing court life as seen in the furniture, costumes, accessories, hairstyles, and makeup. All the costumes and accessories were handmade replicas—by master tailors, embroiderers, and artists—of Qing styles, requiring an enormous amount of time and the highest level of craftsmanship. They were virtually works of art. The same degree of meticulousness and elegance can be seen in *Royal Nirvana*.

More importantly, classicism is seen not only in the re-creation of the material culture and court life of the Song dynasty but also in the way it is an integral part of the main characters and plot development. The frequent references to poetry and other classical texts, calligraphy and painting, tea ceremony and the making of aromatics, and etiquettes and rituals are employed not just for the purpose of ambiance but play a key role in the plot. Poetry in the web drama contains two kinds: classics and original compositions. An example of the former is the repeated lines: "Beautiful ones fill the hall; swiftly your eyes alone meet mine" (滿堂兮美人，忽獨與余兮目成) from "Junior Lord of Fate" (少司命) in *Chuci* 楚辭 (*Songs of the South*) by Qu Yuan 屈原 (339–278 BCE) and later poets. In the drama series, Xiao Dingquan recites these lines to his newly wedded wife, who asks Lu Wenxi, now in the guise of a court servant, to explain them to her, thus suggesting a stronger rapport between the crown prince and Wenxi than that between him and his wife.

An example of original poetry is the quatrain inscribed on the landscape painting by Lu Wenxi. Her painting was done on a decorative screen presented to Minister Lu Shiyu for his birthday, and the crown prince wrote a couplet on the screen at Lu's request. Later, when he met Wenxi at his teacher's residence behind the painted screen, they found an instant affinity with each other in a brief exchange of words, and he asked her to paint the same painting for him. Not only did she give him the painting, but she also added a couplet to complete the quatrain. The screen between the lovers, which appears again at the end of the story, suggests that they are the mirror image of each other. This is a key symbol in the story. Not only do the two characters have the same childhood name, Abao 阿寶 ("Precious"), but they are also the same in their integrity, purity, and courage.

The quatrain reads:

Clouds in Dai, wild geese in western Shaanxi, tide of the Zhe River,
The wandering soul of that man awaits summoning.
How many guests of Golden Valley are there in this world?
The cranes utter a few cries, thoughts drifting far away.

代雲隴雁浙江潮，人有迷魂猶待招
世間多少金谷客，數聲鶴唳念遙遙

According to the author, this poem was one of the four poems that a Mr. Zheng
Xinmiao 鄭欣淼 wrote after he had read the novel in 2014. He then sent them to
the author. When she wrote the screenplay for the web drama, she incorporated
one of the four poems into the plot.[16] The poem is full of classical allusions. The
first line alone contains three. The images of clouds and wild geese both come
from "Rhapsody on Regret" (恨賦) by Jiang Yan 江淹 (444–505), which depicts
the regrets of six historical figures ranging from kings and generals to a beautiful
court lady and talented literati. Evoking the desolate frontier, these two images
allude to Wang Zhaojun 王昭君 (ca. 54–19 BCE), who as a "political bride" was
married to the chieftain of the Xiongnu tribe located to the northwest of Han
China. The image of wild geese is further related to two other allusions: the
migratory bird is emblematic of messages from home, based on the story of Su
Wu 蘇武 (140–60 BCE), the Han diplomat who remained loyal during his deten-
tion by the Xiongnu tribe. It is also associated with Wang Zhaojun in that wild
geese are struck by her beauty and fall to the ground.

The third allusion in line 1 is the high tide of the Qiantang River (錢塘江),
also known as the Zhe River, a celebrated natural spectacle. Around the middle
of the eighth month on the lunar calendar, the thundering tide pushes up like a
wall, reaching eight to ten meters high. The annual tide watching probably started
in the Eastern Han and became a popular trend in the Tang and Song dynasties. "Watching the Tide" (觀潮) by Su Shi 蘇軾 (1037–1191) and Zhou Mi 周密
(1232–98) has immortalized the site.[17]

Line 2 alludes to "Summoning the Soul" (招魂) by Qu Yuan. "That man"
refers to King Huai of Chu 楚懷王 (ca. 355–296 BCE), who, against Qu Yuan's
advice, was tricked into going to the State of Qin, was held there when he refused
to cede a piece of the Chu territory, and died in despondency. The first two lines
are consistent in their theme of regret and melancholy tone, which continue
into the next line, which alludes to Shi Chong 石崇 (249–300), an official at
the end of the Western Jin dynasty, who used his power to amass an enormous
fortune and built a lavish garden named Golden Valley in his residence in the

capital Luoyang. He incurred the resentment of a courtier and was killed, along with his entire family. Before his execution, Shi expressed regret for his greed.

Notably, line 2 uses the noun *ke* in referring to Shi Chong. In Chinese, *ke* means "guest" as well as "visitor." Being a guest at someone's house or a visitor in a foreign country suggests a temporary stay away from home. This notion underscores the classic metaphor of human life as a short journey, which can be traced back to "The Nineteen Old Poems" (古詩十九首) from the end of the Eastern Han. As a "guest" in the Golden Valley Garden, Shi Chong enjoys his wealth only for a short while. The disconsolate connotation of *guest* is brought to the fore in the famous poem by Li Yu 李煜 (937–78), the last emperor of the small kingdom of Southern Tang. He wrote the poem in captivity in the Song capital after his kingdom fell: "In my dream, I no longer remember I am a guest, / and I can steal a happy moment" (夢裡不知身是客，一晌貪歡). Instead of *prisoner*, Li uses the word *guest*, a euphemism rendering his situation even more bitter.

Densely allusive, the quatrain sums up the twofold theme of *Royal Nirvana*: the precariousness and transience of life, on the one hand, and the longing for spiritual freedom, symbolized by the crane, on the other. The poem recurs throughout the story, driving the theme home.

Besides the poems discussed above, there are quite a few references to classical prose. For example, this passage from "An Essay on Mr. Yan's Ancestral Hall" (嚴先生祠堂記) by Fan Zhongyan 范仲淹 (989–1052): "The cloud-veiled mountain is blue, the river is wide and deep. The gentleman's character is a high mountain and a long river" (雲山蒼蒼，江水泱泱。先生之風，山高水長). Fan's essay pays tribute to Yan Guang 嚴光 (39 BCE–49 CE), who turned down the repeated offer of an official post from Emperor Guangwu 光武帝 (5 BCE–57 CE), the founder of the Eastern Han dynasty, and chose the life of a recluse. In *Royal Nirvana* Lu Wenxi cited these lines (with modifications of the third line) when she and the crown prince met at Minister Lu Shiyu's residence. This allusion reiterates the bond between the two protagonists who long for the same ideal life.

Another classical allusion is to the three dishes that Minister Lu craves: watershield (菰菜), water bamboo soup (蓴羹), and braised sea bass (鱸魚膾). He expresses his craving to the crown prince, who visits him at his home in the middle of a political conspiracy. Xiao Dingquan understands what his teacher means immediately and begs him not to retire. The three dishes allude to Zhang Han 張翰, a virtuous scholar in the Western Jin dynasty. According to his biography in *The History of the Jin* (晉書), fed up with court intrigues, Zhang missed the three local dishes from his hometown, in present-day Suzhou, and decidedly resigned from office. In *Royal Nirvana* Minister Lu stays because of the crown prince's plea but, in the end, pays with his life.

Finally, *Royal Nirvana* repeatedly cites from *Sutra of Forty-Two Chapters* (四十二章經), the first Buddhist scripture translated from Sanskrit to Chinese by the Indian masters Kasyapa Matanga and Dharmaratna in the first century CE. From chapter 25 the passage reads: "The Buddha said: 'For a man to have desire and attachment is like walking against the wind holding a torch; his hand is bound to be burned'" (佛言:愛慾於人，猶如執炬逆風而行，必有燒手之患). In *Royal Nirvana* the passage describes the crown prince, who has never been close to his father (who favors his elder brother, Prince Xiao Dingtang 蕭定棠) and lost his beloved mother, Empress Gu, when he was seventeen years old. He does his best to please his father and protect the people he loves, including his teacher; his wife and unborn child; his maternal uncle, General Gu, who is like a father to him; his cousin Gu Fengen 顧逢恩; and Lu Wenxi. In doing so, he repeatedly puts himself in an extremely vulnerable position in the midst of political machinations. In the end, all of them die because of him.

The irony of the story is that none of the fine qualities—moral fortitude, beauty, erudition, artistic talent—and enviable stature of the crown prince give him security and happiness. If anything, they are the cause of his suffering. Thus, understandably and befittingly, the epigraph to the sequel to *Royal Nirvana* reads: "Please come with a lantern, to light up this magnificent hell for me" (請你點一盞 燈來，為孤照亮這叢錦繡地獄). Addressed to Wenxi, these words attest to their love as the only ray of light in darkness.

Besides poetry and painting, classicism is seen in calligraphy. In *Royal Nirvana* Minister Lu Shiyu is the greatest calligrapher in his time, and the crown prince learns the art from him and has developed his own distinctive style, named Gold Dagger (金錯刀). The slim and angled style can be traced to the aforementioned Emperor Li Yu and is similar to Slim Gold (瘦金體), for which Emperor Hui 徽 宗 (1082–1135) of the Song dynasty is famous. Calligraphy also plays a key role in the twists and turns of the plot: Xiao Dingquan teaches Wenxi how to write in the Gold Dagger style, and Prince Xiao Dingkai 蕭定楷, Dingquan's younger brother, tries to frame him for treason by forging his handwriting.

The representation of Song culture would not be complete without tea culture. In *Royal Nirvana* the tea ceremony is extensively and skillfully incorporated into the plot. Tea—*Camelia sinensis*—originated in southwestern China about five thousand years ago. By the early Zhou dynasty, it was cultivated and processed as a beverage, first used in rituals. For many centuries thereafter, tea was enjoyed mainly by the nobles and the upper class. It was not until the Tang that tea drinking spread. The first monograph on the subject, *The Classic of Tea* (茶經) by Lu Yu 陸羽 (733–804), appeared in 780. It is noteworthy that *The Classic of Tea* was the first written record in which the word *cha* (tea) was used, instead of the character *tu* 茶—a bitter herb—up to that point in Chinese history.

Tea culture flourished during the Song dynasty with distinctive features. Unlike the Tang when tea was boiled over fire, the Song boiled water to brew tea. Instead of bowls of metal (copper, silver, gold) used in the Tang, the Song

FIGURE 3. Tea culture in *Royal Nirvana*.

preferred porcelain. As repeatedly seen in *Royal Nirvana*, the elaborate tea cere-mony is called touching tea (點茶)—grinding tea leaves into fine powder, pouring boiled water into the bowl containing the tea powder, and whipping it rigorously with a bamboo whisk so foam—known as liquid flower (湯花)—is formed. Dur-ing the Song dynasty, tea culture evolved into an elegant, leisurely activity that appealed to the senses—not only smell and taste but also sight and sound. Com-petitions on how well one prepared tea—the color of tea and the amount and pattern of "liquid flower"—became a popular pastime in Song society.

In *Royal Nirvana* the tea ceremony serves as a significant metaphor of the relationship between father and son (fig. 3). When the princes were growing up, the emperor patiently taught Xiao Dingtang how to prepare tea but completely ignored the crown prince. In episode 9 the emperor, Dingtang, and the prince's mother gather merrily, and the emperor praises the prince's skill in preparing tea. The perfect picture of a loving family is interrupted by the entrance of the crown prince: the emperor abruptly stops smiling and puts on a stern face. Toward the end of the drama, the reversal of the father-son relationship is also dramatized by tea drinking. In episode 58 the emperor regrets having misunderstood and mistreated the crown prince all these years. He reaches out his hand and asks Dingquan to prepare tea with him. It is a symbolic gesture of reconciliation. In the following scene, the emperor gives his son some tips on how to whip up the foam and reminisces about how he had difficulty when he was a boy, to which Dingquan softly replies, "That was Elder Brother, not me."

Finally, it is rare to see aromatic culture, or the Way of Aromatics (香道), represented in classicist drama in China, whether film, television drama, or web drama. Aromatic substances, or *xiangliao* 香料, come from plants—flowers, herbs, fruits, leaves, roots, and barks—and, in a few cases, from animals (e.g., musk and ambergris). The use of aromatics can be traced to the Spring and Autumn Period, and the culture thrived in the Tang and Song dynasties. Preserved in various forms—from incense to potpourri—aromatics were widely used in everyday life and on special occasions, serving multiple functions that ranged from hygienic and medicinal to aesthetic and religious.[18]

In *Royal Nirvana* the crown prince and his cousin Gu Fengen, who is knowledgeable about aromatics, prepare a potpourri named Plum Flower Fragrance (梅花香). Stored in a small jar, it needs to age for the scent to mature. The crown prince intends to give it to Lu Wenxi, but he never gets around to doing that. The jar ends up sitting on the shelf in his residence for years. In one episode, the crown prince stops his wife from opening it when she comes across it by chance. In my view, the potpourri is emblematic of the relationship between the protagonists. Echoing the notion of purity of the crane, the central symbol of the story, Plum Flower Fragrance intimates the precious love that is kept hidden for most of the story.

Royal Nirvana is an exemplary classicist web drama that represents the "Chinese style" or "Asian aesthetics." *Chinese style* refers to the incorporation of traditional Chinese elements into the design of a creative work, whether it is clothing, accessories, and stationery, or music, furniture, architecture, and landscaping. As an example, in pop music, Jay Chou 周杰倫, along with the lyricist Fang Wenshan 方文山, has led the way in popularizing the Chinese style, which has inspired numerous songwriters and singers in the Chinese-speaking world. As another example, in recent years, it is not uncommon to see young men and women in China wearing *Hanfu* 漢服, modeled on traditional Han-ethnic clothing.

The classicist trend may be seen as a response to socio-politico-cultural development. As China gains prominence in the world with its economic prosperity and political muscle, Chinese people's confidence in their cultural heritage grows, and their desire to create designs that are characteristically Chinese is a natural outcome. Such confidence and desire are partly spontaneous and partly inculcated. The government actively promotes national pride through policies, the educational system, and mass media. Such slogans as "Chinese Dream" (中國夢, proclaimed by Xi Jinping on November 29, 2012) and "Amazing China" (厲害了，我的國, also the title of a 2018 propaganda documentary film) have become part of common parlance in China.

The other side of the government's motivation to promote the Chinese style is to combat what is perceived as excessive influences by foreign cultures, including the West, Japan (e.g., anime and J-pop), and Korea (e.g., Kdrama and K-pop). In the case of Korea, in the 2000s Korean popular culture swept China, like the rest of Asia, and was referred to as the "Korean wave." In July 2016 the United States announced that the antiballistic missile defense system THAAD would be deployed in South Korea, despite protests from the Chinese government. Compounding the tension was that in recent years Korea had claimed that Confucius and Qu Yuan were actually Korean. As a result, the Chinese government issued a ban on Korean popular cultural products and collaborations between Chinese and Korean entertainment industries. Although there have been periods of letting up, it seems unlikely that Korean pop culture will regain the market it once had in China.

Arguably more than any other classicist drama in the contemporary period, *Royal Nirvana* is imbued with the high culture of dynastic China. According to the director, a large team of experts on Song culture was consulted, and the production spared no expense in achieving excellence. For example, the instrumental soundtrack of the drama series was composed by the renowned composer Roc Chen 阿鲲 and performed by the Royal Philharmonic Orchestra in Britain. The level of meticulousness enables *Royal Nirvana* to avoid the pitfall of affectation and kitsch, on the one hand, and crude commercialism, on the other, which are sometimes associated with the Chinese style. By weaving Song cultural elements into the development of characters and the storyline, the web drama displays artistic integrity and beauty.

Case Study 2: *The Untamed*

Like *Royal Nirvana*, *The Untamed* is also based on web literature. The difference between these two original works is that, before they were adapted as drama series, the former had attracted a relatively small but devoted readership online, whereas the latter had achieved a cult status with a huge fan base. This explains why *The Untamed* was widely anticipated by viewers despite "zero publicity" before it streamed online (fig. 4).[19]

The Untamed is an adaptation of *Grandmaster of Demonic Cultivation* (魔道祖师), written by Mo Xiang Tong Xiu 墨香铜臭 (commonly referred to as MXTX). The novel was serialized on Jinjiang Literature City from October 31, 2015, to March 1, 2016, followed by a revision with three new chapters from September 7, 2016, to January 1, 2018. It became so popular that an anime was produced by Tencent (fig. 5).[20] Part 1 of the anime was serialized from July 9 to

FIGURE 4. *The Untamed.*

FIGURE 5. Anime version of *The Untamed*.

October 16, 2018, part 2 in 2019, and part 3 in 2021. Moreover, along with two other web novels by MXTX, *Grandmaster of Demonic Cultivation* was translated into English and published by Seven Seas Entertainment. The first three volumes appeared in 2021–22, volumes 4 and 5 were published in December 2022 and May 2023, respectively. The web novel in translation is readily available on Goodreads, Google Books, and other platforms.

The Untamed belongs to the genre of classicist fantasy, or "immortal knight-errant saga" (*xianxia* 仙俠). In terms of content, it is a *danmei* adaptation (耽改劇). As mentioned in part 1, the first *danmei* work—including web movies and drama series—in China was *Like Love* in 2014.[21] In 2016 there were at least eighteen such adaptations. Up to that point, the most successful one was *Addiction*, based on the web novel *You Got Addicted* (你丫上瘾了) by Chai Jidan 柴雞蛋. After *Addiction* was taken off the internet, the actors who played the protagonists were also forbidden to share the screen again.[22] Both young stars have since remade their careers by playing roles in works on mainstream themes, whether heterosexual romance or patriotic action drama. For example, Huang Jingyu has starred in the military action film *Operation Red Sea* (紅海行動), the uplifting race-car film *Pegasus* (飛馳人生), and the anti-drug drama series *The Thunder*

(破冰行動). Box-office success has catapulted him to the list of "Forbes China 100 Celebrities" twice, in 2019 and 2020.

After *Addiction* was taken offline in 2016, *danmei* web drama completely disappeared for a year, with not a single one aired in 2017. When it did come back in 2018, it employed two strategies to bypass state censorship: first, by switching the focus from homosexual relationship to brotherhood, and second, by giving more airtime to female characters. Understandably, making these changes to the original stories risks protests from the fans; however, it is a matter of survival for the productions. Both strategies are evident in *The Untamed*.

In the web drama, there are two leading female roles: Jiang Yanli 江厭離, the elder foster sister of the protagonist Wei Wuxian 魏無羨, and Wen Qing 温情 from one of the five clans. Both are minor characters in *Grand Master of Demonic Cultivation*. Wen Qing appears in only 2 out of 119 chapters, but in *The Untamed* she appears in approximately two-thirds of the fifty episodes. She takes on a somewhat wifely role in a household that includes her, Wei Wuxian, her younger brother Wen Ning 温寧, and the little boy from the Wen clan, Ayuan 阿苑. As to Jiang Yanli, she is like a mother to Wei Wuxian, who was orphaned when he was little and has been ill-treated by the mistress of the Jiang clan, his foster family. In the web drama, Yanli is the only woman he listens to and reveals his feelings to, more like a son than a younger brother. Her death turns him against the clans and into a "demonic grandmaster."

Enlarging these two female roles is congruous with the ostensible theme of brotherhood. In *The Untamed* Wei Wuxian and Lan Wangji 藍忘機 start out as opposites: Wei is the proverbial "bad boy" while Lan is an exemplary student; Wei challenges authorities while Lan enforces the rules; Wei is extroverted and easygoing while Lan is reserved and straitlaced. In the early part of the drama, Lan would have nothing to do with Wei. In fact, he expresses annoyance and disdain toward the prankish young man. But as the two face dangers and fight alongside each other, they form a bond that defies life and death. The road to brotherhood is long and tortuous, however. Lan regrets that he chose to stand with the alliance of the clans against Wei, who had mastered demonic power, and watched him fall to his death from a cliff. Sixteen years later, Wei is reborn in another body, and this time Lan protects and defends him with his life.

For most of the drama, Wei is dressed in black while Lan wears white. This is significant in two ways. First, it suggests the sharp differences in their personality and style. However, as the relationship evolves, the color contrast also intimates yin and yang, which are opposite but not oppositional. They complement each other and work as one. The harmony at a deeper level is already embedded in their style names: *Wuxian* means "no envy," and *Wangji* means "forgetting scheming." Both names have Daoist-Buddhist overtones in denouncing worldly desires and maintaining spiritual purity.

Does this mean that *danmei* is completely purged from the web drama? By no means. Despite the rewriting of the original story necessitated by self-censorship, the web drama is loaded with suggestive, even titillating hints of homosexual love between the protagonists. There are too many to mention; below are just a few of the most telling details. First, in episode 36, Lan, who has little capacity for wine, gets drunk one night, falls asleep, and starts sleepwalking. He trespasses into a farmer's yard, where there are chickens in a coop. Then he grabs two roosters out of the coop and hands them to Wei, asking him: "Are they big and fat?" Wei replies: "Yes, they are." This episode makes little sense until we understand the role of chickens in traditional Chinese marriage custom. Allowing local variations, it is customary for the groom to give two roosters to the bride's family either as part of the engagement gift or on the day of the wedding. The rooster has several symbolic meanings. First, it stands for virility, thus expressing the wish that the new couple will have many children. Second, *ji* (chicken) is a homophone with the word *auspicious*, again expressing good wishes for the couple. Third, the image is associated with the traditional notion of the wife being subordinate to the husband, as expressed in the Chinese proverb, "Follow the rooster if you marry a rooster, follow the dog if you marry a dog." The fact that the gifting of two roosters takes place between the two protagonists in the web drama cannot but suggest that Lan is proposing to Wei or that they are a couple.

Of course, the bold confession is possible only when the reticent and reserved Lan Wangji is in a drunken stupor; namely, when he no longer has to repress his feelings. He knows too that when he is sober, he cannot express his love for Wei, which is why the next morning he gingerly asks what he said the night before. When Wei recalls by slowing down on purpose, "You said you're very fond of . . . ," the visibly nervous Lan interrupts him: "Fond of what?" Then he finishes the sentence to Lan's relief: "Rabbits! You are very fond of rabbits!" It is obvious that Wei is playing with him, and he knows exactly why Lan gets nervous.

There are other clues that the feeling between the two men is mutual. In an early episode, when Wei has to copy the rules of the Lan clan as punishment for his unruly behavior, he musingly watches Lan from a distance and does a drawing of him. Also, when Wei finishes school and is leaving Endless Cloud, home to the Lan clan, he tries to find Lan to say goodbye to him, even though Lan has been cold to him. In episode 24, Wei asks Jiang Yanli, who we remember is like a mother to him, about matters of the heart. He confesses he likes a certain person: "Why does one person like another . . . I mean that kind of 'like'?"

In episode 46 Wei and Lan pass by the Jiang ancestral hall and stop to pay respect to Wei's foster parents, even though Wei is blamed for their deaths and is ostracized by the clan. The picture of them kneeling side by side before the altar and kowtowing three times bears a close resemblance to the bride and the groom kowtowing to heaven and earth and the groom's parents, which lies at the heart of the traditional wedding ceremony. Finally, the most often-quoted line in the web drama appears in episode 25, where Lan says to his elder brother: "I want to take someone back to Endless Clouds, take him back and hide him there." *Someone* refers to Wei, who is injured and hunted by his enemies. Lan is not only expressing his desire to protect Wei, but the image of hiding also harks back to Lan's own parents' story of forbidden love. Just as his father kept his mother hidden in Endless Clouds to keep her safe, so he wants to do the same for Wei.

In contrast to the explicit homoeroticism in the original story, the web drama is much more subtle. However, even for someone like me who watches the drama without the benefit of having first read the web novel, the charged attraction between the two protagonists is palpable. This is attributed to the screenplay and the directorship, on the one hand, and to the chemistry between the two protagonists both on- and offscreen, on the other. While interpersonal chemistry is natural—and this is an important factor in casting—I argue that it can also be manufactured to some degree.

It is common in show business that a real-life romantic relationship between the leading stars of a movie creates news and attracts eyeballs. There is a natural desire for fans to see romance on the screen transferred to real life, a desire to turn fantasy into reality. What André Bazin says about cinema as "an idealistic phenomenon" applies equally well to other forms of dramatic representation.[23] While romances between leading stars do happen in real life, in most cases it is a marketing ploy to boost the box office or ratings. In the age of the internet, the rapid expansion of fandom seems to have fueled the fantasy. Moreover, fans not only want to see "CPs" (couples) on- and offscreen, but they play an active role in creating the fantasy. This is true of heterosexual couples as well as same-sex couples. Therefore, there are two new terms in Chinese: *CP-fen* (CP 粉), meaning "CP fans," and *weifen* 唯粉, meaning "sole fans," the latter referring to fans of only one member of a group or a couple. As the numbers of fans grow and become powerful, it is not uncommon for CP fans and sole fans to get into nasty fights online, and with real consequences.

When it comes to *danmei* drama, fans' desire to see real-life couples seems to be even stronger.[24] Going back to the web drama *Addiction*, for years many fans believed that the two actors were gay lovers. In 2022, when Xu Weizhou announced on his website that he had married a woman on March 14, his CP fans were devastated. In the case of *The Untamed*, fans have played an active role in constructing the fantasy of Xiao Zhan and Wang Yibo as a real-life CP. These CP fans are like detectives who pore through behind-the-scene tidbits, interviews of the stars, the stars' personal websites, and videos of any occasion when the two stars appear together (e.g., promotional concerts, fan meetings, award ceremonies) to convince themselves and others that Xiao Zhan and Wang Yibo are romantically involved in real life. To this day, the Xiao-Wang CP remains

FIGURE 6: CP in real life.

the most popular among all CPs in show business in China. Hundreds of videos made by their CP fans are available online, attracting views that number from tens of thousands to several millions. It is also important to note that these CP fans come not only from China but also from all over the world. This can be seen in the videos and the comments in various languages, such as Vietnamese, Thai, Spanish, and Russian. It seems that *The Untamed* has come full circle: from the original *danmei* novel to the sanitized web drama that ostensibly tells a story of brotherhood, to the CP fantasy created by fans (fig. 6).

But CP fans could not have done it alone. While the drama was streaming, the production company released some behind-the-scene tidbits. While some showed interactions between the director and the actors on the set and bloopers, others were suggestive of something more than friendly banter between Xiao and Wang. As more and more tidbits became available online, many of which came from unknown sources, the line between the couple in *The Untamed* and the two actors was blurred, even erased. Such details as loving stares, physical touching, and suggestive verbal exchanges seem to point to amorous feelings offscreen. For example, one of those video clips shows Wang Yibo saying how much he loves wearing hats. Immediately Xiao Zhan responds by asking, "How about a green hat?" Wang then raises his voice and forcefully rebukes, "See if you dare!" "Wearing a green hat" is a Chinese expression meaning one is cuckolded. In another video, during a break Wang asks what Xiao would like to eat, and Xiao names a number of Japanese dishes. Later that evening, paparazzi take pictures of them going to a Japanese restaurant.

Besides those titillating behind-the-scene tidbits, fans look for other clues on the actors' websites, such as wearing the same clothes, sneakers, and necklaces, or secret codes in the graphics that express amorous feelings for each other. Similarly, when they appear at a Tencent award ceremony, their body language is analyzed closely. Is it another marketing ploy, is it the CP fans' wishful thinking and willful construction, or is it both? No one can say for sure. What is clear is that, since *The Untamed*, the CP fantasy has become a significant—and hugely profitable—part of fan culture in China.

The success of *The Untamed* as a national and international sensation is singular and cannot be duplicated. Between 2014 and 2020 a total of forty-six *danmei* web drama series streamed online.[25] However, *The Untamed* is the only one that has become a national and transnational sensation. According to Taylor Poulos in the *Masters Review*, as of the first half of September 2021, the drama series has over 10 billion views on the Tencent Video platform.[26] After the phenomenal success of *The Untamed*, as many as fifty-nine *danmei* adaptations were in the works at various stages, from purchasing copyrights to shooting.[27] However, most of these latecomers will never see the light of day in the foreseeable future. *Danmei* was singled out for criticism twice in the *Guangming Daily* (光明日報), a newspaper of the Chinese Communist Party, in spring and summer 2021.[28] As part of the ongoing Clean Action campaign, *danmei* has been banned by the government as a "perverse aesthetics" and a corrupting influence on the youth. Although the *danmei* drama series *Word of Honor* (山河令) premiered online in June 2021, before the ban was announced, it didn't escape the fate of being taken off the air, much like *Addiction* five years earlier.

Finally, *The Untamed* demonstrates the IP business model for web drama at its best. The abbreviation of *intellectual property*, IP is used to refer to a drama series that is an adaptation of web literature and yields high market value.[29] The concept of IP first appeared in China in 2014, and in 2015 several drama series were so successful that the year was dubbed "Originary Year of IP" (IP 元年) in the industry. At the core of IP are the original story and its adaptations in different media, typically drama series, anime, computer games, and musical works. Revolving around the core are countless derivative products. In the case of *The Untamed*, they range from bookmarks, stickers, cell phone cases, notebooks, nightlights, and calendars to hats, scarves, cross-body bags, thermoses, umbrellas, folding fans, throw pillows, and even lipsticks, eyeshadows, and compact mirrors. Moreover, a theme restaurant opened in Shanghai in September 2021, replicating the décor and serving dishes that appear in the web drama. Many of these products cater to female fans, whether in design or in function, a fact that supports the theory that women are the main authors as well as the majority audience of *danmei* literature.[30]

As super IP, *The Untamed* has expanded the IP business model. For example, it started a tier system of subscription. Members who paid a higher fee enjoyed the privilege of accessing new episodes before other members. Concerts and fan meetings were held both domestically and abroad. Magazines that featured the two protagonists sold over a million copies, and the products for which they were spokesmen sold out instantly.

Conclusion

This article has analyzed two classicist drama series in China from 2019, each representing an important subgenre in web drama. *Royal Nirvana* is a splendid example of Chinese style or Asian aesthetics. The re-creation of Song culture goes way beyond "costumes, makeup, and props" (服化道) to fully and skillfully integrate period-specific arts and cultural practices into characterization and plot development. The scope and depth of the representation distinguish the drama series from its predecessors, including both television and web drama. Perhaps an unanticipated contribution of *Royal Nirvana* is that it will inspire later productions to aspire to the high standards it sets in representing classical Chinese culture.

The Untamed remains the most successful classicist drama series in the *danmei* genre in China. If the popularity of the original web novel provided a large built-in fanbase for the drama, it took off immediately after it premiered online thanks to the quality of the production and the beauty and acting of the protagonists. As a supernatural knight-errant saga, it has constructed a CP fantasy for both domestic and international fans with enduring staying power, a fantasy that blurs the boundary between representation and reality, between art and life, and it lives on to this day. The fantasy is so successful that the IP business model of *The Untamed* has generated record-breaking revenues. However, the tightening up of government regulation of the entertainment industry means that *danmei* drama will not be aired online any time soon, if ever. *Danmei* culture in general has been forced to go underground, and *The Untamed* will be a glorious reminder of "the good old days."

In the final analysis, although *Royal Nirvana* and *The Untamed* are both well-made classicist drama series, they reflect opposite forces in Chinese cyberspace with broader sociocultural implications. *Royal Nirvana* is thoroughly classical—even traditional—in its language, Confucian values (loyalty and filial piety in particular), and cultural ambiance, whereas *The Untamed* manages to breathe new life into a *danmei* web novel, albeit in a sanitized form. The love between the male and female protagonists in *Royal Nirvana* exemplifies integrity, purity, courage, and self-sacrifice, whereas the politically correct theme of brotherly love between the male protagonists in *The Untamed* is undermined by telling details in the drama and the offscreen CP fantasy. Ironically, *Royal Nirvana* appeals to a smaller audience, even though it represents mainstream values, whereas *The Untamed* is embraced by millions, even billions, with its subtly disguised transgressions. The contrast suggests an existing tension in Chinese society that is unlikely to be ameliorated, much less resolved, with rules and regulations.

MICHELLE YEH is Distinguished Professor at the University of California, Davis. Her areas of research include modern poetry from mainland China, Taiwan, and Hong Kong; classical Chinese poetry; international modernism; and Taiwan literature. She has also published many Chinese-English translations and books of prose in Chinese.

Notes

1 Feng, *Romancing the Internet*.

2 Inwood, *Verse Going Viral*.

3 Hockx, *Internet Literature in China*.

4 For example, Shao, *Interpreting the Canon of Web Literature*; Wang and Chang, *Studies of Types of Web Fiction*; Zhao, "China's Sprawling World of Web Fiction."

5 The NRTA was established in 2018, but censorship has always existed in China. Prior to the NRTA, censorship was administered by agencies under different names, going all the way to 1946–49. For the time frame covered in this article, the last two predecessors of the NRTA were the National Radio Film and Television Administration (國家廣播電影電視總局) from 1998 to 2013 and National News Publication Radio and Television Administration (國家新聞出版廣電總局) from 2013 to 2018.

6 Relevant documents can be found on the NRTA official website at http://www.nrta.gov.cn/art/2018/11/9/art_113_39686.html.

7 "Bullet screen" was invented by the Japanese Cartoon site NicoNico. Comments fly across the screen while the video is playing. As far as I know, only Japan and China adopt this feature.

8 Kong, "'Affective Alliance.'"

9 Zhang and Ji, "New Demands and New Behavior of Television Drama Audience."

10 See Tencent's announcement on January 14, 2019 (https://news.sina.cn/2019-11-14/detail-iihnzahio917001.d.html).

11 For a comprehensive list of web drama series, see *Baidu Encyclopedia*, https://baike.baidu.com/item/%E7%BD%91%E7%BB%9C%E5%89%A7/10614888; also, Wang, "Existence and Evolution of the Subculture of Chinese Web Drama."

12 The story *Royal Nirvana* is available at https://www.jjwxc.net/oneauthor.php?authorid=225737, from which the number of viewings was obtained on July 6, 2022.

13 All translations of classical poems and prose passages are by the author.

14 Chapter 33 of *A New Account of the Tales of the World*, ctext.org/shi-shuo-xin-yu/you-hui/zh.

15 For a reading of the image, see Tang, "Interpreting the Image of 'Crane' in *Royal Nirvana*."

16 See the author's Weibo account: https://weibo.com/3816347926/L1laWzc9G.

17 Su Shi: "The misty rain on Mount Lu, the tide at the Qiantang River. / If you've never been there, deep regret has no mitigation. / Once you've been there, nothing seems to have happened, / Misty rain on Mount Lu, tide of the Qiantang River" (廬山烟雨浙江潮，未至千般恨不消。到得還來別無事，廬山烟雨浙江潮).

18 For a study of aromatics in China and the world, see Xi, *Fragrance*.

19 Qianchuang Film and Television, "'Chen Qing Ling' Had Zero Publicity before It Was Broadcast."

20 Although the site does not provide the number of views, Jinjiang Literature City uses an algorithm based on the numbers of collections and views, as well as reviewers' scores. *The Untamed* has accumulated 15,314,938,880 points (www.jjwxc.net/oneauthor.php?authorid=1322620, accessed October 31, 2022).

21 The earliest films explicitly depicting gay love are *East Palace, West Palace* (東宮西宮, 1996, directed by Zhang Yuan 張元) and *Lan Yu* (藍宇, 2001, directed by the Hong Kong director Stanley Kwan and featuring two actors from mainland China). Both, however, were banned and only circulated underground in China.

22 It is important to note that although *Addiction* was banned in China, the complete drama was available in Japan, Korea, and Thailand. Because *danmei* drama is subject to ban, USB copies ("U disk" in Chinese) are sold on the market.

23 Bazin, *What Is Cinema?*, 17.

24 Women who love boys' love are called *fu* in Chinese, which came from the Japanese word *fujoshi*. It is commonly believed among scholars that male CPs appeal especially to female readers and viewers, who constitute the majority group of consumers for *danmei*. See, for example, Xu and Yang, "'Obsessive Women' and 'Obsessive Men.'"

25 Jing Nai, "2014 到2020."

26 Poulos, review.

27 For a complete list of *danmei* adaptations, see "Why Are Danmei Adaptations Banned: A Chronology of the Rise and Fall of Danmei-Adaptation Drama" (耽改劇為啥會被禁：盤點耽改劇的興衰歷程), posted on September 24, 2021, m.cidastar.com/repo rts/20210924120446.

28 See Meng, "Danmei Adaptations Lead the Public Astray in Taste" (耽美作品改編盛行帶偏大眾審美), April 7, 2021; Yi, "A Warning against Danmei Leading the Public Taste Astray" (警惕耽改劇把大眾審美帶入歧途), August 26, 2021.

29 Xian, Luan, and Re "Current State and Strategies of the Film and Television Transformations of Domestic IP."

30 See Xue, "Equal Love"; Zhu and Zhao, "Imaginary Politics."

References

Bazin, André. *What Is Cinema?* Translated by Hugh Gray. Berkeley: University of California Press, 1967.

Feng, Jin. *Romancing the Internet: Producing and Consuming Chinese Web Romance*. Leiden, Netherlands: Brill, 2013.

Hockx, Michel. *Internet Literature in China*. New York: Columbia University Press, 2015.

Inwood, Heather. *Verse Going Viral: China's New Media Scenes*. Seattle: University of Washington Press, 2014.

Jenkins, Henry. *Textual Poachers: Television Fans and Participatory Culture*. New York: Routledge, 1992.

Jing Nai 井鼐. 2014 到2020: 中国耽改剧小史 [From 2014 to 2020: A Brief History of Chinese Danmei-Adaptation Drama]. https://zhuanlan.zhihu.com/p/112172906, accessed October 2, 2022.

Kong, Shuyu. "The 'Affective Alliance': *Undercover*, Internet Media Fandom, and the Sociality of Cultural Consumption in Postsocialist China." *Modern Chinese Literature and Culture* 24, no. 1 (2012): 1–47.

Meng, Lei 孟蕾. "Danmei Adaptations Lead the Public Astray in Taste" (耽美作品改編盛行帶偏大眾審美), April 7, 2021. https://www.chinawriter.com.cn/n1/2021/0407/c419388-32071317.html.

Poulos, Taylor. Review of *Grandmasters of Demonic Cultivation*, by Mo Xiang Tong Xiu. Masters Review, February 24, 2022. https://mastersreview.com/book-review-grandmaster-of-demonic-cultivation-by-mo-xiang-tong-xiu/#:~:text=Grandmaster%20of%20Demonic%20Cultivation%20is,romance%20novel%2C%20originally%20published%20online.

Shao Yanjun 邵燕君. *Interpreting the Canon of Web Literature* (網絡文學經典解讀). Beijing: Peking University Press, 2016.

Qianchuang Film and Television. "'Chen Qing Ling' Had Zero Publicity before It Was Broadcast, and 'Chen Qianqian' Was Disliked, but It Became a Popular Drama." *Sina*, June 11, 2020. https://k.sina.cn/article_1340604587_4fe800ab00100n4yj.html.

Tang Yanyan 唐豔豔. "Interpreting the Image of 'Crane' in Royal Nirvana" (解讀《鶴唳華亭》中的 "鶴" 意象). *Art Panorama* (藝術大觀), no. 7 (2020): 83–84.

Wang Guangdong 王光東, and Chang Fangzhou 常方舟, eds. *Studies of Types of Web Fiction* (網絡小說類型專題研究). Shanghai: Dongfang chubanshe, 2019.

"Why Are Danmei Adaptations Banned: A Chronology of the Rise and Fall of Danmei-Adaptation Drama" (耽改劇為啥會被禁：盤點耽改劇的興衰歷程), September 24, 2021. https://m.cidastar.com/reports/20210924120446.

Xi Mi 奚密. *Fragrance: Literature, History, Everyday Life* (香：文學，歷史，生活). Beijing: Peking University Press, 2013.

Xian Bing 冼冰, Luan Yihang 欒一航, and Dila Re 迪拉熱. "The Current State and Strategies of the Film and Television Transformations of Domestic IP" (國產IP影視化轉換的現狀與對策). *News Dissemination* (新聞傳播), October 2021: 94–96.

Xinrubaby. "Why Are Danmei Adaptations Banned? A Chronology of the Rise and Fall of Danmei-Adaptation Drama" (耽改劇為什麼被禁：盤點耽改劇的興衰歷程). *Zhihu* 知乎. https://zhuanlan.zhihu.com/p/421260853 (accessed March 4, 2024)

Xu Yanrui 徐豔蕊 and Yang Ling 楊玲. "'Obsessive Women' and 'Obsessive Men': Danmei, 'Fu' Culture, and the Reconstruction of Male Style in Transnational Cultural Flow" (腐女"腐" 男：跨國文化流動中的耽美、腐文化與男性氣質的再造). *Cultural Studies* (文化研究) 20 (Autumn 2014): 17–39.

Xue Yingjie 薛英杰. "Equal Love: The Rise of *Danmei* Fiction and the Transformation of Women's Expectations" (平等之愛：耽美强强文的崛起與女性訴求的轉型). *Journal of Shandong Women's College* (山東女子學院學報), no. 5 (September 2021): 54–65.

Yi Jun 藝君. "A Warning against Danmei Leading the Public Taste Astray" (警惕耽改劇把大 眾審美帶入歧途), August 26, 2021. https://news.sina.com.cn/c/2021-08-26/doc -ikqcfncc5015686.shtml.

Zhang, Hongjun 張紅軍, and Ji Jing 季靜. "New Demands and New Behavior of Television Drama Audience in the Age of Convergence Media" (融媒體時代電視劇受眾的新需求和新行). Jiangsu Thinktank (江蘇智庫網), October 13, 2021. https://www.jsthinktank .com/jiangsuzhiku/jszjcmzk/yjdt/202110/t20211013_7264611.shtml.

Zhao, Jin. "China's Sprawling World of Web Fiction." China Project, August 17, 2022. https:// u.osu.edu/mclc/2022/08/22/chinas-sprawling-world-of-web-fiction.

Zhu Lili 朱麗麗 and Zhao Tingting 趙婷婷. "Imaginary Politics: Text Writing and Gender Practices of 'Danmei' Fan Groups" (想像的政治： "耽美" 迷群體的文本書寫與性別實踐). *Jiangsu Social Sciences* (江蘇社會科學), no. 6 (2015): 202–8.

LIANG LUO

The Digital Classicism of the Cantonese Opera Film
White Snake

ABSTRACT This article examines the 2019 Cantonese opera film *White Snake* as an important case of an evolving "digital classicism," making use of audience-based digitally produced and transmitted Chinese-language materials, among other sources. The article contextualizes the Cantonese opera film as continuing the tradition of experimenting with the White Snake theme, using the genres of local opera and opera film, and special and visual effects enabled by the newest technology. It then moves to a close reading of a series of *danmu*, anonymous live comments on the Cantonese opera film trailer posted on Bilibili, as important entry points for the study of audience participation in digital times. The digitally produced "ink painting–style Chinese aesthetics" of the film, its digital breakthrough as a "musical with Chinese characteristics," as well as various forms of fan and anti-fan digital labor triggered by the film, provide further evidence on the importance of "the digital" as "processes of sense making." The article concludes with thoughts on what difference "the digital" might be able to make in this long history of representing what has become a "classical" Chinese legend.

KEYWORDS digital classicism, Cantonese opera film, *danmu*, visual effects, digital fan/anti-fan labor

Baishe zhuan · qing 白蛇傳 · 情 (White Snake), which opened in mainland China on May 20, 2021, and was branded as a 4K surround-sound Cantonese opera (*yueju* 粵劇) film representing an "ink painting–style Chinese aesthetics" (*shuimo guofeng meixue* 水墨國風美學), provides an excellent case for the study of "Sinophone classicism" in digital times.[1] As an opera film with 90 percent of the scenes created by computer graphics (CG), it was said to have broken wide open the small circle of opera fans (*poquan* 破圈)[2] and has been widely regarded as a Cantonese opera film tailored for the young. The film indeed won a major following among young fans in Chinese movie theaters in May 2021.[3] Owing to popular demand, it began streaming for a fee on one of the leading Chinese streaming sites, *B zhan* B站 (Bilibili), in October 2021, and it was released again in theaters in May 2022.

Considering the 2019 Cantonese opera film *White Snake* in the context of "Sinophone classicism" reminds us that the film's use of Cantonese, the Sinitic language with one of the largest population of speakers second only to Mandarin,[4] speaks both to the multilingual nature of the Sinitic-language spaces and the importance of including mainland China in our continued exploration of

PRISM: THEORY AND MODERN CHINESE LITERATURE • 20:2 • SEPTEMBER 2023
DOI 10.1215/25783491-10992790 • © 2023 LINGNAN UNIVERSITY

the "Sinophone" and its dynamic, multilayered, and evolving engagements with "classicism." As emphasized in the introduction to this special issue, it is important to call out "cosmopolitan homogenization" as well as "Han nationalism or cultural essentialism" in our explorations, especially when such engagements are reinventing and reimagining the Chinese cultural past in our increasingly hyperconnected digital age.

Situating "Sinophone classicism" in digital times, I employ "digital classicism" as an analytical tool to examine the recent popular breakthrough of the Cantonese opera film *White Snake*, making use of audience-based digitally produced and transmitted Chinese-language materials, among other sources. Inspired by this special issue's focus on "the conceptual, emotional, and even ontological shake-ups brought about by digital engagement *and* entanglement with classicism," I first contextualize the Cantonese opera film in the history of experimenting with the White Snake theme, with a focus on special effects and visual effects and the genres of local opera and opera film. I then move to a close reading of a series of *danmu* 彈幕 (bullet screen), anonymous live comments on the Cantonese opera film trailer posted on the popular video streaming platform Bilibili, as important entry points for the study of audience participation in digital times. The digitally produced "ink painting–style Chinese aesthetics" of the film, its digital breakthrough as a "musical with Chinese characteristics" with more than 90 percent of CG, as well as various forms of fan and anti-fan digital labor triggered by the film, provide further evidence of the importance of "the digital" as "processes of sense-making."[6] The article concludes with thoughts on what difference "the digital" might be able to make in this long history of representing what has become a "classical" Chinese legend.

Cantonese Opera, Special Effects, and Opera Films Encountering the White Snake Theme

Cantonese opera's rise to popularity and major influence throughout the Chinese-speaking worlds can be traced back to the early decades of the twentieth century, if not earlier, when Cantonese opera rose to be among the three leading performance genres used to render the White Snake legends on Shanghai stages, together with Peking opera (*jingju* 京劇) and *tanci* 彈詞 storytelling.[7] The Cantonese opera actress Li Sut-fong (Li Xuefang)'s 李雪芳 (1898–?) 1919 charity performance in Shanghai was famous for its "new costumes, electric lights and colorful special effects, which complemented her singing."[8] There is quite a resemblance between this 1919 performance and the 2019 film version of *White Snake* starring the head of the Guangdong Cantonese Opera Institute Zeng Xiaomin 曾小敏 (1977) as the White Snake, exactly a hundred years later.

Both the 1919 stage performance and the 2019 film seem to have focused on spectacular appearances and visual stimuli, which came under attack in theater reform movements in mainland China from the early 1950s onward, as both the Cantonese style and the "Shanghai School" (*haipai* 海派) of traditional Chinese theater performance were condemned as superficial or, worse, decadent, in the changed climate of the new communist regime. Li Sut-fong's returning to the stage in Hong Kong in 1950 as Mrs. Henry Wei, and appearing in two nights of White Snake performances for the Hong Kong Society for the Protection of Children, speaks precisely to the power of the Cantonese opera to move beyond geopolitical borders.[9]

The rise of Cantonese opera, as well as many other regional operas using local dialects or, rather, other important Sinitic languages in addition to Mandarin, has been narrated as a response to Peking opera's presumptive cultural dominance. The story of Cantonese opera's popularity in republican Shanghai and its far-reaching impact on Southeast Asia and in Cantonese-speaking communities all over the world enriches our understanding of the importance of the genre and the intertwined cultural history between the local, the national, and the transnational, of which *White Snake* and its digital breakthroughs are but some of the most recent manifestations.

Related to the development of visual spectacles in Shanghai-style operatic performance and of staging techniques in Cantonese opera aided by new technology, as early as the 1890s, special effects have become a selling point on the White Snake stage, according to *Shenbao* 申報 (Shanghai Times) advertisements.[10] Development of special effects was also central to White Snake–themed films across East Asia, with the 1956 Japanese film *Byaku fujin no yōren* 白夫人の妖恋 (Madame White Snake) featuring special-effects director Tsuburaya Eiji 円谷英二 (1901–70) of *Godzilla* fame as a prime example.[11] Indeed, *Madame White Snake*'s all-out fantasy provided fertile ground for Tsuburaya's experiments. Most notably, his work on the film was credited as the first use of the "blue-back" ブルーバック, or blue-screen/green-screen system in the history of Japanese filmmaking.[12] Similarly, in the 1960 Korean film *Paeksa buin* 백사부인 (Madam White Snake), director Shin Sang-ok 신상옥 (1926–2006) portrays White Snake's "humanity of the nonhuman" through the use of special effects.[13]

The 2011 special effects–heavy, 3D film *Baishe chuanshuo* 白蛇傳說 (It's Love), starring Jet Li (Li Lianjie 李連傑; 1963–) as Abbot Fahai, continues to accentuate the gray zone between the human and the nonhuman, and good and evil, using cutting-edge technology. It does so with a newly created character, Nengren 能忍, a young disciple of Abbot Fahai who not only falls in love with Green Snake but also turns out himself to have a hybrid identity of human and demon.[14] The film, as a high-tech martial arts romantic fantasy film, creatively reflects the genre-blending trends in the legend's Japanese and Korean cinematic adaptations throughout the Cold War, in which fantasy, romance, comedy, martial arts, and horror long intersected through the meticulous use of cutting edge special effects techniques. In this context, the 2019 *White Snake* film, 90 percent of which uses CG effects, again represents the latest development in using special effects, in this case, computer-generated visual effects to bring the White Snake performance to life in the digital age.

Similarly, experimentation with the genre of opera film has long been used in representing the White Snake on-screen. Runje Shaw (Shao Zuiweng) 邵醉翁 (1896–1975), who directed the *Yiyao Baishe zhuan* 義妖白蛇傳 (The Righteous Snake) films in Shanghai in 1926 and 1927, codirected with Li Pingqian 李萍倩 (1902–84) a Cantonese opera film *Shilin jita* 仕林祭塔 (Memorial at the Pagoda) in 1934 through the Naam Yuet Movie Company (南粵影片公司) in Hong Kong. More attempts at using Cantonese opera to approach the White Snake theme were made in the early 1960s, with Wong Fung's 王風 (1923–) *Duanqiao chanzi* 斷橋產子 (Giving Birth on the Bridge) from the Chiu Ming Film Company (超明影業公司) and Chan Pei's 陳皮 (1904–66) *Gechang Shilin jita* 歌唱仕林祭塔 (Till Death Do We Part) from the Hing Fat Film Company (興發影業公司), both made in Hong Kong in 1962, as prominent examples.

Other local operatic forms, including *Huangmei diao* 黃梅調 (Huangmei opera), also heavily influenced White Snake films from the 1960s onward, with the 1962 film *Baishe zhuan* 白蛇傳 (Madam White Snake) produced by Shaw Brothers Studio in Hong Kong as the most influential throughout the Sinophone worlds in Southeast Asia and beyond. Intriguingly, the White Snake iconography popularized by the phenomenally successful 1992 Taiwanese TV series *Xin Bainiangzi chuanqi* 新白娘子傳奇 (New Legend of the White Snake) again points to the aesthetic beauty of traditional Chinese costumes and the Huangmei opera–style singing in opera films from the mid-twentieth century. This historical context helps us position the 2019 4K surround-sound version of *White Snake* as but a continuation of attempts to marry the genres of opera and film in representing the White Snake theme, with the aid of the most innovative technology for its times.

Danmu, Audience Participation in Digital Times

On May 8, 2021, a final trailer for the 2019 *White Snake* film,[15] scheduled to open in Chinese movie theaters less than two weeks later on May 20, 2021, was released on Bilibili, the most popular digital video-sharing platform among young people in China. This one-minute, twenty-second trailer attracted some 2 million views overnight and rose to be the most popular video on Bilibili, garnering tens of thousands of enthusiastically favorable "bullet screen" (*danmu*) comments, a form of massive anonymous live chats shown as comment lines emerging from the right to the left of the screen and sometimes forming a dense curtain over the video content they comment on, overwhelmingly from the young people frequenting the site. The advertised release date of May 20, or 520, when reading in

Mandarin Chinese, sounds like *wo ai ni* 我愛你 (I love you). By titling the new Cantonese opera film with an added keyword *qing* 情 (emotion, love) and choosing a date conveying the meaning of romantic and sexual love to the younger Mandarin-speaking mainland Chinese audience, the creators and promotors of the film set out to capture the younger generation, who are also the majority of internet users, through the digital promotion of the film trailer.

In this sense, the viral film trailer and the abundant *danmu* comments it generates became a set of fitting digital texts worthy of close reading, for the study of audience participation in digital times. Recent scholarship has focused on the spontaneity and virtual heterotopia expressed in *danmu*,[16] as *danmu* comments are completely anonymous and temporally fixed to appear at the point of insertion, allowing future audiences to view the video with all the accumulated anonymous comments simultaneously and experience a false sense of live interaction. In particular, Leticia-Tian Zhang and Daniel Cassany's 2020 study can help us better appreciate the importance of *danmu* as ways of not only forming complex interpretative communities but also guiding future interpretations of the contents they comment on.[17]

The digitally conceived and produced film trailer opens with the Buddhist abbot Fahai 法海 calling out Bai Suzhen 白素貞, the name of the White Snake spirit after she assumes the form of a beautiful woman, instantly attracting bullet-screen comments on how skilled the Cantonese opera performer is in his enunciation of words and how expressive his eyes are in conveying his authority (00:03). The scene then fades to a wall of defense (*luohan zhen* 羅漢陣) formed by more than a dozen monks (only fourteen rather than the expected eighteen in number, as in the set phrase *shiba luohan* 十八羅漢). With black smoke-like traces morphing from the robes of the monks, the scene takes on the effect of ink spreading on rice paper and melting into its surrounding background (00:03). The trailer then presents the title character, White Snake, wielding her sword to form a flowery pattern (*jianhua* 劍花) and striking a dignified pose, again with superb sound effects and with a closeup on the snake woman's determined gaze as she confronts Fahai and his wall of defense (00:05). Here the background continues to show the effect of ink morphing on rice paper, forming what would be characterized as "ink painting–style Chinese aesthetics" (*shuimo guofeng meixue* 水墨國風美學) by the creative team, audience comments, and popular press coverage of the film.

After prominently listing the three coproduction agencies, including the Guangdong Cantonese Opera Institute (00:16), the trailer frames the White Snake in front of a half-covered moon gate, with an opaque bamboo forest seemingly shrouded in a dense fog framed by the gate, and weathered tree branches in the style of Chinese ink painting stretching out on a faded gray wall connected to the gate, all appearing with fuzzy edges and the effect of ink morphing into its surroundings. The bullet screen accompanying this frame (00:18) presents viewer comments branding the film as "a new direction for traditional theater" and its aesthetics as "Chinese-style ink painting" or simply "Chinese-style," in big, imposing fonts and bright red colors. The trailer strategically capitalizes on many recent successes in terms of "Chinese-style aesthetics." This includes the design of Jinshan si 金山寺 (Golden Mountain Temple), where the climactic fight between the White Snake and Abbot Fahai takes place (00:20), in the style of Yunshen buzhichu 雲深不知處 (Cloud Recesses), the mountain base of the Lan Clan in the extremely popular *Chenqing ling* 陳情令 (The Untamed), a fifty-episode web drama based on a "boys love" fantasy novel.[18] The ink painting–style animation sequences (01:14–20) leading to the final appearance of the film title also recall the title sequence in the animated film *Baishe: Yuanji* 白蛇：緣起 (White Snake: The Legend Begins), which opened in theaters nationwide in China in January 2019 and became an instant success with both audiences and film critics.

Such echoes should also be considered in the larger context of the rise of a polyphonic "Chinese-style aesthetics" (*Zhongguo feng* 中國風, literally, "China wind") in Sinophone popular culture in recent decades. For example, a celebrated duo, the Taiwanese megastar and singer/songwriter Jay Chou 周杰倫 (1979–) and famed lyricist Vincent Fang (Fang Wen-shan 方文山; 1969–), are at the center of a Mandopop sensation featuring lyrics deeply saturated with the beauty of classical Chinese poetry, with songs such as "Dongfeng po" 東風破 (East Wind Breaks), "Fa ru xue" 髮如雪 (Hair like Snow), "Qinghua ci" 青花瓷 (Blue and White Porcelain), and "Juhua tai" 菊花台 (Chrysanthemum Terrace).[19] Such imagined and romanticized versions of a nostalgic Chineseness may not correspond to a specific historical period and may have never existed in such a form in the first place. Now presented as a treasured "classical Chinese aesthetics" encroached upon by everyday life and needing restoration in contemporary times, it conditioned some of the bestselling digital cultural products across the Sinophone worlds, with the pervasive web presence of "Chinese-style" Mandopop—such as the rising popularity of the singer Zhou Shen 周深 (1992–), web drama series such as *The Untamed*, reality shows featuring songs based on classical Chinese poetry such as *Jingdian yong liuchuan* 經典詠流傳 (Everlasting Classics), and programs showing celebrities learning different local opera highlights such as *Zuimei Zhongguo xi* 最美中國戲 (Most Beautiful Chinese Theater), among many others—as prime examples from mainland China and widely popular on various digital platforms.

"Classical Chinese aesthetics" is at the center of the promotional video for *White Snake*. Only a few seconds into the trailer of the film, comments such as "every frame is a painting" (00:06) appear on the bullet screen, as the Bilibili viewers are very attuned to the visual qualities of the film. Other comments alerted the viewers to the film's superb sound effects and urged others to wear their earbuds when watching the trailer, stating that "the operatic enunciation is truly exquisite" and "every sound makes you feel electrified" (00:23). Yet another comment mentioned that the Guangdong Cantonese Opera Institute, where the performers are from, has been experimenting with online games in addition to film (00:10), attesting to the young viewers' keen perception of the formal experimentations of the film. At the same time, these predominately favorable comments also open up *danmu* to possible interpretations as potentially manipulative, as they could also have been posted by hired hands.[20]

The bullet-screen comments continue to point out how the film embodies the confrontation between traditional theater and its televisual and filmic adaptations, how it presents lavish enjoyment both visually and auditorily, and how the film is of outstanding quality, both materially and textually (00:35). When the White Snake uses her *shuixiu* 水袖 (water sleeve) to control water in her fight against Fahai, many commented on the joining of CG and theatrical conventions, emphasizing how this film could be considered as carrying on the tradition of the musical theater but with Chinese characteristics (00:43).[21]

The trailer proper seems to anticipate and echo these comments by means of intertitles, which brand the film as "the first 4K surround-sound Cantonese opera film" (00:53) and emphasize the themes of the film: "reincarnation and transmigration" (00:57), "committing to love for a thousand years" (01:04), and, centrally, "a human without emotion is less than a demon, a demon with emotion can be human" (01:05–14). The digital trailer and the digital *danmu* continuously collaborate to foster a sense of live interaction and simultaneous participation among readers of the *danmu* and viewers of the trailer, shaping future interpretations of the advertised film while also leaving room for heterogeneous, critical voices to surface among predominantly positive comments.

Ink Painting–Style Chinese Aesthetics, Digitally Produced

Significantly, the discussions surrounding the aesthetics of the film consolidated around the more specific *Songdai meixue* 宋代美學 (Song dynasty aesthetics). Why Song dynasty (960–1279) specifically? In an English-subtitled promotional video interview posted on YouTube,[22] the director Zhang Xianfeng 張險峰 highlights how "the whole movie shows the Song-dynasty aesthetics," with the accompanying promotional video showing two celebrated Song-dynasty paintings, Guo Xi's 郭熙 (ca. 1000–ca. 1087) *Zaochun tu* 早春圖 (Early Spring) and Fan Kuan's 范寬 (ca. 950–ca. 1032) *Linliu duzuo tu* 臨流獨坐圖 (Sitting Alone by a Stream) (02:22–23).

The "literati painting" tradition of the Song dynasty is highlighted here by the producers of the film to foster a distinctive classical aesthetics, one that is infused with a strong sense of Han ethnic nationalism. The emphasis on "Songness" suggests an attempt to dissociate the classical aesthetics from the perceived cosmopolitanism of the preceding Tang dynasty and the ethnic hybridity of the succeeding Mongol Yuan dynasty. The irony is that it was during the early Yuan dynasty (1271–1368) that Northern Song (960–1127) painters like Guo Xi were rediscovered as part of a broader revival of early landscape painting practices, shifting away from the highly decorative blue-and-green style and reinterpreting the scholar-recluse image to magnify the grandeur of the state.[23] It is thus important to point out that the film producers' use of an imagined "Song-ness" to represent the peak of literati aesthetics of classical China could fall into the pitfall of cultural essentialism and should be interrogated throughout our analysis.

Zhang continues to emphasize how Song-dynasty aesthetics is reflected in the film's costumes, all of them "dyed with plants," and the YouTube video shows how Green Snake's costumes are created with such natural green dye in mind (02:26). In terms of portraying the snake women's flying movements in the film, the director asks, "How should the Chinese fly?," and answers his own question by stating that the team studied "Dunhuang murals" and "tried many poses" to "find something Oriental [*dongfang* 東方]" (02:47). This self-orientalization move dominated the thinking of the production team, as many other interviews reveal.

This emphasis on Song-dynasty aesthetics is echoed in the "Chinese Style: Interview with Designers" column on Sohu Fashion.[24] The column invited art designer Li Jinhui 李金輝 and stylist Wang Xiaoxia 王曉霞 to share their creative thinking behind their designs for the film. Li claims that the film follows "the traditional color spectrum of Chinese painting," as the paint materials in Chinese painting come from plants and minerals and hence are closer to the experience of everyday life. Li uses the opening scene of the film featuring the "lotus-picking girls" as an example. For that scene, the art design team used mountain green (*shanlü* 山綠) and rock blue (*shiqing* 石青), colors most frequently used in Chinese painting, to foster a lively dancing and singing sequence.[25] In addition, the team used bean green/blue (*douqing* 豆青), a frequently appearing color in Song-dynasty porcelain such as Ru ware (*Ruyao* 汝窯),[26] to try to represent the exquisite beauty of the unfolding love story between Bai Suzhen and Xu Xian 許仙. Although the film is in color, the ending scene of "lingering snow on the broken bridge" (*duanqiao canxue* 斷橋殘雪) features an abundant use of the "leaving blank" (*liubai* 留白) technique in Chinese ink painting, largely reducing the temperature and saturation of the color spectrum to foster an atmosphere of heartbreak, sorrow, and desolation and echoing the plot of the film, according to Li.

The Sohu Fashion interview continued to highlight how the film conveyed such a distinctive aesthetics through costume design. The stylist Wang Xiaoxia had long been interested in dyeing costumes according to traditional methods, and she was very excited to bring such an idea to fruition for the film. For example, a piece of the costuming for White Snake's sister/maid, Green Snake (Xiao Qing 小青), was first dyed blue using true indigo (*landian* 藍靛), then dyed yellow using cape jasmine (*zhizi* 梔子). The resulting color is a gentler and more natural light green, close to the color effect of rock blue or mountain green and more fitting for the kind of traditional aesthetics the film is pursuing. Similarly, although White Snake's more than twenty pieces of clothing in eight different styles all seem to be white, the whiteness of every piece is different, some with a hint of gray, others the light pink color of a lotus root. Such delicate color variations and their natural-looking, subtle color spectra could be achieved only through traditional plant-based dyeing techniques, according to Wang.[27]

Crucially, such Song-dynasty aesthetics is largely conceived, produced, transmitted, and consumed digitally. The film's digital qualities were further highlighted when Zhang announced that more than 90 percent of the film's seventeen hundred scenes were made with computer graphics, created by three top-notch visual effects teams from New Zealand, Australia, and Shenzhen, China. According to *Dazhong dianying* 大眾電影 (Popular Movies), one of the most influential and long-lasting film magazines in China,[28] the creators changed their designs three times during the shooting process, creating 210 concept designs and 10 scene-setting locations.

This kind of "cinematic quality" in terms of visual effects is most prominently expressed in the key scene at the Golden Mountain Temple. For audiences familiar with the Cantonese opera stage version of the scene, surprises await. Instead of presenting the charging waves in abstraction, with twenty Cantonese opera actresses flinging their "water sleeves" to symbolize the waves, the film pushes the use of CG to the extreme, realistically presenting the effects of raging waves reaching the sky. Zhang referred to this as a cinematic means of presenting a grand form of the "painting of the spirit" (*da xieyi* 大寫意) tradition, a tradition in Chinese painting in which extreme realism and grand symbolism converge.

In an interview with Zhang by Diyi daoyan on Douban,[29] the Cantonese opera film was proclaimed the "king of CG," highlighting its advanced use of CG-produced visual effects, especially in the climactic fight at the Golden Mountain Temple. Zhang specifically responded to why the creators gave up the way Cantonese opera has staged this scene in the past. Inspired by the famous Japanese woodblock print *Kanagawa oki nami ura* 神奈川沖浪裏 (The Great Wave Off Kanagawa) by Katsushika Hokusai 葛飾北斎 (1760–1849), Zhang was determined to bring out the powerful human spirit amid the great waves in that painting, and, rather paradoxically, he attempted to release the same human spirit of the nonhuman snake women in the film, using CG-produced visual effects.

Computer Graphics and "Musical with Chinese Characteristics": A Digital Breakthrough
Despite the popularity of the trailer and its rising to be the most popular video on Bilibili in May 2021, the public's exposure to the film itself was limited because of the way the Chinese film market functions and its extreme restrictions on such a genre film (showings of the film made up only 1 percent of the total available screenings when it opened in the movie theaters). Still, the film was reported

to have attracted many more young people to the theaters as paying customers than any other opera film in Chinese film history. Zhang mused on why the film was able to broaden the small circle of traditional opera fans and reach out to the young. He claims that the film constitutes a "system of oriental aesthetics" and "directly incorporates traditional opera with film." These claims are continuously being echoed in the digital *danmu* and other online audience comments and reviews.[30]

How are the visual effects loved by the younger generation achieved? As mentioned earlier, the climactic flooding scene was designed by leading visual-effects experts both from China and from abroad. In the same interview by Diyi daoyan on Douban, Zhang particularly highlighted the difficulties in getting the foreign teams to tone down the "Hollywood-style waves" seen in disaster films. Zhang pointed out to them that what he was aiming at was the framing (*goutu* 構圖) and spirit (*qiyun* 氣韻) of a scene, rather than light and shadow. He consequently showed the foreign teams many Chinese paintings and asked them to reduce the contrast between light and shadow and to add floating fog and fleeting clouds among the waves.[31]

Furthermore, the film's success with the younger generation, according to its creators, does not lie in reproducing the traditional "stage documentation" style of opera films from the past, which often employed a static camera and simply recorded stage performance in a documentary style; instead, it strives to become a "musical with oriental characteristics," produced according to the industry processes of filmmaking in digital times. The creators believe that only with a work that is fully integrated in the genre (of musical) and full of visual impact and emotional tension can they get rid of the notion that traditional opera films are fitting only for opera fans, hence bringing opera film to the younger generation and even moviegoers outside the country, enlarging the audience for opera film from "opera fans" to the general populace.[32]

In fact, long before its official release in the Chinese market in May 2021, the film had been touring film festivals,[33] garnering prizes and attracting attention both in China and internationally since late 2019.[34] According to the aforementioned *Popular Movies* article, on October 18, 2019, at the Pingyao International Film Festival in Shanxi, China, this Cantonese opera film, often perceived as belonging to a niche (*xiaozhong* 小眾) genre, won "the most popular film" title in the genre film category, with the results determined solely by votes of the audiences, whose members were mostly young people.[35] As a result, already in 2019 and long before the "final trailer" went viral on Bilibili in May 2021, bits and pieces of the film, including short promotional scenes and behind-the-scenes shots, have been voluntarily uploaded by young audience members to popular platforms such as Bilibili B站, Douban 豆瓣, and Zhifu 知乎, attracting increasing numbers of hits online.[36] These activities helped bring fresh "China Wind" to both domestic and international audiences and prepared for the film's success with the younger generation once it opened in mainland China in May 2021. Such audience activities would then be amplified through fan and anti-fan labors on digital platforms.

Reviews, Comments, and Other Forms of Fan/Anti-fan Labor on Digital Platforms

In an audience post on Douban, a viewer by the name of Xingzi wu 杏子塢 (Apricot Dock)[37] based in Toronto, Canada, wrote in detail about how the costumes and makeup (including a reference to the Morandi color made famous by the Italian painter Giorgio Morandi),[38] the Chinese-style garden, and the framing of the scenes worked together with the Cantonese opera structure the film follows—five sequences (*zhe* 折) and one epilogue (*weisheng* 尾聲)—to foster a distinct aesthetics for the film. Another audience review gave a brief historical overview of Cantonese opera in North America and attributed the film's popularity to the marrying of opera with film and to Cantonese opera's historical status as popular culture.[39] The same reviewer's real encounter with the film was, however, through a staging of one scene from the film by Zeng Xiaomin, the White Snake actress in the film, and Liang Hanwen 梁漢文 (1971–), a Hong Kong actor and singer, at Bilibili's New Year Gala, live-streamed on its site. This staging of "Dengni guilai" 等你歸來 (Waiting for Your Return) was in fact one of the most frequently mentioned moments of enchantment for many young audiences, who first saw this highlight of the film (with a different Xu Xian) at the Bilibili New Year Gala online. Realizing that they had missed the opportunity to see the film in theaters, they started to serve as volunteer promoters of the film by reposting bits and pieces of videos of this staging and of the film.

An extreme case of volunteering fan labor could be seen in a lengthy 17,500-word review of the film on Zhihu, a popular question-and-answer website, with a fan-created performance script of the film appended to the same post in a later update.[40] The performance script is identified as a "fan-made script," which not only lists the full cast and crew of the film but also meticulously highlights the differences between the stage and the film scripts. The plot summaries, chapter titles and settings, singing parts, speaking parts, and what may serve as stage directions are all color coded in the fan-made script, with names of different set tunes in Cantonese opera such as *changju gunhua* 長句滾花 (long line rolling), *fanxian zhongban* 反線中板 (reverse medium tempo), and *shigong manban* 士工慢板 (*shigong* slow tempo) clearly marked out in the script. The full lyrics of the opening aria sung by the White Snake that enchanted the young commentators on Bilibili read as follows:

> Fulfilling my wishes, my heart lingers for a thousand years,
> waiting only for a chance encounter with you.

Raising a sunny sky for me in the rain along the West Lake.

Under the umbrella, I smile shyly, like a lotus flower in late summer.

Love rises, hearts follow.

Love rises, too late to regret.

Who cares he is a young man of the human realm,

stop saying I am a snake who cannot love.

For him, I search for the immortal herb.

For him, I flood the Golden Mountain.

For him, I can forego life and death.

For him, I am willing to be imprisoned for another thousand years.

Love rises, even longings and memories are sweet.

圓我的願，心事千年，只等你遇見，
西湖雨裡為我撐起一片晴天。
傘下，羞得嫣然，是六月蓮。
情已生，心相至；
情已生，悔也遲；
哪管他是人間少年，莫再說我是蛇兒不能戀。
為了他，求仙草;
為了他，漫金山;
為了他，舍生死;
為了他，我願塔裡再困千年，
情已生，思憶點點甜。[41]

The opening aria summarizes in a nutshell the plot of the film from the perspective of the White Snake. In an interview, Mo Fei 莫非, the script writer of both the Cantonese opera (she also directed the stage version) and the opera film, emphasized the title keyword *love* (*qing*) in her adaptations.[42] Mo Fei grew up watching White Snake performances with her grandmother. The young viewer and young female fan later emerged as a scriptwriter and director who, before embarking on the Cantonese opera *White Snake*, had already directed a blackbox musical version of the play, *Green Snake*, as a labor of love. For the Cantonese opera, Mo Fei attempted to instill a contemporary spirit in the plot to maintain the dynamics and liveliness of the art of Cantonese opera. In a related interview, she listed seven behind-the-scenes details that would help the audience better appreciate her attempt at scripting the Cantonese opera *White Snake* for a contemporary audience: the emphases on White Snake's relentless pursuit of love, maintenance of Fa Hai's dignified image, insistence on White Snake's human frailty, restoration of Xu Xian's sincerity in love, infusion of strong emotion in the abundant fighting scenes, intense cinematic visualization of the use of water sleeves in the fighting scenes, and the use of real people to form the "wall of defense" rather than using visual effects.[43] These details speak to the new Cantonese opera film's thematic and technical preoccupations, with a focus on fusing human emotions with visualization in the digital context of contemporary filmmaking.

A master's thesis, another kind of labor of love, has also been written on the spatial issues in opera films, with the 2019 film version of *White Snake* as a central case study; it is digitally accessible as an appendix to the author's review of the film on Douban.[44] The thesis focuses on the creation of stage space through poetic movements, and the relationship between abstraction in realistic scene setting and poetic realism. Through the confrontation between the genres of opera and film, the author finds a vast space for research into spatial issues in opera film, including into the genres' shared and distinct formal qualities with respect to song and dance as storytelling. The author further investigates the implication of using a circle motif and traditional garden and landscape design to shape the spatial qualities of modern opera theater, and the relationship between these formal visual qualities and the deep-focus camera work used in filmmaking.

One of the most devastatingly critical reviews of the film, or a sort of anti-fan labor reflecting a love-hate relationship, however, took the form of a podcast that went live online on June 18, 2021.[45] The host and the two interviewees appeared to be experts on opera performance and opera films, and they had a lot to say about the problems of *White Snake*. One of the guests was more accommodating than the others, in that she was able to look at both the successes and problems of the film, including the film's creative use of CG and the successful scene in which snake scales emerge from White Snake's face as she looks in the mirror. Both examples suggest that this guest was more receptive to the experimental qualities of the film.

The rest of the two-hour interview, however, focused exclusively on how problematic the film is. One of the deadliest flaws of the film, according to the podcast, lies in its omission of the gong sounds and drumbeats (*luogu dian* 鑼鼓點) that are supposed to serve as the onstage drivers that move the plot forward. In this context, Fei Mu's 費穆 (1906–51) 1947 opera film *Zhan jingtang* 斬經堂 (Murder in the Oratory) was mentioned as a positive model, with an interesting twist: the opera performer Zhou Xinfang 周信芳 (1895–1975) hoped to achieve realist effects in the film, while the film director Fei Mu advocated for operatic qualities, as if they traded positions in the process of finding the best way to synthesize the two genres, opera and film. The podcast discussions continued to center on how *White Snake* pursues high visual qualities at the cost of operatic aesthetics and at the risk of forgoing the preservation of performance conventions. The speakers cited as an example the episode in which the crane and deer spirits survey the mountain and encounter the White Snake attempting to steal the magic herb. The more tolerant guest talked about how the CG-created crane and deer and the live-action humanized figures of the two spirits form a dynamic relationship; however, all involved in the podcast criticized that the scene did not work with the required theatrical conventions and named Gai Jiaotian's 蓋叫天 (1888–1971) portrayal of Wu Song 武松 in the 1963 Peking opera film *Wu Song* as a much more successful precedent.

Similarly, the podcast rather cynically criticized the film's claim of pursuing the effect of a grand form of the "painting of the spirit" tradition as rather "a PowerPoint style," with an emphasis on its use of color and props as befitting "a studio photo." The speakers also complained that the whole film seemed to be shot with filters that were too strong, making the settings so abstract that viewers feel they are watching the four main characters in front of an empty background. They attributed this effect to the film's being shot in front of green screens and on studio film sets rather than in outdoor settings. They also could not wrap their heads around the opening and ending, with densely colored dancing and singing scenes introducing and concluding the film.

However, quite contrary to the podcast's ranking of *White Snake* as subpar (five or six out of ten), the film was enthusiastically received by the public on its first release in May 2021, its digital release in October 2021, and its rerelease in theaters in May 2022. A May 31, 2022, online article quoted the producer of the film as saying that the filmmakers' goal was precisely to get young people to the theater to appreciate opera film and get closer to traditional culture.[46] The president of the Chinese Association for Film Criticism was also quoted as saying that when adapting traditional theater into film, faithful "representation" of the "authentic" qualities of the opera would not attract the attention of the younger generation, and thus would fail in its responsibility of cultural transmission. In this sense, the artistic and technical maneuvers in the cinematic adaptation of this Cantonese opera film were said to provide a model for the modernization and "youthification" of other traditional operatic genres.

The same article further connects the success of the Cantonese opera film *White Snake* to a new wave of films, including the Cantonese animation film *Xiongshi shaonian* 雄獅少年 (I Am What I Am, released in theaters on December 17, 2021), the Chaoshan-language 潮州話 (Teochew) film *Daini qujian woma* 帶你去見我媽 (Back to Love, in theaters on January 7, 2022), and other films featuring Cantonese cultures. A new Cantonese opera film, *Qiaoguo furen* 譙國夫人 (Lady of Qiaoguo), featuring the same creative team from the Guangdong Cantonese Opera Institute, is in the works, and according to the Pear River Film Group, the coproducer of *White Snake*, it will help create a "Cantonese opera film phenomenon."[47] Such a rhetoric of presenting the Cantonese opera film *White Snake* as a trailblazer in the modernization of a traditional performance genre, however, should be conditioned in the long history of using special effects and the genre of opera film in representing the White Snake theme, as discussed at the opening of this article.

Digital Classicism: What Difference Does the Digital Make?

Historically speaking, just as the 2019 *White Snake* film inherited the "ink-painting aesthetics" from earlier White Snake films, including the 1953 Japanese black-and-white film *Ugetsu* 雨月物語, the success of *White Snake* as a youth film must also be attributed to its immediate predecessor, the 2019 animation film *White Snake: The Legend Begins*. The Cantonese opera film took inspiration from recent Chinese animation films, and its visual effects incorporated many digitally animated sequences. The opening of the film, for example, features the snake women chasing butterflies, with the aid of animated colorful butterflies filling the sky, echoing the legend of the Butterfly Lovers, reminding the viewer of Zhuangzi's dreaming of butterflies, and recalling the butterfly-chasing Shi Xiangyun 史湘雲 in the canonical Chinese novel *Dream of the Red Chamber*. Here, digital production provides a superb tool for the creation of kitsch extravaganza. The creation, circulation, and consumption of such "digital kitsch" has become an important cultural phenomenon worthy of our critical attention.

The animated butterflies, always appearing at the most affective moments throughout White Snake and Xu Xian's love story, serve as an important mechanism for fostering the romantic ambience of the film. Echoing the flying butterflies are pink peach-blossom petals at the height of the love story and snowflakes after the separation of the lovers, all digitally produced and filling up the whole sky with their imposing presence. Such animated atmospheric props gave concrete shapes and colors to a range of complex emotional entanglements between White and Green Snakes, White Snake and Xu Xian, and, to a limited extent, the largely overlooked relationship between White Snake and her son in the film. Digital technologies reshaped the film through CG-produced visual effects, and the high-tech ink-painting aesthetics was able to attract young audience members and lure them into the affective web of relationships fostered by the Cantonese opera performance.

We have considered the formal experimentations of the 2019 *White Snake* to better appreciate its success as a high-tech Cantonese opera film. Tracing the popularity of Cantonese opera in early twentieth-century Shanghai and its major influence on diasporic Chinese populations, we have realized that the pursuit of rich visual stimuli and the use of cutting-edge special and visual effects have become an enduring tradition in White Snake performances. At the same time, Cantonese-language film has also established its own tradition in contemporary popular culture. In this sense, the high-tech *Snake White* was able to combine the rich traditions of Cantonese opera and Cantonese film, which established a good base for its mass appeal.

However, formal avant-gardism does not necessarily lead to radical content and activism. The reason *White Snake* has won over more audience members than earlier experiments in opera film may lie in its exclusive focus on the keyword *qing* (emotion, love), as highlighted in its Chinese title, and its predominant use of CG.

It has been argued that it is precisely this "purification" of love that distinguishes the film as a "new edition" of the White Snake, through the reframing of the story and reshaping of the characters via digital postproduction. The White Snake in this version of the Cantonese opera and film, who willingly returns to the pagoda to receive punishment, of course would not require any salvation from her son or her sister/maid. This also returns the Buddhist abbot Fahai to the role of a "warner," as in Feng Menglong's 馮夢龍 (1574–1646) 1624 story collected in *Jingshi tongyan* 警世通言 (Stories to Warn the World), and the abbot would eventually become a "protector" of the White Snake so as to ensure the future reunion of the lovers. Such a harmonious happy ending, compared to Tian Han's revolutionary, "anti-feudal" version of the mid-1950s and the Green Snake–centered "postmodern" narratives advocating for gender transgression and activist revolt, is rather conservative. However, such conservatism seems to be in sync with the demands of contemporary audiences and the spirit of the Xi Jinping 習近平 (1953–) era, when renewed expectations for tradition-themed and revolution-fused "core values" increasingly dominate the public consciousness and everyday life. At the same time, such a pervasive conservatism also suggests the necessity of maintaining the rebellious spirit of the snake women as outlets for transgression.

So what exactly does the digital do to the White Snake legend's contemporary cinematic revamping in the form of a high-tech Cantonese opera film? Many of the young audience members frequenting the Bilibili site and producing the tens of thousands of positive *danmu* comments on the film trailer, as discussed earlier in this article, are indeed already "living hyperhistorically," according to Luciano Floridi, as information and communication technologies and their data-processing capacities become essential for the functioning and flourishing of everyday life.[48] In this sense, digital media in the form of video streaming and other online platforms that brought the film to larger circles, as well as the digital technologies involved in the making and post-producing of the film itself, became both technical infrastructures and "processes of sense-making," which not only provided the means but also the ways of thinking in understanding how today's social worlds come into being.[49] *White Snake*, as a cultural phenomenon enabled by the digital age, and the critical role played by fan and anti-fan digital labor in the process, suggest that the digital could help engineer new formations of humanity. This is shown in the transformation of all characters in the story into protagonists, rather than maintaining a critical distance toward Abbot Fahai and Xu Xian's characters. At the same time, the digital could also open critical and potentially productive spaces for grassroots engagement, resistance, and deconstruction of such new formations.[50]

Chinese ink painting and garden design, and their monochrome aesthetics, along with the use of the Cantonese language and the adaptation of opera conventions to suit a digitally produced film, the subdued colors, the plant-dyed costumes, and hand-crafted accessories, among many other markers of a "classical"

Chinese aesthetics, dominate this contemporary, experimental, and avant-gardist digital project. The case of the 4K surround-sound *White Snake* and its digital breakthrough showcase how digital mediations have transformed the way we produce, disseminate, understand, and appreciate the Chinese legend of the White Snake. Moreover, such a cultural phenomenon of the relatively popular success and critical acclaim of the Cantonese opera film *White Snake* pushes us to wrestle with the conceptual implication of digitality and its manifestation in classicism, which has created new critical spaces and invited new grassroots participation in producing, transmitting, and consuming contemporary popular culture.

LIANG LUO is professor of Chinese studies at the University of Kentucky and a Distinguished Visiting Researcher at the Institute of Folklore at East China Normal University. She is the author of *The Global White Snake* (2021) and *The Avant-Garde and the Popular in Modern China* (2014). She is working on a creative nonfiction project connecting the European avant-garde, Black internationalism, and the Chinese Revolution.

///////////////////////////////

Notes

1   Z. Yang, "Sinophone Classicism," 659–60.
2   *Zhongguo wenhua bao*, "Yueju dianying *Baishezhuan · qing* heyi 'poquan'?"
3   Ibid.
4   Mair, "What Is a Chinese 'Dialect/Topolect'?"
5   Wang, "Introduction," 316.
6   Couldry and Hepp, *Mediated Construction of Reality*, 5.
7   Luo, *Global White Snake*, 55.
8   *Shenbao*, November 30, 1919.
9   *South China Morning Post*, July 9, 1950.
10   *Shenbao* (Shanghai edition), February 16, 1895.
11   *Global White snake*, 122.
12   Tanaka, *Tōhō tokusatsu eiga zenshi*.
13   *Global White snake*, 158–59.
14   Yang H., "Duoyuan yu baorong."
15   This final trailer is posted on Bilibili on May 8, 2021: www.bilibili.com/bangumi/play /ep425052?theme=movie&spm_id_from=333.999.0.0.
16   Chen, "Poetic Prosumption of Animation."
17   Zhang and Cassany, "Making Sense of *Danmu*."
18   For more on *The Untamed*, see Michelle Yeh's article in this special issue.
19   Lin, "Multidimensionality of Chineseness"; Lin, "Jay Chou's China Wind Pop."
20   It is possible that *danmu* comments could be subject to possible manipulations by hired *shuijun* 水軍 (water troops), those who are paid to leave positive or negative comments online to sway other viewers' opinions.
21   Tian Han 田漢 had proposed to develop and advocate national, scientific, and popular content, and he used these as criteria in striving for a new democratic theater, *minzu gewuju* 民族歌舞劇, or "national musical." See Tian, "Zenyang zuo xigai gongzuo?," 99.
22   Yit, "Gorgeous Movie Praised by Millions."

23 Hearn, "Shifting Paradigms in Yuan Literati Art," 80–83.

24 Sohu Fashion, "Meishushi, zaoxingshi jiemi."

25 This emphasis on blue and green in fact deviates from the "Song-ness" of literati painting and the general tone of the film as more refined and more subtle. The heterogeneity in the film's color choices speaks to the invented nature of the "Song-ness" and how such "classical" Chinese aesthetics are in fact hybrid cultural imaginations conditioned by the contemporary moment of filmmaking.

26 For more details, see www.sothebys.com/en/auctions/ecatalogue/2012/ru-hk0367/lot.101 .html?locale=en (accessed November 18, 2023).

27 Sohu Fashion, "Meishushi, zaoxingshi jiemi."

28 *Dazhong dianying*, "*Baishezhuan · qing*."

29 Zhang X., "Zhuanfang *Baishezhuan · qing* daoyan."

30 Nie, "*Baishezhuan · qing* weishenme chenggong 'chuquan'?"

31 Zhang X., "Zhuanfang *Baishezhuan · qing* daoyan."

32 *Dazhong dianying*, "*Baishezhuan · qing*."

33 The film was China's entry in the Seventy-Eighth Golden Globe Awards in its non-English-language films category in 2020 and in the 2021 Academy Awards in its best international feature competition.

34 In addition to its success at Pingyao 平遥 in October 2019, the film was also nominated as one of the best opera films/musicals for the Golden Rooster Award, won best film award in the opera and musical category at the Canada Golden Maple Film Festival, and won best technology award at the Second Hainan International Film Festival in 2019.

35 *Dazhong dianying*, "*Baishezhuan · qing*."

36 We can debate about the legality of these fan posts, but we cannot deny that such fan labors helped create and amplify desire for seeing the film in theaters when it was released in China in May 2021.

37 Xingzi wu, "Renjian haozai nali?"

38 Zhang L., "Culture of Color."

39 Shiyaobaya, "Cong Yueju dao dianying."

40 Shizhichunye, "Ruhe pingjia Yueju dianying *Baishezhuan · qing*?"

41 From "*Baishezhuan · qing* fanzhi taiben" 《白蛇傳·情》飯制台本 [*White Snake* Fan-Created Performance Script], available at Shizhichunye, "Ruhe pingjia Yueju dianying *Baishezhuan qing*?" Translations are by the author.

42 Zhou and Ding, "*Baishezhuan · qing* bianju Mo Fei."

43 Liu and Wang, "Zhe qige muhou xijie."

44 Huabuguo, "Yi *Baishezhuan · qing* weili."

45 "'Youxi meixi.'"

46 "Yueju dianying *Baishezhuan · qing* chongying."

47 Ibid.

48 Floridi, *Fourth Revolution*, 4.

49 Couldry and Hepp, *Mediated Construction of Reality*, 5.

50 Frischmann and Selinger, *Re-engineering Humanity*, 42.

References

Chen, Zhen Troy. "Poetic Prosumption of Animation, Comic, Game and Novel in a Post-socialist China: A Case of a Popular Video-Sharing Social Media Bilibili as Heterotopia." *Journal of Consumer Culture* 21, no. 2 (2021): 257–77. https://www.doi.org/10.1177 /1469540518787574.

Couldry, Nick, and Andreas Hepp. *The Mediated Construction of Reality*. Cambridge: Polity, 2017.

Dazhong dianying. "*Baishezhuan · qing*: Dianying rang xiqu geng youxi" 《白蛇傳·情》：電影讓戲曲更有戲 [*White Snake*: Film Makes Traditional Theater More Popular]. *Sina*, June 22, 2020. k.sina.com.cn/article_3133440825_bac48339020000ine.html.

Floridi, Luciano. *The Fourth Revolution: How the Infosphere Is Reshaping Human Reality*. Oxford: Oxford University Press, 2014.

Frischmann, Brett, and Evan Selinger. *Re-engineering Humanity*. Cambridge: Cambridge University Press, 2018.

Hearn, Maxwell K. "Shifting Paradigms in Yuan Literati Art: The Case of the Li-Guo Tradition." *Arts Orientalis* 37 (2009): 78–106.

Huabuguo 花不果. "Yi *Baishezhuan · qing* weili, tan xiqu dianying zhong kongjian de xiangguan wenti (xiying yanjiusheng lunwen fushang)" 以《白蛇傳·情》為例，談戲曲電影空間的相關問題 (戲影研究生論文附上) [On Spatial Issues in Opera Films—Centered on *White Snake*, with MA Thesis Appended]. Douban, March 13, 2022. https://movie.douban.com/review/14272485/.

Lin, Chen-yu. "Jay Chou's China Wind Pop Made in Taiwan and Its Transnational Audiences." *Taiwan Insight*, February 13, 2020. https://taiwaninsight.org/2020/02/13/jay-chous-china-wind-pop-made-in-taiwan-and-its-transnational-audiences/.

———. "Multidimensionality of Chineseness in Taiwan's Mandopop: Jay Chou's China Wind Pop and the Transnational Audience." In *Made in Taiwan: Studies in Popular Music*, edited by Eva Tsai, Tung-Hung Ho, and Miaoju Jian, 189–200. New York: Routledge, 2019.

Liu Changxin 劉長欣, and Wang Xintong 王昕桐. "Zhe qige muhou xijie, youzhuyu ni 'kantou' *Baishezhuan · qing*, dujia zhuanfang bianju" 這七個幕後細節，有助於你"看透"《白蛇傳·情》，獨家專訪編劇 [These Seven Behind-the-Scene Details Will Help You 'See through' *White Snake*: Special Interview with the Scriptwriter]. *Nanfang baoye*, reposted on *Renmin zixun*, May 22, 2021. https://baijiahao.baidu.com/s?id=1700453652323073489&wfr=spider&for=pc.

Luo, Liang. *The Global White Snake*. Ann Arbor: University of Michigan Press, 2021.

Mair, Victor H. "What Is a Chinese 'Dialect/Topolect'? Reflections on Some Key Sino-English Linguistic Terms." *Sino-Platonic Papers* 29 (September 1991): 12–13.

Nie Qing 聶青. "*Baishezhuan · qing* weishenme chenggong 'chuquan'?" 《白蛇傳·情》為什麼成功出圈? [Why Did *White Snake* Successfully 'Break Circles'?]. *Xin kuaibao*, reposted on *Xinhua wang*, May 20, 2021. http://www.xinhuanet.com/ent/2021-05/20/c_1127467682.htm.

Shiyaobaya 是窈八丫. "Cong Yueju dao dianying: Tianshi dili renhe de yitiao xinlu" 從粵劇到電影：天時地利人和的一條新路 [From Cantonese Opera to Film: A New Road Opened Up at the Right Moment]. *Douban*, June 12, 2022. https://movie.douban.com/review/14451784/.

Shizhichunye 是枝春野. "Ruhe pingjia Yueju dianying *Baishezhuan · qing*?" 如何評價粵劇電影《白蛇傳·情》? [How to Evaluate Cantonese Opera Film *White Snake*?]. *Zhihu*, May 20, 2021. www.zhihu.com/question/362956135. (Includes "*Baishezhuan · qing* fanzhi taiben" 《白蛇傳·情》飯制台本 [*White Snake* Fan-Created Performance Script], updated on the seventh day of the seventh lunar month, 2021.)

Sohu Fashion 搜狐時尚. "Meishushi, zaoxingshi jiemi: Yueju dianying *Baishezhuan · qing* pingshenme mei chuquan?" 美術師、造型師揭秘：粵劇電影《白蛇傳·情》憑什麼美出圈? [Art Designer and Stylist Uncovering the Secrets: How Did the Beauty of the

Cantonese Opera Film *White Snake* Break Circles?]. *Sina*, June 25, 2021. https://k.sina.cn /article_3180303821_bd8f95cd02000u4zq.html?from=fashion.

Tanaka Tomoyuki 田中友幸, ed. *Tōhō tokusatsu eiga zenshi* 東宝特撮映画全史 [A Complete History of Films Made by Tōhō]. Tokyo: Tōhō kabushiki kaisha shuppan jigyōshitsu, 1983.

Tian Han 田漢. "Zenyang zuo xigai gongzuo?—Gei Zhou Yang tongzhi de shi feng xin" 怎樣做戲改工作？一給周揚同志的十封信 [How to Conduct Opera Reform?—Ten Letters to Comrade Zhou Yang]. In *Tian Han quanji*, vol. 17. Shijiazhuang: Huashan wenyi chubanshe, 2000.

Wang, David Der-Wei. "Introduction: Chinese Literature across the Borderlands." *Prism: Theory and Modern Chinese Literature* 18, no. 2 (2021): 315–20.

Xingzi wu 杏子塢. "Renjian haozai nali?" 人間好在哪裡? [What Good Is the Human Realm?]. *Douban*, June 18, 2022. https://movie.douban.com/review/14461461/.

Yang Hong 楊紅. "Duoyuan yu baorong: Baishe chuanshuo de houxiandai zhuyi jiedu" 多元與包容：白蛇傳說的後現代主義解讀 [Multiplicity and Tolerance: A Postmodern Reading of Legend of the White Snake]. *Dianying wenxue*, no. 12 (2012): 96–97.

Yang, Zhiyi. "Sinophone Classicism: Chineseness as Temporal and Mnemonic Experience in the Digital Era." *Journal of Asian Studies* 81, no. 4 (2022): 657–71. https://doi.org/10 .1017/S0021911822000596.

Yit. "Gorgeous Movie Praised by Millions [of] People with Every Frame Breathtaking." YouTube video, 4:41. June 7, 2021. www.youtube.com/watch?v=kWdkAyt9Q2A.

"'Youxi meixi': Yueju dianying *Baishezhuan qing* de 'xinhuan' yu 'jiuhen'" 「有戲沒戲」：粵劇電影《白蛇傳情》的 "新歡" 與 "舊恨" ["A Love-Hate Relationship": The "New Love" and "Old Hate" of the Cantonese Opera Film *White Snake*]. *ShrimpTalk*, podcast, episode 31, June 18, 2021. https://mp.weixin.qq.com/s /qZNbFlN_9wIoTDoSwTsLaQ.

"Yueju dianying *Baishezhuan · qing* chongying, zaixu poquan rechao" 粵劇電影《白蛇傳·情》重映，再續 "破圈" 熱潮 [Cantonese Opera Film *White Snake* Rereleased, Continuing Its Heat Waves of "Breaking Circles"]. *Zhongguo xinwen wang*, May 29, 2022. https://www.chinanews.com.cn/cul/2022/05-29/9766613.shtml.

Zhang Lei. "A Culture of Color." *China Daily*, September 4, 2021. http://global.chinadaily .com.cn/a/202109/04/WS6132d2eda310efa1bd66d4f3_1.html.

Zhang, Leticia-Tian, and Daniel Cassany. "Making Sense of *Danmu*: Coherence in Massive Anonymous Chats on Bilibili.com." *Discourse Studies* 22, no. 4 (2020): 483–502. https:// www.doi.org/10.1177/1461445620940051.

Zhang Xianfeng. "Zhuanfang *Baishezhuan · qing* daoyan: Nüquan benzhi shang shi tiaozhan nanquan zhong meiyou renxing de bufen" 專訪《白蛇傳·情》導演：女權本質上是挑戰男權中沒有人性的部分 [Special Interview with Director of *White Snake*: Feminism Is Essentially a Challenge to the Inhumane Elements in Patriarchy]. Interview by Falanxi jiaopian, Diyi daoyan, *Douban*, May 31, 2021. https://movie.douban.com/review /13581447/.

Zhongguo wenhua bao. "Yueju dianying *Baishezhuan · qing* heyi 'poquan'?" 粵劇電影《白蛇傳·情》何以 "破圈" [Why Did Cantonese Opera Film *White Snake* "Break Circles"?]. *Gmw*, June 22, 2021. https://m.gmw.cn/baijia/2021-06/22/1302371315.html.

Zhou Yu 周宇, and Ding Huifeng 丁慧峰. "*Baishezhuan · qing* bianju Mo Fei: Wanwu youqing ji gongtong gongming" 《白蛇傳·情》編劇莫非： 萬物有情即共通共鳴 [*White Snake* Scriptwriter Mo Fei: Love Enables the Communication among All Things]. *Nanfang dushibao*, May 14, 2021. http://rsstoutiao.oeeee.com/mp/toutiao /BAAFRD000020210514486920.html.

TARRYN LI-MIN CHUN

Surface Classicism
Aesthetics, Poetics, and Remediation in Digitally Enhanced Chinese Performance

ABSTRACT This article examines digital classicism in contemporary Chinese performance through the case study of an excerpt of the dance-drama *Zhici qinglü* 只此青綠 (Journey of a Legendary Landscape Painting) performed at the 2022 CCTV Spring Festival Gala. It argues that the mobilization of digital performance technologies in *Zhici qinglü* and other contemporary large-scale performance in the PRC generates what might be termed "surface classicism"—an engagement with the past that sublimates elements of classical art and literature into the realm of digitally enhanced visuality. Surface classicism lends itself to critiques of superficiality and inauthenticity, but this article demonstrates that its ubiquity in contemporary culture also creates new networks of relationality among remediations of classical poetics and imagery. Ultimately, the mediation of both liveness and spectacular technologies in contemporary, digitally enhanced performance establishes classicist poetics and imagery as a core component of shared contemporary Chinese culture and may even engender new, more accessible modes of classical erudition.

KEYWORDS surface classicism, theater, performance, technology, media

Midway through the 2022 CCTV Spring Festival Gala (Zhongyang guangbo dianshi zong tai Chunjie lianhuan wanhui 中央廣播電視總台春節聯歡晚會), the annual extravaganza's dazzling special effects and glittering costumes gave way to a comparatively austere scene: fifteen female dancers, draped in turquoise and celadon fabric, stood motionless on an unadorned stage. The elegant costumes, arrangement of bodies, and unusual peaks created by their tall hairstyles evoked the colors and shapes of a classical blue-and-green landscape painting (*qinglü shanshui hua* 青綠山水畫) (fig. 1). Haze seeped onto the stage, forming rings of clouds around the bases of the human mountains. As they danced, the backdrop too came alive. Swirling golden streaks moved along with the dancers and in time to a *guqin*-dominated soundtrack. At one point, calligraphy splashed across the proscenium wall; later in the dance, a larger-than-life landscape painting in black ink appeared on the backdrop and auditorium walls. Vibrant greens and blues filled in the outlines of mountains and rivers, revealing a digitized version of the famous Song dynasty painting *Qianli jiangshan tu* 千里江山圖 (A Thousand Li of

PRISM: THEORY AND MODERN CHINESE LITERATURE • 20:2 • SEPTEMBER 2023
DOI 10.1215/25783491-10992800 • © 2023 LINGNAN UNIVERSITY

FIGURE 1. Opening vignette of *Zhici qinglü* excerpt performed at the 2022 CCTV Spring Festival Gala. Screenshot from 2022 CCTV Spring Festival Gala livestream/recording. Source: https://www.youtube.com/watch?v=OZIUvIV50Ww.

Rivers and Mountains) by Wang Ximeng 王希孟 (1096–1119).[1] Becoming three-dimensional, the projections then expanded into the audience space and replaced the piece's opening austerity with full-blown spectacle.

Only one of many acts featured during the four-hour Spring Festival Gala, this excerpt from *Zhici qinglü* 只此青綠 (Journey of a Legendary Landscape Painting) proved to be a highlight—and perhaps the most widely discussed event—of the evening.[2] The full-length "poetic dance-drama" (*wudao shiju* 舞蹈詩劇) choreographed by Zhou Liya 周莉亞 and Han Zhen 韓真, both members of the "80 *hou*" (80 後) or post-1980 generation, had premiered only months earlier at the National Centre for the Performing Arts (Guojia da juyuan 國家大劇院, or NCPA) in Beijing. Its national tour then took the country by storm, with many venues adding performances to accommodate demand.[3] Subsequent appearances on the Bilibili New Year's Eve Gala on December 31, 2021, and the CCTV Spring Festival Gala on January 31, 2022, as well as widespread media coverage, only served to increase its circulation and popularity—but did so in large part by moving the live performance into the digital realms of streaming, social media, and microblogging. *Zhici qinglü* therefore constitutes an important case study of classicism in digital times. To begin, its engagement with landscape painting and poetic traditions participates in the broader resurgence of interest in the classics seen across contemporary Sinophone literature, film, television, performance, and popular culture. The role of online technologies in disseminating video and images of the production and providing platforms for audience discussion accords with Zhiyi Yang's argument that "current trends in classicism" are "powered by the new digital media that knit global Sinophone communities into an increasingly tight network."[4] At the same time, the fact that *Zhici qinglü* is in its primary form a *live* performance enhanced by cutting-edge stage technologies complicates the way that classicism operates and connects to individual reader/viewer/user experience.

Moreover, *Zhici qinglü* does not stand alone as a unique case study; rather, it represents a growing trend whereby elaborate Chinese theatrical productions capitalize on the latest advancements in performance technologies to "bring to life" well-known poetic images, literary tropes, and local landscapes. Perhaps most prominent among such performances are the 2008 and 2022 Beijing Olympics opening ceremonies, helmed by film and theater director Zhang Yimou 張藝謀 (b. 1950). However, similar aesthetics, uses of technology, and connections to classicism can be found across political propaganda performances, exhibitions and expos, tourist shows, and theatrical productions designed for grand theater venues such as the NCPA. Increasingly, both media publicity for and audience responses to these productions also circulate online, creating digital doubles that extend and remediate the ephemerality of live performance. Like *Zhici qinglü*, these productions raise questions about the relationship between spectacular, digitally enhanced visual displays and classicist refinement—aesthetic modes that may seem at odds with one another, but which in these productions come together to produce different layers of audience engagement, meaning making, and cultural identity.

Analysis of contemporary performance therefore enables a reconsideration of the relationship between classicism and cutting-edge technology, materiality and immateriality, topos and text in the digital age. Framed by a close reading of the *Zhici qinglü* excerpt performed for the 2022 CCTV Spring Festival Gala, this article first examines the multiple ways in which digital enhancement has become a standard feature across many genres of contemporary Chinese theater and performance. Then it turns to the question of how digital technologies are mobilized specifically in the service of translating classicist aesthetics and poetics for the stage. This process of translation, or transmediation, generates what might be called "surface classicism"—an engagement with the past that relies heavily on the literal projection of classical text and image onto performance surfaces and sublimates the more ornate elements of classicist style into the realm of digitally enhanced visuality, but which also lends itself to critiques of superficiality and inauthenticity. Rather than dismissing such productions as a result of these tensions, I argue that the ubiquity of surface classicism in contemporary culture creates new networks of relationality among remediations of classical poetics and imagery. Ultimately, the mediation of both live performance and spectacular performance technologies in digitally enhanced performance works to establish classicist poetics and imagery as a core component of shared contemporary Chinese culture and may even engender new, more accessible modes of classical erudition.

Digitality in Live Performance

In contemporary Chinese performance—and indeed, contemporary performance worldwide—digital technologies can and do work on many levels, but they function most notably as infrastructural components of the live event itself and as mediating interfaces that extend the live into virtual spheres. The *Zhici qinglü* excerpt from the 2022 CCTV Spring Festival Gala functions as a case study for both aspects of digitality in live performance. As staged for the Gala, *Zhici qinglü* featured the successful application of some of the most cutting-edge stage, recording, and display technologies available in the People's Republic of China (PRC). It was also immediately mediated, as part of the Gala broadcast and livestream, and later *re*-mediated via clips, commentary, and news reports posted online. *Zhici qinglü* thus connects to and represents a much broader trend in the twenty-first century wherein digital enhancements and mediation have become key components of scenic design, audience appeal, and the ability of live performances to reach well beyond their in-person venues.

The Gala has long been a platform for showcasing the latest in performance technologies, with the use of virtual elements further heightened during the COVID-19 pandemic. As a major annual state-sponsored event and the purportedly most watched television program in the PRC, the Gala has been analyzed extensively for its role in promoting ideology, attempting to create a sense of kinship and shared culture, and highlighting national priorities (as defined by the party-state).[5] Technology, unsurprisingly, has featured prominently in both content and form in recent Galas. In 2016, for example, 540 "smart robots" danced in synchrony beneath a laser light show at the Gala's Guangzhou venue, while the 2021 Gala premiered artificial intelligence (AI) plus virtual reality (VR) naked-eye three-dimensional (3D) displays and used a combination of holograms and virtual environments to incorporate remote performers.[6] The 2022 Gala was no exception. Media reports in both Chinese and English highlighted its use of AI-driven VR, augmented reality (AR), and extended reality technologies, as well as the 720-degree screen of LED panels covering the main performance auditorium at the CCTV studio.[7] At-home viewing options were also enhanced, with 130 cameras capturing the live performance and digital effects added to its broadcast and streamed versions. Large ultra-high definition 8K screens set up in cities across the PRC provided another alternative to in-home or personal device viewing.

While these technologies were used across the various song-and-dance numbers featured in this year's gala, the *Zhici qinglü* excerpt engendered a unique tripartite relationship between an original two-dimensional work of art, live performers, and digital technologies. To begin, the LED panels and AR technologies were used to add texture to the stage space and directly reference Wang Ximeng's *Qianli Jiangshan tu* painting. At the beginning of the number, for example, the color of

the screen reflected that of a warmly colored silk scroll, while flashes of light skim-
ming across their surface added a luminescent glow to the "cloth." Remote audiences also perceived the presence of a pool of water at the front of the stage—a
feature that was added digitally and clearly *not* present to live audiences in recording shots that show the physical space of the auditorium (fig. 2). The virtual pool
seemed to reflect and double the dancers' bodies but also accentuated the impression of a *shanshui* painting materialized, with the performers as the mountains
and digital effect as the water of that dyad. As one article on the production commented, through the holographic projections and AR technologies, the dancers
and the painted scroll were "combined as one" 舞蹈詩劇《只此青綠》運用全息,

FIGURES 2a–b: Digital effect producing a reflective pool of water at dancers' feet, with alternate camera angle
showing edge of stage and audience. Screenshot from 2022 CCTV Spring Festival Gala livestream/recording. Source:
https://www.youtube.com/watch?v=0ZIUvIV50Ww.

FIGURE 3. Digitized rendering of *Qianli jiangshan tu* displayed on 720-degree surround screen and via 3D holographic effects. Screenshot from 2022 CCTV Spring Festival Gala livestream/recording. Source: https://www.youtube.com/watch?v=OZIUvIV50Ww.

AR技術，讓舞蹈演員與《千里江山圖》畫卷合而為一.[8] Later in the performance, the screens shifted to display the larger-than-life digital reproduction of *Qianli jiangshan tu* surrounding the in-person audience, followed by holographic technologies extending three-dimensional renderings of the green-and-blue landscape beyond the stage (fig. 3). Technology thus contributed to creating a more immersive experience for both the in-person audience and viewers at home—a desired effect not only for this segment but also for the entire gala performance.[9]

Two other segments in the 2022 gala similarly engaged with artifacts from China's cultural and material history, with even more advanced digital visualization technologies. One was a dance duet entitled "Jinmian" 金面 (Golden Mask), which used an AI multimodal motion capture system (AI *duomotai dongbu xitong* AI 多模態動捕系統) to enable choreography between live performers and their avatars in a VR environment.[10] In the other, a partly prerecorded segment entitled "Yi Jiangnan" 憶江南 (Remembering Jiangnan)—named after the Tang dynasty poem by Bai Juyi 白居易 (772–846)—individual actors embodied characters inspired by famous poems from the Tang, Song, and Yuan dynasties. The actors were filmed in a blue-screen studio and then digitally woven into a 3D virtual re-creation of the landscape painting *Fuchun shan ju tu* 富春山居圖 (Dwelling in the Fuchun Mountains) by Huang Gongwang 黃公望 (1269–1354).[11] These segments shared with the *Zhici qinglü* excerpt an impulse to use technology to enliven famous cultural artifacts and, by doing so, to simultaneously showcase historical artistic achievement and contemporary technological prowess.

Yet while the use (and some might say, overuse) of cutting-edge stage, display, and recording technologies is undeniably a characteristic of the Gala, it is also a trend that extends to other holiday extravaganzas, opening ceremonies, propaganda performances, tourist and commercial theater, and even seemingly more "highbrow" productions designed for grand theaters (*da juyuan* 大劇院).[12] The trend has important antecedents in late imperial court pageants and twentieth-century political propaganda performances like *Dongfanghong* 東方紅 (The East Is Red).[13] Over the first two decades of the twenty-first century, however, productions defined by their scale and reliance on digital technologies have become a particularly prominent and popular segment of the performing arts market, especially in theatrical productions developed for large proscenium venues that typically seat upward of a thousand audience members. These venues themselves often function as a kind of showpiece; as scholars like Aihwa Ong, Anne-Marie Broudehoux, and others have discussed, the architecturally distinctive buildings that have sprung up in cities across the PRC since the turn of the twenty-first century belong to another kind of performance, one of architectural modernity and cosmopolitanism.[14] Grand theaters also display their technological modernity through cutting-edge infrastructure, such as the revolving, raising and lowering stage installed in the NCPA in Beijing.[15] *Zhici qinglü* is an example of the genre created for such theaters, and while its original staging did not feature holograms or AR, it did make full use of the high-tech lighting, sound, and mechanical systems of the theaters in which it was performed.

Two other major examples of this trend can be found in the growth of large-scale real-scenery landscape performances (*daxing shanshui shijing yanchu* 大型山水實景演出), exemplified by Zhang Yimou's "Yinxiang xilie" 印象系列 (Impressions Series), over the past two decades and in "mega-events" such as festival or expo opening ceremonies. The Impressions Series was inaugurated in 2003 with the premiere of *Yinxiang Liu Sanjie* 印象劉三姐 (Impression Liu Sanjie) in Yangshuo, Guilin. Several more productions followed, such as *Yinxiang Lijiang* 印象麗江 (Impression Lijiang) in 2006 and *Yinxiang Xihu* 印象西湖 (Impression West Lake) in 2007; the producing company has spun off several other projects such as the "Youjian xilie" 又見系列 (Encore Series) and "Zhiyou xilie" 只有系列 (Unique Series) under director Wang Chaoge 王潮歌 (b. 1965) and the "Zuiyi xilie" 最憶系列 (Living Poem Series).[16] These performances take place at well-known destinations throughout the PRC such as West Lake in Hangzhou, Wutai Mountain in Shanxi Province, and Dunhuang in Gansu Province. They mobilize, and at times exploit, connections between these topoi and local culture, classical poetry, religious practices, and the Chinese national imaginary. As Audrey Yue has discussed, each of the Impressions productions also uses "large-screen technologies" to "tap into a global Chinese visual culture resonant with public screens" in a way that both enchants and disenchants audiences.[17] Factors including the popularity of these productions, collaborations with government entities and tourist industries, and the evangelism of theater producers have made real-scenery landscape performance burgeon into an enormous industry in the PRC.[18] Meanwhile, opening ceremonies perform on an even grander scale in sports stadiums and large auditoriums, with international draw, thousands of spectators in attendance, and live broadcast/streaming further augmenting audience size. Most emblematic are, of course, the opening ceremonies for the 2008 Summer Olympics and 2022 Winter Olympics in Beijing, although many other mega-events (like the Shanghai World Expo in 2010) also have held opening-ceremony performances.

Across these works of theater and performance, the digital may be defined on multiple levels. At the most fundamental, many commonly used technologies, like LED screens, increasingly operate in the realm of the digital. Analog projection is a mechanical process whose optics are governed by the materiality of the power source, the lighting unit, the lenses, the physical slide, and the screen onto which it is projected. In contrast, digital displays like LED screens rely on electronic inputs to control their light-emitting diodes and computerized control systems to play images on their surfaces. When LED displays and similar technologies such as digital projections, projection mapping, and computer-controlled lighting systems are used, then, a given production moves toward the realm of what Steve Dixon has called "digital performance." Digital performance, as defined by Dixon, includes "all performance works where computer technologies play a *key* role rather than a subsidiary one in content, techniques, aesthetics, or delivery forms."[19] This includes a range of work from theatrical productions that incorporate digital projections to onstage robotics to virtual reality or cyber theater, and it is one of many terms that have been coined to describe the increasing presence of media and technology in live performance. Indeed, how to conceptualize and theorize digital media in performance has been a contested issue in theater and performance studies for several decades, and not all digitally engaged performance meets the standards of Dixon's definition.[20] The same is true of contemporary Chinese performance, wherein use of the digital ranges from central, as described by Dixon, to more subsidiary or even superficial. The productions discussed in this piece are therefore best described as "digitally enhanced" rather than fully digital performance.

Because the layering of digital enhancements onto live performance occurs most perceptibly in the realm of scenic and lighting design, it also contributes to a distinctly digital aesthetics in these productions. This digital aesthetics varies slightly, depending on the specific technologies used, but is generally characterized by features such as a color palette determined by the properties of LED diodes (which has broadened over time but favors strong, bright hues) and digital projectors, as well as a high degree of luminosity (brightness) due to the same technologies. In *Zhici qinglü*, for instance, the rich golden hue of the LED screens imitates, but also enhances and brightens, the color of a physical silk scroll. Likewise, a painting from the blue-and-green school of landscape painting, which is characterized by vibrant, jewel-tone hues of paint, translates particularly well into the color range best displayed by LEDs.

A final layer of digitality operates beyond the live performance and on-screen in the recording, streaming and broadcasting, and online posting of video clips, artist interviews, and images via websites and social media platforms. In general, intellectual property concerns and the desire to sell tickets to ongoing live performances limit the content that producing organizations make available online. Here again, *Zhici qinglü* provides a typical example. The performance is still touring and selling tickets, and no full-length recording is readily available online.[21] In contrast, the Gala provides a rare example of a live performance that is broadcast and livestreamed but also remains widely available in its recorded entirety after the performance. The specific excerpt of *Zhici qinglü* performed for the Gala is available online both as part of the full-length Gala recording and as a stand-alone six-minute video; the same dance number also appears as a teaser-trailer for the performance and was performed as part of the livestreamed Bilibili New Year's Eve Gala. Beyond this particular signature scene, one other scene and additional clips from the full-length performance have appeared online as part of advertisements and media coverage of the production. A large number of still images and written descriptions of the performance, as well as audience reactions, can be found on microblogs and on Wechat, as well as in journal and newspaper articles. The creative team and performers have appeared in media interviews and a special behind-the-scenes documentary that also circulated online.[22] In a digital age, these online materials should be viewed not merely as a window onto audience response but also as a form of essential paratext that is in fact a core component of the live performance.

Surface Classicism

As digital technologies have gained popularity and prevalence in twenty-first-century Chinese performance, two significant trends have emerged. First, as noted above, the role played by digital and multimedia technologies has increased and become a defining feature of large-scale performance, across genres. This leads to not only a distinctly digital aesthetics but also a more exaggerated aesthetics of technological excess whereby the performance *of* technological prowess—sometimes digital, sometimes not—becomes a focal point. Second, while many theatrical productions in this mode participate in the staging of local or national history, memory, and culture, a narrower engagement with what might be identified as "classicism" has emerged in a number of high-profile productions.[23] From *Zhici qinglü* to the Impressions Series to the Olympics opening ceremonies, contemporary Chinese productions often employ digital performance technologies specifically to enliven poetic images, textural tropes, and landscape topoi that are rooted in premodern literary and visual culture.[24] This entanglement produces what I refer to as "surface classicism," borrowing a term used by art historian Erwin Panofsky to describe the imitation of general composition, motifs, facial types, and surface textures in European proto-Renaissance art and architecture.[25] In contrast to Panofsky's definition, however, surface classicism in contemporary Chinese performance suggests not an immaturity of engagement with ancient models but, rather, a targeted mobilization of seemingly superficial qualities to map the classical onto the contemporary.

In the Gala *Zhici qinglü* excerpt, this mapping took place first and foremost in the display of landscape across the stage backdrop, proscenium opening, and auditorium, as LED screens and holograms shaped the digitized rendering of Wang Ximeng's *Qianli jiangshan tu* to the contours of the performance space. In other words, the display of the painting took place quite literally on the surface of the auditorium walls, with the glossy stage and digital pool of water providing additional reflective surfaces. The walls of the space thus became what Yue terms a "media skin" for the projection of a specific vision of Chinese literature and culture, with *Qianli jiangshan tu* defining that vision.[26] Popularly known as one of the "ten great masterpieces of ancient Chinese painting" (Zhongguo shi da chuanshi minghua 中國十大傳世名畫), *Qianli jiangshan tu* is widely recognizable as a "classic." On one level then, like Panofsky's observations of surface classicism in proto-Renaissance artwork, the image displayed was an imitation—or more precisely, a direct reproduction—of a work that holds a privileged place in the canon of Chinese landscape painting. More specifically, *Qianli jiangshan tu* has long stood as an exemplar of the blue-and-green school of landscape painting and of the Northern Song court painting patronized by Emperor Huizong 宋徽宗 (r. 1100–1126 CE). It therefore is already in a classicist or "recovering antiquity" (*fugu* 复古) mode, since Song blue-and-green styling harkens back to Tang dynasty painting practices, making the Gala projections doubly classicist.[27] As Patricia Buckley Ebrey writes, however, the painting is also notable for pushing the boundaries of its style through its enormous size (11.9×5.1 meters high) and by using brighter pigment than other blue-and-green landscapes.[28] Part of the function of the original painting therefore may have been to demonstrate "that the court could cultivate painters capable of spectacular paintings, ones that showed mastery of illusionistic technique and grand imaginative powers."[29] Chinese visual culture as defined through the use of this painting, then, is characterized both by a quintessential form—the landscape painting—and by (state-sponsored) spectacle.

The choice to term *Zhici qinglü* a "poetic dance-drama" and to include poetry in the production's scenographic design further illustrates surface classicism by connecting it to the Chinese literary canon and echoing the traditional practice of landscape painting inscription. Descriptions of the full-length production even explicitly emphasized its shared lineage with ancient classics, as in the following:

> The histories of poetic drama and literature are in the same vein, our country's pre-Qin *Nine Songs* can be seen as the earliest embryonic form of poetic drama, and Yuan songs can be seen as poetic drama that can be either read or performed. As theater in the form of poetry, poetic drama both carries a strong poetic sentiment and quality and also has the plot and scenes of the theater.

> 詩劇與文學史同脉，我國先秦時期的《九歌》可以看作最早的詩劇雛形，元曲並可看作是可讀可演的詩劇。作為詩歌體戲劇，詩劇既帶有濃烈的詩情詩意，也有著戲劇的情節和場面。[30]

The description continues to detail how poetic dance-drama transmutes lyricism not into spoken text but, rather, into the language of bodily movement. In the Gala excerpt, in particular, this mode of lyricism is augmented by how the dancers' costumes, hair styles, and bodily positions mirror the mountains in Wang Ximeng's painting. The dancing body thus also becomes a surface for the projection of classicist poetics and imagery.

When written poetry does appear, it is displayed in digital calligraphic script on the proscenium at two points in the performance. Like the use of *Qianli jiangshan tu*, these poetic entanglements are again in a sense both literally surface and superficial. The poems read, respectively:

If your heart can hold the hills and valleys	心中若能容丘壑
Then your brush may bring together the mountains and rivers.	下筆方能匯山河
With no name and no inscription,	無名無款
Just this one scroll,	只此一卷
Green and blue for thousands of years,	青綠千載
Mountains and rivers without bounds.[31]	山河無垠

Wang Ximeng's painting famously features an inscription written by the minister Cai Jing 蔡京 (1047–1126) in 1113, which is the main source of information on the painter and circumstances of the painting's composition.[32] Yet the poems used in the performance are not drawn from that text. Instead they are evocative of classical verse: a seven-syllable rhymed couplet for the former, and four tetrasyllabic lines for the latter.[33] The two poems therefore operate not by specific allusion to the painting's inscription but instead through a formal connection to *types of poetry* that are easily recognizable as classical. The first couplet echoes the seven-syllable regulated verse (*qi yan lüshi* 七言律詩) most associated with famed poets of the Tang dynasty, and it even loosely follows some of that style's rules of rhetoric, composition, and structure. It attempts parallelism, for example, with both lines ending with a character pronounced *he* and the landscape image of "hills and valleys" in the first line pairing with "mountains and rivers" in the second. The second, tetrasyllabic poem, meanwhile, nods to even earlier forms of verse such as those found in the *Shijing* 詩經 (Classic of Poetry) and the classical poetic practice of juxtaposing human and nature between its two sets of lines.

Similar to these broad references, even though the LED display of *Qianli jiangshan tu* occurs in high fidelity and references a specific painting, the landscape reproduced can also be seen as one of broadly recognizable imagery. After all, Wang Ximeng's painting is not associated with a specific historical or local landscape. Rather, what is depicted is a *type of landscape* that represents the idyllic topography of southern China, or the Jiangnan region. The use of the term "Qinglü" 青綠 (Blue and Green) in the dance-drama title, rather than the painting name, then further abstracts the reference and lays claim to representing an entire style of painting whose practice historically spanned several dynasties. Across both image and text, the piece—and surface classicism in general—works in generalizations and widely recognizable tropes.

Surface classicism also might be compared with what Shengqing Wu has described as "ornamental lyricism" in late Qing and Republican-era poetry. Wu defines ornamental lyricism as "an expression of intensified emotion with heightened formal consciousness and rhetorical execution" that "designates the extensive use of literary conventions, allusions, tropes, and the rhetorics of *bi* 比 (metaphorical comparison) and *xing* 興 (affective images), thereby conveying a feeling of excessiveness or overdecoration."[34] As can be seen from the example above, surface classicism shares the use of allusions, tropes, and rhetoric, and especially the feeling of excessiveness, with ornamental lyricism. Yet whereas ornamental lyricism tends to be densely allusive, surface classicism is only loosely so. It does not require the classical erudition that would enable a reader or viewer to identify arcane allusions from the literary canon and interpret their meaning in reference to the work at hand. To be sure, as Xiaofei Tian has argued, "Classical poetry could be erudite and densely allusive, but it could also be so simple and direct in diction that even an illiterate person or someone with basic school education could understand it."[35] With surface classicism in large-scale performance, both impulses are at work: text and allusion move toward the simple and direct, while ornamentalism is retained but sublimated into the visual realm through the use of spectacular performance technologies.

This mode of surface engagement with classical poetic and aesthetic traditions is a phenomenon that can be found across many of the large-scale, digitally enhanced productions described in the previous section. For instance, the original production of *Impression West Lake*, which premiered in 2007, opened with video projection onto a round, moon-like surface seemingly floating just above the surface of the lake. The projections featured a long poem, in even less strictly classical verse than the lines in *Zhici qinglü*, overlain on a series of filmic and painterly images associated with West Lake. A remounting of the production as *Zuiyi shi Hangzhou* 最憶是杭州 (Hangzhou: A Living Poem) for the G20 Summit in Hanghzou in 2016 then simultaneously added more specific allusions to the Chinese poetic tradition, such as by titling itself after the same Bai Juyi poem referenced by the 2022 Gala segment "Remembering Jiangnan," and broadened its content to include music, images, and references recognizable to a more global audience, like the use of Beethoven's Ninth Symphony. Likewise, the stage production *Chang hen ge* 長恨歌 (Song of Everlasting Sorrow), which takes place on-site at the Huaqing Hot Springs outside Xi'an, is based on the story of Yang Yuhuan 楊玉環 as told in the well-known Bai Juyi poem of the same name.[36] As with the other large-scale, digitally enhanced performances in this vein, it layers spectacular stage technologies over a loosely adapted literary and historical narrative. Contemporary performance is thereby yoked to the artistry and longevity of landscape painting, poetic inscription, and literary classics. Digitally enhanced visuality then accentuates this connection and awes the audience with both visual splendor and technological prowess.

Remediation, Density, and Depth

What to make, however, of the fact that the spectacular use of digital enhancements in large-scale performance seems so often to go hand in hand with a superficial appropriation of classical aesthetics and poetics? Classicism is already, as Yang points out, prone to critiques of being derivative and inauthentic; the replacement of erudite allusion with direct reference, digital reproduction, and large-scale screen surfaces only seems to exacerbate such complaints.[37] Surfaces themselves similarly "are the external appearance of things, easily manipulated, and within many traditions of thought, are held to be of lesser consequence than 'deeper' or more 'substantive' interiorities," as Glenn Adamson and Victoria Kelley note.[38] Moreover, surface classicism features most prominently in performances that have clear ties to state agencies and commercial ventures, which for all their structural opacity have seemingly transparent motives: ideology and profit. Scholars may parse the specific messages conveyed by each year's Gala skits and dance numbers, for example, yet it is widely accepted that they are meant to reinforce and disseminate current ideological directives. Meanwhile, theoretical formulations such as Siegfried Kracauer's mass ornament or Guy Debord's society of the spectacle have for so long pointed to spectacle's underlying manipulation of bodies and audiences that this, too, ought to be all too apparent. The marriage of surface classicism with spectacular visuality in large-scale Chinese performance, then, teeters on many edges of easy dismissal.

Yet, as media studies scholar Giuliana Bruno reminds us, "In visual culture, surface matters, and it has depth."[39] This is perhaps even more true when visual culture is married to performance, with all its corporeality and liveness. And indeed, if one moves beyond the *Zhici qinglü* Gala excerpt to consider the full-length performance from which it was derived, a more recognizable depth of historical engagement and artistry does become apparent. The full-length performance centers on a fantastical act of art historical research: a Palace Museum researcher called the "Scroll opener" (Zhan juan ren 展卷人) travels back in time to witness the creation of *Qianli jiangshan tu*. Actual time travel was not, of course, involved in the scripting and staging of *Zhici qinglü*, but the playwright and choreographers did conduct extensive research into the painting and painter, Song dynasty culture and history, and the craft trades connected to classical painting (such as the production of paper, silk, ink, pigment, and brushes).[40] These areas of craftwork then became the focus of individual scenes, making for a highly original dramatization of the artistic process. Scenography and stage technology were also employed to create a more immersive feeling of traveling between vignettes and viewing a landscape painting scroll for the audience, through the use of multiple turntables, flying panels, and lighting effects.[41] These details of research and behind-the-scenes technology, moreover, have been widely reported in interviews, media reports, and scholarly articles on the production.[42] While visually stunning, then, the performance also projects an impression of depth.

"Surface classicism," in fact, seems a less fitting description for the full-length *Zhici qinglü* and instead may be a condition engendered specifically by the dance-drama's excerption and redesign for the Gala. Cutting the performance piece down to one emblematic scene and adding a fully digitized, LED-powered moving-image backdrop impressed audiences but also diluted the sense of engagement with the past. In a thread on the popular question-and-answer site Zhihu 知乎, for instance, the question "How to rate the 2022 Spring Festival Gala dance *Journey of a Legendary Landscape Painting*?" (Ruhe pingjia 2022 Chunwan de wudao *Zhici qinglü*? 如何評價2022春晚的舞蹈《只此青綠》?) generated 563 responses and 2,367,133 views (as of June 20, 2023).[43] While many responses were positive, a number of viewers complained about the color scheme and the brightness of the LED backdrop, or they compared the Gala version unfavorably to the original or the Bilibili New Year's Eve online program. Others felt that the piece was difficult to understand, which may have been a result of extracting only one scene from the longer dance-drama.

At the same time, however, the same properties that arrest the viewer at the surface level also generate tensions that gesture toward new, potentially productive ways of understanding how classicism operates in a digital age. That is to say, we should not automatically dismiss the *Zhici qinglü* Gala excerpt because of its seemingly superficial and spectacular engagement with the past. Instead, turning attention to the specific technologies and forms of mediation at work can reveal new sets of intertextualities and interconnections among the works of art in question, as well as between art and audience. Following Bruno, the screen (as surface) can be taken as a point of connection on equal footing with the work of art that is remediated. In Jay David Bolter and Richard Grusin's oft-cited formulation, remediation is defined as the representation of one medium within another, which engenders a tension between the desire to deny or erase and to call attention to the presence of the medium(s) and act(s) of mediation.[44] In the *Zhici qinglü* excerpt, there is in fact a constellation of acts of remediation: the landscape painting, for instance, is remediated both through the bodies of the dancers and through the display of its digitized double. Likewise, classical poetry appears both as an aesthetic mode absorbed into the dance choreography and visually as digitized calligraphy writ large against the LED screen–covered proscenium. Surfaces themselves are multiplied and layered in the surface of the river within the painting, the (digital) scroll as a painted surface, the skin of LED screens on the auditorium walls, and the screens mediating the experience for at-home viewers.

The screen as the medium of display for these multiple layers of painting, calligraphy, and performance also reaches beyond the temporality of the performance itself to interface with other recent on-screen appearances of classical art and literature—and even of the same painting. *Qianli jiangshan tu* has in fact been repeatedly remediated over the last decade and a half, especially through high-profile events with large audiences. Perhaps the most prominent of these was the 2008 Beijing Olympics opening ceremony, where the painting was one of many images displayed on an enormous LED scroll that unfurled across the Bird's Nest Stadium floor. Not unlike the full-length version of *Zhici qinglü*, the 2008 Olympics vignette featuring *Qianli jiangshan tu* began with a short video depicting the process of making paper and mounting a scroll; when the LED scroll unrolled in the stadium, then, images of archaeological artifacts and pieces of art moved across the screen as dancers used their bodies to paint a new piece and a *guqin* musician played. The image then dissolved into a digital reproduction of *Qianli jiangshan tu* scrolling across the screen as the newly created painting was lifted up into the air.

Nearly a decade later, an immensely popular exhibition of the actual *Qianli jiangshan tu* at the Palace Museum in Beijing occasioned another layer of screened mediations. The original painting was exhibited along with other pieces in the blue-and-green style held by the Palace Museum from September 15 to December 14, 2017, generating extensive media coverage and circulation of images of the painting online.[45] The Palace Museum also digitized the painting and developed an interactive AR exhibit around it, as well as collaborated with Netease Games to release a mobile game based on the painting in 2018.[46] Meanwhile, *Qianli Jiangshan tu* also appeared on several popular television shows, such as *Guojia baozang* 國家寶藏 (National Treasure) in December 2017 and *Wenming zhilü* 文明之旅 (Journey of Civilization) in January 2018. Once again, a shared premise across remediations is notable: the *Guojia baozang* episode featured well-known actor Li Chen 李晨 (Jerry Li, b. 1978), who introduced the painting and then "time traveled" back to the Song dynasty to play the character of Emperor Huizong as he received the painting from Wang Ximeng.[47] A central element of the reenactment was the display of a digitized version of the painting on a rounded LED-screen backdrop. As Li Chen/Huizong inspects a material reproduction of the scroll, the audience in studio and watching at home see what he sees, enlarged and enhanced on a 180-degree screen encircling the stage.

Even the act of excerpting the dance-drama for on-screen performance was itself in dialog with previous instances of recorded segments appearing in television shows and documentaries, media publicity, and the earlier streamed piece done for the Bilibili New Year's Eve Gala. In a self-referential move, *Guojia baozang* itself aired an episode on *Zhici qinglü* on October 23, 2021, four years after its segment on *Qianli jiangshan tu*. The episode included interviews with key creative personnel, behind-the-scenes video clips of the rehearsal process, and a recording of the "Ruhua" 入畫 (Entering the Painting) scene from the performance.[48] Cutting-edge technology was also on display: at one moment, show host Zhang Guoli 張國立 (b. 1955) expressed a desire to truly "enter the painting," and the stage space transformed into a digitally enhanced immersive environment based on the painting; at another, the two choreographers and actor Zhang Han

FIGURE 4. Choreographers Zhou Liyan and Han Zhen, along with actor Zhang Han, promote *Zhici qinglü* on a Vivo-sponsored episode of *Guojia baozang*. Screenshot from CCTV *Guojia baozang* broadcast/recording. Source: https://youtu.be/HNPgzMykZW4?si=mWth2GW3p8QozNUo.

張翰 (b. 1984), who plays Wang Ximeng, place a cell phone displaying a close-up image from *Qianli jiangshan tu* on a podium center stage (fig. 4).[49] The host even referenced the 2017 episode of his own show, and the choreographers also described their inspiration for *Zhici qinglü* as related to the 2017 Palace Museum exhibition. Throughout the episode, then, viewers were constantly reminded not only of connections between the painting, performance, and Song dynasty culture but also of recent live and media events that featured *Qianli jiangshan tu* and, via the cell phone, the omnipresence of technological remediation.

Yet another layer of cross-platform reference was created by the overlap in performances for the Bilibili New Year's Eve and CCTV Spring Festival galas. The same scene, "Green and Blue," was performed at both galas, but there were notable differences in how it was staged for each.[50] To begin, the Bilibili version was nearly two minutes longer than the Gala performance (about eight minutes versus six minutes), suggesting that a substantial amount of choreography was cut to fit the standard length of a Gala dance segment. The use of stage and display technology also diverged; the Bilibili stage featured a large, curved screen upstage of the dancers that was similar to the CCTV stage backdrop, but without the full-surround LED screens. The background projections also remained much more muted throughout the performance, with the full painting appearing only about forty-five seconds from the end of the number. When it did appear, moreover, it was projected onto a scrim that had descended mid-stage, which created a hazy, abstract effect that starkly contrasts with the high fidelity of the Gala display.

These various remediations not only reference *Qianli jiangshan tu* but do so via similar screen technologies of digital reproduction, display, and reenactment. As Bruno writes, "The screen becomes the surface that connects and mediates between art forms."[51] In this case, the art forms that are remediated exist not only in a past-present, vertical, and cross-temporal relationship (from Song dynasty classic to present) but also in a contemporaneous, lateral, and transmedial network—not dissimilar to the rhizomatic networks of identity and performance in transnational Chinese theater theorized by Rossella Ferrari.[52] In other words, the connections among the various screen reproductions of the painting online, on television shows, onstage in the 2008 Beijing Olympics ceremony and *Zhici qinglü*, and in reports of these events on social media are as significant as the relationship between "original" and "copy."

In the case of surface classicism, this network is both implicitly composed of connections such as those detailed above and explicitly perceived by audience members and viewers and linked to the current trend of classicism. As one commentator for *Wenhuibao* 文匯報 writes, television shows like *Guojia baozang* and mediatized dance like *Tanggong yeyan* 唐宮夜宴 (Tang Palace Banquet), which was premiered by the Zhengzhou Song-and-Dance Theater (Zhengzhou gewu juyuan 鄭州歌舞劇院) in 2020, are related to *Zhici qinglü* as part of the "traditional culture fever" (*chuantong wenhua re* 傳統文化熱) or "national style" (*guochao feng* 國潮風) movement that is currently sweeping the PRC—a movement that is further characterized by its melding of art and technology.[53] Scholarly articles on *Zhici qinglü* likewise note the cross-platform nature of the performance's popularity and situate it in relation to other performances based on cultural artifacts and works of art.[54] As exemplified by the *Zhici qinglü* Gala excerpt, then, surface classicism connects and mediates not only between new and old art forms but also between the many remediations of classical art forms already present in contemporary media culture. The result is a network of transmedial associations wherein the density of connections *across* media matters as much as the depth of engagement with the real or imagined past.

Conclusion: Erudition for All?

When discussing contemporary mobilization of classical poetics and aesthetics in large-scale, digitally enhanced performance, it is tempting to dwell primarily on the relationship engendered between present and past in works such as *Zhici qinglü*. In tracing such genealogies and accreted allusions, however, it becomes all too easy to assume a connection between textual density and depth of meaning. In contrast, refocusing our attention on the surface nature of much of the Sinophone classicism in circulation today calls attention to the properties that Bruno identifies: "The surface holds what we project into it. It is an active site of exchange between subject and object. The surface, like the screen, is an architecture of relations. It is a mobile place of dwelling, a transitional space that activates cultural transit. It is a plane that makes possible forms of connectivity, relatedness, and exchange."[55]

In a counterintuitive sense, then, the very superficiality of surface classicism may engender a more accessible form of cultural connection through the easy identification of classics and the participatory nature of online engagement. In other words, if a shared sense of Chinese identity is created through large-scale digital performance, it operates as much in the realm of remediation as in that of the historical or the mnemonic. When an audience member sees a performance featuring a classical painting, they might be reminded of (a) seeing the real painting exhibited, (b) seeing the performance based on the painting, (c) seeing a television show about either of the above, (d) participating in online conversations about either, even just as an observer—or any combination of the above. The sense of shared "Chineseness" produced, therefore, is both accessible and multiply mediated. In one sense it is shared and open to anyone with internet access, but it is also entirely unique to the individual viewer.

TARRYN LI-MIN CHUN is assistant professor in the Department of Film, Television, and Theatre at the University of Notre Dame. She is author of *Revolutionary Stagecraft: Theater, Technology, and Politics in Modern China* (2024).

////////////////////////////////

Acknowledgments

Research for this article was funded by a fellowship from the National Endowment for the Humanities. I would like to thank my research assistant, Wu Xiyun, for her help in gathering materials; David Der-wei Wang, Zhiyi Yang, Xiaofei Tian, and all my fellow participants at the Harvard-Frankfurt-Lingnan Symposium on "Classicism in Digital Times" for their helpful feedback on early versions of this article; and the two anonymous reviewers for their comments.

Notes

1 The painting is currently held by the Palace Museum in Beijing. On the painting itself, see Gesterkamp, "Thousand Miles of Streams and Mountains."

2 For a recording of the excerpt performance, see CCTV, "Hongbian quanwang! Bei mei dao le!" For one disgruntled audience member's enumeration of the reasons why the segment generated so much discussion, see "Tao," "*Zhici qinglü* wei shenme zheme huo?" All websites referenced in this article have been archived using the Internet Archive Wayback Machine (web.archive.org/).

3 The dance-drama opened in August 2021 and was coproduced by the Palace Museum (Gugong bowuyuan 故宫博物院), the China Oriental Performing Arts Group (Zhongguo dongfang yanyi jituan youxian gongsi 中國東方演藝集團有限公司), and People's Daily Online (Renminwang gufen youxian gongsi人民網股份有限公司), with additional support from the Yushang Harmony Culture Development Company (Yushang hemei wenhua fazhan youxian gongsi 域上和美文化發展有限公司). Its title translates literally as "Only Blue and Green," but the website for the official premiere uses the English title *Journey of a Legendary Landscape Painting*, while the Spring Festival Gala CGTN livestream translated the title as *Journey on a Painted Landscape*. See National Center for the Performing Arts, "China Oriental Performing Arts Group."

4 Yang, "Sinophone Classicism," 659.

5 See, for example, Xinyu Lu, "Ritual, Television, and State Ideology"; Wang, "From Court Fools to State Puppets"; Wang, "Between the Past and the Future"; and Zhao, "Popular Family Television and Party Ideology."

6 Popular singer Andy Lau, for example, was unable to perform in person and so appeared dancing with virtual oxen (for the Year of the Ox) in a fully digital environment. Allen-Ebrahimian, "China Celebrates"; CGTN News, "2021 Spring Festival Gala."

7 CGTN News, "2022 Spring Festival Gala."

8 Jiang, "Chuangxin wei yinling," 6.

9 In one report on previews of the Gala, for example, China Media Group president and deputy minister of the Central Propaganda Department Shen Haixiong 慎海雄 praised the program's scenography and use of technology specifically for its "immersive visual effect" (*chenjinshi shijue xiaoguo* 沉浸式视觉效果). "Zongtai lingdao shenkan 2022nian Chunwan wumei sheji."

10 Jiang, "Chuangxin wei yinling," 7.

11   *Fuchun shan ju tu* was burned and split into two halves. One half is held by the Zhejiang Provincial Museum in Hangzhou and the other by the National Palace Museum in Taipei. The selection of this painting for a segment of the CCTV Spring Festival Gala thus had contemporary political implications in addition to its function as representative of classical Chinese landscape painting. For behind-the-scenes details on the making of this segment, see CCTV, "Guyi angran huazhong xian."

12   The producing organizations for such performances can include government organizations, state-sponsored performing troupes, and commercial entities, or a combination of these.

13   On visual spectacle and "post-epic theatricality" in political performance, see Chen, *Staging Chinese Revolution*, 245–86.

14   See, for example, Broudehoux, "Spectacular Beijing"; Ong, "Hyperbuilding." For a discussion of grand theater architecture in particular, see Lu Xiangdong, *Zhongguo xiandai juchang de yanjin*; Xue, *Grand Theater Urbanism*.

15   Zheng, "Guojia da juyuan de dixia 'moshu shi.'"

16   There is a large body of published scholarship, critical reviews, and audience responses to *shanshui shijing yanchu* in Chinese; in English see, for example, "Staging China: The Art of *Yijing*" in Xuelin Zhou, *Globalization*, 85–114. For a list of performances, see Sanxiang Impressions website: www.guanyinxiang.com/yinxiangyanchu/yinxiangxilie/.

17   Yue, "New Media," 367.

18   On the intersection of tourism and performance in China, see, for example, Zhu, "When the Global Meets the Local"; Denton and Xu, "Lu Town."

19   Dixon, *Digital Performance*, 3.

20   See, for example, Klich and Scheer, *Multimedia Performance*; Chapple and Kattenbelt, *Intermediality in Theatre and Performance*; Bay-Cheng et al., *Mapping Intermediality in Performance*; Giannachi, *Virtual Theatres*.

21   In fact, *Zhici qinglü* became embroiled in an intellectual property controversy when another dance troupe seemingly plagiarized the show's choreography and costumes. Ji and Lou, "Chinese Dance Show Suspected of Plagiarism."

22   For example, the China Oriental Performing Arts Group disseminated the documentary on its YouTube channel, and the choreographers shared it via their Weibo accounts. See www.youtube.com/watch?v=ThmvrNm1bSU.

23   This article is primarily concerned with the interface between classicism and digital technologies. For a nuanced discussion of concepts of the "classical" in relation to Chinese dance choreography, see Wilcox, "Han-Tang 'Zhongguo gudianwu.'"

24   On literary references and intermediality in landscape performance, see, for example, Wang, "Shijing yanchu," 52–63.

25   Panofsky, "Renaissance and Renascences," 214.

26   Yue, "New Media," 366.

27   Ebrey, *Emperor Huizong*, 215. On the relationship between classicism and *fugu*, see the work of Martin J. Powers, John Hay, Wu Hung, and others, such as Powers, "Dialectic of Classicism," 20–25; Hay, "Some Questions Concerning Classicism," 26–34; and Wu H., *Reinventing the Past*.

28   Ebrey, *Emperor Huizong*, 213.

29   Ibid., 216.

30   "Wudao shiju *Zhici qinglü*." Translated by the author.

31   The first couplet appears at 2:00 and the second at 5:47 in the full video of the dance performance posted by CCTV on YouTube. See www.youtube.com/watch?v=OZlUvIV50Ww. Translated by the author.

32 For further discussion of Cai Jing and his role in Emperor Huizong's court, see Ebrey, *Emperor Huizong*: translation of inscription at 186; further discussion of *Qianli jiangshan tu* at 213–16.

33 Online articles repeatedly reference that choreographers Han Zhen and Zhou Liya quoted the first couplet as one of many poems that served as inspiration during rehearsals, but none gives a source for the poem. See, for example, Li, "Hunian Chunwan."

34 S. Wu, *Modern Archaics*, 2.

35 Tian, "'Each Has Its Moment,'" 520–21.

36 On stage design in *Changhen ge*, see Xun, "Daxing shijing lishi wuju."

37 Yang, "Sinophone Classicism," 661.

38 Adamson and Kelley, introduction, 1.

39 Bruno, *Surface*, 5.

40 China Oriental Performing Arts Group, "*Zhici qinglü* jilupian."

41 For further discussion of scenography and the use of stage technology in the full-length *Zhici qinglü*, see, for example, Yuan, "Shixing, chenjin, kua meijie," 78; Tian, "Wumei zai wutai."

42 See, for example, Ye, "Bentu ticai xiandai yishi dangdai zhuanhua"; and Yuan, "Shixing, chenjin, kua meijie," among a cluster of articles on *Zhici qinglü* published by *Wenhua yishu yanjiu* in April 2022.

43 The thread can be found at Zhihu forum, "Ruhe pingjia 2022 Chunwan de wudao *Zhici qinglü*?" The original performance and Gala version also generated widespread discussion and reviews on other popular sites such as Douban or Weibo and on Wechat.

44 Bolter and Grusin, *Remediation*, 5, 45.

45 For the official press release, see en.dpm.org.cn/exhibitions/current/2017-09-13/2702.html.

46 Wang et al., "'Smart Museum' in China," 12, 14. The digitized version of *Qianli jiangshan tu* has subsequently been exhibited by other museums and cultural centers, in various visual and interactive formats.

47 The homepage and description of the first season of the show can be found online at tv. cctv.com/2017/11/29/VIDAjmY28VSqK4hfQtHwoyJE171129.shtml; the Li Chen episode first aired on December 3, 2017, and can be viewed on the CCTV website (as well as on YouTube): tv.cctv.com/2017/12/03/VIDEO2mvCYPcVUdHwpCrl2HY171203.shtml.

48 MCT, "Wudao shiji"; a full recording of the episode can be found online at youtu. be/HfMXaEkY-4w.

49 The show is sponsored by Vivo, a Chinese technology company headquartered in Dongguan, Guangdong, that manufactures popular smartphones. Their X70 Pro+ model was advertised prominently throughout the *National Treasure* episode.

50 The Bilibili performance is available online: ""Wenhua zixin Zhongguo dongfang yanyi jituan *Zhici qinglü* yanhuo le qianli jiangshan tu."

51 Bruno, *Surface*, 115.

52 My description of these networks is deeply indebted to Ferrari's discussion of relationality and transnational networks among Sinophone theater artists and their work, which in turn builds on Gilles Deleuze and Félix Guattari's concept of the rhizome. See Ferrari, *Transnational Chinese Theatres*, 1–15.

53 Like *Zhici qinglü*, a scene from *Tanggong yeyan* was excerpted and digitally enhanced for performance at the Henan Television Spring Festival Gala in 2021. Tang Baijing, "Zai Yangshi Chunwan shang kan wudao yu keji."

54 Yuan, "Shixing, chenjin, kua meijie," 78; Ye Zhiliang, "Bentu ticai," 74.

55 Bruno, *Surface*, 8.

References

Adamson, Glenn, and Victoria Kelley. Introduction to *Surface Tensions: Surface, Finish and the Meaning of Objects*, edited by Glenn Adamson and Victoria Kelley, 1–12. Manchester: Manchester University Press, 2013.

Allen-Ebrahimian, Bethany. "China Celebrates Lunar New Year with 540 Disco Robots and 29 Drones." *Foreign Policy*, February 8, 2016. https://foreignpolicy.com/2016/02/08/china-monkey-lunar-new-year-dancing-robots-drones-gala/.

Bay-Cheng, Sarah, Chiel Kattenbelt, Andy Lavender, and Robin Nelson, eds. *Mapping Intermediality in Performance*. Amsterdam: Amsterdam University Press, 2010.

Bolter, J. David, and Richard A. Grusin. *Remediation: Understanding New Media*. Cambridge, MA: MIT Press, 1999.

Broudehoux, Anne-Marie. "Spectacular Beijing: The Conspicuous Construction of an Olympic Metropolis." *Journal of Urban Affairs* 29, no. 4 (2007): 383–99.

Bruno, Giuliana. *Surface: Matters of Aesthetics, Materiality, and Media*. Chicago: University of Chicago Press, 2014.

CCTV. "Guyi angran huazhong xian | CCTV Chunwan" 古意盎然畫中仙 | CCTV春晚. [Ancient Immortals within a Painting | CCTV Spring Festival Gala]. 2022 Chunwan wei jilu 2022春晚微紀錄 [2022 Spring Festival Gala Micro Documentary Series]. YouTube video, 4:27. February 2, 2022. https://www.youtube.com/watch?v=_Y358OcX6ac.

———. "Hongbian quanwang! Bei mei dao le! Cangzhe qianli Jiangshan de *Zhici qinglü* jiang Zhongguo gudianshi chuanqi wei wei daolai '2022 yangshi chunwan'" 紅遍全網！被美到了！藏著千里江山的《只此青綠》將中國古典式傳奇娓娓道來「2022央視春晚」 [Popular across the Internet! Slayed by Beauty! *Journey of a Legendary Landscape Painting* Holds the Beauty of a Thousand Mountains and Rivers, Eloquently Bringing Chinese Classical Style Legends to the 2022 CCTV Spring Festival Gala]. YouTube video, 5:59. February 2, 2022. https://www.youtube.com/watch?v=OZlUvIV50Ww.

CGTN News. "2021 Spring Festival Gala Dazzles Viewers with High Tech." February 12, 2021. https://english.cctv.com/2021/02/12/ARTI228CmLGBoHCEfoV2GMoa210212.shtml.

———. "2022 Spring Festival Gala to Present Innovative Audio-visual Feast." January 28, 2022. https://english.cctv.com/2022/01/28/ARTIjRijcVuFfXxbB9uOHHKy220128.shtml.

Chapple, Freda, and Chiel Kattenbelt, eds. *Intermediality in Theatre and Performance*. Amsterdam: Rodophi, 2006.

Chen, Xiaomei. *Staging Chinese Revolution: Theater, Film, and the Afterlives of Propaganda*. New York: Columbia University Press, 2016.

China Oriental Performing Arts Group. "*Zhici qinglü* jilupian: Shanzhong shuifu, fanglan baichuan" 《只此青綠》紀錄片：山中水復，方覽百川 [*Journey of a Legendary Landscape Painting* Documentary: Mountain Waters Restored, a Hundred Rivers Viewed]. YouTube video, 18:09. May 7, 2022. https://www.youtube.com/watch?v=ThmvrNm1bSU.

Denton, Kirk, and Yichun Xu. "Lu Town: Theme Parks and the Commodification of Literary Culture in China." *Cultural Heritage* 11, no. 2 (2022): 148–80.

Dixon, Steve. *Digital Performance: A History of New Media in Theater, Dance, and Performance*. Cambridge, MA: MIT Press, 2007.

Ebrey, Patricia Buckley. *Emperor Huizong*. Cambridge, MA: Harvard University Press, 2014.

Ferrari, Rossella. *Transnational Chinese Theatres: Intercultural Performance Networks in East Asia*. Cham, Switzerland: Palgrave Macmillan, 2020.

Gesterkamp, Lennert. "A Thousand Miles of Streams and Mountains: Daoist Self-Cultivation in Song Landscape Painting." *Journal of Daoist Studies* 15, no. 1 (2022): 31–65.

Giannachi, Gabriella. *Virtual Theatres: An Introduction.* New York: Routledge, 2004.

Hay, John. "Some Questions Concerning Classicism in Relation to Chinese Art." *Art Journal* 47, no. 1 (1988): 26–34.

Ji Yuqiao and Lou Kang. "Chinese Dance Show Suspected of Plagiarism, Raises Concerns about Copyright Protection." *Global Times,* May 23, 2022. https://www.globaltimes.cn /page/202205/1266397.shtml.

Jiang Wenbo 姜文波. "Chuangxin wei yinling, keji zhu chuangzuo: quanmian tisheng 2022 nian Zongtai Chunwan ronghe chuanbo xiaoguo" 創新為引領，科技助創作：全面 提升2022年總台春晚融合傳媒效果 [With Innovation as a Guide, Technology Assists Creativity: Comprehensive Enhancements in the Integrated Media Effects of the 2022 CCTV Spring Festival Gala]. *Dianshi yanjiu* 電視研究 [Television Research] 2 (2022): 4–8.

Klich, Rosemary, and Edward Scheer. *Multimedia Performance.* New York: Palgrave Macmillan, 2012.

Li Ming 李明. "Hunian Chunwan wudao shiju *Zhici qinglü* shuaping biandao pilu zhouhong milu 虎年春晚舞蹈詩劇《只此青綠》刷屏 編導揭露走紅秘密 [Year of the Tiger Spring Festival Gala Poetic Dance-Drama *Journey of a Legendary Landscape Painting* Smash Hit Directors Reveal the Secret to Gaining Popularity]. *China Press,* February 2, 2022. https://www.uschinapress.com/static/content/SH/2022-02-02 /938419259800170496.html.

Lu Xiangdong 盧向東. *Zhongguo xiandai juchang de yanjin: Cong da wutai dao da juyuan* 中國現代劇場的演進：從大舞台到大劇院 [On the Evolution of Modern Theaters in China: A History from Grand Stage to Grand Theater]. Beijing: Zhongguo jianzhu gongye chubanshe, 2009.

Lu, Xinyu. "Ritual, Television, and State Ideology: Rereading CCTV's 2006 *Spring Festival Gala.*" In *TV China,* edited by Ying Zhu and Chris Berry, 111–26. Bloomington: Indiana University Press, 2009.

MCT (Ministry of Culture and Tourism of the PRC). "Wudao shiji *Zhici qinglü* zai *Guojia baozang zhanyan ji* bochu" 舞蹈詩劇《只此青綠》在《國家寶藏》展演祭 出 [Poetic Dance-Drama *Journey on a Legendary Landscape Painting* Broadcast on *National Treasure* Festival], November 2, 2021. https://www.mct.gov.cn/whzx/zsdw /zgdfyyjtyxgs/202111/t20211101_928668.html.

National Center for the Performing Arts. "China Oriental Performing Arts Group: *The Journey of a Legendary Landscape Painting.*" https://en.chncpa.org/whatson/zdyc/202207 /t20220720_243409.shtml (accessed June 27, 2023).

Ong, Aihwa. "Hyperbuilding: Spectacle, Speculation, and the Hyperspace of Sovereignty." In *Worlding Cities: Asian Experiments and the Art of Being Global,* edited by Ananya Roy and Aihwa Ong, 205–26. Malden, MA: Wiley-Blackwell, 2011.

Panofsky, Erwin. "Renaissance and Renascences." *Kenyon Review* 6, no. 2 (1944): 201–36.

Powers, Martin J. "The Dialectic of Classicism in Early Imperial China." *Art Journal* 47, no. 1 (1988): 20–25.

Tang Baijing 唐白晶. "Zai Yangshi Chunwan shang kan wudao yu keji xiangyong de 'Zhongguo shi langman'" 在央視春晚上看舞蹈與科技相擁的 '中國式浪漫' [The "Chinese-Style Romance" of the Embrace of Dance and Technology as Seen in the CCTV Spring Festival Gala]. *Wenhui bao* 文匯報 [Wenhui Daily], February 11, 2022. https://www .chinanews.com.cn/yl/2022/02-11/9673707.shtml.

"Tao 濤." "*Zhici qinglü* wei shenme zheme huo?" 只此青綠為什麼這麼火？ [Why Is *Journey of a Legendary Landscape Painting* So Popular?]. Zhihu online forum, February 25, 2022. zhuanlan.zhihu.com/p/463945330.

Tian Fenying 田奮穎. "Wumei zai wutai biaoyan Zhong de zhongyao zuoyong: Yi wudao shiju *Zhici qinglü* weili" 舞美在舞台表演中的重要作用：以舞蹈詩劇《只此青綠》為例 [The Importance of Stage Design in Stage Performance: Taking the Poetic Dance-Drama *Journey of a Legendary Landscape Painting* as an Example]. *Yishu pinjian* 藝術品鑑 [Appreciation] 15 (2022): 97–99.

Tian, Xiaofei. "'Each Has Its Moment': Nie Gannu and Modern Chinese Poetry." *Frontiers of Literary Studies in China* 12, no. 3 (2018): 485–525.

Wang, Hongjian. "From Court Fools to Stage Puppets: Country Bumpkins in the Skits on CCTV's Spring Festival Gala, 1983–2022." *China Quarterly* 250 (June 2022): 552–71.

Wang Keyue 王柯月. "Shijing yanchu iang de wenxue yu kua meijie zhuanhua" 實景演出中的文學與跨媒介轉化 [Literary and Cross-media Transformation in Real-Scenery Performance]. *Yishu pinglun* 藝術評論 [Arts Criticism] 4 (2022): 52–63.

Wang, Min. "Between the Past and the Future: The Rise of Nationalist Discourse at the 1983 CCTV Spring Festival Gala." *Inter-Asia Cultural Studies* 23, no. 2 (2022): 203–19.

Wang, Siyi, Yong Duan, Xiaofei Yang, Chenxing Cao, and Shouyong Pan. "'Smart Museum' in China: From Technology Labs to Sustainable Knowledgescapes." *Digital Scholarship in the Humanities* (2023): 1–19. https://doi.org/10.1093/llc/fqac097.

"Wenhua zixin Zhongguo dongfang yanyi jituan *Zhici qinglü* yanhuo le qianli jiangshan tu" 文化自信：中國東方演藝集團《只此青綠》演活了千里江山圖 [Cultural Confidence: *Journey of a Legendary Landscape Painting* by the China Oriental Performing Brings to Life a Thousand Li of Mountains and Rivers." Bilibili video, December 31, 2021. https://www.bilibili.com/bangumi/play/ep454140.

Wilcox, Emily. "Han-Tang 'Zhongguo gudianwu' and the Problem of Chineseness in Contemporary Chinese Dance: Sixty Years of Creation and Controversy." *Asian Theatre Journal* 29, no. 1 (2012): 206–32.

Wu, Hung, ed. *Reinventing the Past: Archaism and Antiquarianism in Chinese Art and Visual Culture*. Chicago: Center for the Art of East Asia, University of Chicago and Art Media Resources, 2010.

Wu, Shengqing. *Modern Archaics: Continuity and Innovation in the Chinese Lyric Tradition, 1900–1937*. Cambridge, MA: Harvard University Asia Center, 2013.

"Wudao shiju *Zhici qinglü*—wuhui *Qianli Jiangshan tu* Shanghai zhan" 舞蹈詩劇《只此青綠》—舞繪《千里江山圖》上海站 [Poetic Dance-Drama *Journey of a Legendary Landscape Painting*—Dance Painting *A Thousand Li of Mountains and Rivers* Shanghai Performance]. www.shgtheatre.com/project/wudaoshijuzhiciqinglu-wuhuiqianlijiangshantu (accessed May 31, 2022).

Xue, Charlie Qiuli, ed. *Grand Theater Urbanism: Chinese Cities in the Twenty-First Century*. Singapore: Springer, 2019.

Xun, Lijie 荀麗潔. "Daxing shijing lishi wuju *Chang hen ge* de wumei jiedu" 大型實景歷史舞劇《長恨歌》的舞美解讀 [A Reading of the Scenography in the Large-Scale Real-Scene Historical Dance-Drama *Song of Everlasting Sorrow*]. *Dazhong wenyi* 大眾文藝 [Mass Literature and Arts] 15 (2019): 174–75.

Yang, Zhiyi. "Sinophone Classicism: Chineseness as a Temporal and Mnemonic Experience in the Digital Era." *Journal of Asian Studies* 81, no. 4 (2022): 657–72.

Ye Zhiliang 叶志良. "Bentu ticai xiandai yishi dangdai zhuanhua—wudao shiju *Zhici qinglü* de dangdai yiyi" 本土題材·現代意識·當代轉化—舞蹈詩劇《只此青綠》的當代意義

[Local Themes, Modern Consciousness, Contemporary Transformation—The Contemporary Significance of the Poetic Dance-Drama *Journey of a Legendary Landscape Painting*]. *Wenhua yishu yanjiu* 文化藝術研究 [Culture and Arts Research] 15, no. 2 (2022): 73–77.

Yuan Yi 袁藝. "Shixing, chenjin, kua meijie: wudao shiju *Zhici qinglü* de meixue jiangou" 詩性、沉浸、跨媒介：舞蹈詩劇《只此青綠》的美學建構 [Poetry, Immersion, Transmedia: The Aesthetic Construction of the Poetic Dance-Drama *Journey on a Legendary Landscape Painting*]. *Wenhua yishu yanjiu* 文化藝術研究 [Culture and Arts Research] 15, no. 2 (2022): 78–83.

Yue, Audrey. "New Media: Large Screens in China." In *The Oxford Handbook of Chinese Cinemas*, edited by Carlos Rojas and Eileen Chow, 359–76. Oxford: Oxford University Press, 2013.

Zhao Bin. "Popular Family Television and Party Ideology: The Spring Festival Eve Happy Gathering." *Media, Culture & Society* 20, no. 1 (1998): 43–58.

Zheng Rongjian 鄭榮健. "Guojia da juyuan de dixia 'moshu shi'" 國家大劇院的地下 '魔術師' [The "Magician" Underground at the National Center for the Performing Arts]. *Zhongguo yishu bao* 中國藝術報 [Chinese Art News], April 18, 2012. http://www.cflac .org.cn/ys/xwy/201204/t20120418_134386.htm.

Zhihu forum. "Ruhe pingjia 2022 Chunwan de wudao *Zhici qinglü*?" 如何評價2022春晚的舞蹈《只此青綠》？ [How to Rate the 2022 Spring Festival Gala Dance *Journey of a Legendary Landscape Painting*?], January 31, 2022. https://www.zhihu.com/question /514238732.

Zhou, Xuelin. *Globalization and Contemporary Chinese Cinema*. Singapore: Palgrave Macmillan, 2017.

Zhu, Yujie. "When the Global Meets the Local in Tourism—Cultural Performances in Lijiang as Case Studies." *Journal of China Tourism Research* 8, no. 3 (2012): 302–19.

LAURA VERMEEREN

Writing the Heart Sutra Online

ABSTRACT Online calligraphic handwriting has taken on various creative forms: from WeChat handwriting communities to digital teaching apps and downloadable calligraphic fonts. This article proposes to consider online calligraphy practice a means to connect to an imagined past. Calligraphy, then, is employed for a haptic reconnecting with the past through movements of brush and wrist by restoring and reenacting an (imagined) classical Chinese culture on digital screens. This article focuses specifically on the affective modes of writing the Heart Sutra (Xin Jing 心經) in the online environment of the platform Kuaishou (快手). It analyzes how the affordances of the social media platform allow for various forms of affective engagement with the classicist text. This article suggests that the specific modalities underpinning Heart Sutra writings are informed by the nostalgic desire to perform a type of Chineseness. Instances of online sutra writings on Kuaishou further contest the widespread misconception that content uploaded on the specific platform is mostly subsumable under the cultural mode of *tuwei* 土味 or "vulgar content."

KEYWORDS Heart Sutra, calligraphy, Kuaishou, social media, Chineseness

> Whether we believe in Buddhism or not, we have certainly all seen it appearing in
> poetry, read it in books, seen it in movies, and lying in the arms of our grandparents
> at night, heard them softly reciting the sentences.
> —Lin Xi, 2019

In her twenty-seven-second Kuaishou 快手 video, we see the post-1980s (*baling hou* 八零後) calligrapher Yan An 顏安 writing the last characters of the Heart Sutra (Xin Jing 心經).[1] The video is played at double speed, catering, possibly, to the short-lived attention span of the digital generation. We see a split second of Yan An's long black hair and traditional *qipao* 旗袍 before the camera zooms in on the brush in her hand out of which beautiful cursive characters flow—thanks to the technical affordances of the media recorder—with impressive swiftness. The background music counters this fast rendition: we hear the calming tones of a bamboo flute and a female voice chanting the Heart Sutra. The video exudes a sense of both "Buddhism" and "traditional Chineseness," the latter an increasingly, as Zhiyi Yang 楊治宜 notes, "ill-fitting notion"[2] that I will attempt to complicate in this article. The video ends with Yan An standing back from her written piece

PRISM: THEORY AND MODERN CHINESE LITERATURE • 20:2 • SEPTEMBER 2023
DOI 10.1215/25783491-10992810 • © 2023 LINGNAN UNIVERSITY

and stamping it with her seal, after which she glances bashfully and proudly at the camera for less than a second. The video gathered 291,000 views on Kuaishou. We find that Yan An, who proudly claims descendancy from the famous Tang calligrapher Yan Zhenqing 顏真卿 (709–85 CE) in her online bio, has uploaded the same video on Douyin 抖音 (thirty-nine thousand views and twenty-three thousand comments) and Bilibili 哔哩哔哩 (a puzzling nine views)—and the video currently appears on five calligraphy WeChat channels. On at least four different social media platforms, Yan An has made an embodied addition to the ancient ritual practice of calligraphic sutra copying.

The Heart Sutra (Xin Jing 心經, sk. Prajñāpāramitā Hridaya Sutra) is one of the most widely known, loved, recited, and copied Mahayana Buddhist texts in China. The text is so well-known that it is difficult not to speak about it in superlatives: it is one of the longest-living texts in the history of printing;[3] there is no other single text "that has been interpreted by such a long and virtually unbroken list of illustrious authorities;[4] and no Buddhist text "has ever been so widely deployed for such a diverse range of uses."[5] There are two versions of the sutra, a short and a longer one. The short version, only 260 Chinese characters long, is considered the authoritative version across China and larger East Asia and serves as the basis for all Chinese commentaries on the sutra, as well as most English translations. Its translation from Sanskrit into Chinese has been attributed to the seventh-century translator and monk Xuan Zang 玄奘 (602–64 CE)—we know Xuan Zang from the novel *Journey to the West* (*Xiyou ji* 西遊記) (ca. 1500–ca. 1582), in which his travels to India are fictionalized. On this infamous journey to India, so the story goes, Xuan Zang was given the sutra by a scruffy and sick old monk. Along the way, the thirsty and tired Xuan Zang found himself suddenly surrounded by evil spirits, and he invoked the name of his guardian bodhisattva Avalokiteshvara. It was to no avail, and the spirits persisted. Only when he started chanting the Heart Sutra would the spirits disappear. Because of the sutra's power as a protective talisman, a cult started to develop around the text in medieval China.[6] The Heart Sutra has since then been widely studied; copied; recited; used as a text for devotion, exorcism, and tantric meditation; and used as a source for comparative philosophy.[7] The copying of sutras serves several purposes: it initially aided the spread of Buddhism, and it further helps the copyist to internalize its teachings and works as an act of piety and devotion. Such an act of devotion can, according to Buddhist doctrine, alter one's position in the continuous cycle of life, death, and rebirth. "This is," argues Sarah Mattice, "a sutra that lives in the complicated space between conceptual thought and daily embodied activity."[8]

The practice of sutra writing has remained a devotional activity to the present day. But today, hand copying the sutra is increasingly done for a wider array of purposes. In Japan the practice of sutra copying (*shakyo*) arrived in the eighth century and is still practiced in communal settings all over Japan, where one can join a session of collective writing organized by various temples. At the same time, it is marketed and propagated as an act of self-care and cultivation—an activity to resort to when feeling overwhelmed or faced with uncertainty. A 2006 study showed how *shakyo* is effective in preventing dementia[9]—nudging the practice ever more toward a technology of the self. Sutra writing was brought to Korea in the third century and remains both a popular and devotional practice. The text is pulsating with life and activity today, and as a living piece of writing, it is heard daily all around the world: as a chanted meditation in religious communities but also in pop songs, tear-jerking ballads, rapped by Korean nuns and even churned out on a loop by robot-monk Mindar in Japan. It materializes on objects as well: we see the Heart Sutra inscribed on jewelry, printed on T-shirts, written on prayer beads, and even imprinted on noodles.[10] Taking into account that the sutra means and does many different things for a wide variety of people, I choose to approach the Heart Sutra here specifically as a site of calligraphic practice in China that affords affective modes of "being Chinese" in online environments. The Heart Sutra lives and sings, perhaps unsurprisingly, just as loud through digital space. I have argued elsewhere, taking cues from David Miller and Don Slater, that separating the digital realm from "normal life" has become wholly untenable. Information and communication technology allow instead for an extension of quotidian social life.[11] This assertion implies that our everyday lives might be somehow stretched, even enriched by digital space, but what we *do there* might be rather like (and just as mundane as) what we do in our everyday lives. Ben Highmore suggests that, "if everyday life, for the most part, goes by unnoticed (even as it is being revolutionized), then the first task for attending to it will be to make it noticeable."[12] Here lies the premise of this article: I attempt to unpack how the everyday practice of writing the Heart Sutra has moved to the social media platform Kuaishou and, importantly, how that affords affective modes of "being Chinese."

Methodology

By means of narrowing down this research, I look specifically at home videos on which amateur content makers are writing the Heart Sutra, published on the online environment of Kuaishou, a Chinese smartphone app platform. Kuaishou boasts over 346 million daily active users in 2022 and is the fourth-largest social media platform in China after WeChat, QQ, and SinaWeibo.[13] The platform started out in 2011 as an animated GIF maker and changed to its current form in 2012. Kuaishou now mainly functions as a short video (varying from seven seconds to one minute) and livestream provider, the latter introduced in 2016 and highly influential in facilitating the emergence of a *wanghong* 網紅 or micro-celebrity culture. During the livestream of a performer, usually a female, a viewer can gift them digital gifts with actual money. The performer can cash this after the livestream is over, but not before the platform takes its share.[14] This feature, Lin Jian and Jeroen de Kloet stress, provides economic and creative opportunity for less educated and rural *wanghong* entrepreneurs.[15] With that demographic orientation, Kuaishou is different from other Chinese social media platforms, as it is specifically designed to appeal and cater to uneducated young Chinese living in rural areas or third- and fourth-tier cities.[16]

Kuaishou offers user-generated entertainment that reflects the socioeconomic particularities of the app's subscribers and distinguishes itself by facilitating the distribution of what is often described as "unsophisticated" or abrasive content.[17] Registered users create many types of videos for (live) broadcasting on Kuaishou, showing activities ranging from makeup tutorials, cooking, and slapstick to hunting, but also official sponsored content that actively promotes core socialist values and traditional Chinese culture. The "coarseness" of Kuaishou's content has been labeled over the past few years as belonging to what is termed a "*tuwei* 土味 aesthetic." *Tuwei* refers to a type of raw and real visual quality, almost exclusively associated now with Kuaishou videos. Such *tuwei* videos seem to deliberately take a position opposite of the stylized and highly edited videos featuring urban celebrities seen on other platforms, and instead they celebrate a coarse and "real" portrayal of rural life. We see red-cheeked farmer girls harvesting crops, ironic cooking shows, toddlers playing with pig heads, or eating contests where people eat octopus still alive, grinning at the camera with mouths full of tentacles. Or videos that are full of ironic play on viral fads, such as lip-sync and dance videos with absurd and exaggerated movements. Instead of the highly stylized portrayal of urban life, or the Zen-like rural idyll depicted by bloggers such as Li Ziqi 李子柒, these *tuwei* videos are "tacky-cool" and full of satire. Kuaishou has taken the internet by storm: it functions as both an outlet for the rural population and a type of nostalgic rural retreat for urbanites, who can dream with it for a simpler life. The content of these types of videos have helped in conjuring Kuaishou as a "platform of the people." Kuaishou targets rural users, has adopted a decentralized algorithm so that users with fewer followers are promoted, and has for years managed to evade celebrity endorsement.[18] And although this is now changing, as Kuaishou has recently started to include celebrity endorsements, is trying to attract more urban users, and has an increased focus on spreading "positive content," the platform is also continuously allowing for user-generated content portraying the everyday lives of rural and small-town residents. This focus on portraying "everyday life" is of interest to me, first because I am eager to probe calligraphic sutra writing specifically as a quotidian mediated practice. And second, there is a palpable tension in a ritualistic exercise such as sutra writing being displayed on a platform that distinguishes itself as a provider of coarse portrayals of rural life. Surely, there is nothing "raw" or "tacky-cool" about sutra writing?

To unpack this tension, I focus both on the content itself as well as Kuaishou's interface and affordances. To that end, the methodology supporting this research consists first of an analysis of the Kuaishou app following the "walkthrough" method developed by Ben Light, Jean Burgess, and Stephanie Duguay.[19] This method, Light and colleagues argue, "involves the step-by-step observation and documentation of an app's screens, features and flows of activity—slowing down the mundane actions and interactions that form part of normal app use in order to make them salient and therefore available for critical analysis."[20] By understanding the digital infrastructure, we can better understand the intended purpose of the app, and its ideal user base. This article furthers draws its insights from a qualitative visual content analysis of a selection of Heart Sutra videos on Kuaishou generated through a hashtag search and the subsequent algorithmic recommendations. These are amateur videos that do not generate money through the livestream. The pitfall, if left unattended, of this methodology is what Florian Schneider refers to as a "digital bias."[21] My Kuaishou account now features almost exclusively sutra-writing and calligraphy-writing content. Acknowledging that the data I am receiving is not well balanced and is based on algorithmic interpretation can avoid this pitfall. Moreover, this article benefits from gaining insights into the algorithmic feed. I ask: What kinds of Heart Sutras are written, and who writes them? What kind of visual cues can we discern and how do we interpret them in the context of cultural recreation and appropriation: colors, textures, props or objects, mise-en-scène, sound, and narration? How do we make sense of kinesis and the bodily engagement in mediated calligraphy writing: Do we see hands, brushes, heads; how does the body move; and what cues can we take from the stylistic choices of the creator in making the home video? What is shown and what, importantly, is left out? In my selection of the videos of twenty-five followed accounts, their everyday user activity as well as the algorithmic recommendations, I identified four main modes of calligraphic sutra writing: (1) Buddhist devotion, (2) Chinese traditional culture and purity, (3) education, and (4) creative writing. First, let us turn to how Chineseness is indexed in relation to calligraphy, and how we might start to unpack this concept in relation to calligraphic online practice on Kuaishou.

Calligraphy and Chineseness

As calligraphy has almost entirely lost its practical use—we use ballpoint or pencil if we write at all, and increasingly type pinyin on our phones or computers—the calligrapher and his or her calligraphy today have moved to a position somewhere within the very contested territory of "art." There the calligrapher performs an art that is readily and enthusiastically indexed as quintessentially "Chinese." It might be useful to give a working definition of Chinese calligraphy (*shufa* 書法) here. In its most undressed definition, *calligraphy* refers to writing

Chinese characters with ink and brush on rice paper (*xuan* 宣), according to a traditional set of rules widely known and taught in China. Around the beginning of the 1980s, the field of calligraphy expanded drastically into different domains. Contemporary calligraphy (*dangdai shufa* 當代書法) was one of such domains, in which bold experiments were made with the Chinese character: from distortion of form and space and using newly discovered archaic script types to a complete erasure of lexicalized meaning. Artist calligraphers started to leave rice paper as their main surface of writing and began to venture toward creating calligraphies on a wide range of surfaces—photographs, bamboo, leftover foods, or walls—or leave the concept of writing surfaces altogether and interpret calligraphy as dance or as a video game. And alongside these artistic explorations, calligraphy has become an increasingly popular everyday practice for many people who do not identify as either artists or calligraphers. People write, for example, hard-pen calligraphy during work time, write with water on the streets, or make spring festival couplets (*duilian* 對聯) with friends and family. We are in the middle of an ongoing calligraphy fever (*shufa re* 書法热) that has not yet given any signs of breaking since the opening of the arts in the 1980s. Private schools are bourgeoning, and an increasing number of primary schools are now able to offer the state-mandated (*bixiuke* 必修課) calligraphy class. The number of universities that offer calligraphy as a specialized subject at their departments of fine arts is also growing substantially. This growth is partly incentivized by the need for skilled calligraphy teachers to teach those state-mandated classes all over China.

One result of this rise of calligraphy education is that today's youth are remarkably well educated in calligraphy. Of course, then, calligraphy is also happening in digital environments. At first sight, calligraphy does not seem to be a great match for a digital screen: brush, ink, and paper (*wenfang sibao* 文房四寶) are so quintessentially *analog* that it is challenging to envisage a calligraphy practiced online. But a multitude of apps allow calligraphy enthusiasts to upload handwritten pieces to their online environment of choice to exhibit, compare, or sell. Digital calligraphic fonts are also increasingly employed, and scanned original calligraphy is integrated into much-used online dictionaries and copybooks or virtual online museum galleries. All these digital tools make calligraphy consumption increasingly accessible and mobile, and mediated experiences of calligraphy have become commonplace by now. Throughout the ongoing diffusion of calligraphic practices to online platforms, a commonly held conviction has, however, remained intact: the Chinese written character continues to be seen as an ideal articulation of Chineseness. The idea of a five-thousand-year-old cultural China throughout which the Chinese sign was uninterruptedly employed remains a forceful and easily legible one. Based on this idea, the Chinese nation is conjured, a nation that cherishes and cultivates an art form that is so deeply understood as quintessentially *theirs*. And *theirs* now increasingly applies to *all* Chinese people, as it has become a quotidian practice for everyone—both voluntarily and involuntarily—to participate in.

Andrea Bachner maintains that the Chinese character, apart from being an instrument of communication, "has to carry the additional semiotic burden of Chineseness."[22] This remark is specifically apt when we talk about calligraphy, in which Chinese characters do not have to be distinctly legible. Alongside aesthetic pleasure, artistic and technical accomplishment, the only communicative task for calligraphy, then, to use Bachner's term, might be Chineseness. But the concept of Chineseness is far from straightforward and has been evaluated thoroughly for decades now, for its problematic identity politics, the hegemony of mainland China in using the notion, and for its close connection to nationalism.[23] It has become such a catch-all term that its heuristic power is waning and becomes something that conceptually might be close to what Claude Lévi-Strauss has called a "floating signifier": it "represents an undetermined quality of signification, in itself void of meaning and thus apt to receive any meaning."[24] Indeed, how to still use this term effectively after such rigorous deconstruction? Zhiyi Yang proposes an alternative and open-ended way to conceptualize Chineseness: as a "subjective, intimate, and reflexive way to experience an individual's culturally acquired 'Chineseness' that is temporal, mnemonic, and often mediated by digital media."[25] Through what Yang calls a "rhizomic and dynamic process of cultural re-creation,"[26] people attempt to (re)connect with an (imagined) classical Chinese culture on digital screens. The Chinese party-state is more and more set on imposing a monolithic, nationalistic, and mainland-centered definition of Chineseness, staying close to the vision of Xi Jinping, who urges all to "tell China's stories well." Calligraphy is in that constellation a resourceful discourse—one that can be mobilized by government structures as an expression of love for and dedication to the motherland, as well as an embodied participation in a strong and culturally confident China. At the same time, a subjective, quotidian, and intimate storytelling takes place, and it is at this junction between governmental instrumentalization and subjectivity that we should place calligraphic sutra writings on digital platforms.

Kuaishou's Sutras

Our lives are increasingly structured through a wide array of digital platforms, in China actively supported by the government's Internet Plus and China 2025 policies.[27] These platforms are user-friendly apps, and we use them to organize and maintain our friendships, order food, get our news, buy the things we need, and shape and test our opinions on all kinds of matters. While the early rhetoric on platformization first lauded its democratic potential, and the way in which it could provide marginalized communities opportunities to engage in cultural production, the platform society is now a "contested concept."[28] Contested, because all our social and economic interactions are interconnected, which alters the ways in which power is distributed.[29] Contested too, because of the type of labor it facilitates, a type of labor that is founded on a precarious and zero-liability model.[30] Cultural producers, the platforms on which they operate, and global markets have become intricately connected, as Thomas Poell, David B. Nieborg, and Brooke Erin Duffy argue, which has large consequences for the "sustainability of cultural production, and the diversity and vitality of culture at large."[31] The online platform, in short, is not an empty and neutral podium for anyone to climb on and perform freely, but a state-sponsored mechanism whose technological affordances restructure and manage our economic activity, sociability, and, importantly for my argument here, our cultural preferences.

Taking the above into account, I now move to a "walkthrough" of the Kuaishou app. Kuaishou's platform design is intuitive and straightforward, featuring buttons for "followed accounts," "trending videos," "live broadcasting," and "nearby" that are placed at the top of screen. A "plus" button at the bottom of the screen allows the user to upload a video. The followed accounts appear on the home screen as soon as the app is opened. I have selected twenty-five accounts to follow based on their usage of the hashtags: #抄寫心經 (hand copying Heart Sutra), #寫心經 (writing Heart Sutra), and #心經書法 (Heart Sutra calligraphy). As I tracked the everyday activities of these accounts from the home screen, the algorithmic recommendation system suggested an increasing number of videos that aligned with the topic of my followed accounts and hashtag searches: movies of people writing calligraphy, carving the sutra, chanting the sutra, explanatory videos on the sutra, or moving imagery of tranquil landscapes anchored by the sutra written in digital font. By following the everyday activities of these accounts for a period of two months, as well as the algorithmic recommendations, I identified four main modes of calligraphic sutra writing: (1) Buddhist devotion, (2) Chinese traditional culture and purity, (3) education, and (4) fun and creative writing. All videos last between eleven and fifty-seven seconds, and although Kuaishou has been testing a long-video feature with videos up to ten minutes since 2019, this feature is not available to everyone yet. The videos subsumed under the first category of Buddhist devotion are all sequenced in a strikingly similar format. The background music is either a soft chanting or a more upbeat, poppy version of reading the sutra out loud in Chinese. Or we hear soundtracks of babbling brooks, birdsong, soft piano, or guqin 古琴 and flute melodies. In this mode, we rarely see anything of the maker except for their hand holding the brush in a shot from the calligrapher's point of view. When camera and sound are rolled, the hand starts moving. We see how the brush is dipped into ink and placed on the sheet of rice paper, which in this mode is often a quadrille paper. Now characters start to flow from the brush in real-time speed. The video is usually cut off after

FIGURE 1. Writing the sutra with golden ink. Video of Shufa Tingting 書法婷婷. Kuaishou, October 2022. www.kuaishou.com/shortvideo /3xscb74psw2d9uw?authorId=3xhf3kmhzahccku&streamSource=profile& area=profilexxnull.

around eight characters—the abruptness of the cut-off suggests that the writing will go on in real life. Interesting is how, in this mode, makers are inclined to write large seal script or clerical script, often paired with blue grid paper and golden ink. Historically, Tang dynasty (618–907) sutra copies were written on indigo-colored paper and gold or silver pigment made from gold powder and glue. These objects became sacred in themselves, and the production of such sutras are an act of devotion. The Heart Sutra advocates the principle that wisdom resides in emptiness, and the Kuaishou videos in this mode seem to align themselves with this doctrine: they are relatively short and unembellished videos in which the maker remains largely absent. The focus is on writing a few characters of the sutra, which should be understood as acts of devotion (fig. 1).

In the second mode, we see more of the maker and their surroundings. In these videos, recognizable indicators of Chinese traditional culture are deliberately featured in the mise-en-scène, as in, for example, the videos of Tang Wanyun 唐婉芸, a young female calligrapher with currently 556,000 followers. The Heart Sutra is one of her subjects of choice, along with other commonly used subjects for calligraphy writing such as Wang Xizhi's 王羲之 orchid pavilion, spring festival couplets (*duilian* 對聯), and four-character idioms (*chengyu* 成語). Her videos often start with an establishing shot in which she stands in the middle of the frame, behind her writing desk in a studio. Framed calligraphy and traditional Chinese ink-wash paintings adorn the walls, and we see a traditional Chinese cabinet and wooden stands holding seals, brushes, and ink stone. Often, fresh flowers are placed strategically in one of the corners of the frame. Tang Wanyun is always meticulously dressed, sometimes in traditional Chinese *qipao* with jade bracelets, or in flowing white cotton dresses—not exactly dressing in *Hanfu* 漢服 style, but clothes that are more generically suggestive of purity and femininity. The video starts when she begins her writing, and we see her upper body in full. Resting her left arm on the desk, her right arm holds the brush and moves fast, because the video is played in double speed. The double speed not only allows us to see more of what she does, as a whole idiom can be seen written in a short time span, but the fast rhythm underscored by the Chinese popular music also gives the video an almost magical quality, as if the writing appears out of nowhere. Makers of videos in this mode are intent on showing their calligraphic skill in a setting that exudes an atemporal sense of traditional Chinese exquisiteness. This "Chinese exquisiteness" is not limited to mise-en-scène, objects, or the calligraphy writing itself; rather, it extends to the bodies of the makers. There is a feminine quality to these videos, which are indeed often made by young women. They dress in *qipao*, or pure cotton or silk clothes, and, with their black hair and minimal makeup and pale face, seem to obey a certain beauty standard of purity and innocence, referred to as the first love face (*chulianlian* 初戀臉).

The aesthetics of these videos are redolent of the #thatgirl aesthetics that have become all the rage over the last two years on TikTok. "That girl" performs her daily rituals on a digital platform—she gets up in the morning, gets dressed, eats a healthy breakfast, and gets ready for work—in an extremely polished, clean, and jealousy-inspiring organized fashion. There is a tinge of holiness attached to the term *ritual*, as it is most readily associated with a performance embedded in religion. But ritual is also an ordinary everyday act that cements our being in the world. Media extends this and gives it an audience, *signals* something: it becomes a ritual performance. I identify a ritual-like performance in these sutra-writing videos. We see a sequence of ritualistic events being performed: first, the preparation of the proper tools, then a meticulous and faultless calligraphic writing performed by bodies that connote an explicitly Chinese purity. These makers often have many similar videos of calligraphy writing in the same setting (see figs. 2 and 3), which hints at their calligraphy practice being a daily ritual, one that links them to the constellation of "being Chinese." "Chinese" here is imagined as rooted in a (more) ideal past and as something pure, feminine, and beautiful. On the personal homepage of these accounts, we find that these subscribers predominantly post calligraphy performances, interspersed with videos of them drinking Chinese tea, folding dumplings, or more rural activities such as picking corn or gathering tea leaves. But evidently, this imagination of Chineseness is not just about pureness and innocence. This is also a Chineseness associated with being a highly skilled calligrapher: literate, educated in ancient Chinese classics, and, because of these two attributes, perhaps a pure manifestation of being Chinese.

FIGURE 2. Young woman in silk dress writing the sutra. Video of Wenxian Shuyu 文賢書語. Kuaishou, September 2022. 自幼练习书法，酷爱书法，如果您无意间刷到这个视频，请给我一个红心和一个关注，可以吗?-快手 (kuaishou.com).

FIGURE 3. Young woman in silk dress writing the sutra. Homepage of Lushan Guniang 麓山姑娘. Kuaishou. 麓山姑娘-快手 (kuaishou.com).

A large strand of sutra writing falls into the category of "education" (fig. 4). Here, objects, mise-en-scène, and kinesis are much less important or even entirely absent, and the focus is on narration and demonstration. These videos zoom in on only one grid of a sheet of rice paper, and a single character will be demonstrated in one video. Throughout the narration, sometimes with soft background music, a few words are said about the sutra, but mainly technical instructions are given about brush placement and hand or wrist movement. Sometimes nothing is said at all, and we only hear music and see the brush move slowly—inviting the audience to write along. Although narration is often lacking, we see how an online community of calligraphers is imagined and created using hashtags. These videos typically post hashtags such as #一起練字 (*yiqi lianzi*, practice calligraphy together), #傳統文化 (*chuantong wenhua*, traditional culture), #日常練字 (*richang lianzi*, daily practicing calligraphy), or #練字是一種生活 (*lianzi shi yi 14hong shenghuo*, practicing calligraphy is a way of life). Hashtags are evocative of a collective narrative that can bring people with shared ideals or ambitions together. This narrative connects people who see calligraphy practice as a way of life, as a traditional practice that should be sustained in the present, with help of new technologies that can be used for teaching and forming learning communities.

A final and much smaller mode of calligraphic sutra writing can be subsumed under "fun and creative writing." The content of these videos is more in line with the earlier mentioned *tuwei* aesthetic associated with a mode of video making in which one does not shy away from sharing failures, ugliness, and ironic gesture.

FIGURE 4. Educational video on how to write the thirteenth character of the Heart Sutra. Video of Xiezi Bai Xiaoseng 寫字白小僧. Kuaishou, January 2022. #欧楷书法 #一起练字 #心经 最近生病了，离开了写字台一个月的时间，甚是想念各位书友-快手 (kuaishou.com).

In one video we see, for example, a man writing the Heart Sutra in his studio. Most videos stop there, but here we see him rolling up the sutra and placing it in a cardboard tube. He walks out of his studio with the scroll in one hand, filming the street and the scroll in front of him with his other hand. He narrates as he goes and decides to hide the scroll in an abandoned traffic cone. Once he has placed the sutra in the cone, the video stops. A video of a man using the claw of a hammer as a brush to write a few characters of the Sutra is another example, and another in which we hear a loud and coarse female voice praising her exhausted-looking friend for spending three days and three nights writing the Heart Sutra in his own creative, graffiti-like calligraphic script (fig. 5). Instead of beaming with the Zen-like contentment we have come to recognize in the videos categorized under the previously mentioned modes, in this video the protagonist looks grumpy, tired, and dissatisfied. He points at his final work, showing his audience how he skipped a couple of characters instead of writing the full 260 characters of the sutra, making the work useless. In these examples we see a rare show of failure, dissatisfaction, faulty writing, and ironic play.

Conclusion

In this article I approached the Heart Sutra as a site of calligraphic practice in China that affords affective modes of "being Chinese" in online environments. I suggested a tension between the ritualistic exercise of sutra writing on the one

FIGURE 5. Writing the Heart Sutra in creative style. Video of Zhu Jingyi Guo chao Shufa 朱敬一國潮書法. Kuaishou, January 2022. #心经 #艺术 #书法-快手 (kuaishou.com).

hand, and its display on a platform that distinguishes itself as a provider of coarse portrayals of rural life on the other. The technical affordances of Kuaishou permit forms of affective engagement with the classicist text. One of those seemingly banal but very powerful affordances is the "plus" button at the bottom of the screen that allows one to easily upload a short video. It is that simple to add a contribution, and that simple to join an imagined online community. In the first mode of sutra writing, we saw how such a community of devotees write the sutra by hand, showing not themselves but merely the product of their labor. In an act of imagined cultural remembrance, these sutras are often written in seal or clerical script on blue paper with golden paint, taking cues from the indigo and gold Tang-dynasty sutra calligraphy that are sacred objects in themselves. Backed by an imagined Chinese past, their practice becomes a mnemonic exercise: strategies to remember, embody, and exercise a Chinese aesthetic and religious practice to create "a community of memory."[32] In the second mode, "being Chinese" here is imagined as pure, feminine, and beautiful. We see sutra writing, but equally important in the video are the makers' body movements and dress, and the objects positioned in the frame. All these elements work together tell a story: a nostalgic imagining of a beautiful Chinese past, in which beautiful women leisurely wrote sutras. One might even argue that this is "telling China's stories well," pur sang. But this is not just about being aesthetically pleasing: their sutra writings are highly skilled and reveal a solid education in calligraphy. In these videos,

makers combine this privileged access to cultural capital with a corporeal investment in the project of displaying Chineseness. Such "cultural capital," however, is
increasingly easier to access in the digital age. Calligraphy education on Kuaishou
is a case in point: we find a large community connected through hashtags who
practice their calligraphy with the help of short explanatory videos.

And finally, we identified how a much smaller group writes unconventional
Heart Sutras. In this mode, their writing is not readily identified as an act of
devotion, nor is it showing an ideal world in which the sutra takes the main stage.
Here the sutra again reveals itself as the highly popular object that conveys Chineseness. The sutra might be a holy text, but it is also a text for every Chinese to
chant, sing, write, or hide in a traffic cone. Kuaishou as a "platform of the people"
stages such affective engagements. Although far from vulgar, these instances of
"playing with" the sutra are significant and align with the *tuwei* aesthetic in its
"tacky-cool" and ironic capacities. They are yet another way of building cohesive
connections between the text and all it connotes, and the domain of everyday
subjectivity. Michael Billig has famously argued that "the world of nations is the
everyday world, the familiar terrain of contemporary times."[33] Performing everyday national acts, Billig argues, and making them routines rather than performing grand sacral displays of national ceremony, are more effective with regard
to constructing a sense of nation and belonging. Where Billig mainly mentions
official national symbols, such as in raising flags or singing anthems, I contend
that the online quotidian calligraphic sutra writings work similarly. In all modes
we see an intimate storytelling that might subliminally work toward a national
agenda, but always remains subjective.

///////////////////////////

Notes

1   Yan An, *Kuaishou*, March 2021. 通篇下来一口气完成，不折纸不画线只因线在心中，
    不错字不漏字只因意在笔先 。 #书法 #心经-快手 (kuaishou.com) (accessed April 21,
    2022).
2   Yang, "Sinophone Classicism," 2.
3   Campany, "Notes on the Devotional Uses."
4   McRae, "Ch'an Commentaries on the Heart Sutra," 87.
5   Lopez, *Elaborations on Emptiness*, 6.
6   Campany, "Notes on the Devotional Uses"; Wong, *Making of a Saint*.
7   Lopez, *Elaborations on Emptiness*, 6.
8   Mattice, *Exploring the Heart Sutra*, 121.
9   Otake, "Sutra-Writing by Hand to Boost the Brain."
10 Creative 72, 《心經》麵條.
11 Miller, *Internet*; Vermeeren, "Chinese Calligraphy in the Digital Realm."
12 Highmore, *Everyday Life and Cultural Theory*, 23.
13 La, "TikTok rival boasts profitability in China."

14 Liu et al., "Zhibo gonghui."

15 Lin and de Kloet, "Platformization of the Unlikely Creative Class."

16 Ibid.

17 Tan et al., "The Real Digital Housewives."

18 Meng, "Is Kuaishou Still China's Short Video 'Platform of the People'?"

19 Light, Burgess, and Duguay, "The Walkthrough Method," 882.

20 Ibid.

21 Schneider, *China's Digital Nationalism*, 64.

22 Bachner, *Beyond Sinology*, 250.

23 See, for example, Chow, "Introduction"; Reid, "Escaping the Burdens of Chineseness"; Ang, "Can One Say No to Chineseness?"; Chun, "Fuck Chineseness."

24 Lévi-Strauss, *Introduction to Marcel Mauss*, 63.

25 Yang, "Sinophone Classicism," 11.

26 Ibid., 4.

27 Keane, "Internet + China."

28 Van Dijck, Poell, and de Waal, *Platform Society*, 4.

29 Ibid., 8.

30 Van Doorn, "Platform Labor," 901.

31 Poell, Nieborg, and Duffy, *Platforms and Cultural Production*, 200.

32 Yang, "Sinophone Classicism," 3.

33 Billig, *Banal Nationalism*, 6.

References

Ang, Ien. "Can One Say No to Chineseness? Pushing the Limits of the Diasporic Paradigm." *Boundary 2* 25, no. 3 (1998): 223–42.

Bachner, Andrea. *Beyond Sinology: Chinese Writing and Scripts of Culture*. New York: Columbia University Press, 2014.

Billig, Michael. *Banal Nationalism*. London: Sage, 1995.

Campany, Robert. "Notes on the Devotional Uses and Symbolic Functions of Sutra Texts as Depicted in Early Chinese Buddhist Miracle Tales and Hagiographies." *Journal of the International Association of Buddhist Studies* 14, no. 1 (1991): 28–72.

Chow, Rey. "Introduction: On Chineseness as a Theoretical Problem." *Boundary 2* 25, no. 3 (1998): 1–24.

Creative 72. (@创意72变). 《心經》麵條，吃飯變修行，中國也有了 ["Heart Sutra" Noodles: Eating Becomes Practice; China Has It Too]. Bilibili.com, April 22, 2017. https://www.bilibili.com/video/BV1Vx411U7gM?spm_id_from=333.337.search-card.all.click.

Chun, Allen. "Fuck Chineseness: On the Ambiguities of Ethnicity as Culture as Identity." *Boundary 2* 23, no. 2 (1996): 111–38

Highmore, Ben. *Everyday Life and Cultural Theory: An Introduction*. London: Routledge, 2002.

Keane, Michael. "Internet + China: Unleashing the Innovative Nation Strategy." *International Journal of Cultural and Creative Industries* 3, no. 2 (2016): 68–74.

La, Tao Lam. "TikTok Rival Boasts Profitability in China, Overseas Business Soars." Tech in Asia, August 24, 2022. https://www.techinasia.com/kuaishou-boasts-profitability-home-overseas-business-soars.

Lévi-Strauss, Claude. *Introduction to Marcel Mauss*. London: Routledge, 1987.

Light, Ben, Jean Burgess, and Stephanie Duguay. "The Walkthrough Method: An Approach to the Study of Apps." *New Media and Society* 20, no. 3 (2018): 881–900.

Lin Jian and Jeroen de Kloet. "Platformization of the Unlikely Creative Class: Kuaishou and Chinese Digital Cultural Production." *Social Media and Society* 5, no. 4 (2019): 246–56.

Liu, Tingting, Chris K. K. Tan, Xiaobing Yang, and Miao Li. "Zhibo gonghui: China's 'Live-Streaming Guilds' of Manipulation Experts." *Information, Communication, and Society* 26, no. 6 (2021): 1–16.

Lopez, Donald S. *Elaborations on Emptiness: Uses of the Heart Sutra*. Princeton, NJ: Princeton University Press, 1996.

Mattice, Sarah. *Exploring the Heart Sutra*. Lanham, MD: Lexington Books, 2021.

McRae, John. "Ch'an Commentaries on the Heart Sutra: Preliminary Inferences on the Permutation of Chinese Buddhism." *Journal of the International Association of Buddhist Studies* 11, no. 2 (1988): 87–115.

Meng Siyuan. "Is Kuaishou Still China's Short Video 'Platform of the People'?" Radii, January 8, 2021. radii.co/article/kuaishou.

Miller, David, and Don Slater. *The Internet: An Ethnographic Approach*. New York: Berg, 2000.

Nattier, Jan. "The Heart Sutra: A Chinese Apocryphal Text?" *Journal of the International Association of Buddhist Studies* 15, no. 2 (1992): 153–223.

Otake, Tomoko. "Sutra-Writing by Hand to Boost the Brain." *Japan Times*, December 24, 2006. https://www.japantimes.co.jp/life/2006/12/24/general/sutra-writing-by-hand-to-boost-the-brain/.

Poell, Thomas, David B. Nieborg, and Brooke Erin Duffy. 2022. *Platforms and Cultural Production*. Cambridge: Polity.

Reid, Anthony. "Escaping the Burdens of Chineseness." *Asian Ethnicity* 10, no. 3 (2009): 285–96.

Schneider, Florian. *China's Digital Nationalism*. New York: Oxford University Press, 2018.

Tan, Chris, Jie Wang, Shengyuan Wangzhu, Jinjing Xu, and Chunxuan Zhu. "The Real Digital Housewives of China's Kuaishou Video-Sharing and Live-Streaming App." *Media, Culture, and Society* 42 (2020): 1243–59.

Tanahashi, Kazuaki. *The Heart Sutra: A Comprehensive Guide to the Classic of Mahayana Buddhism*. Boulder, CO: Shambhala, 2014.

Van Dijck, Jose, Thomas Poell, and Martijn de Waal. *The Platform Society: Public Values in a Connective World*. New York: Oxford University Press, 2018.

Van Doorn, Niels. "Platform Labor: On the Gendered and Racialized Exploitation of Low-Income Service Work in the 'On-Demand' Economy." *Information, Communication, and Society* 20, no. 6 (2017): 898–914.

Vermeeren, Laura. "Chinese Calligraphy in the Digital Realm: Aesthetic Perfection and Remediation of the Authentic." *Concentric: Literary and Cultural Studies* 43, no. 2 (2017): 163–91.

Wong, Dorothy. "The Making of a Saint: Images of Xuanzang in East Asia." *Early Medieval China* 8 (2002): 43–95.

Yang, Zhiyi. "Sinophone Classicism: Chineseness as Temporal and Mnemonic Experience in the Digital Era." *Journal of Asian Studies* 81, no. 4 (2022): 657–71.

CHIEH-TING HSIEH

The Body That Counts
On the Digital Techniques of the Chinese Modern Dance

ABSTRACT This article is intended to analyze the "digital techniques of dance" implied in the different dance notations from the perspective of *Medienwissenschaft*. *Medienwissenschaft*, which is often translated as German "media theories," regards media as techniques through which concepts are developed. The digital technique is therefore redefined here as the technique of counting in general through which the concept of number is developed. The *digital technique of dance* in this article is also defined as the "technique of counting number with the body in dance." This article's analysis of the digital techniques of dance begins with the notation developed by Rudolf Laban for the Western modern dance and that developed by Zhu Zai-yu for the ancient Chinese dance. These notations were once researched by one of the most important dance researchers and choreographers, Liu Feng-hsueh, for her Chinese modern dance. The analysis of these notations indicates that the digital technique of Laban's notation is based on partition of time and space and the digital technique of Zhu Zai-yu's notation is based on interpretation of force. The article argues that it is only through the analysis of the digital technique of dance that "Chineseness" in modern dance can be based not only on the "spirit of the arts," which haunts dance like a ghost, but also on digital technique as the technique of the body. For research on Chinese modern dance, it is the body that counts.

KEYWORDS German media theories, digital technique, cultural technique, dance notation, Rudolf Laban, Zhu Zai-yu, Liu Feng-hsueh

01100010 01101111 01100100 01111001. These are the numbers on which the modern digital technique is based. What do these os and 1s mean? How to decipher them? They seem to be more mysterious than the numbers one, two, three, and so forth. These os and 1s are more like ciphers than numbers. Nonetheless, one often ignores that all the other numbers are also ciphers. A B Γ Δ and ٤ ٣ ٢ ١ , as signs that indicate numbers, are also ciphers. Nonetheless, to decipher does not only mean to figure out which sign indicates which number—as A and ١ indicate the number 1, B and ٢ indicate the number 2, Γ and ٣ indicate the number 3, and Δ and ١ indicate the number 4. It also means to figure out what these numbers mean: Do they indicate a sum? The order of things? A position in time or space? The way force acts? The sign that indicates number is a cipher, for it is the number itself that requires decipherment. The numbers 0 and 1, on which the modern digital technique is based, are not as mysterious as they seem. They differ from other numbers only because they are in binaries. They are no more mysterious than other numbers. They are also numbers to be counted. One must not forget that the machine that is used to decipher 0s and 1s is the *computer*. It clearly indicates that to decipher is to compute and therefore to count. The argument that 0s and 1s are mysterious and therefore different from other numbers is only a delusion. It ignores the actual digital technique, that is, the actual technique of counting those 0s and 1s. Moreover, as I argue in this article, there is no technique of counting—including the modern digital technique based on the numbers 0 and 1—without the body. The body—particularly the body in dance—is precisely one of the most important concerns in the research here.

Nonetheless, does the definition of the body change for the modern digital technique? As media researcher Sybille Krämer indicated, the body can no longer be limited to actual space. Through digitalization, the body can also be in digital space. The body in digital space, as Krämer implies, is like the body in a mirror: they come from the body in actual space.[1] Nonetheless, while the body in the mirror is the body of light, the body in the digital space is the body of number. Like the body, dance can also be in digital space through digitalization. While the question of whether the dance in the digital space is one of the body or one of number is one of the most important concerns in research on the digital body and digital dance, this article is not intended to analyze dance in the digital space.[2] Rather, it is intended to analyze the digital techniques of dance.

I define the digital technique of dance as the technique of counting with the body in dance. This definition is not intended to overturn the common definition of the digital technique as being based on the numbers 0 and 1. Rather, it returns to the etymological meaning of *digit* as a number or the finger with which one counts number. In German *Medienwissenschaft* (media theories), media are regarded as the techniques through which concepts are developed. From the perspective of *Medienwissenschaft*—which reflects on the prioritization of concept over technique in the Western tradition of *Geisteswissenschaften*, that is, the humanities—there is no concept without technique. It is the same with the concept of number. The technique of number through which the concept of number is developed is counting.[3] As media researcher Thomas Macho indicates, there is no concept of number before the technique of counting.[4] The digital technique, which is redefined as the technique of counting, is not limited to the modern technique based on the numbers 0 and 1. Rather, it includes the techniques of counting in ancient times.

It is important to note that not only the technique of counting but also the concept of number that is developed through counting is culture specific. There is more than one concept of number. Those concepts of number have also changed through time. For instance, it is widely known that the number 0 was not regarded as a number from the beginning in Western culture.[5] Only later was it regarded as the number that refers to absence and therefore as the counter to the number 1, which refers to presence. It is based on this conception of 0 and 1 that the modern digital technique, which uses them to indicate the electromagnetic signals – and +, was developed. Moreover, 0 and 1 correspond to the concept of *yin* 陰 and *yang* 陽 in ancient China. *Ying* and *yang* are also one of the Chinese translations for the electromagnetic signals – and +. I argue that *yin* and *yang*, which are often regarded as concepts notorious for their ambiguous meanings, are also numbers to be counted. The conception of *yin* and *yang* as numbers reflects a culture-specific concept of numbers that implies a different technique of counting.

The technique of counting implies the body. It means that the technique of number is the technique of counting number with the body. The digital technique is therefore closely related to the dance. When one dances, one also counts with the body. It is interesting to note that there is almost no dance notation without an indication of how dancer counts. As my analysis indicates, there are different ways to count in different notations: in the Western modern dance notation developed by German dance theorist Rudolf Laban around 1920, one counts the numbers one, two, three, and so forth in order to know how to move the body in space and time, and in the ancient Chinese dance notation developed by Chinese music and dance theorist Zhu Zai-yu 朱載堉 (1536–1611) in the Ming 明 dynasty, one counts the numbers *yin* and *yang* in order to know how to use force with the body. This article analyzes these different digital techniques of dance in these notations, which Liu Feng-shueh 劉鳳學 (1925–2023), one of the most important modern dance choreographers, once researched in order to choreograph her Chinese modern dance. The analysis begins with these questions: Why did Liu Feng-hsueh research these notations for her Chinese modern dance? How is the dance not only modern but also Chinese? How does one examine the "Chineseness" of modern dance?

The word *Chineseness* is notorious for the ambiguous meanings particularly with regard to dance. While some modern choreographers search for Chineseness through Chinese traditions, for instance, the practice of *qi* 氣 or the art of *shufa* 書法, Liu Feng-shueh, one of the earliest who tried to choreograph Chinese modern dance, based the Chineseness on the laws of ancient dance, that is, the ways the ancient dancers danced.[6] As most of the ancient dances are lost, how to know the ways the ancient dancer danced? For Liu Feng-shueh, reconstruction is the only way. She therefore researched ancient dance notations, including those preserved in the Japanese *gagaku* 雅楽 and those developed by the Chinese music and dance theorist Zhu Zai-yu in the Ming dynasty. Although it is said that some of the Chinese court music and dance of the Tang 唐 dynasty are preserved in the *gagaku*, *gagaku* is Japanese rather than Chinese. Also, while Japanese *gagaku*—unlike the lost Chinese court music and dance—is still in practice, it is also not without reconstruction under *Gagakukyoku* 雅楽局 in modern times.[7] It is therefore difficult to argue that the court music and dance in *gagaku* are the same as those in the Tang dynasty. While most of Liu Feng-shueh's reconstructions are based on the *gagaku*, there are also some dances preserved in Zhu Zai-yu's notation in the Ming dynasty. It is important to note that some of the Zhu Zai-yu's dances are also reconstructions of ancient dances, for which Zhu Zai-yu developed the dance notation to demonstrate the laws of dance. Liu Feng-hsueh also used notation to demonstrate the laws of dance. Nonetheless, for her the laws can be demonstrated more clearly with the Western modern dance notation developed by Germen dance theorist Rudolf Laban around 1920. She therefore researched Laban's notation, which is known as Labanotation, for reconstruction of ancient dances. Her Chinese modern dances, such as *Vast Desert, Solitary Smoke Rises Straight* (*Damo Guyenzhi* 大漠孤煙直, 2000), were also notated with Labanotation.

The notations developed by Laban and Zhu Zai-yu are the beginning of my analysis of the digital technique of Chinese modern dance. For me, dance notation is not only de-scription in the sense of writing down, but also, and more important, pre-scription in the sense of writing that sets up the laws for the dance a priori. It is clearly reflected in the notations that Liu Feng-shueh researched. They are intended to set up the laws for her Chinese modern dance. How does dance notation set up the laws? For me, it is through the digital technique as the technique of counting with the body. As mentioned, there is almost no notation without indication of how dancer counts with the body.

While I begin with Liu Feng-hsueh's search for Chineseness in modern dance, I do not intend to analyze her Chinese modern dance. Neither do I intend to examine the Chineseness in her dance. Rather, I intend to analyze the different digital techniques implied in the different notations that she researched. For me, the Chineseness is not only the spirit of the arts that are reflected through concepts from ancient China, such as *qi* 氣 or *yin* and *yang*. Rather, it is based more on the laws of dance. The importance of research on the laws of dance in the search for Chineseness is also emphasized by Liu Feng-shueh. For me, the laws implied in the digital techniques of the notations are the most important laws of dance. As the digital technique is the technique of counting with the body in dance, it is also the technique of the body. It is therefore important to analyze the different digital techniques as different techniques of the body in the different notations for the research on Chineseness based on the laws of dance.

The Technique of Counting as the Technique of the Body: A Perspective of *Medienwissenschaft*

Before the analysis of the different digital techniques in the notations developed by Laban and Zhu Zai-yu, it is important to explain more about the perspective of German media theories, that is, *Medienwissenschaft*. As already mentioned, media is regarded more as technique through which concept is developed from the perspective of *Medienwissenschaft*, which reflects on the prioritization of concept over technique in the humanities, that is, *Geisteswissenschaften*.[8] As the word *Geisteswissenschaften* implies, the interpretation of the meanings of concept is considered to be the work of *Geist*, that is, spirit. Therefore, the body and technique are often ignored in the *Geisteswissenschaften*. Nonetheless, as media researcher Friedrich Kittler indicates, *Medienwissenschaft* is intended to cast the *Geist* out of *Gesiteswissenschaften*.[9] What is the "ghost" in *Geisteswissenschaften*? From the perspective of *Medienwissenschaft*, it is spirit without the body, or more precisely, the (mis-)conception of spirit without the body that haunts *Geisteswissenschaften*. How to cast the *Geist* out of *Geisteswissenschaften*, which can be translated as ghost-*wissenschaften*? For the researchers of *Medienwissenschaft*, it is through the analysis of techniques, or more precisely, through the analysis of how concepts are developed through techniques. Kittler's reflection on spirit as a ghost is an important reminder to dance research that emphasizes Chineseness interpreted only as the spirit of the arts reflected through concepts and ignores techniques through which concepts are developed, for instance, the technique of counting as the technique of the body. Without the analysis of the technique of counting as the technique of the body, Chineseness, interpreted only as the spirit of the arts, is nothing more than the ghost that haunts dance.

From the perspective of *Medienwissenschaft*, there is no concept per se. Or more precisely, there is no concept without technique. It is the same with the concept of number. It is through the technique of counting that the concept of number is developed. This is clearly implied in the Chinese and German words for "number" and "counting." In Chinese the word for both is the same: *shu* 數. In German the word for "number" is *Zahl* and the word for "counting" is *zählen*. These words clearly indicate that it is through the technique of counting that one gets the number. How does one count to get the number? It is implied in the etymological meaning of *digit* as finger. The word *digit* derives the meaning of number from finger, or more precisely, from counting with the finger. The digital technique is therefore also the technique of the body. When one counts, one often counts with the body. One counts with the fingers one after another. For instance, one can count the number one with the thumb, count the number two with the thumb and the second finger, and count the number three with the thumb, the second finger, and the middle finger, and so forth. In Western culture the fingers are one of the most important body parts to indicate number.[10] It is interesting to note that the musicians also use the fingers to count the beats in the Chinese traditions of music. For instance, the *kunqu* 崑曲 musicians touch the counter with the second, middle, and fourth fingers to count the first beat, with the second finger the second beat, with the middle finger the third beat, with the fourth finger the fourth beat; the *nanguan* 南管 musicians touch the thumb with the second finger to count the first beat, touch the thumb with the middle finger to count the second beat, and touch the thumb with the fourth finger to count he third beat. In some of the extremely long meters, the technique of counting the beats with the fingers is important for the musicians to know which beat is being counted now. With the fingers, the beats are set in order.

The technique of counting with the fingers implies that numbers are discrete and come one after another in order. While two can be regarded as a sum of ones, one and two are discrete numbers. That numbers are discrete is clearly reflected in the body by the fingers, which are discrete. One can count number with the finger only because the fingers are discrete. It is important to note that number also implies order. They come one after another in order. After one comes two, after two comes three, and so forth. Although counting often means counting up to a sum, counting up means counting one after another. It is the same with counting down. Counting down from a sum is also counting one after another.

The modern digital technique based on the numbers 0 and 1 is no more mysterious than counting with all the numbers in the sense that those 0s and 1s are counted one after another. The modern digital technique based on the discreteness of the numbers 0 and 1 is already implied in the discreteness of the fingers.[11] The only difference is that those 0s and 1s in the modern digital technique are counted in binaries. For instance, how to decipher 01100010 01101111 01100100 01111001? These 0s and 1s in the first set, 01100010, are counted from the right: the first number (from the right) indicates how many 2^0 is there, the second indicates how many 2^1, the third how many 2^2, and so forth. Therefore, 01100010 indicates that there is 0 of 2^0, 1 of 2^1, 0 of 2^2, 0 of 2^3, 0 of 2^4, 1 of 2^5, 1 of 2^6, 0 of 2^7, that is:

01100010
$2^7\ 2^6\ 2^5\ 2^4\ 2^3\ 2^2\ 2^1\ 2^0$
$0+64+32+0+0+0+2+0=98$

In sum, 01100010 is $(0 \times 2^0) + (1 \times 2^1) + (0 \times 2^2) + (0 \times 2^3) + (0 \times 2^4) + (1 \times 2^5) + (1 \times 2^6) + (0 \times 2^7) = 98$. There is also no difference in the technique of counting 98: 98 indicates that there is 8 of 10^0 and 9 of 10^1, that is:

9 8
$10^1\ 10^0$
$90+8=98$

01100010 01101111 01100100 01111001 in binaries is, therefore, 98 111 100 121, which refer to the order of the signs in one of the widely used character encoding systems: 98 refers to the 98th sign, *b*; 111 refers to the 111st sign, *o*; 100 refers to 100th sign, *d*; and 121 refers to the 121st sign, *y*—*body*. If these 0s and 1s are not counted in order, their meaning would be garbled. To decipher is therefore to count numbers and sets of numbers one after another in order. One must not forget that the machine that is used to decipher those os and 1s is *computer*, which is translated as *jisuanji* 計算機 in Chinese. The meaning of *jisuanji* is manifest: it is a machine (*ji* 機) that computes or counts (*jisuan* 計算). Counting numbers one after another implies not only the discreteness but also the order, which implies laws. From the perspective of *Medienwissenschaft*, the number is one of the most important concepts that set up laws. It is also one of the most important techniques of dance that sets up the laws of dance for the body.

There is no technique without the body. There is also no technique of counting without the body. When the body counts number with the body, the body is also being counted by number. It means that number that one counts with the body also counts the body. In other words, the body is numbered. For instance, when one counts the number one with the thumb, on the one hand, one counts it with the thumb, but on the other hand, it also counts the thumb in the sense that it numbers the thumb as the "first" finger. The body is therefore the body of the number. It indicates that not only one who counts but also that which one counts *has* the body or, more precisely, *is* the body. It indicates that number is not a concept without the body. It is clearly implied in the etymological meaning of *calculation* as *calculus*, which means the stone used in an abacus. The stone that one counts is already the body. Moreover, the stone used in an abacus, like the finger, is already a number. It is interesting to note that an abacus is also a computer in the sense that it is a machine that counts. The machine counts with the body, for the machine itself is the body. It is the same with the numbers 0 and 1 in the modern digital techniques. As they are used to indicate the electromagnetic signals – and +, they come from the electromagnetic body such as chromium dioxide or silicon. As the dancer also counts with the body, the body is important to the analysis of the digital techniques of dance. This article is intended to analyze the laws which the dance notation sets up for the body through the digital techniques.

The Digital Technique of the Western Modern Dance Notation: Counting Number as Partition of Space and Time

When one dances, one often counts the numbers one, one two, one two three, and so forth. What does it mean to count? What does the number indicate? Doesn't it mean that when one counts the number one, at this first position in time one must move the body part to that first position in space, and when one counts two, at this second position in time one must move the body part to that second position in space? Doesn't it mean that time and space are partitioned? As I am going to argue, the digital technique of the Western modern dance notation developed by Laban is partition of space and time.

The notation, which is known as Labanotation, was developed from Laban's earlier dance notations in his work *Choreographie*. The word *choreographie*, which means writing of dance, is clearly derived from one of the earliest systems of dance notation, which Pierre Beauchamp and Raoul-Auger Feuillet developed for the Western court dance around 1700. The notation, which was developed under the order of the King Louis XIV, was intended to set up the laws for the dance.

Laban's dance notation was also intended to set up the laws for Western modern dance. It is therefore not only description but also prescription. The laws that he set up through the notation are the laws of the body based on the space of the body. Laban defined the space of the body with the directions of front and back, left and right, high and low. As Laban mentioned, the directions of front and back, left and right were implied in the positions of the Western court dance that were numbered in Feuillet and Beauchamp's notation.[12] For instance, the second position, which is having one foot placed on the left or right to the other, indicates that the body has the directions of right and left, and the third position, which is having one foot placed to the front or back of the other, indicates that the body has the directions of front and back. Apart from the directions of right and left, front and back, the directions of high and low are also of the body. They come from the position of the weight of the body, which is emphasized in the Western modern dance.

It is with these directions that Laban set up the laws of dance. It is clearly reflected in Laban's *Schwungskala*, the practice of movement for dance. In *Schwungskala*, the movement is based on the directions defined with the positions in space. For instance, the movement in *Schwungskala* A begins with *lz* going to *hr*, and ends at *vt* going back to *lz*, and the movement in *Schwungskala* B begins with *rz* going to *tl* and ends at *vt* going back to *rz*.[13] The notation *lz*, *hr*, *vt*, *rz*, and *tl* indicate the positions in space at the left back (*links-zurück*), high right (*hoch-rechts*), front low (*vor-tief*), right back (*rechts-zurück*), and low left (*tief-links*) to the body. Therefore, going from *lz* to *hr* means to move the body from the position left back to the position high right, and going from *rz* to *tl* means to move the body from the position right back to the position low left.

In Labanotation, the movement of the body is also notated with the signs that indicate the direction of movement.[14] They are notated on the lines that indicate the space of the body: the lines on the right indicate the right part of the body, and the lines on the left indicate the left. The lines on which the signs are notated indicate which part of the body must move. For instance, a sign on the line for the right part of the body such as the right arm or the right leg indicates that the right part of the body must move in the direction the sign indicates, and a sign on the line for the left part of the body such as the left arm or the left leg indicates that the left part of the body must move in the direction the sign indicates. The sign that indicates the direction of the movement also indicates the movement's duration: the longer the sign is, the longer the duration is. The line in Labanotation that indicates the space of the body is a timeline. The position in space is also a position in time. The positions from which and at which the movement begins and ends in space are also the positions from which and at which the movement begins and ends in time. It indicates that durations, like directions, are defined with positions. To notate the movement with the signs that indicate directions and durations in space and time therefore means to partition. Although the movement in the *Schwungskala* begins and ends at the same position in one circle movement, it is partitioned into different directions that are defined with different positions. As Laban numbered the directions in *Schwungskala*, to count numbers also means to partition space and time. When one counts the number one, one must move the body part in the first direction to the first position in space within the first duration which is defined by the first position in time, and when one counts the number two, one must move the body part in the second direction to the second position in space within the second duration which is defined by the second position in time. The digital technique of Laban's notation is therefore partition. It is partition of space and time.

The Digital Technique of the Ancient Chinese Dance Notation: Counting Number as Interpretation of Force

The concepts of *yin* and *yang* in ancient China are notorious for their ambiguous meanings. The meanings of *yin* and *yang* are ambiguous, for they are used to refer to many different things: heaven, earth, sun, moon, thunder, wind, and so forth. They are also used to describe dance in Zhu Zai-yu's notation. What do *yin* and *yang* mean? Are *yin* and *yang* concepts? Aren't *yin* and *yang*, which correspond to the numbers 0 and 1 in the modern digital technique, also numbers to be counted? How does one count *yin* and *yang*? As I am going to analyze, while the digital technique of Laban's notation is partition of space and time, the digital technique of Zhu Zai-yu's notation is interpretation of force.

Yin and *yang* are not only concepts but also numbers to be counted. According to some research, the signs of *yin* and *yang* are derived from the number of the stems that are decided by lot in the prophetic practice *shi* 筮.[15] *Shi* is the practice of drawing stems from a lot to get the sign of *yin* and *yang* based on the number of the stems that one draws for interpretation. It is therefore important to note that *yin* and *yang* are often not indicated directly in the ancient writings of *Yi* 易 (Change). Rather, in the ancient writings of *Yi*, *yang* is indicated with the number 9 and *yin* with the number 6. It clearly indicates that *yin* and *yang* are numbers. That *yin* and *yang* are numbers is also implied in the way the signs are interpreted. To interpret *gua* 卦, a composite sign that is composed of *yao* 爻, the signs of *yin* and *yang*, one must "count" *yin* and *yang* from the lowest part to the highest part. As the lowest part implies how things begin and the highest part indicates how things end, the position of *yin* and *yang* in a composite sign implies time. The position of *yin* and *yang* in a composite sign also implies space: the lowest part refers to earth, the highest part refers to heaven, and the part between refers to man. To interpret *yin* and *yang* therefore means to count *yin* and *yang* one after another from the lowest part to the highest part in a composite sign. To count *yin* and *yang* at different positions in a composite sign also means to interpret how things begin and end, how heaven and earth work, and how man takes care of the changes.

In the interpretation of *yin* and *yang*, the question of how man takes care of the changes is particularly important. It is because the way man takes care of the changes also changes the way things change. Therefore, although *yin* and *yang* are regarded as the signs that manifest the way things change, such changes are not set. Therefore, the signs of *yin* and *yang* are not only description but also prescription. They not only describe the way things change but also prescribe how man can change the way things change. As there is no change without force, *yin* and *yang* are also the signs of force. They manifest the way force works.[16] According to some research, the signs of *yin* and *yang* are derived from the ruptures of the oracle bones used in the prophetic practice of *bu* 卜.[17] *Bu* is the practice of burning bones to get the signs from the ruptures on the bones for interpretation. As the ruptures on the bone manifest the way force works, they are the signs of force, and therefore the prophetic signs that have prophetic force.

As *yin* and *yang* are the signs derived from prophetic practice, they ask for interpretation. It is through interpretation that they ask for that *yin* and *yang* are used to refer to many different things: heaven, earth, sun, moon, thunder, wind, and so forth. They are also used to describe dance in Zhu Zai-yu's notation. While Zhu Zai-yu uses figures of dancers to indicate in which direction the dancer is positioned, these figures are so simple that they are almost of no use without Zhu Zai-yu's descriptions of dance. In one of Zhu Zai-yu's descriptions, *yin* and *yang* are particularly important. As Zhu Zai-yu indicates, "The grandness [of the dance] must be like that of earth, and the clearness [of the dance] must be like that of heaven. The way the dancer turns must be like the way the times of the year end and begin and the way the wind and rain take in turn."[18] He also mentions that the open gesture in the dance must be of the "straightness" of *qian* 乾, the composite sign that is composed of the signs of *yang*, and the close gesture in the dance must be of the "roundness" of *kun* 坤, the composite sign that is composed of the signs of *yin*.[19] What do *qian* and *kun* that refer to heaven and earth in the interpretation of *yin* and *yang* mean for dance? What do the "straightness" of *qian* and the "roundness" of *kun* mean? Do they mean the "straightness" of heaven and the "roundness" of earth? Aren't *yin* and *yang* also numbers to be counted? I argue that to count *yin* and *yang* is to interpret *yin* and *yang* with the body, that is, to use force in the specific ways which are implied in the signs.

As mentioned, *yin* and *yang* are the signs that manifest the ways the force works. Therefore, the signs of *qian* and *kun* are more than references to heaven and earth. They also refer to the way heaven and earth repose or act. As the ancient writings of *Yi* indicate, the repose (*jing* 靜) of *qian* is of "roundness" (*zhuan* 專) and the act of *qian* is of "straightness" (*zhi* 直), from which "grandness" (*da* 大) emerges; the repose of *kun* is of "closeness" (*yi* 翕) and the act of *kun* is of "openness" (*pi* 闢), from which "wideness" (*guang* 廣) emerges.[20] What do "roundness" and "straightness" mean? What do "closeness" and "openness" mean? I argue that they are not concepts. Rather, they are descriptions of how heaven and earth act or repose that indicate the ways force works. Therefore, they are heaven's "holding-within-roundness" and "going-with-straightness" and the earth's "being-in-closeness" and "being-in-openness." The "roundness" of *kun* and the "straightness" of *qian* in Zhu Zai-yu's description of dance are therefore also not concepts. Rather, they are descriptions of the ways the body uses force. When one regards them as descriptions of force, it becomes manifest that the "roundness," which Zhu Zai-yu used to describe the close gesture, is the body's "holding-within-roundness," and the "straightness," which Zhu Zai-yu used to describe the open gesture, is the body's "going-with-straightness." They are descriptions of the ways force works. Therefore, it is only when the force is used in the specific ways which are implied in the signs of *yin* and *yang* that the grandness and the clearness of the dance emerge. Zhu Zai-yu's description of the dance is prescription. The laws that he set up for dance are the laws of force. The digital technique of Zhu Zai-yu's notation is interpretation of force.

The "Chineseness" of Modern Dance: The Digital Technique of the Body

My analysis of the digital techniques of dance began with Liu Feng-shueh's Chinese modern dance. It began with the notations of Laban and Zhu Zai-yu that Liu Feng-shueh researched for her Chinese modern dance. Liu Feng-shueh used notation to demonstrate the laws of ancient Chinese dance based on which she choreographed her Chinese modern dance. Nonetheless, notation not only demonstrates the laws. It also sets up the laws for the dance through the digital technique, that is, the technique of counting with the body. The analysis in this article has indicated that the digital technique of Laban's notation is partition of space and time and the digital technique of Zhu Zai-yu's notation is interpretation of force. As there is no technique of counting without the body, the technique of counting is also a technique of the body. It is therefore for the body that the notations set up the different laws of dance through the different digital techniques. In Laban's notation, the positions are the laws in the sense that one must move the body according to the durations and directions that are defined with the positions in space and time. In Zhu Zai-yu's notation, the signs of *yin* and *yang* are the laws in the sense that one must use force in the ways that are implied in the signs. The different laws that the different notations set up for the dance also reflect the different concepts of dance: while dance in Laban's notation is regarded as movement defined by positions in space and time, dance in Zhu Zai-yu's notation is regarded as the work of force.

Having analyzed the different digital techniques of dance in the different notations, there are more questions for reflection: Can the laws set up in the notation that Zhu Zai-yu developed for ancient Chinese dance be demonstrated with the notation that Laban developed for Western modern dance? Isn't there conflict between the laws of the dance set up in Zhu Zai-yu's notation and in Laban's notation? Isn't there conflict between the digital techniques of ancient Chinese dance and Western modern dance? What are the laws on which the Chineseness in Liu Feng-hsueh's Chinese modern dance is based? These questions clearly require not only the analysis of the digital techniques of ancient Chinese dance and Western modern dance in the notations but also the analysis of Liu Feng-hsueh's Chinese modern dance that is beyond the concern of this article.

While this article begins with the notations that Liu Feng-shueh researched, it is not intended to examine the Chineseness of her dance. Nonetheless, as the Chineseness must be based on the laws of ancient Chinese dance, I argue that it is only when the dancer moves the body according to the durations and directions that are defined in space and time and at the same time use force in the specific ways that are implied in the signs of *yin* and *yang* that the digital technique can be modern and Chinese. While the research in this article is clearly limited, the analysis of the digital techniques is intended to emphasize the importance of the laws of dance to the research on Chineseness. From the perspective of *Medienwissenschaft*, the research on the Chineseness of Chinese modern dance requires the analysis of the digital techniques as the techniques of the body. Kittler's reminder of the ghost in *Geisteswissenschaften* is important. Without the analysis of the digital techniques as the techniques of the body, the Chineseness can be nothing more than a ghost that haunts dance like the spirit of the arts. Therefore, it is the body that counts.

Acknowledgments
This work is supported by NSTC (Taiwan) Research Project Grant No. NSTC 111-2410-H-004-225-MY2.

Notes
1   Krämer, "Verschwindet der Körper?"
2   See deLahunta and Jenett, "Making Digital Choreographic Objects Interrelate"; Portanova, *Moving without a Body*.

3   On the number as "culture-technique" (*Kulturtechnik*), see Krämer and Bredekamp, "Kultur, Technik, Kulturtechnik."

4   Macho, "Zeit und Zahl."

5   On the historical development of the number 0 in Western culture, see Kaplan, *Nothing That Is.*

6   On Liu Feng-shueh's concept of "Chinese modern dance," see Li, *Liu Fengxue fang-tan.*

7   See Naoko, "Beyond the Court."

8   For the introduction to the perspective of *Medienwissenschaft* on *Kulturtechnik*, see Siegert, "Introduction"; Winthrop-Young, "Cultural Techniques"; Parikka, "Afterword."

9   Kittler, *Austreibung des Geistes aus den Geisteswissenschaften.*

10 Williams and Williams, "Finger Numbers in the Greco-Roman World and the Early Middle Ages."

11 See also Puskar, "Counting on the Body."

12 Laban, *Choreographie*, 6–7.

13 Ibid., 29–31.

14 For the complete introduction to Labanotation, see Guest, *Labanotation.*

15 Zhang, *Xianshu yixue*, 117–30.

16 On the interpretation of *yin* and *yang* as signs of force, see also Hsieh, "Dynamics, Writing, Figure," 144–50.

17 Zhang, *Xianshu yixue*, 117–30. See also Qu, "Yigua yuanyu guibu kao."

18 Zhu, *Yueluquanshu*, 39.40–41.

19 Ibid., 39.42.

20 Wang and Kong, *Zhouyi zhengyi*, 273.

References

deLahunta, Scott, and Florian Jenett. "Making Digital Choreographic Objects Interrelate: A Focus on Coding Practices." In *Performing the Digital: Performativity and Performance Studies in Digital Cultures*, edited by Timon Beyes, Martina Leeker, and Imanuel Schipper, 63–79. Bielefeld: Transcript, 2017.

Feuillet, Raoul Auger. *Chorégraphie, ou l'art de décrire la danse.* Paris, 1700.

Guest, Ann Hutchinson. *Labanotation: The System of Analyzing and Recording Movement.* New York: Routledge, 2005.

Hsieh, Chieh-ting. "Dynamics, Writing, Figure." PhD diss., Freie Universität zu Berlin, 2018.

Kaplan, Robert. *The Nothing That Is.* New York: Oxford University Press, 1999.

Kittler, Friedrich, ed. *Austreibung des Geistes aus den Geisteswissenschaften: Programme des Poststrukturalismus.* Paderborn, Germany: Schöningh, 1980.

Krämer, Sybille. "Verschwindet der Körper? Ein Kommentar zu virtuellen Räumen." In *Raum, Wissen, Macht*, edited by Rudolf Maresch and Niels Werber, 49–68. Frankfurt: Suhrkamp, 2002.

Krämer, Sybille, and Horst Bredekamp. "Kultur, Technik, Kulturtechnik: Wider die Diskursivierung der Kultur." In *Bild, Schrift, Zahl*, edited by Sybille Krämer and Horst Bredekamp, 11–22. Munich: Fink, 2009.

Laban, Rudolf. *Choreographie.* Jena: Eugen Diederichs, 1926.

Li Xiao-hua 李小華. *Liu Fengxue fang-tan* 劉鳳學訪談 [Conversation with Liu Feng-shueh]. Taipei: Shibao wenhua 時報文化, 1998.

Macho, Thomas. "Zeit und Zahl: Kalender- und Zeitrechnung als Kulturtechniken." In *Bild, Schrift, Zahl*, edited by Sybille Krämer and Horst Bredekamp, 179–92. Munich: Fink, 2009.

Naoko, Terauchi. "Beyond the Court: A Challenge to the *Gagaku* Tradition in the 'Reconstruction Project' of the National Theatre." In *Performing Japan*, edited by Henry Johnson and Jerry C. Jaffe, 93–125. Leiden: Brill, 2008.

Parikka, Jussi. "Afterword: Cultural Techniques and Media Studies." *Theory, Culture and Society* 30, no. 6 (2013): 147–59.

Portanova, Stamatia. *Moving without a Body: Digital Philosophy and Choreographic Thoughts*. Cambridge, MA: MIT Press, 2013.

Puskar, Jason. "Counting on the Body: Techniques of Embodied Digitality." *New Media and Society* 21, no.10 (2019): 2242–60.

Qu Wan-li 屈萬里. "Yigua yuanyu guibu kao" 易卦源于龜卜考 [Examination of the prophetic practice of oracle bone reading as the origin of the signs in *Change*]. In *Zhouyi yanjiu lunwenji* 周易研究論文集 [Collection of writings of Zhou-yi research], vol. 1, edited by Huang Shou-qi 黃壽祺 and Zhang Shan-wen 張善文, 43–63. Peking: Beijing shifan daxue 北京師範大學, 1987.

Siegert, Bernhard. "Introduction: Cultural Techniques, or, The End of the Intellectual Postwar in German Media Theory." In *Cultural Techniques: Grids, Filters, Doors, and Other Articulations of the Real*, translated by Geoffrey Winthrop-Young, 1–18. New York: Fordham University Press, 2015.

Wang Bi 王弼 and Kong Ying-da 孔穎達, annos. *Zhouyi zhengyi* 周易正義 [The Righteous Meaning of *Change*]. Edited by Li Xue-qin 李學勤. Peking: Beijing daxue 北京大學, 1999.

Williams, Burma P., and Richard S. Williams. "Finger Numbers in the Greco-Roman World and the Early Middle Ages." *Isis* 86, no. 4 (1995): 587–608.

Winthrop-Young, Geoffrey. "Cultural Techniques: Preliminary Remarks." *Theory, Culture and Society* 30, no. 6 (2013): 3–19.

Zhang Qi-cheng 張其成. *Xiangshu yixue* 象數易學 [Semiology and Numerology of *Yi*]. Guangxi: Guangxi kexue jishu 廣西科學技術, 2009.

Zhu Zai-yu 朱載堉. *Yuelu quanshu* 樂律全書 [Complete Writings on the Laws of Music]. Taipei: Taiwan shangwu yinshuguan 臺灣商務印書館, 1983.

Keep up to date on new scholarship

Issue alerts are a great way to stay current on all the cutting-edge scholarship from your favorite Duke University Press journals. This free service delivers tables of contents directly to your inbox, informing you of the latest groundbreaking work as soon as it is published.

To sign up for issue alerts:

1. Visit **dukeu.press/register** and register for an account. You do not need to provide a customer number.

2. After registering, visit **dukeu.press/alerts**.

3. Go to "Latest Issue Alerts" and click on "Add Alerts."

4. Select as many publications as you would like from the pop-up window and click "Add Alerts."

read.dukeupress.edu/journals